This b

A Introduction to Early Childhood Studies

THE LIBRARY
NEW COLLEGE
SWINDON

WITHDRAWN

An Introduction to Early Childhood Studies

Second Edition

Edited by
Trisha Maynard and
Nigel Thomas

Los Angeles | London | New Delhi
Singapore | Washington DC

20060034 01

Editorial arrangement, introduction and part introductions © Trisha Maynard and Nigel Thomas 2009

Chapters 1, 12, 15 and 17 © Bob Sanders
Chapter 2 © Roy Lowe
Chapters 3 and 10 © Nigel Thomas
Chapter 4 © Helen Penn
Chapter 5 © Ruth M. Ford
Chapter 6 © Tricia David
Chapter 7 © Thea Cameron-Faulkner

Chapter 8 © Justine Howard
Chapter 9 © Sonia Jackson and Mary Fawcett
Chapter 11 © Iram Siraj-Blatchford
Chapter 13 © Liz Noblett
Chapter 14 © Guy Roberts-Holmes
Chapter 16 © Alison Clark
Chapter 18 © Carol Aubrey

First edition published 2004. Reprinted 2005, 2007, 2008
Second edition published 2009

Apart from any fair dealing for the purposes of research or private study, or criticism or review, as permitted under the Copyright, Designs and Patents Act, 1988, this publication may be reproduced, stored or transmitted in any form, or by any means, only with the prior permission in writing of the publishers, or in the case of reprographic reproduction, in accordance with the terms of licences issued by the Copyright Licensing Agency. Enquiries concerning reproduction outside those terms should be sent to the publishers.

SAGE Publications Ltd
1 Oliver's Yard
55 City Road
London EC1Y 1SP

SAGE Publications Inc.
2455 Teller Road
Thousand Oaks, California 91320

SAGE Publications India Pvt Ltd
B 1/I 1 Mohan Cooperative Industrial Area
Mathura Road
New Delhi 110 044

SAGE Publications Asia-Pacific Pte Ltd
33 Pekin Street #02-01
Far East Square
Singapore 048763

Library of Congress Control Number: 2008939390

British Library Cataloguing in Publication data

A catalogue record for this book is available from the British Library

ISBN 978-1-84787-167-1
ISBN 978-1-84787-168-8 (pbk)

Typeset by C&M Digitals (P) Ltd, Chennai, India
Printed and bound in Great Britain by TJ International Ltd, Padstow, Cornwall
Printed on paper from sustainable resources

Mixed Sources
Product group from well-managed forests and other controlled sources
www.fsc.org Cert no. SGS-COC-2482
FSC © 1996 Forest Stewardship Council

CONTENTS

NOTES ON EDITORS AND CONTRIBUTORS

Carol Aubrey is Professor of Early Childhood and Director of Research at the Institute of Education, University of Warwick. She trained as a primary school teacher and educational psychologist and spent a number of years in primary teacher education, with a particular focus on the early years, first at University College Cardiff and then at the University of Durham. Her research interests lie in the policy-to-practice context of early childhood education and care, including multi-agency working, leadership, early learning and development, with an interest in mathematics development and inclusion/special educational needs. She is editor for *Journal of Early Childhood Research*.

Thea Cameron-Faulkner is a Lecturer in the School of Social Sciences at Cardiff University. She taught English as a Foreign Language for six years before studying for a PhD in Psychology. Her research is situated within a constructivist approach to language development and focuses on the role of the linguistic input in the early stages of the developmental process.

Alison Clark is a Senior Lecturer in Childhood and Youth Studies at the Open University. Her research interests include listening to children, children's experiences of place and the development of participatory research methods. Working with Professor Peter Moss at Thomas Coram Research Unit she developed methods for listening to young children in research called the Mosaic approach. Her research studies have included a three-year longitudinal study exploring young children's involvement in the design of new buildings. She is interested in how qualitative research methods can facilitate communication between children and adults in a range of professional roles.

Tricia David has worked in the field of Early Childhood Education and Care for almost forty years. Having officially retired, she is honoured to have been awarded the titles of Emeritus Professor at Canterbury Christ Church University and

Honorary Emeritus Professor of Early Years Education at the University of Sheffield. Tricia's publications have included studies of international comparisons and, more recently, the review for *Birth to Three Matters*. Tricia is delighted that her 1990's works on multi-professionalism, apparently still read during current developments in provision, are spurring others to create contemporary studies in this complex and exciting field.

Mary Fawcett trained as a teacher of young children and taught in nursery and infant classes and was active in the early years of the Preschool Playgroups Association. She lectured at the University of East Anglia and, with Sonia Jackson, founded and later directed the degree in Early Childhood Studies at the University of Bristol. Her publications include: *Learning Through Child Observation* (1996) Jessica Kingsley Publishers; *Focus on Early Childhood: Principles and Realities* edited with Margaret Boushel and Julie Selwyn (2000) Blackwell Science; and *Researching Children Researching the World: 5x5x5=creativity* with Susi Bancroft and Penny Hay (2008) Trentham Books.

Ruth Ford is a Senior Lecturer in Developmental Psychology at Griffith University in Brisbane, Australia, and her research focuses on the development of memory and thinking skills during early childhood. Ruth is especially interested in sociocultural theories of cognitive development and the implications of such theories for efforts to raise the educational attainments of disadvantaged children through early intervention. While working in the United Kingdom, Ruth was instrumental in founding a Sure Start project that was successful in developing the self-regulation and school readiness of low-income preschoolers by increasing their experience of one-on-one, scaffolded interactions with their primary caregiver.

Justine Howard is a Senior Lecturer at the Centre for Child Research at Swansea University and the Programme Director of their Masters in Developmental and Therapeutic Play. She is a Chartered Psychologist and Associate Fellow of the British Psychological Society, holding a first degree in psychology, a postgraduate diploma in research methods and a PhD in the psychology of education. She is also trained in Developmental and Therapeutic Play. Her research is principally concerned with children's perceptions of play and how these perceptions are influenced by social and environmental interaction. Her recent experimental work focuses on the benefits of playful practice. She is also the editor of *The Psychology of Education Review*.

Sonia Jackson is Professor of Social Care and Education at the Institute of Education, University of London. Before moving into university teaching and research, she worked as a clinical psychologist, teacher and social worker. She is co-author of *People Under Three: Young Children in Day Care*, (two editions and five languages) and many other publications on early years and children in care. She was responsible for initiating the first degrees in Early Childhood Studies at the Universities of Bristol and Swansea and was awarded the OBE for services to children in 2003.

Roy Lowe retired recently as Visiting Professor at the Institute of Education, University of London. He has published widely on aspects of the history of education in Britain and North America. His books include *Education in the Post-War Years* (Routledge, 1988), *Schooling and Social Change* (Routledge, 1997) and *The Death of Progressive Education: How Teachers Lost Control of the Classroom* (Routledge, 2007). His five-volume collection on the history of universities has recently been published by Routledge, following his four-volume collection of essays on the history of education published in 2000. He has been President of the History of Education Society of the United Kingdom, and was awarded an OBE in the 2002 New Year's Honours for services to education.

Trisha Maynard is Professor of Early Childhood Studies in the Centre for Child Research, Swansea University. Trisha taught at an infant school before joining the Department of Education at Swansea in 1991 where she worked on the Primary PGCE. In 1999 Trisha took on the role of Course Director of the BSc in Early Childhood Studies and in 2003 became Head of Department. Trisha's research interests have included student teachers' school-based learning and the role of the mentor, and young children and gender (in particular, boys and literacy). In recent years she has been researching outdoor play and learning.

Liz Noblett began her career as a paediatric nurse. Having qualified as a health visitor, she practised in a rural community while also being employed as a tutor on the BSc in Early Childhood Studies at Swansea University. Liz left the University to play a key role in the development of a new child health programme for Carmarthenshire. She went on to design the health strand for Flying Start Carmarthenshire, which she then managed until ill-health forced her retirement from full-time work. Liz has recently returned to her role as tutor in the Centre for Child Research, Swansea University, where she specialises in child health.

Helen Penn is Professor of Early Childhood in the Cass School of Education, University of East London (UEL), UK, and co-director of the International Centre for the Study of the Mixed Economy of Childcare (ICMEC) at UEL. She was previously a teacher and a senior administrator of ECEC services, before becoming an academic. She has worked for a number of international organisations including OECD and EU and on large-scale international aid projects in Southern Africa and in Central Asia. Her latest book, the second edition of *Understanding Early Childhood, Issues and Controversies* (OUP) has just been published.

Guy Roberts-Holmes is a Senior Lecturer and Programme Director for MSc in Early Childhood in the Centre for Child Research at Swansea University. Guy's research interests include the professionalisation of early years teachers in a range of international contexts; the effects of privatisation upon early childhood education and care; young children's understandings of 'race' and ethnicity; and men in childcare. He is the author of *Doing Your Early Years Research Topic: A Step by Step Guide* (2005) published by Paul Chapman.

Bob Sanders is Senior Lecturer in the School of Human Sciences at Swansea University. He worked in social work for 15 years before becoming a lecturer in 1992. From the mid-1970s he specialised in work with children and families and maintained that interest in his teaching and research activities. His research has focused on child protection, the effectiveness of family support, the impact of family adversity and stress on sibling relationships, and more recently the representation of childhood in the cinema. His publications include *The Management of Child Protection* (1999) and *Sibling Relationships: Theory and Issues for Practice* (2004).

Iram Siraj-Blatchford is Professor of Early Childhood Education at the Institute of Education, University of London. Her recent research projects include: Evaluation of the Foundation Phase across Wales and she is principal investigator of the major DCSF 16-year study on Effective Pre-school, Primary and Secondary Education (EPPSE 3-16) Project (1997–2013). She is working on longitudinal studies in a number of countries including Australia and Ireland. Iram is the President of the British Association for Early Childhood Education and has published over 40 major reports and books, and over 120 peer-reviewed articles and chapters in scholarly books.

Nigel Thomas is Professor of Childhood and Youth Research at the University of Central Lancashire. He was previously a social work practitioner and manager, before becoming a Lecturer in Applied Social Studies, and then Senior Lecturer in Childhood Studies, at Swansea University. His research interests are principally in child welfare, children's rights and participation. His publications include *Children, Family and the State: Decision-Making and Child Participation* (Policy Press, 2002); and *Social Work with Young People in Care* (Palgrave, 2005). He is co-editor of the journal *Children & Society*.

INTRODUCTION

Trisha Maynard and Nigel Thomas

In the introduction to the first edition of this text, published in 2004, we noted that in recent years early childhood appeared to command a much higher place on the agenda of politicians and policy makers in the UK. In 2009 this has not changed; indeed, if anything, there is an increased recognition that the health, wealth, education and well-being of young children and their families really do matter.

This growing recognition of the importance and significance of early childhood has resulted in many additional employment opportunities for those wishing to work with young children and their families. It has also, unsurprisingly, resulted in a proliferation of undergraduate degrees which have children and childhood as a key area of study. The primary purpose of this book is to provide a core introductory text for the many undergraduate students who are now studying early childhood. While numerous texts now exist, we felt that there was the need for a text that would introduce students to the significant ideas in each of the key areas of study, so providing them with a sound basis for further reading, thinking and research. Of equal importance, we reasoned, was the need for a text that would introduce students to a number of interwoven themes within the field of early childhood studies, and would help to show how these themes are reflected and played out within different areas. This seemed to be of particular importance given that most undergraduate courses are now modular; it can be hard for students to make the links between the various topics or modules studied.

As well as being useful to students, we hope this text will also be of interest to those already working with young children. We believe that all practitioners need to have a sound knowledge of different theoretical perspectives if they are to evaluate and attempt to improve their own practice. That is not to suggest that the theory–practice relationship is straightforward; indeed, the characteristics of the 'reflective practitioner' (Schön, 1983) have been debated for many years. There does appear to be a consensus, however, that practical experience, while essential in developing expertise, is not in itself sufficient.

So what are the key themes addressed in this text? We have identified four: political, social and economic changes; the social construction of childhood and children's rights; the impact of globalisation; and dominant and competing theories.

1   Political, social and economic changes

As Jackson and Fawcett note in Chapter 9, over the last decade billions of pounds have been committed to reforming early childhood services in the UK, although when compared with the provision available in Scandinavian countries (particularly Sweden) it appears that there is still some way to go. Unsurprisingly, then, a strong theme within this text is the concern that there is a growing divide between the rich and the poor, with those in greatest need of, for example, high quality health provision or childcare being the ones least likely to receive it (see for example Chapters 9, 11 and 14).

The changes resulting from devolution have also become more significant since the first edition of the text was published. There has been an increasing divergence between policies and between the types, and arguably the levels, of provision available in the 'four nations' of the UK. This is noticeable in relation to, for example, the training of the early childcare workforce (Chapter 9 and 18), child health policy and provision (Chapter 13), and social policy (Chapter 12). It is also visible in the differing aims, structure, curriculum and pedagogy of educational provision for our youngest children (see, for example, Chapters 9 and 11). It is unclear how far the four nations are simply adopting different approaches to meeting the same aim, possibly to ensure that young children are prepared for later schooling or the future workforce, or how far they are adopting different frames of reference – for example, seeing childhood as important in its own right and prioritising young children's well-being over their attainment in literacy and numeracy.

2   The social construction of childhood and children's rights

This leads to a further theme that is emphasised in this edition as in the last: that of the social construction of childhood. This is the idea that childhood is not a naturally given phenomenon, but the result of social processes of discourse, definition and interaction. As a result, the characteristics of children and childhood are not the same in different times and places (see Chapters 1 to 4). That said, within many chapters we find the idea of the child as *subject*: in scientific terms, as active in their own development and learning (Chapters 5 to 8) and in political terms, as young citizens with rights to autonomy and to participation in decision making (Chapters 3, 10, 11, 12 and 16). Indeed, the idea of children's rights (and of seeing children as having 'rights' as well as 'needs') is arguably one of the most significant themes underpinning a study of early childhood.

3   The impact of globalisation

The social construction of childhood can be linked to a further issue noted by several writers: the ongoing process of globalisation (see, in particular, Chapters 1 and 4). The opening up of the world allows us to find out about different childhoods; challenges our perceptions about what we consider to be 'normal' and thus good practices and approaches – for example, models of parenting (Chapter 4); and even facilitates the 'borrowing' of early childhood policies, provision or practices from different cultures and countries. However, while learning from different countries is viewed positively (see Chapter 9), concerns have been raised about the export of theories and practices, and with them particular embedded values, especially when this is from the relatively wealthy North to the relatively poor South (Chapters 1 and 4). A specific anxiety for some writers is the imposition of what are seen as dominant theories of child development (Chapter 1). These theories, along with concepts such as 'culture' and 'quality' are now being explored and problematised (see, for example, Chapters 1, 3, 4, 9 and 14).

4   Dominant and competing theories

Despite, or rather alongside these concerns, it goes without saying that 'dominant' theories – particularly dominant theories of child development (Chapters 5 to 8) – are still extremely powerful; an understanding of these theories, along with the ability to be critically reflective (Chapters 14 and 18) and the development of skills in, for example, child observation (Chapter 15), are seen as imperative for a highly qualified early childhood workforce.

However, given that they derive from different disciplines, within each area of interest different theories are often in tension (or competition) one with another. Within this text, for instance, some writers consider a range of perspectives and propositions when discussing a particular issue – for example, when exploring children's cognitive development or how they acquire language (Chapters 5 and 7). However, it is also possible to identify competing theories when pursuing an area of interest across different chapters. This is well illustrated in relation to the issue of play. For example, it is maintained that play is fundamental to young children's learning and development – cognitive, social and emotional – (Chapters 5, 6 and 8), as well as to the development of adaptable and flexible thought (Chapter 8). It is also argued that play is central to an inclusive curriculum (Chapter 14). We are warned, however, that not all play promotes learning and development and that when considering children's education, the prioritising (and even the existence) of 'free play' is challenged (Chapter 11). Indeed, when considering play in a global context, the idea that children should be allowed simply to play, rather than making a contribution to the family and community, is raised for consideration (Chapter 4).

Of course, these tensions between competing theories and discourses remind us of the demands and significance of interagency and multidisciplinary working (Chapter 17). They also emphasise the complexity, challenges and excitement of the interdisciplinary study of early childhood!

Organisation of the book

The 18 chapters in this book between them cover a very extensive territory, ranging from the history of childhood to the place of play in the early years curriculum. In order to make the text more manageable and accessible we have organised the book into four parts:

1   Perspectives on childhood
2   The developing child
3   Policy and provision for young children
4   Developing effective practice.

We do not suggest that these four dimensions are in any significant way independent of each other. Readers will find that the interrelationships between child development, historical and cultural perspectives on childhood, local and national policy and the nature and quality of provision, and the implications of all this for professional practice, are emphasised throughout the text.

Part One considers how childhood differs culturally, historically and globally, and introduces sociological approaches to the study of childhood. Part Two includes chapters on cognitive, emotional and social development, on language acquisition and on play. Part Three includes an overview of early years policy and services, as well as specific chapters on children's rights and the law, education, welfare and child protection, health, and inclusion.

Finally, Part Four focuses on some particular aspects of practice – child observation and undertaking research with children, interagency and multidisciplinary working and leadership. Each part of the book begins with a brief editorial introduction that explains what is in the chapters that follow and which draws attention to some common themes and to differences of emphasis.

Each individual chapter aims to introduce its subject to an intelligent reader with limited previous knowledge, and also to indicate some of the important areas of debate within the field. Some chapters include case examples or practical exercises. Each chapter concludes with some questions or ideas for further work, and with suggestions for further reading. The full list of all sources referred to is at the end of the book.

For this new edition all the chapters have been updated, and most have been extensively revised, and we thank our original authors for this. We have also commissioned eight new contributions which we think have strengthened the book considerably. We are particularly pleased to have new chapters by Helen Penn, Iram Siraj-Blatchford, Alison Clark, Carol Aubrey and Thea Cameron-Faulkner as well as contributions from Swansea colleagues Justine Howard, Liz Noblett and Guy Roberts-Holmes. Mary Fawcett assisted with the revision of Sonia Jackson's chapter, for which we are grateful.

Each of our chapter authors is an expert in her or his own field, and their professional backgrounds are very diverse, reflecting the multidisciplinary nature of the subject as well as the strong interchange between theory and practice.

Although there are differences of emphasis in the chapters that follow, and many changes from the first edition, one perspective still runs through the whole book. This is our theoretical and practical commitment to respecting the rights of children and seeing children as active participants in all matters relating to their health, care, welfare and education. Children, we are convinced, should be seen *and* heard!

PART ONE

PERSPECTIVES ON CHILDHOOD

This first part of the book is concerned with perspectives on childhood and on how children grow up. If there is one message from all that has been written about childhood in the last 25 years, it is that childhood is not at all the same thing in different times and places. That childhood differs in important ways according to where in the world we are, what period of history we are in, or which social group we are considering, is not in dispute. What is sometimes disputed, however, is whether we can use the words 'childhood' and 'children' to apply to what we find in different times and places or among different social groups. Unsurprisingly, some authors prefer to speak of a multiplicity of 'childhoods' rather than a single 'childhood'.

It is now generally accepted that childhood is, in a significant sense, socially constructed – that is, it is something produced in social interaction and discourse rather than being a purely natural phenomenon. That is not to say that there is not a physical and biological base to some of the important characteristics that distinguish children from adults – but the form which these differences take is a social production. In no way is this more evident than in the enormous variation between the appearance of childhood in different times, places and social settings.

The following chapters approach the issue of differences in childhood from four different angles.

In Chapter 1, Bob Sanders focuses on the differences in childhood in different cultures, and explores the power issues that lead to the defining of childrearing patterns in some parts of the world as 'proper' while other parts of the world are seen as failing. The chapter introduces an issue which has long challenged anthropologists – finding the right balance between *ethnocentrism* and *cultural relativism*.

In Chapter 2, Roy Lowe turns his attention to the history of childhood and considers how the pioneering work of Ariès and others has redefined the way in which we understand childhood. Key themes in this chapter are the tension between views of children as innocent or corrupt, how far childhood is socially constructed or biologically given, and how far childhood in history differs in different places. Lowe looks in particular at the significance for childhood of key social changes that took place in Britain during the sixteenth century in domestic life and in education.

In Chapter 3, Nigel Thomas reviews developments in the sociological study of childhood and the potential of sociology for advancing our understanding in this area alongside other disciplines. He shows how theoretical models such as Corsaro's 'interpretive reproduction' help us to understand how children can be at the same time determined by their culture and society and active in making meanings and transformations. A strong message is that children do not simply exist in relation to the family or the school, but may have to be understood differently in different settings. This echoes the point made earlier that there is not one 'childhood' but a multiplicity of childhoods, and that children themselves help to define and make those childhoods what they are.

In Chapter 4, Helen Penn argues that while it is possible to identify some general features of early childhood, all of them are shaped and modified by cultural contexts to the extent that, rather than searching for what is shared, it may be more useful to understand what is particular: that is, local conceptions of childhood. Penn illustrates some of these particularities through a consideration of traditional African values and attitudes – in particular, the principle of *ubuntu*. Turning to the globalisation of early childhood, Penn notes the tension in the South (the majority world) between the need to provide early years education and care and the importing of inappropriate Euro-American models of good practice.

1

CHILDHOOD IN DIFFERENT CULTURES

Bob Sanders

Contents:

- **Introduction**
- **Why study the development of children in a cross-cultural context?**
- **Culture, ethnocentrism and cultural relativism**
- **Globalisation**
- **International conventions**
- **Conclusion**

Introduction

This chapter asks why it is important to understand how different the experience of being a child can be, depending upon where in the world a child is growing up. It begins by considering why we should study childhood in different cultures – not only because it helps us provide better care for children, but also because we need to understand the power issues that lead to the definition of childrearing patterns in some parts of the world as 'proper' whilst those in other parts are seen as failing to live up to Westernised notions of what all children should aspire to. The chapter discusses culture and introduces an issue which has long challenged anthropologists – finding the right balance between *ethnocentrism* and *cultural relativism*.

Why study the development of children in a cross-cultural context?

There are many reasons for studying the cross-cultural context of children's development. First, there are practical reasons. Trawick-Smith (1997) gives an illuminating example of a relatively experienced care provider who encounters difficulties in her new post in a large urban childcare centre, when trying to soothe a young child from a different cultural background. The usual things that she has tried in the past do not seem to work with this child. He asks the question: 'How is it that this lesson had escaped her until now?' (1997: 577). The answer he suggests is:

> Children in her previous family child care home were of very similar cultural and socio-economic backgrounds. They were primarily sons and daughters of white middle-class professionals. Their family lives were very much like her own. Her new child care setting includes children of many different cultural and social economic backgrounds. (Trawick-Smith, 1997: 577–8)

To operate effectively with young children, the worker needs not only to learn 'what works?', but 'what works for this particular child, from this particular socioeconomic and cultural background?'

Another reason for studying children's development across cultures is to appreciate the value of, and the necessity for, diversity in adaptation to different environments. Darwinian principles apply not only to the physical adaptation of living organisms to their environment, but also to their social adaptation. Harkness and Super (1994) have suggested the concept of 'developmental niche', which is conceived in terms of three basic components: the physical and social settings of the child's everyday life; the culturally-regulated customs of childcare and childrearing; and the psychology of the caretakers. It is important to remember that childrearing patterns vary from culture to culture and represent an adaptation to different environments (physical and social). Given the dynamic nature of the adaptation, they may represent the optimal survival patterns within that particular environment. Child development is a continuing dynamic of an individual interacting with, and adapting to, his/her environment – an 'ecological' model of child development that has gained considerable attention in recent years (Bronfenbrenner, 1979; Barrett, 1998).

A third reason is to remind us that the process of attaching values to different cultural practices, whether in relation to childrearing or to other customs and practices, contains a *power* component. In this sense there is a postmodern construction of cultural differences. The 'discourse' within cross-cultural childrearing can be construed as a set of events and circumstances defined and evaluated by those with power, in relation to those without (or with less). Sanders (1999), for example, looks at child abuse in a cross-cultural context, and argues that it is essential to understand the power to define 'abuse'. There is a danger that Westernised concepts of child abuse are taken on board in other cultures and societies where there may be far more urgent threats to children's well-being and survival, certainly dangers that are at least as pressing as the risks posed by intra-familial abuse.

A fourth reason for studying culture in relation to children is to gain a new perspective on our own society. As Rogoff and Morelli put it:

> An important function of cross-cultural research has been to allow investigators to look closely at the impact of their own belief systems . . . Working with people from a quite different background can make one aware of aspects of human activity that are not noticeable until they are missing or differently arranged. . . . (1993: 18)

It is helpful to understand just how different child upbringing can be, so that one's own cultural approach can be set in the context of a range of different approaches. It provides a 'You are here' marker in relation to a world map of diverse cultural childrearing.

Related to this is a fifth and final reason – the value of a 'decentring' exercise, so that one's own experience of being on the receiving end of childrearing does not become the yardstick against which other methods of childrearing are compared. There are other yardsticks for looking at differing childrearing approaches, which will be discussed below, but using one's own upbringing is a potential pitfall to be avoided. It should be remembered that differences are just that – differences. They should not be seen or interpreted as deficits.

This chapter does not describe the different patterns of childrearing throughout the world: there is simply not enough space. Instead, it considers some of the issues around looking at childrearing patterns across cultures. The chapter considers the issues of culture, ethnocentrism and cultural relativism, globalisation, and the development of international conventions to promote the welfare of children.

There is, however, a wealth of information available for students to consider in depth the experiences of growing up in particular societies and cultures. Not all of this is in the form of textual material, and students are also advised to look at the portrayals of children and childhood in film. Childhood has long been a favourite theme of film-makers, and they will often use children as the protagonist in films to highlight issues such as the impact of large-scale adversity (for example, war and political turbulence) on children, or use the 'uncontaminated' eyes of the child to present to the audience a particular view of society. Such films can be seen to contain profound themes in relation to the social construction of childhood, a theme of this book, but on a more immediate level, they contain depictions of everyday life involving children in other societies and cultures.

Several highly worthwhile films include:

- *The Blue Kite* (China)
- *My Life as a Dog* (Sweden)
- *Kolya* (Czech Republic)
- *The Bicycle Thieves* (Italy)
- *The 400 Blows* (France)
- *The Boy Who Stopped Talking* (Netherlands and Kurdistan)
- *Ma Vie en Rose* (France)
- *The Spirit of the Beehive* (Spain)
- *Pather Pachali* (India)
- *Los Olvidados* (Mexico).

For some of these films the societal context is peripheral to the theme of the film, and we see an unselfconscious depiction of a child in a particular culture at a particular time as conveyed through the eyes of the director. In others – for example, *The Boy Who Stopped Talking, The Blue Kite, Kolya, Ma Vie en Rose, Pather Pachali, Los Olvidados* – the focus is on the interaction between a young child and some powerful influence of the society within which he or she is growing – for instance war, political ideology, sexist ideology, or third world poverty.

Culture, ethnocentrism and cultural relativism

So how are we to understand culture? At its most basic, culture can be understood as the 'rules and tools' of a society. White (1959: 3) defines culture as comprising 'tools, implements, utensils, clothing, ornaments, customs, institutions, beliefs, rituals, games, works of art, language, etc.' (cited in Kottak, 1994: 36).

Kottak (1994) describes aspects of culture which provide us with a clearer understanding. Culture is *learned* and relies on symbols to convey meaning. Culture is imposed upon nature ('natural lakes don't close at five, but cultural lakes do'). It is both general and specific: all people have culture, but individuals have different cultures. It is all-encompassing, in the sense that it includes everything that people do, not just the more 'aesthetic' activities. Culture is *shared*: it is learned through interaction with others in the society. Consider, for example, children who have not had that experience – so-called 'feral' children brought up by animals away from human society (Newton, 2002). Not only do they miss out on learning human language, and that part of thinking that is dependent upon language, but they have also not been *encultured*; they have not engaged in that process through which babies and young children acquire culture. Culture is *patterned* in the sense that aspects of it are linked, so that if one cultural institution changes, for example, employment practices, other connected institutions, such as domestic roles within families, may change as a result.

Consider, for example, the way in which our conceptualisations of the needs of children changed before and after the Second World War, with women first contributing to the war effort (and children being provided with day care to enable this) and then being told that they were needed back in the home in the role of mothers and caretakers for their children, leaving the jobs for those returning from the war.

On other hand, although people may be clear about cultural requirements, people don't always follow rules, reflecting the tension between the individual and society identified by child development theorists and criminologists alike. We expend considerable effort in trying to understand why some individuals don't conform to what we expect, and it is arguable that we should spend as much time studying why people *do* conform. And, indeed, following the rules may require a great deal of sophistication, perhaps much more than we are sometimes aware of. Waksler (1991a) reminds us that, for a kindergarten school child, knowing what the unwritten and implicit rules are (such as stopping dancing when the music stops) can be very difficult. As she notes:

> Being a rule-abiding kindergartner is no mean accomplishment; it involves extensive, sophisticated knowledge and the grasp of a wide array of subtleties and nuances of words and action. (Waksler, 1991a: 105)

Another aspect of culture described by Kottak (1994) is that it has universality, particularity, and generality at the same time. By *universality* is meant those cultural aspects that distinguish human beings from other species and which are present in all people. *Particularity* refers to the uniqueness of every culture: it is like no other. *Generality*, on the other hand, refers to aspects of culture that may link some cultures together into groupings, but not all. In relation to people, there is an expression: 'Every person is, at any one time, like all other people, like some other people and like no other people.' The same could be said to apply to cultures.

Cultures do not exist in a vacuum. They are in a social world within which there is increasing contact at all different levels (see discussion of globalisation below). The early anthropologists were aware of the dangers of imposing external cultural values on the societies they were studying. They began to articulate such notions in the concepts of ethnocentrism and cultural relativism, which may be seen as opposite ends of a continuum. These are difficult concepts to fully understand, and indeed because one (ethnocentrism) has tended to become value-laden as a 'bad thing', and the other (cultural relativism) as a 'good thing', it is sometimes difficult to appreciate that extremes of either can be unhelpful.

What is ethnocentrism?

Schultz and Lavenda (1990: 32) offer the view that ethnocentrism is 'the opinion that one's own way of life is natural or correct, indeed the only true way of being fully human'. Seymour-Smith (1986: 97) offers as a definition 'the habit or tendency to judge or interpret other cultures according to the criteria of one's own culture', and considers it to be a universal tendency. Applebaum (1996) considers that one of the greatest achievements of multiculturalism has been a better understanding of the 'indignity' of ethnocentrism, arguing that appreciating diversity and finding value in other cultures does not imply belittling one's own culture. Kottak (1994: 48) describes it as 'the tendency to view one's own culture as best and to judge the behaviour and beliefs of culturally different people by one's own standards.' In connection specifically with childrearing practices, Barnes (1995: 102) refers to the 'ethnocentric fallacy', which holds that 'what any one culture considers to be optimal childrearing practices (for example, firm control with clearly explained reasons embedded in a climate of warmth: the authoritarian style...) will also be optimal for every other culture.' In the same vein Sprott observes, 'Polarized ideas about parental control dominate the Anglo Dominant Culture's value orientations, reflected in both popular and scientific literature. Parental permissiveness is cast into an opposing category of "noncontrol", imbuing it with negativism' (1994: 1111). Prejudice against 'Eskimo' childrearing as being over-indulgent is examined in that context and a method is offered to 'loosen' the grip of Anglo beliefs about parenting.

However, it is not as simple as it might seem to avoid some degree of ethnocentrism. It can be tantamount to trying to achieve a completely value-free perspective, or a viewpoint that is not based on the history of one's own experiences. A particular dilemma posed by Seymour-Smith (1986) is how anthropologists should deal with ethnocentrism encountered in the populations they study. He asks:

> ... should 'native ethnocentrism' be respected as part of the indigenous world view, or should the anthropologist combat prejudice and misinterpretation in the community by providing more information about the values and customs of other people? (1986: 97)

What is cultural relativism?

If ethnocentrism is an evil to be avoided, what then is cultural relativism? It is understanding another culture well enough and sympathetically enough so that the culture is comprehensible as a plan for how to live. Kottak (1994: 48) defines it as, 'the position that the values and standards of cultures differ and deserve respect. Extreme relativism argues that cultures should be judged solely by their own standards.' Seymour-Smith (1986: 63) defines it as, 'An approach or theory in anthropology [in which] each culture or each society possessed its own rationality and coherence in terms of which its customs and beliefs were interpreted.' In all three of these definitions we see a pattern of internal consistency emerging as a defining characteristic. If then indeed, a culture were to be understood in its own terms, and not according the standards and dictates of other cultures, 'what business did members of one culture have telling those of another what to do?' (Gardner and Lewis, 1996: 28).

But as with ethnocentrism, there are dilemmas. Seymour-Smith (1986: 64) notes, 'One of the major problems in the concept of cultural relativism when held dogmatically is that it leaves the anthropologist without a theoretical basis for comparative generalizations regarding human societies or cultures.' Korbin (1981), in her anthropological examination of child abuse, notes that 'a stance of extreme cultural relativism, in which all judgments of humane treatment of children are suspended in the name of cultural rights, may be used to justify a lesser standard of care for some children.' Barrett also addresses the issue of abusive cultural practices:

> The time-honoured way in which anthropologists have attempted to avoid ethnocentrism is relativism. It has generally been assumed that there are no good or bad cultures or cultural practices. This approach carries with it the danger of slipping into the more radical position of amoral relativism, in which there are no standards whatever. In other words, under the guise of culture, anything goes, because moral judgment is ruled out. This seems to be one of those problems incapable of rational solution. If we criticize someone else's cultural practice, such as clitoridectomy (female circumcision), we would seem to be guilty of ethnocentrism; but if we fail to do so, where do we draw the line? The obvious way around this dilemma is to articulate a set of universal values, but that is easier said than done. (1996: 21)

How then is one to approach the issue of cultural practices, particularly as they apply to children, which might be acceptable within the context of one culture, but unacceptable when judged by another? At a time when there was much less contact between different cultures, when that contact was limited to anthropologists from Westernised developed nations visiting so-called 'primitive' societies, the issue might have been less significant than it perhaps is today when most nations now have majority and minority ethnic groups, and many countries have a significant number of different cultural groups establishing communities within national borders. These globalising trends place different cultures in contact with each other much more than previously, and this trend is likely to continue. As I have noted elsewhere:

> The dangers of an ethnocentric perspective are relatively clear. It is a manifestation of the exercise of power imbalances between different cultures and societies. With ethnocentrism one has cultural hegemony; however, with cultural relativism one lacks a foundation from which to censure female circumcision, the internment of Jewish children (and adults) in concentration camps, the historical practice of foot-binding in China, and ultimately, the practice of child sacrifice as practised in some societies in former times. At its most extreme, cultural relativism would imply the acceptance of such practices. (Sanders, 1999: 27–8)

Are there universal standards which one can apply? One may perhaps consider the UN Convention on the Rights of the Child as such a set of universal standards. However, as noted by Hodgkin (1994), implementation of the Convention can produce difficulties when violations of the rights of children are justified on the basis of cultural practice.

Globalisation

Globalisation is 'the rapidly developing and ever-densening network of interconnections and inter-dependencies that characterize modern social life' (Tomlinson, 1999: 2). Hall (1992: 229) describes it as 'those processes, operating on a global scale, which cut across national boundaries, integrating and connecting communities and organisations in new space–time combinations, making the world in reality and in experience more interconnected.' In both of these cases, it could be argued that the writers, by emphasising the intercommunication aspect, are describing the causes of globalisation rather than the consequences, and as such only focusing on a part of the definition. Pugh (1997) describes it as a 'process in a world in which time and space have become compressed because of the operation of modern transport, communications and the increasing internationalisation of economic activity. Thus, actions in one part of the globe have consequences elsewhere' (Pugh, 1997: 101, cited in Pugh and Gould, 2000).

Among these other usages, the concept reflects the increasing trend of cross-influence between different cultures on a world level. It also reflects power differentials within that process of reciprocal influence, which mean that the traffic is predominantly one-way. Despite the proliferation of exotic restaurants within Western societies (very frequently beginning with previously colonised nations – for example British-Indian, French-Vietnamese, Dutch-Indonesian), there is arguably more influence of Westernised, developed and industrialised countries on non-Westernised, non-developed and non-industrialised countries than the other way round. In large part this is because of the desire for overseas markets on the part of multinational companies. Hirst and Thompson (1996: 1) observe:

> It is widely asserted that we live in an era in which the greater part of social life is determined by global processes, in which national cultures, national economies and national borders are dissolving.

With others being more influenced by us and *vice versa*, one aspect of concern about globalisation is the trend from a planet of diverse societies and cultures towards a planetary cultural homogeneity. It is possible, however, to overstate this. For example, Hall provides a number of reasons why the concept of cultural homogeneity is 'too simplistic, exaggerated and one-sided' (1992: 304). Reasons include the continuing fascination with difference, and the fact that this kind of globalisation is 'unevenly distributed around the world', affecting more so countries in the Western world.

A perhaps more powerful argument against the ultimate threat of cultural homogeneity emerges when we consider the reasons why we have different cultures. From a Darwinian perspective, it could be argued that one reason human societies differ from each other in the first place is because the world consists of tropical rain forests, vast plains, mountainous areas, deserts, areas of permafrost, and so forth. Culture is perhaps largely a reflection that human species have been compelled to adapt to different environments, thereby reflecting a diversity at least as wide-ranging as the ecological niches within which people are born, grow, live and die. The argument against the threat of eventual cultural homogeneity therefore would be that as long as the world has a variety of different environments within which people can and do survive, and as long as people continue to derive an advantage from living in social groupings rather than in isolation, there will continue to be a wide range of variations in cultures. However, whilst this may reassure us about the threat of the eventual demise of all cultures but one, it does not necessarily reassure us about variations in the levels of cultural diversity around the world.

Let us now consider some further aspects of this concept. It would not be possible to have such a worldwide trade in culture without the incredibly rapid technological advances of the twentieth century. Transportation and communication developments in particular have effectively made a reality of the phrase 'It's a small world' – and becoming smaller all the time. Whereas at the end of the nineteenth century it would have taken a month to cross the Atlantic, now one can do it in a matter of hours. Communications technology over the last two centuries has gone from telegraph systems (1837) to transatlantic cables (1858) to the invention (1876) and subsequent development of the telephone, the development of wireless radio (1895), and the subsequent development of public broadcast radio, the development and marketing (1936–1938) of televisions, the large-scale distribution of personal computers and the development of the Internet during the 1990s. During the same time cars have revolutionised the ability of people to move around within and between countries, and air travel, once the prerogative of the affluent elite, has developed into a widespread necessity of life, enabling people to live and work further and further afield from the place where they may have originated.

These technological advances have also contributed to another facet of globalisation, which has been highlighted through 'McDonaldization' and 'Coca-Cola-ization' metaphors: 'Wherever you go in the world you will find a McDonalds.' Apart from wonder at the successful marketing of a product that is less than forty years old, and aside from the astounding economic success of the product, there are other cultural implications. Firstly, it is not only bringing an American product, but an American ideology (entrepreneurial enterprise) to many other countries. As noted by Fukuyama (1991, cited in Pugh and Gould, 2000: 124), 'For some writers, globalisation marks the triumphal spread of the capitalist free market influence over the world's economic and political systems.' Nothing exports capitalism nearly as effectively as the fast-food delivery of a Big Mac. The product is both standardised and adapted to the local customs. The success of McDonalds draws on the love–hate relationship with the USA throughout the world. Whilst people may have deplored the engineered involvement of the USA in numerous overseas conflicts, protested outside American embassies over a range of political activities, etc., there has ever been a deep fascination with American cultural symbols, and companies in the USA have been quick to exploit these. Levi and Wrangler Jeans, Hollywood icons such as James Dean, Marilyn Monroe, Humphrey Bogart, entertainers such as Elvis Presley, Chuck Berry, Buddy Holly – all are 'products' that have been deliberately marketed overseas and have been voraciously devoured by consumers of various nationalities, eager to import American culture, if not American imperialism, into their part of the world.

Let us now briefly consider the role of language in globalisation. The Biblical story of the Tower of Babel tells of the origin of different languages. It was God's punishment for the arrogance of mankind, that they should contemplate building a Tower that would reach to heaven. To punish them he made them all speak in different tongues, and with that, the ability, and necessity, to collaborate in the building of the Tower was lost and the Tower was abandoned. The tale highlights the necessity to be able to communicate, and the ability to sell products and services overseas has historically required the ability to communicate in local languages. However, English had become the 'lingua franca' of the world by the end of the twentieth century. Europe provides a very interesting illustration of the ethnocentric orientation of the English language. In virtually every Western European country except the UK, children are taught a second and sometimes a third language at an age when they are most receptive – in primary school, usually starting around age seven. By the time that European children are eight or nine, they are generally extremely proficient in English. In the UK, other European languages are not taught until children enter secondary school (although in Wales children learn Welsh in primary school). In effect, children of other countries are expected to learn English, but English-speaking countries make little effort to teach their children European languages. However, this is likely to change. It was announced by the Education Secretary, Alan Johnson in March 2007 that by the year 2010, children aged 7–14 in England will be required to take a modern foreign language as part of the National Curriculum.

To further highlight the significance of language, Sanders (1999) demonstrates how child protection can be influenced across national boundaries, in ways that reflect linguistic similarities (USA and UK; Belgium, Netherlands and France). If the models adopted to address social problems are indeed, as suggested, derived predominantly from interactions with countries speaking the same language, and if English appears to be headed towards being the Esperanto dream of a language spoken around the world, regardless of what other language is spoken, then it would seem to follow that there is a likelihood, and a danger, that the future holds the prospect of more and more solutions to social problems being derived from the English-speaking nations.

Why is understanding these concepts so important in relation to children and childhood? The answer is that there is a danger, in the context of unbridled ethnocentrism and an increasingly globalised world culture, that certain ideologies about children and childhood (derived predominantly from Western, affluent countries) will come to dominate the discourse about childhood and displace the vital diversity of experience of being a child that there is at present. Colton et al. (2001), for example, note the limited range of countries (USA and Europe) from which are derived contemporary notions of child development, that is, how children do and should develop, and which are accepted as universal.

International conventions

The United Nations Convention on the Rights of the Child, ratified by all countries in the world except Somalia and the USA, sets minimum standards against which the treatment of children in different countries can be judged. Provisions such as the right to life, to a name and a nationality, the prevention of kidnapping and abduction, the right to free primary education, the prohibition of torture, cruelty, capital punishment, or life imprisonment of children, and protection from the effects of war, appear to relate to issues that are not of pressing concern within the UK. However, it would be a mistake to be complacent or regard the Convention simply as a tool to promote minimum standards in non-Western countries. The UK is a long way from adequately addressing children's right to express views on matters concerning them. There are concerns about protection for asylum seeking children – the UK was singled out in a European report as providing poor services in this respect (*Guardian,* 3 April 2001). Kohli (2007) attributes this to an 'ambivalence' of policy at national level about such children which reflects at local level.

Even the Articles requiring countries to provide support to both parents to bring up a child, and to promote a child's right to an adequate standard of living, could be said to have been dramatically undermined between 1979 and 1997 in the UK, as increasing numbers of British children found themselves growing up in impoverished households. Government targets to reduce child poverty by 25% by 2004, by 50% by 2010 and to eliminate it by 2020 remain elusive, and despite some 700,000 children being lifted out of poverty, the government failed to reach the first target (Harker, 2006).

Likewise, if we look at the European Convention of Human Rights, we see that there are significant differences within Europe in the extent to which children are treated as citizens in their own right (for instance, by countries banning corporal punishment), or the extent to which the state is seen as having a role in the care of children (for instance, by countries providing pre-school programmes for young children). In these ways the interpretation of international standards is coloured by each country's own cultural values.

The final point to be mindful of when looking at provision across countries is whether rich and powerful countries are using their power and economic influence to coerce others to adopt their standards. In other words, the process of implementing international Conventions also brings us back to the tension we identified earlier, between ethnocentrism, cultural relativism and globalisation.

Conclusion

This chapter has focused on themes arising from a better understanding of children's development when located in a cross-cultural context. The focus has been to provide the student with a rationale for studying childrearing in different cultures, an examination of issues of power in defining 'normality' in child development (with particular references to discourses concerning ethnocentrism and cultural relativism), a discussion of globalisation, and a brief reference to international conventions affecting the welfare of children.

Questions and exercises

1. What are the most important reasons for studying the cross-cultural context of children's development?
2. How can we find out about cultural differences in childrearing?
3. What do we mean when we talk about 'culture'?
4. What is 'ethnocentrism' and what is wrong with it?
5. What is 'cultural relativism' and what are the problems with it?
6. What is 'globalisation' and what are its implications for childrearing and child development?
7. What is the impact of international conventions on the upbringing of children? Can such conventions help us to overcome the problems we have identified with 'ethnocentrism' and 'cultural relativism'?

Further reading

Bronfenbrenner (1979) is indispensable as an introduction to thinking about global differences in children's upbringing. Trawick-Smith (1997) is a useful starting point for understanding what sort of differences there are and provides a particularly good critique of traditional child development theories, when examined from a multicultural perspective. Konner (1991) is an excellent source (with a range of interesting illustrations), highlighting cross-cultural variations in specific aspects of childrearing. Likewise, Keats (1997) focuses on specific aspects of different societies. Tomlinson (1999) is helpful on the issue of globalisation and its implications for culture. Harwood et al. (1995) and Kağitçibaşi (1996) both reflect powerfully on precisely what difference culture makes in the way children develop and finally, Valsiner (2000) describes the relatively new field of cultural developmental psychology and provides interesting cultural contexts of various aspects of children's lives and development.

2

CHILDHOOD THROUGH THE AGES

Roy Lowe

Contents:

- **Introduction**
- **Origins**
- **Underlying issues**
- **A framework for understanding the history of childhood**
- **Conclusion**

Introduction

This chapter examines the ways that childhood has been studied by historians. It looks at the origins of the historical study of childhood, picks out some of the issues which have been seen as important and then goes on to give one account of the changing nature of childhood in the period since the Middle Ages.

Origins

Two books can be identified as starting points for the study of childhood in history. First and most significantly, Philippe Ariès' *Centuries of Childhood* was initially published in French in 1960 and was translated into English in 1962. Its appearance marked the beginning of the systematic study of the history of childhood.

It is perhaps hardly surprising that this sub-discipline should originate in France. After the Second World War the *Annales* school of history, which was extremely popular in France, stressed the need for new approaches to the study of society by historians. Ariès was a leading protagonist of this school and sought to open up a whole new field of enquiry by turning his attention to the history of childhood.

In the book, which remains influential today, he came up with several hypotheses. First, he stressed the extent to which there was little precision during the mediaeval period in respect of counting things such as years of age. One result of this was that the idea of childhood remained ill-defined, if recognised at all, and was not in any sense quantified with reference to any particular age or stages of development. He found numerous examples of the brutal treatment of children and of their being introduced to an adult world at a very early age through both sexual play and exploitation and as a commodity within the labour market. Ariès went on to argue that during the early modern period, most probably the seventeenth century, although most social groups continued to be very imprecise in the use of their term 'child', it became possible to discern a new usage, first among the middle classes, by which 'childhood' began to assume some of its modern meanings. Ariès argued that somewhere between the thirteenth century and modern times 'childhood' was discovered. Whereas during the Middle Ages children were depicted and seen as being small adults by the eighteenth century there was a general understanding that 'childhood' meant a stage of life which was widely recognised in a number of ways. This involved the coming of children's clothing, distinctive from that of adults, an end to their being depicted as small adults in books and illustrations, as well as the appearance and wider recognition of children's games and pastimes and a growing sense of the innocence of childhood.

There were several reasons why Ariès' arguments proved very persuasive and are still taken seriously. First, as he pointed out, it was the common lot of humankind that a significant proportion of infants did not survive to adulthood. In many societies more than a half of the child population was lost through one cause or another. He suggested that the likelihood of losing children made it very difficult for parents at earlier times to draw too close to their children or to sentimentalise them lest they suffer emotional torment at their likely loss. Although this argument is conjectural, it carries some weight for earlier historical periods.

It should be remembered too that in most societies children were needed as part of the workforce to sustain the economy. In this context it would have been an inappropriate luxury to spend too much dwelling on the particular needs of childhood. Only with the coming of affluence and the appearance of a more comfortable middle class did it become possible to postpone the entry of some children to the labour market thus allowing a growing number of parents to consider their offspring as 'children' in the modern sense. In brief, Ariès located the appearance of childhood within the sixteenth and seventeenth centuries.

Ariès' work sparked off an interest in the history of childhood among historians and a growing number of authors began to focus on this phenomenon. In 1974 an American scholar, Lloyd DeMause, brought together a collection of essays under the title *The History of Childhood*. Here, in a lengthy introductory chapter on the evolution of childhood, DeMause developed his 'psychogenic theory of childhood' and set about turning Ariès' ideas on their head by suggesting that childhood, in particular the way in which children were treated by adults, was central to any understanding of the human past. He argued that the habits and practices which were imposed on children throughout history offered the only meaningful explanation of how they subsequently performed as adults. Therefore, DeMause argued, it is not possible to understand human history without first understanding how the main protagonists had been reared: the kind of childhood they had experienced. He extended this argument to suggest that the maltreatment of children was a constant factor in human history and explained much of the social involvement of adults at a later stage in their lives.

DeMause remains active to the present day and continues to disseminate his ideas. He is currently actively involved in debates in a website exchange on the history of childhood and is still seeking, almost 30 years after his initial pronouncements, to publicise the importance of understanding child psychology in history. His ideas have been enormously influential and certainly have had the effect of 'psychologising' the study of childhood.

Underlying issues

As the study of childhood developed during the years that followed a number of underlying issues quickly became evident. It is important for anyone approaching the history of childhood to have some awareness of these issues and to have thought through their own beliefs in respect of each of them.

First, running through European history there is a tension between two opposed views of childhood which appear to contradict each other. On the one hand, there is a vast literature which suggests that the child is at birth intrinsically evil, or at least in need of improvement, and that it is the duty of parents and adults to school the child, to get rid of unfortunate characteristics and behaviours and, in brief, to redeem it so that it can become an effective adult. This view is, of course, underpinned by much Christian literature which stresses the need for redemption and the extent to which humankind is innately evil. The idea that humankind is innately wicked is an enduring and pervasive one and it has underpinned much of the thinking about childhood during the last two millennia.

Set against this, quite contradictorily, is the view which also is frequently found in European literature that children are born innocent but are corrupted by their growing

experience of and acquaintance with the adult world. Ironically, this thread car
discerned within the Christian church. For example, during the Middle Age
usual at religious ceremonies to dress children in white as a symbol of their inn

During the eighteenth and nineteenth centuries, in particular, a school of literature appeared which stressed the innocence of the child. Jean Jacques Rousseau's book *Emile* (1762) took this view, as did Wordsworth who subscribed to the neo-Platonist view that it was possible to look back to an age of innocence during which various insights into the nature of being were possible which were denied the corrupted adult:

There was a time when meadow, grove, and stream,

The earth, and every common sight,

To me did seem

Apparelled in celestial light,

The glory and the freshness of a dream.

It is not now as it hath been of yore; –

Turn wheresoe'er I may,

By night or day,

The things which I have seen I now can see no more.

In his 'Ode on Intimations of Immortality from Recollections of Early Childhood', from which these words are taken, Wordsworth reflected on the loss of childish innocence and the loss of insight and understanding that went with it. These two views of childhood appear to be mutually contradictory, and yet they have stood against each other for the best part of two millennia.

A second underlying issue is the question of the extent to which childhood has been socially constructed in history or whether it is a stage of life which all human beings necessarily pass through. On the one hand, much recent child psychology, such as the work of Piaget, would suggest that there are stages of development through which all children must pass on their journey to adulthood. Against this is the consideration that in many contexts childhood has necessarily been abbreviated and curtailed allowing no possibility of a childhood in the form that we currently understand it. In these historical contexts, does it make sense to talk of childhood as though it were comparable, for the vast majority of children, with the experiences undergone by a modern day child? Equally, there is in recent times, an idealisation of childhood in books, films and on television which suggest to any thinking observer that childhood may be being redefined as well as described by these treatments. The possibility of the social construction of childhood is one which has to be to the fore in the thinking of any historian of childhood.

A third issue is the question of what adult characteristics are socially constructed during childhood. Central to this is the question of gender. Are the differences and distinctions in male and female adult behaviour and the differing roles ascribed to them within society the result of differing hormones and a differing genetic endowment or are they the result of the social conditioning which takes place during the early years? What other adult characteristics and attitudes can be shown to be, to some extent at least, moulded during childhood? Is personality ultimately genetic or socially conditioned? These are all questions which can be illuminated by the study of the emergence of childhood as a historical phenomenon.

Fourthly, it is important to bear in mind the extent to which childhood may differ and may have differed in history in differing locations. There are today very clear contrasts between the Developed World, the Developing World and the Third World in respect of experiences which children undergo. It is likely that this has always been the case. These variations in experience exist both across continents and countries and within individual nations. In Britain, for example, during the period of industrialisation, childhood meant different things in differing locations depending upon particular local patterns of industrialisation. These contrasts persist to the present time and some would say have always been there. It is important for anyone approaching the history of childhood to bear this consideration in mind and to have a sense of the limits which have to be placed on any generalisation. This also gives rise to the possibility of fascinating local studies which unearth local experiences of childhood which have been lost or are as yet unknown to historians.

A framework for understanding the history of childhood

As the study of the history of childhood has become more extensive during the past thirty years, it has become possible to distinguish a number of key elements in the historical development of childhood which, together, constitute a framework which helps us to conceptualise childhood over the past four or five centuries. First, a number of detailed studies have thrown far greater light than ever before on the relative ill treatment of children across Europe during the Mediaeval period (Shahar, 1990; Schultz, 1995). This work has led us to a greater realisation of the significance for childhood of key social changes that took place in Britain during the sixteenth century. The growth of the wool trade and the swift growth of a number of towns in response to this meant that a growing number of merchants and yeoman farmers could afford, for the first time, to build larger homes than had been usual throughout the Middle Ages. These buildings often incorporated a first floor to enable separate sleeping arrangements for parents and children. This kind of domestic arrangement was unknown before and was critical for the development of the family and of childhood since it instituted in a growing number of homes for the first time the concept of privacy. It also made it easier for the children to be separately identified and treated differently in a number of respects within the home. This subtle but very significant shift tied in with other changes that were going on in society. A restructuring of apprenticeship and a complete restructuring of the education system meant that the preparation for work became far more codified and far better organised during the sixteenth century than had ever been the case before. Society was beginning to put in place the mechanisms for the codification and organisation of childhood. It is no coincidence that in 1545 Thomas Phayre wrote the first English book on paediatrics, *The Regiment of Life*. In addition, at this time, the Reformation meant not only the redirection of the religious life of Northern Europe but also that education itself became far more secular than had previously been the case. This too had a massive impact upon the lot of many children. Another key development at the end of the century was the 1598 Poor Relief Act which, for the first time, made poor children the responsibility of the Parish. The parochial overseers of the poor became for the next three centuries those who took responsibility for the welfare of children whenever parenting failed or was absent. This was to determine for ever the way in which children were perceived and treated in Britain.

Nonetheless, although there was a prospect of some kind of schooling for a minority of the luckier ones, for the vast majority of children life remained hard. In many rural areas over the next two centuries gang systems of agricultural labour developed with women and children being used for weeding, stone picking, root gathering and other menial tasks. In other parts of Britain local trades such as lace making, hosiery, straw plaiting, glove making and shoe making, each generated a demand for unskilled child labour. Some industries, such as the making of straw hats in Bedfordshire and other parts of the Home Counties, were almost entirely dependent upon child labour. The textile industries placed particular demands on children, whether it was wool manufacture in West Yorkshire, East Anglia or the West Country or lace manufacture in some Midlands towns. The well-established tradition of out-working by which much of the manufacturing took place on a small-scale in the homes of weavers and spinners led to a situation in which children were notoriously exploited for their nimble fingers and their availability. By the end of the eighteenth century there was hardly any corner of Britain in which children were not being exploited on a vast scale for one form or other of cheap labour (Horn, 1994).

Set against this, the responsibility of the Parish to take care of orphaned and penurious children resulted in a significant network of charity schools. From 1699 these were co-ordinated and founded by the Society for Promotion of Christian Knowledge with a welter of new foundations in England down to 1740. By the mid-eighteenth century there was hardly any middle-sized town in England which did not have its 'blue coat' or charity school, the blue uniforms being a token of the poverty of the children who were being cared for. Without exception the supporters of these schools stressed the need for a basic education to be provided. Isaac Watts wrote in 1724:

> there are none of these poor who are, or ought to be, bred up to such an accomplished skill in writing and accounts as to be qualified for superior posts: except here and there a single lad whose bright genius and constant application and industry have outrun all his fellows.

The tradition that the education of the poor should not extend beyond the 'three Rs' and the catechism was well established in these charity schools during the eighteenth century.

If the lot of the poor child was hard during the early modern period, the coming of industrialisation served only to make it worse. Industrialisation, involving the appearance of factories and a rapid increase in population and in the size of the towns and cities generated a situation which was too tempting for unscrupulous employers to resist. In large towns, such as London, clergymen and parish officers realised they had a new opportunity to solve the problem of child pauperism. Equally, the factory owners saw the possibility of gaining a new and remarkably cheap labour force from the towns. The consequence was that literally thousands of young orphaned children were taken long distances from their homes and confined in near prison conditions for long hours of industrial labour. At the start of the nineteenth century this traffic in children had passed its peak, but still during the first decade of the century over 2,000 pauper apprentices were sent from London to work in a variety of textile mills, three-quarters of them going into the cotton industry. Most of these were below the age of 11 (Horn 1994: 18–34). Parish children were a key source of labour enabling the swift expansion of industrialisation between 1750 and 1850. Many of the tasks they did were dangerous and the conditions in which they lived, usually in apprentice houses, were overcrowded and unhealthy. Survival rates were dreadful and those that did make it to adulthood were often stunted, puny and unhealthy. Conditions in other industries such as mining were hardly any better and in some cases worse.

All of this led to a relatively new construction during the nineteenth century: the child as the object of pity or of philanthropy. A growing number of reformers such as Peel and Wilberforce, alarmed at the conditions in which children were working in the factories, set about the establishment of legislation which would control these practices. The outcome was, by the end of the century, a plethora of Acts of Parliament which made it increasingly difficult for unscrupulous employers to exploit children as had been the case a hundred years before. This was the first serious engagement of the state in its modern form with children. By controlling the conditions of their employment and seeking to set minimum standards, the state, perhaps unwittingly, set itself up as the ultimate arbiter of the well-being of children. The other leg of this nineteenth-century reform movement was the drive to establish systems of popular education which would be increasingly accessible to all and ultimately universal. By 1870 provisions were in place for every child in England and Wales to be served by elementary schools and by 1891 schooling was de facto compulsory for all except the children of itinerant workers such as bargees and travelling showmen (Stephens, 1998).

But for much of the century the emphasis was on a schooling that was basic and confined in reality to reading, writing, arithmetic and the catechism. As Andrew Bell, one of the founders of the monitorial system of elementary education, observed in his book *The Madras School* in 1808:

> it is not proposed that the children of the poor be educated in an expensive manner or be taught to write or cypher. Utopian schemes for the universal diffusion of general knowledge would soon realise the fable of the belly and the other members of the body and confound that distinction of ranks and classes of society on which the general welfare hinges ... There is a risk of elevating by an indiscriminate education, the minds of those doomed to the drudgery of daily labour above their conditions and thereby rendering them discontented and unhappy in their lot.

Thus, in practice, the coming of popular education seems to have been driven as much by a determination to impose some kind of social control as by any sprit of charity. It is surely no coincidence that regular hours, submission to the demands of the bell, and the ready acceptance of a system of rewards and punishment (all characteristics of the industrial system) were central elements in what was offered to children through elementary schools throughout the nineteenth century. Only towards the end of the century, with a series of extensions to the revised code which had been introduced in 1862, was there a prospect of a fuller education for the ordinary child.

It is impossible to understate the significance of universal schooling for understandings of childhood. First, schooling enabled childhood to be perceived as a set of stages through which young people progressed naturally: nursery, infant, junior and secondary. The processes of transition defined and identified what was thought to be taking place. Further, schooling in this way involved a standardisation of childhood which otherwise would not have happened. It became increasingly easy for commentators, policy-makers and critics to identify templates of childhood to which 'template' solutions could be applied. One spin-off from this was the identification of the 'normal'. In 1956, C. W. Valentine wrote a book entitled *The Normal Child* reflecting these perceptions.

Moreover, schooling enabled a heightening and codification of the gendering of childhood. Boys and girls were separated from an early age in classrooms, into different schools and into differing curricula routes. All of this made it far easier to fashion 'little women' and 'little men' through the education system. An extreme version of this was the code of masculinity which was perpetrated in the boys' preparatory schools and public schools (Heward, 1988). These schools developed during the

Victorian period and have persisted. They provide an elite education for a privileged few (roughly 7% of the population) who, among other things, acquire distinct perceptions of their gender roles through their schooling. Conversely, the schools for girls, which grew greatly in number at the start of the twentieth century, marketed their own versions of 'domesticity' and 'femininity' in order to prove attractive to potential fee-paying parents (Dyhouse 1989). Thus, schooling meant gendering. The processes that were set in train with the coming of industrialisation appear, in retrospect, to be almost irreversible.

A third concomitant of universal schooling was the discovery of child poverty towards the end of the nineteenth century. The success of school attendance officers appointed by the School Boards after 1870 in getting the vast majority of the child population into schools meant that teachers were brought abruptly face-to-face with the spectre of urban poverty. It was an issue that was seized on by the nascent socialist movement. Two investigators, Charles Booth, a Liverpool shipowner and Seebohm Rowntree independently investigated the extent of poverty in London and York. Their findings, which were published at the turn of the twentieth century were shattering in their impact. In both cities they found that about one-third of the population was living below the poverty line but, equally significantly in our context, that it was possible to identify cycles of poverty during one individual's lifetime. Those families most likely to fall into poverty were those with large numbers of children. Hence, the number of children living in poverty at the beginning of the twentieth century was disproportionately higher than the overall percentage in poverty. These findings coincided with the realisation of the ill-health of the urban proletariat during the recruiting campaign for the Boer War. Even worse, it became evident that child poverty correlated with ill-health. Children in poverty were far more likely to be suffering from tuberculosis, to die of scarlet fever or to suffer dental caries. All of this became evident as a direct result of universal schooling and of politically inspired, privately funded research projects (Englander and O' Day, 1995).

The outcome was a permanently changed view of the ways in which the state should deal with the child. At the beginning of the twentieth century the medical inspection of school children was introduced. At the same time, a school meals programme was allowed by Parliament. In addition, it became clear that in future the process of educating children was to involve far more than instruction. A number of welfare initiatives were intended to alleviate the lot of poor and unhealthy urban children. The first of these was the Open Air School movement which took off during the Edwardian period and resulted, by the time of the First World War, in most large cities having Open Air Recovery Schools (usually for tubercular children) in rural locations away from the urban centres.

One other significant result of the discovery of child poverty was the appearance of a Child Study movement in the late nineteenth century. In 1895 James Sully produced a book entitled *Studies in Childhood*. This appeared at exactly the moment that organisations were being set up in both England and America to study children and the child's mind. Between 1889 and 1906 the medical profession organised five large-scale enquiries into the condition of children in London alone. In 1894 the Child Study Association was set up. Two years later, the more medically oriented Childhood Society was established. This immediately launched a journal, *The Paidologist*. During the Edwardian period, these two organisations merged and in 1907 they formed the Child Study Society (Hendrick, 1994). In these initiatives we can see the origins of child psychology in modern Britain. Many of the early leaders in the child psychology movement were members of one or other of these organisations.

However, in Britain the Child Study movement took a particular slant as a result of the foundation of the Eugenics Society, a London-based organisation committed to racial improvement. Founded by Charles Galton at the turn of the century, this quickly became the basis of an international movement. The Galton Laboratory was established in 1905 at the University College London where Galton's collaborator, Karl Pearson, set about experimental work on the human mind. Several of the pioneers of child psychology were attracted to the Eugenics movement, perhaps most notably Cyril Burt. Within a few years Burt and his associates, working from within the Eugenics Society, had shifted child psychology in Britain to a position where it was very firmly focused on intelligence testing and on the separation and streaming of children rather than on the identification of a whole range of psychological needs (Hearnshaw, 1979). Britain became one of the 'stamping-grounds' for early intelligence tests and over a forty-year period before the Second World War most Local Education Authorities were beginning to use intelligence tests to diagnose children for entry to schools of one type or another (Wooldridge, 1994). It is possible, to greater or lesser degree, to show that each of these initiatives stemmed in large part from the coming of universal schooling.

Meanwhile, other agencies were appearing which would work to stereotype and to idealise childhood. The popular press emerged in its modern form in the years following the foundation of the *Daily Mail* in 1896 and universal schooling, leading to universal literacy resulted in a mass reading public which enabled a vast growth in book publishing at the turn of the twentieth century. Books were written about children, and for them (Turner, 1976). A number of authors from the mid-Victorian period onwards established their reputation on writing at least some of their major works for children: G. A. Henty, Rudyard Kipling, Jack London, C. M. Ballantyne, Robert Louis Stevenson, Anna Sewell, to name but a few. They conjured a world in which children were brave, adventurous, loyal and patriotic. They provided the stereotypes which enabled children to have an image of what they were meant to be and which at the same time offered the adult world a stereotype of childhood which they found acceptable and worthwhile. This stylisation of childhood has continued apace during the intervening 100 years. New agencies such as radio, television, popular film and, more recently, the record, tape and CD have all offered images of childhood which are widely admired and extremely influential. In brief, during the period since the 1880s agencies have appeared which are deeply influential in determining society's view of childhood. If schooling began the process of standardisation and stereotyping, the media have extended and confirmed it.

More recently, the range of areas in which the state has felt it appropriate to intervene towards children has expanded dramatically. Perhaps the first signals of this were apparent when schemes to send orphaned Dr Barnardo's children to Australia and Canada became popular during the inter-war years (Bean and Melville, 1990). This preparedness to arbitrarily move large numbers of children in what was perceived to be their own interests was followed by the evacuation scheme introduced in 1939 to save urban children from the perils of a German bombing campaign. This scheme proved largely ineffective, since thousands of children and their parents simply returned to their own homes rather than sit the war out in strange rural locations, but it was evidence of the preparedness of the state to take far wider responsibility for the well-being of children. Since then the expansion of the work of Juvenile Courts, the 'statementing' of children with emotional and behavioural difficulties in schools, the accretions to the powers of the Youth Service and the introduction of Young Offender schemes are all clear tokens of the preparedness of the state to take responsibility for more or less every aspect of the life of the child (Pilcher and Wagg, 1996).

Conclusion

Thus, in brief, what emerges from this sketch of key developments in the history of childhood over the last 200 years is that childhood does appear to have changed irreversibly, that the powers of society to govern and control childhood have been greatly enhanced, and in the process childhood itself seems to have become irreversibly stereotyped. All of this has generated a vast research literature, some of which is hinted at in the references.

This phenomenon of the emergence of childhood as a historical phenomenon also raises questions for anyone embarking on a study of the early years. Whatever aspect of childhood is being examined, it is always important to bear in mind the historical context within which we work today and the historical influences which have come to bear on childhood. These are still working themselves out in adult perceptions of children and in the self-images that children acquire as they grow up. The study of the history of childhood is necessarily central to any proper understanding of what it means to be a child at the beginning of the twenty-first century.

Questions and exercises

1 Explore the books in the reading list which deal with the history of childhood to find out how far you agree with the ideas in this chapter. Be ready to incorporate your growing knowledge of the history of childhood into your other work on this course.
2 Consider how far and in what ways childhood as you know it today has been conditioned by this historical legacy.

Further reading

Ariès (1962) is in some ways the best introduction to the subject – after all, this was the book that established the discipline. DeMause (1974) is a stimulating exploration of the psychological aspects of the subject, with links to other elements of early childhood studies. Heywood (2001) is the best recent summary of the field. Cunningham (2006) is a wonderfully accessible and expert guide to the history of British childhood, and comes with an accompanying CD which is highly recommended.

3

SOCIOLOGY OF CHILDHOOD

Nigel Thomas

> **Contents**
>
> - **Introduction**
> - **What is sociology?**
> - **Socialisation theory**
> - **Psychologists, sociology and childhood**
> - **Anthropologists, sociology and childhood**
> - **The 'new paradigm'**
> - **Studying children in society**
> - **Recent developments and future directions**
> - **Conclusion**

Introduction

The aim of this chapter is to introduce some key elements of the sociological study of childhood, and to see how it can help us to a better understanding of childhood and children's lives. We will look first at how sociologists have traditionally studied childhood (or more often, have failed to). We will consider some of the problems with socialisation theory and with views of childhood as a preparation for adult life, and consider the critique of socialisation theory from an interactionist perspective. We will also look at some recent work in psychology and anthropology which has dealt with some of the same issues. We then review what has been called the 'new paradigm' of the sociology of childhood.

The second part of the chapter looks at a number of areas of children's lives to see what can be learned about them through sociological research. This part includes some simple exercises based on research texts, which you can do by yourself or with a partner.

What is sociology?

In general terms, sociology is concerned with the study and understanding of *social processes* and *social structures*. These may be studied at a number of different levels:

1   The 'macro' level is concerned with demographic patterns (population and so on) and with global changes in social patterns and relations.
2   The 'meso' level looks at social institutions – the family, work, leisure, schooling and so on.
3   The 'micro' level studies social interaction – sometimes in a very detailed way.

The key organising concepts used by sociologists include:

1   Ideas about social relations – authority, social cohesion, conflict.
2   Social categories such as class, ethnicity and gender.
3   Broader social processes – for instance 'modernisation'.

Early European sociologists such as Emile Durkheim and Max Weber, at the beginning of the twentieth century, were interested in social organisation and in the relationship between the individual and society. They asked questions such as: 'What binds people together in social groups?' 'How do people come to share belief systems, and why are belief systems different?' 'Why do people obey authority? In the middle of the century the dominant voices were American – sociologists such as Talcott Parsons who aimed to build a comprehensive theory that would explain everything from global social structures to the detail of social relations in terms of *function*, and critics such as C. Wright Mills who were more interested in the conflicts of interest between different groups in society. In the 1960s a branch of sociology developed that was concerned much more with social interaction – for instance, Erving Goffmann who studied how individuals present themselves in society, and Harold Garfinkel who focused on the minute detail of interaction, in particular the rules governing conversations.

More recently the dominant voices have included Michel Foucault, with his complex exploration of power and knowledge, and in Britain, Anthony Giddens. Giddens' central preoccupation is with one of the key tensions in social theory, which he characterises as the relationship between *structure* and *agency*. On the one hand, our lives are governed by social structures and social processes, so that it might be said that we have no existence outside society. On the other hand, these social structures and processes are nothing but the result of human activity. So which is prior – do individuals create society, or does society create individuals? Are we free agents, or are our lives

determined? A moment's reflection may suggest to us that in some way
are true – but the task then is to explore the relationship between t'
ologist of major significance is Pierre Bourdieu, who has responde
developing the concept of *habitus*, by which he means the laye
tions from which we draw our routines for thinking, speaking and
it, *habitus* is 'embodied history, internalized as a second nature and ʒ
history … the active presence of the whole past of which it is the product' ʲ.
So we do make choices, but from a repertoire which is more or less limited bʲ
social positioning and experience.

What has all this to do with childhood? From a cursory reading of much of the sociological literature, one might say 'very little'. Many of the standard texts have in the past
had no index entry for childhood, or if they have it has been simply a cross-reference
to 'the family' or 'education'. This has begun to change, but only slowly, and it is rare to
find any book of general sociology with a chapter on childhood. The questions about
social structures and social processes have not been asked specifically in relation to
childhood; the questions about social relations, authority and power have not been
applied to adult-child relations; and the social categories used – class, ethnicity, gender –
have not been extended to include childhood. Where we do find books in the past
about 'the sociology of childhood' they tend to be specifically about the process of *socialisation* (for instance, Bossard and Boll, 1966). Children are studied, not as actual and
participating members of society, but as *prospective* members. What is interesting about
children, from this perspective, is the process by which they are made into adults.

Socialisation theory

A child is born into a world that already exists. From the point of view of society, the function of socialization is to transmit the culture and motivation to participate in established
social relationships to new members. (Elkin, 1960: 7)

The central idea of classical socialisation theory (note: it is often spelt 'socialization', especially in American texts) is that we are in effect *produced* in childhood by
social conditioning. It is only through this process that we become *social*, and
because human beings are essentially social animals, this means that it is only
through this process that we become fully human. More specifically, we are
socialised into understanding and accepting the conventional norms and values of
our particular society, and into becoming part of a culture; we are socialised into
our particular role (s), social status and social class; and according to some our own
individual personality is also the result of a socialisation process. The idea that individual personality is the result of socialisation was put forward most strongly by the
behaviourist J.B. Watson, who wrote:

Give me a dozen healthy infants, well-formed, and my own specified world to bring them up in, and I'll guarantee to take any one at random and train him to become any type of specialist I might select – doctor, lawyer, artist, merchant-chief and, yes, even beggarman and thief, regardless of his talents, penchants, tendencies, abilities, vocations, and race of his ancestors. (from 'Behaviorism', 1930; quoted in Elkin 1960: 46)

Socialisation theory identifies a number of socialising institutions or 'agencies of socialisation': principally the family, the school, the peer group and the mass media. Some theorists distinguish between *primary* socialisation, which includes the laying down of fundamental characteristics of personality, basic values, and so on; and *secondary* socialisation, representing the continuing effect of group interaction and culture on our habits, thoughts and values throughout life. Most of the attention tends to be on primary socialisation; some conceive of this as taking place throughout childhood and into adolescence, whilst others confine it to early childhood. For instance, Bossard and Boll argue that 'the social conditioning of the personality during the first years of life is of primary importance ... the basic patterns of personality are laid during the period of childhood', and that 'the sociological processes of personality formation can best be studied during the earlier stages' (Bossard and Boll 1966: 7–8). From this perspective the family is clearly the most important socialising institution.

Socialisation theory came under increasing criticism in the 1970s from sociologists who took an *interactionist* approach such as Norman Denzin. Studies of adult–child interaction and child–child interaction, and reflections on them, led to dissatisfaction with 'socialisation' as a model for what was observed to take place. Mackay (in Waksler, 1991b) uses the example of an observed interaction between a child and a teacher about the child's understanding of a story, to show how the teacher treats the child as incompetent throughout in respect of the task, but how in fact an analysis of the interaction shows that it presumes a high degree of competence on the child's part to make it work.

Matthew Speier puts the criticism forcefully. He argues that traditional interests in development and socialization have neglected 'the interactional foundation to human group life':

The traditional perspectives have overemphasised the task of describing the child's developmental process of growing into an adult at the expense of a direct consideration of what the events of everyday life look like in childhood ... the intellectual and analytic position of sociologists is essentially ideological in the sense that they have used an adult notion of what children are and what they ought to be that is like that of the laymen in the culture. (Speier 1976: 170)

In other words, it is the job of sociologists to bring distinctive analytic tools, and an open and enquiring mind, to the study of childhood, rather than simply recycle conventional ways of seeing and understanding.

Psychologists, sociology and childhood

The key organising concepts of developmental psychology are very different from those used by sociology – concepts such as *learning, conditioning* or sometimes *unfolding*. Most discussions of child psychology start with Piaget, whose key insight was that the child learns to understand the world better as she or he progresses through a series of developmental stages characterised by increasingly sophisticated conceptual schemes. Margaret Donaldson and others revised Piaget, using research that showed that children were able to understand concepts that had been thought to be beyond their reach, if the tasks were presented in a way that 'made sense' to the child. This linked with the ideas of Vygotsky, an early contemporary of Piaget, about the 'zone of proximal development' – the area into which the child is able to move on with support.

There are other differences between Piaget and Vygotsky. Piaget is sometimes thought to view the child as a solitary learner, and Vygotsky seen as adding a social perspective on the process of development. In fact Piaget did emphasise a social element in learning, but he also seemed to see what was learned as in some sense *natural* – there is a natural progression from one conceptual framework to another, which it is the child's task to discover. For Vygotsky what the child learns is above all a culture, and therefore the role of other people in learning is indispensable. Building on these ideas, a number of psychologists including Jerome Bruner, Martin Richards and Paul Light began to explore the social dimension of psychological development in more depth.

It might on the face of it appear that psychology has converged with socialisation theory, in that it has gone from seeing development as a natural process of 'unfolding', or of the child discovering what is already there in the world, to a focus on the process of transmission of cultural norms and ways of seeing and doing things. In fact the new psychology is very different from traditional socialisation theory precisely because of what Piaget taught us about the child's active participation in learning, and Vygotsky's revelation of the processes of dialogue and negotiation inherent in cultural learning. These strands in the theory are much more convergent with, for instance, the interactionist perspective of Denzin than they are with classical socialisation theory. Barbara Rogoff (1989) writes of 'the joint socialization of development by young children and adults'; she argues that the child from the earliest age is an active participant in the socialising processes of development.

Anthropologists, sociology and childhood

Anthropology is literally 'the study of people'. It developed as an academic discipline in the late nineteenth and early twentieth centuries. First in the field was physical anthropology (the study of variations in physical types around the world), followed closely by cultural anthropology (the study of habits and mode of life),

from which developed modern social anthropology with its focus on kinship relationships and belief systems. From the beginning anthropology developed a distinctive method based on close observation and detailed recording in 'field notes', known
as *ethnography*. The focus was very much on 'primitive' or 'tribal' societies – people
who are 'different' from 'us' in what were thought to be significant ways, although in
recent years the same methods and concepts have been applied to Western societies.

Like sociologists, anthropologists for many years were backward in applying their
concepts and methods to children and childhood. Anthropologists tended to rely on
adult informants, to study adult behaviour and adult beliefs, to be interested in the
social networks of adults, and to share adult concerns with their subjects. In 1973
Charlotte Hardman delivered a paper which argued that children were a 'muted
group' who had been ignored by anthropologists and given no voice in the anthropological record. She suggested that children deserved to be studied in their own
right as a group with their own *culture*, their own network of relationships, their own
beliefs and their own values. Gradually more and more anthropologists have turned
their attention to childhood and the lives of children. This has been important for
the study of childhood for the following reasons:

1   It implies looking at children not just as developing adults or adults-to-be, but as
    people in their own right.
2   It implies looking at children not just in their families or at school, but in their
    peer group, in work, in interaction with other children and with adults both
    within and outside their family group.
3   It implies taking children's own explanations and their beliefs seriously, in the
    same way that anthropology respects adults' accounts of their own culture.

The 'new paradigm'

The contemporary sociology of childhood is distinguished by two central ideas. The first
is that childhood is a social construction. Historical and cross-cultural studies have
shown us that the 'nature' of childhood is enormously variable according to the social
context, and that childhood is in a sense socially defined and created. The biological
processes involved in growing up and getting older are real; but the pattern and the
meaning of these changes is structured and mediated by society and culture. The second idea is the increasing recognition we have seen in sociology, psychology and anthropology that children must be seen as social actors in their own right. Children's lack of
active presence in society has been mirrored by their lack of active presence in theory.

These two insights, that childhood is a social construction and that children are social
actors, are the key elements in what has been called a *new paradigm* for the sociology of
childhood. (A paradigm is a theoretical framework, a fundamental way of understanding reality that underlies specific theories; for instance, when Newton's physics

based on gravity was overturned by Einstein's physics based on relativity, a new paradigm was created in which different questions were asked and different kinds of answers were given.) This new sociological paradigm was clearly articulated by Alan Prout and Allison James (1990). They describe it as an 'emergent' paradigm, because it is not yet fully developed but still in the process of formation.

Prout and James identify the distinctive features of the new paradigm as follows:

1 Childhood is understood as a social construction. As such it provides an interpretative frame for contextualizing the early years of human life. Childhood, as distinct from biological immaturity, is neither a natural nor universal feature of human groups but appears as a specific structural and cultural component of many societies.
2 Childhood is a variable of social analysis. It can never be entirely divorced from other variables such as class, gender, or ethnicity. Comparative and cross–cultural analysis reveals a variety of childhoods rather than a single and universal phenomenon.
3 Children's social relationships and cultures are worthy of study in their own right, independent of the perspective and concerns of adults.
4 Children are and must be seen as active in the construction and determination of their own social lives, the lives of those around them and of the societies in which they live. Children are not just the passive subjects of social structures and processes.
5 Ethnography is a particularly useful methodology for the study of childhood. It allows children a more direct voice and participation in the production of sociological data than is usually possible through experimental or survey styles of research.
6 Childhood is a phenomenon in relation to which the double hermeneutic of the social sciences is acutely present (see Giddens, 1976). That is to say, to proclaim a new paradigm of childhood sociology is also to engage in and respond to the process of reconstructing childhood in society. (Prout and James, 1990: 8–9)

This perspective has produced a great deal of stimulating research, much of it in Northern Europe and Scandinavia. At the same time sociologists in North America have continued to develop research and theoretical work in understanding childhood. Corsaro (1997) made a substantial contribution to thinking about the relationship between *structure* and *agency* in childhood, with his concept of *interpretive reproduction*. The idea behind this concept is that children work to reproduce themselves, their culture and their social relationships, but that in doing so they interpret them for themselves. As he puts it:

1 Children actively contribute to cultural production and change.
2 They are constrained by the existing social structure and by societal reproduction.
3 Within these constraints, children's participation is *creative* and *innovative*.

Studying children in society

The methods used by sociologists to study children in society vary in relation to a number of different factors, in particular the level of analysis:

1   At the *micro* level research is concerned with the study of children as individuals or in social interaction. Research at this level may be qualitative or quantitative, but is more likely to be qualitative. Such research often favours the use of methods of communication that are accessible to children and elicit their competence – for instance drawing, writing and using stories.
2   At the *meso* level research is concerned with the study of children's lives on a larger scale, in relation to institutions such as school, family or the media, in activities such as leisure, sport or travel, or in terms of 'problems' such as poverty, illness, disability, homelessness, divorce and separation, crime, abuse, pornography, war and famine. Such research tends to use survey methods, statistical data, or the compilation of findings from a number of 'micro' studies.
3   At the *macro* level research is concerned with the study of children's lives on a larger scale. This might include historical changes in the nature of childhood and in patterns of child–adult relations, or global and generational relationships between children and adults. This research uses statistical data, or analytical and theoretical work based on existing theory or research.

Most of the research we will consider in this chapter is at the *micro* level, because that is where most of the work in the 'new paradigm' is done. However, there is also some important work being done at the other levels.

Children and their peers

Corsaro uses his concept of 'interpretive reproduction' in studying children's *peer cultures*. For Corsaro, peer culture is defined in interaction, but this takes different forms at different ages. Children's early participation in peer culture is mediated by adults – for instance, it takes place in pre-school settings to which parents arrange access for their children. In these settings children first encounter ideas of sharing and collective ownership, and of friendship. The central themes in children's 'initial peer cultures', according to Corsaro, are: attempts to *gain control* of their lives, attempts to *share* that control with each other, and the importance of *size* and of the idea of 'growing up'. He explores these themes through studies of play routines, of children's protection of their interactive space, and of sharing routines and rituals. Corsaro shows how children learn about autonomy and control through challenging and mocking adult authority and by confronting fears and conflicts in fantasy play. In contrast to the traditional psychologist's view of children's innate capacities unfolding as they mature, or the traditional sociologist's view of roles and values being inculcated by external social institutions and processes, he emphasises the importance of viewing such phenomena as conflict and friendship as *collective* and *cultural* processes.

In later age stages Corsaro focuses on social differentiation: gender differentiation, status hierarchies, core groups and 'rejected, neglected or controversial' children. He advises caution about assuming that these processes are the same everywhere, arguing that cultural differentiation is always important. However, some themes tend to be consistently present: for instance, in pre-adolescent peer cultures he notices the different patterns and issues that typically emerge in the seven-to-thirteen age group, the greater stability of friendship patterns and the phenomenon of 'best friends', of friendship groups and alliances and of gossip.

Children in families

Sociologists might ask different kinds of questions about children in families, depending on what paradigm they are using. For instance, someone using a *socialisation* paradigm might ask questions like: How are children socialised? How do families 'raise' children? What difficulties do parents encounter in 'raising' children? What are the different patterns of family socialisation? How does family socialisation interact with school and peer culture?

Someone working within a *family sociology* paradigm might ask questions such as: Why do parents have children? What is the significance of changes in family composition? What are the different patterns of family life and how are they experienced?

On the other hand, for those following the new paradigm of the sociology of childhood the salient questions might be: What is the meaning of 'family' to children? How are the lives of children in families negotiated? What is the relationship between children's lives in their families and children's other social worlds? What is the relationship between how childhoods are negotiated in families and the social construction of childhood?

Exploring the implications of the new paradigm for the relationship between childhood and family sociology, James and Prout (1996) draw attention to the ways in which children construct and manage their identities differently in different settings – school, family, peer group and so on – and also in response to the particularities of individual families. O'Brien et al. (1996), in the same volume, report on research into children's views on what counts as a family. Presented with vignettes of different household types and relationships (married couples with and without children, unmarried couples with children, single parent and step families, separated parents), children were asked to say whether these counted as families or not. Younger children tended to emphasise conventional criteria such as marriage, while older ones placed more stress on quality of relationships. Children's views tended to reflect their own personal experiences, and in discussion children were prepared to adapt their views in response to each other's arguments. Smart et al. (2001) studied children's perspectives on divorce and separation, and use children's accounts of family life to show how childhood is changing and the status of children in families is being transformed.

Regardless of the approach taken, some features will be important from any perspective, illustrating common concerns of all sociologists:

1   Changes in family life
2   Changes in family composition
3   Children's place in families
4   Children who are outside families.

Children in school

Now let us look at the kind of questions that sociologists might ask about children in school. The socialisation paradigm produces questions like: How are children socialised in schools? How do schools inculcate social values and norms in children? How does school socialisation interact with family socialisation?

Traditional sociology or social policy approaches, on the other hand, might lead one to ask: What is the nature of the school as an institution – how does it operate, where does the power lie? What are the objectives of schooling, and how are they effectively achieved? What is the effect of schooling on social inequalities (in terms of class, gender, ethnicity)?

In the new paradigm the questions that are asked tend to be: What is the meaning of 'school' to children? How are the daily lives of children in schools patterned? How is the experience of children in schools structured in terms of, for example, age, gender, ethnicity? How is meaning negotiated in the classroom between children and teachers? What is the relationship between children's lives in the classroom and in the playground? How does school have an impact on transitions in children's lives? What is the relationship between how childhoods are negotiated in schools and the social construction of childhood?

To take just one recent example, Seung Lam and Pollard (2006) analyse the transition from home to kindergarten, in terms of children crossing a cultural boundary and, in effect, commuting between two cultural settings. The authors present a conceptual framework for understanding children as agents in the transition, employing elements from sociocultural theory such as the concept of *rite of passage*. They conclude that:

> children bring to kindergarten what they learned (including patterns of strategic action, competencies, child identity) at home. They are active in making sense of, responding and adapting to the new kindergarten classroom in terms of separation from caregiver, transition programme, physical environment, play and learning, rules and routines and relationships. This is a dynamic and continuous negotiation process of adaptation. (2006: 137)

Children and work

If we consider the questions that sociologists in different paradigms might ask about children and work, we find a different picture. Within the socialisation paradigm very little attention has been paid to this subject, although someone using this paradigm might ask questions about the role of work experience in socialising children into adult culture and values; nor are questions about children and work often asked within traditional sociology and social policy approaches. However, sociologists working in the new paradigm have looked at this aspect of children's lives more fully, asking questions like: What counts as children's work? What is the meaning of 'work' to children? What is children's experience of work? What are children's views of work? Why do children work? What are the benefits and losses to children from working?

Morrow (1994) studied work done outside school by children aged 11 to 16. She collected children's written accounts of their everyday lives outside school, and followed these up with interviews and classroom discussions. She found that the work done by children outside school fell into four categories: wage labour; marginal economic activity such as baby-sitting, car-washing and odd jobs; non-domestic family labour (e.g., helping in a family business); and domestic labour (including housework, household maintenance and repair, caring activities). Some older children held positions of responsibility involving safety, money, animals, or valuable equipment. Many children took responsibility for the care of their siblings, and some took responsibility for the care of adult family members with disabilities. Many older children looked after other people's young children. Morrow comments:

> It is interesting that supposedly 'incompetent' children are given responsibility for looking after younger children and babies. Thus, the social construction of childhood and the reality of children's activities do not correspond, with the result that children who do assume responsibility are hidden from view, and occupy an ambiguous, and unacknowledged, place between adulthood and childhood. (1994: 137)

Morrow's conclusion was that there is a need for a re-evaluation of childhood in relation to ideas of dependency and responsibility, in the light of the evidence of their experience of work.

Children and the media

There is a growing body of sociological work on children's relationship with communications and digital media – television and video, the Internet, mobile phones and so on. Reflecting the preoccupations of the 'new paradigm', much of the focus is on how children use these new media to extend their social networks and their interaction with a wider world, and sometimes on how they adapt technology to new purposes and in unexpected ways. Research also addresses questions about 'risks' to children from electronic media, reflecting public concern in this area. Key authors include Buckingham (2000) and Livingstone (2002).

Children, place and environment

There is a healthy interchange between sociology and geography in the field of childhood studies. The growing sub-discipline of 'children's geographies' has its own (eponymous) journal and many other publications (for example, Holloway and Valentine, 2000). Research here is concerned with children's use of place and space which, as sociologists and anthropologists have noticed, are key factors in shaping children's lives. Related to this is a substantial body of research and practice around children's relationships with their environments and the part which children may play in environmental change at all levels. The journal *Children, Youth and Environments* is of key significance here.

Recent developments and future directions

The flourishing of new sociological approaches to childhood has tended to be dominated methodologically by small-scale research with children in different settings, and theoretically by an emphasis on children's agency. At the same time there have always been sociologists whose focus was on the bigger picture, and who continued to ask questions about the structure of society and children's place in it (for example, Qvortrup et al., 1994; Qvortrup, 2005). More recently there has been increased questioning of the emphasis on 'agency', and a renewed interest in the ways in which children's lives are more or less determined by social structure. Coincident with this has been a growing interest in the concept of *generation* and in the relationships between generations – particularly, but not exclusively, those between adults and children. Examples include Alanen and Mayall (2001) and Mayall (2002).

In relation to early childhood, there is a growing body of work that applies sociological theory to the understanding of young children's lives, especially in daycare and early education settings – see for instance, Clark et al. (2005). There is also continuing interest in the cross-cutting of the category 'childhood' with other kinds of social stratification – gender, ethnicity, (dis)ability and class. Lareau (2000, 2003) has shown in particular how in the USA social class is hugely significant in shaping the patterns of children's lives in the present, as well as their opportunities in the future. There is no reason to suppose that the same does not apply in the UK and other countries.

Other writers are concerned with the ways in which childhood is changing, and the impact of social change on childhood. Lee (2001) argues that as adult lives become more fluid and uncertain the old dichotomy, with childhood seen as a preparation for adult life, becomes increasingly irrelevant, and that arguments for seeing children as 'being' rather than 'becoming' need to be reframed to reflect these changes. Prout (2005) questions the adequacy of a purely social understanding of childhood for understanding lives that are so shaped by technology, and argues that we need to conceptualise the construction of contemporary childhood in ways that take account of the inseparable part played by artefacts and machines. Nonetheless, a sociological framework is still of key importance in understanding contemporary childhood.

Conclusion

We have seen how sociology can help us to understand children's lives and children's place in society in a fuller and more rounded way – especially a sociology that takes as its starting point that children are people and participants in social life, not just 'adults in the making'. The insights being developed by sociologists have a lot in common with recent work in psychology and anthropology, and to some extent there has been a convergence between the disciplines. However, the distinctive sociological emphasis on social structures and social processes remains important.

It has only been possible in this chapter to introduce some of the ideas behind contemporary sociological research in childhood, and to look at a few examples of the work that is being done. If you want to find out more about the ideas contained in this chapter, do make use of some of the further reading suggested below.

Questions and exercises

Exercise 1

Take an example of research into children's peer culture and relationships – for instance, the paper 'Children's negotiation of meaning' by Nancy Mandell (1991b). Ask yourself (or your partner, if you are working in a pair) the following questions:

1 What aspects of children's lives does the study address?
2 What is the main purpose of the study (what is the author trying to achieve)?
3 What concepts or categories are used in the paper?
4 How might we develop this analysis further?

Exercise 2

Read an account of some research into children's experience of families – for instance, Chapters 1 and 3 in *Understanding Families: Children's Perspectives* by Virginia Morrow (1998), or Chapter 3 of *Connecting Children: Care and Family Life* by Brannen et al. (2001). Ask yourself (or your partner, if you are working in a pair) the following questions:

1 What are the main aims of this research?
2 What concepts or ideas do(es) the author(s) start with?
3 What are the principal methods used in the research?
4 What are the most important findings of the research?
5 What questions are left unanswered (or unasked)?

Exercise 3

Read a research paper on children's lives in school – for instance, the chapter 'Making sense of school' by Margaret Jackson in Pollard (1987). Ask yourself (or your partner, if you are working in a pair) the following questions:

1 What are the main aims of this research?
2 What assumptions does the researcher start with concerning children's lives in school?
3 What methods does the researcher use?
4 What are the most important findings of the research?
5 What questions deserve to be explored further?

Further reading

For sociology in general there are many sound introductory texts, such as Giddens (1993). For the sociology of childhood specifically, the most useful sources are probably James and Prout (1990; revised edition 1997), Corsaro (1997), Waksler (1991b and 1996), Jenks (1996; revised edition 2005), James et al. (1998) and Wyness (2006). There are useful research collections edited by Mayall (1994), Pollard (1987), and Qvortrup et al. (1994). A good general book on childhood in society is Hill and Tisdall (1997). For a brief overview of trends in developmental psychology, see Woodhead (1999). For those interested in exploring some of these issues further, Thomas (2002) attempts to link the sociological understanding of childhood to issues of children's rights and participation.

4

THE GLOBALISATION OF EARLY CHILDHOOD EDUCATION AND CARE

Helen Penn

Contents:

- **How childhoods vary**
- **Caution about culture**
- **International perspectives – a view from the South**
- **An example from Africa**
- **The globalisation of early childhood**
- **Conclusion**

How childhoods vary

One of the most puzzling aspects about how children grow and learn is the importance of context. Take a very simple example, that of food. All children need to eat, but how their food is obtained and prepared, when they eat, what they eat, where they eat, how they eat and what they are taught to think about what they eat is almost entirely determined by where they live and whom they live with. A child living in the UK is likely to have a diet high in processed foods, will graze throughout the day and be petulant about many foods; a child in Italy will be encouraged to savour food, and consider its consumption as a social occasion; a child living in France will eat to the clock; and a child living in Spain will also eat to the clock, but the clock will be set to a much later time. The staple food – the bulk – that children eat may be based on wheat, rice, sorghum, barley, maize, millet, potato, yam, or many other kinds of crop. Children living in nomadic groups in very cold regions of the world will thrive on a diet extremely high in animal fat. Those accustomed to one type of food may view another staple food as inedible (I shall never forget being given raw whale blubber in Northern Canada by an Inuit woman, and being told that it was 'soul food' and she always felt better for having eaten it. I could barely swallow it!). In some parts of the world there is a surplus of food, but in many parts of Africa or Asia, a child will typically experience hunger as an everyday aspect of life, and will never have a choice about the food she or he eats.

Food preparation and consumption, as Goody (1982) pointed out in his classic anthropological text, are deeply embedded in cultural and geographical contexts. This extraordinary variation in food and eating habits means that it is difficult to set nutritional or any other kind of norms that it is possible for all children to follow, except at the very broadest level of generality. Children need certain levels of essential nutrients for growth – although even that minimum level is debatable – but the form in which they obtain them is anything but standard.

The example of food consumption is a metaphor for other aspects of young children's lives. The argument being put forward in this chapter is that whilst there are some very general features of early childhood, all of them are shaped and modified by cultural context. So much so, that rather than understanding the generalities, it may be more useful to understand the particularities. Bruner argues that 'perhaps even more than with most cultural matters, childrearing practices and beliefs reflect local conceptions of how the world is and how the child should be readied for living it' (Bruner, 2000: xi).

This chapter explores some of these local conceptions of childhood, and then considers how and if they are recognised and acknowledged in the early childhood literature. In describing globalisation in early childhood, that is, the spread of ideas about child development derived from understandings and research in European and Anglo/American countries, I use the terms 'North' (Euro-Anglo/American countries/developed countries/the minority world/rich countries/Western countries) and 'South' (Africa, Latin America Asia/developing countries/the majority world/the poor countries).[1]

---

1 These categories are not clear cut: there are some countries which do not fit easily into any categories (e.g. Brunei or Qatar). In most countries there is a small elite who are rich even although their country is poor; and, conversely, there are rich countries with some very poor people indeed amongst their citizens. The terminology shifts with fashion; relatively few people now use the words 'First World' and 'Third World' which used to be the standard terminology. However, the shorthand of 'North' and 'South' is commonly used to describe the large differences that exist between the richest and poorest countries of the world.

Caution about culture

Right at the beginning I want to give a word of caution about using the word culture. 'Culture' is itself a difficult concept, on the verge of being unusable. 'Culture' describes a set of related beliefs and practices of a particular community, although not everyone in the community will understand or practise them in the same way. These beliefs and patterns are manifested in surface differences – diet, games, clothes, eating habits and folklore – but they also draw on implicit and embedded assumptions and values, what the historian Catriona Kelly (2007) calls the 'elusive invisible network'. 'Culture' is usually thought of as belonging to a particular geographical space or country, but from a historical perspective, people are always on the move, and calamity is always round the corner. As Nederveen Pieterse (2004) has claimed in his book *Globalization and Culture: Global Melange*, 'cultures' are always porous, hybrid, shifting, and contradictory and reflect the frequently forced interchanges of ideas and practices that take place over time. For instance, almost all European countries now have large immigrant populations, and even small countries like Ireland or Finland are changing rapidly. On the other hand, in many countries, the nation state is a relatively recent historical imposition, a reflection of past battles and especially of colonialism and empire. Countries like India, Nigeria, Sudan or Iraq or the (now ex) Soviet Union, brought together – sometimes very unhappily – many very different communities, traditions, languages, and religions. So culture is rarely static or unchanging, it shifts from one generation to the next, and certainly over time; it is displayed differently by one individual to another, but is (just about) coherent enough to be recognised and at least partly described. Rather than use the word 'culture' in this chapter, I prefer to use words like 'local community' or 'cultural context' even although these words, too, should be used with care.

International perspectives – a view from the South

Much of the work in child development focuses at a micro-level, about the understandings and interpretations of what children can do and the kinds of explanations that can account for their behaviour. LeVine and New point out that the study of child development has been largely confined to 'America, Europe and other Western countries who comprise less than ten per cent of all children in the world' (2008: 1). In their recent book they try to redress the balance by collecting together accounts of anthropologists working in unusual (to us) corners of the world. They sum up these accounts as follows:

- Every human society recognises a distinction between children and adults and the age-linked emergence of children's abilities to learn, work, and participate in community activities. At the same time societies vary considerably in the way they interpret children's readiness and ability to do these things.

- Schooling is a relatively recent idea. Until the late twentieth century most children participated in economic and domestic tasks; most were involved in multi-age children's groups; and the distinction between work and play was often blurred.
- Childhood environments differ considerably. In material terms, where children live, whether they have water, sanitation and shelter, what they eat and whether they have enough, what kind of health care is available to them; and in cultural terms, who they consider to be part of their family, how they speak and who to and in what language etc. will vary tremendously between societies.
- The ideas of parents are strongly influenced by culture; norms of parenting reflect and help to sustain the moral standards of a community. Parents have strong views about following these norms, yet they also reinterpret them and adjust them to changing circumstances.
- Children are not passive recipients of cultural practices – they are active interpreters. They acquire the conventions of communication and norms of behaviour that give them entrée to their local social world, but they use and modify them for their own purposes.

An example from Africa

LeVine and his colleagues are trying to broaden the traditional discussions about child development, and to point out the narrowness of the knowledge base. My most recent research has been in South Africa, and in Africa more generally the African Charter on the Rights and Welfare of the Child (1999) highlights 'the preservation and strengthening of positive African morals, traditional values and attitudes' and 'the promotion and achievements of African Unity and Solidarity' as an aspect of the welfare of children. How does this manifest itself in practice?

One of the much discussed aspects of 'African' culture, although not specifically referred to in the African Charter, is the principle of *ubuntu*. It has been romanticised and sentimentalised, but it means something like togetherness, sharing and mutual responsibility. As we reported recently, (Penn and Maynard, forthcoming) one of our respondents in a recent trip to South Africa described *ubuntu* to us as a kind of smoothing over, an insistence on trying to maintain harmony and resolve differences, whatever the circumstances. Here is an extract of our description of her stance:

> Children were taught to respect adults and other children, not to have unnecessary arguments or disagreements. She said that in her own childhood, children were expected at all times to sit and be quiet in the presence of adults, but she could see that this had sometimes been inhibiting and prevented children from 'venturing out' and exploring for themselves. However, she felt that even young children should be able to act with dignity, helpfulness, respect and politeness, and to fail to teach them self-restraint was to deny them their culture. (Penn and Maynard, forthcoming)

Very generally *ubuntu* means prioritizing of collective obligations over personal concerns; rootedness in a particular community rather than within a nuclear family; independence within a community rather than dependency in an isolated family setting; spirituality; and issues of gender, patriarchy and gerontocracy. This view of how children should be and act is built into the language they speak. African languages contain in their very grammar terms of relationship and deference (e.g., different ways of saying 'you' according to whom you are speaking – older, younger, boy, girl, etc.). Briefly, these understandings of childhood are outlined below.

1   Individual – collective

The dichotomy between individual and collective, the extent to which the self is seen as a separate bounded individual, or as gaining identity only from nests of relationships, is one of the classic insights of anthropology (Geertz, 1973). In many societies people define themselves in terms of their relationships – as a mother or father or as a brother or a son or a daughter or a sister, or from a village or a community, but never as a unique and isolated individual making his or her own way in the world. We think it is important to respect individuality; but for others being an individual – on your own and without the constant intimate presence of others – is the worst kind of punishment.

Sharing is not something which must be painfully learnt – as in so many pedagogic manuals – but something which is as natural and as human as talking and thinking. In early childhood guidance manuals comes across the phrase: 'Every child should be treated as an individual.' But a guidance manual following the principles of *ubuntu* might have as a starting point: 'Every child should be treated as a member of the group.'

Part of this collective ethos is that children are seen as contributors to the household. Everyone pulls together, and small children have tasks to do like everyone else. Serpell (1993) described how in his Zambian village, all children were trained to run errands from the moment they could toddle. Paula Fass (2007), the American historian of childhood, has argued that over time, one of the biggest shifts in the interpretation of childhood has been in the amount of time children are expected to work and contribute to the household, or play and be non-contributors to the household. In rich countries the notion of helpfulness and obligation is rarely seen as an integral part of childhood and childrearing; and indeed there is a fraught debate around working children. As Fass remarks, some commentators consider it to be morally wrong to 'exploit' children, whereas more nuanced approaches might value children's satisfaction and pride in being able to contribute to the economy of their household, and be part of a family collective, however young, and whatever the arduous nature of their tasks.

2   Family – community

As suggested above, life for many young children is intensely collective. Families are diffuse and fused into their local community. Wole Soyinka, the Nobel Prize winning novelist, in his autobiography *Ake* describes his early childhood in Nigeria, and his experiences of compound life, and that of all the women on whose backs he was carried, none was as comfortable as Mrs B's – a vignette of an utterly communal, although gendered life, where mothers and children were almost, but not quite, interchangeable. Many children slept with his mother in her room, sharing the bed and mattresses on the floor, some of them relatives, others children of friends or visitors who were staying for shorter or longer periods. Many other accounts of African childhood give a similar picture.

By contrast, childhood in rich countries takes place in small and isolated families. It is not uncommon for a mother to say she has never been separated from her child and has had a continuous responsibility for looking after him or her until nursery offers some relief from the 'burden' of parenting. Families are tiny, inward-looking and self-preoccupied; children themselves have become the individual possessions of their parents, a 'lifestyle' choice. This particular dyadic and narrow model of parenting is continually re-echoed and re-emphasised in the services we provide and the way we write about them.

3   Independent – dependent

These ideas of community, collectivity and family, and the notion of the inseparability of the child from everyday life, produces an understanding of the child as physically and emotionally independent and robust, at least far more so than would be allowed in developed countries. The idea of attachment and the need for a continuous, sensitive caregiver is part of the understanding of infancy in most countries where there is a literature about child development. But in African *ubuntu* the child is one amongst many; a child of the community as well as of the family. This quotation which I have used many times, because it indicates such an extraordinary difference of interpretation of early childhood, is from the anthropologist Alma Gottleib, who studied from the Beng community in the Côte d'Ivoire.

> Chantal, a feisty two-year-old in our compound disappeared from sight many mornings, only to emerge at noon for lunch and then around 5pm for dinner preparations. Although she was too young to report on her day's travels, others would chronicle them for us; she regularly roved to the farthest ends of this very large village and even deep into the forest

to join her older siblings and cousins working and playing in the fields. With such early independence even toddlers are expected to be alert to dangerous wildlife such as snakes and scorpions and they should be able to deal with them effectively – including locating and wielding a large machete (2004: 32).

What Chantal is doing is nearly inconceivable to Euro-American childhood experts pre-occupied as they are with physical risk and the need for protective environments. Despite her lack of language, at two years old Chantal is secure, autonomous, curious and very capable. She has a sense of direction and a sense of time. She can use tools effectively. She and her parents are confident that if there is any kind of hazard she is sufficiently compe-tent to deal with it, by recognising and avoiding it or by calling upon others to help her.

4   The world of spirits

A pervasive theme of African folklore about the family is the spiritual world. Dead ancestors and animal spirits are part of the understanding of family life and commu-nity obligation. Children may inherit the spirit of departed relatives. This animist view, nature as continuous, rather than a belief in the distinctiveness and uniqueness of human life, sits alongside more traditional Christian or Muslim beliefs. This ani-mism seems to represent the antithesis of modern scientific thought, although the contemporary ethicist and philosopher Pete Singer (2001) has also suggested that human life is over-valued as part of the spectrum of living things on earth. Many African novelists include this spiritual dimension in their books – for instance the prize-winning novelists Zakes Mda and Ben Okri write about how people live alongside the spirit world and are influenced by the voices of their ancestors.

5   Gender, patriarchy and gerontocracy

Wisdom and knowledge come with age and experience (even if energy disappears!) and *ubuntu* means respecting the elders of a society. Especially in a society where almost all communication is oral and little is written down, an old person dying is like losing an irreplaceable book. It would be unthinkable for a child to be rude or cheeky to an older person, to ignore the embodied experience and wisdom that an older person represents. This lack of respect is often seen by Africans (like our infor-mant above) as part of the damage and corruption of prosperous Western societies.

By the same token, gender differences are often marked. Women in many places are seen as living a different life to men, and these differences are enshrined in language, in dress, in visible as well as invisible ways. 'Equal opportunities' may be an improbable goal in many places. Girls and boys are treated differently, although this does not necessarily mean that they are inferior. It is regarded as *practical* to see them as having different roles.

6   Language

The different understandings of childhood encapsulated in the notion of *ubuntu* are reflected in the very languages African people speak. For example terms of respect, deference and gender are built into most African languages, and communication is meaningless without them. Similarly, the expectations of solidarity are implicit in the language. Zulu for example has more tenses than English, which requires more subtlety in the interpretation of events; and it is more rhythmic and musical, more given to recitation and performance than to private and solitary reading.

Language structures thinking and communication. In one way, children in the South might be regarded as fortunate; often they grow up in bilingual or multilingual environments (Bloch, 2007). Depending on the language you speak, you see and hear the world differently. English is a global language, and most native English speakers see no reason to learn another language. But if ways of thinking and relating to other people is built into language, those who are multi-lingual are automatically at an intellectual advantage.[2] Those who come from oral traditions tend to be acute listeners. Pre-school and schooling experiences sometimes damage rather than enhance language learning by inappropriate methods, including a failure to appreciate the importance of oral learning, rhyme, chanting and recitation.

Ubuntu and the morals and values that underpin it are, of course, much more complex, variable, renegotiated – and made unrecognisable by poverty, war and colonialism – than this brief summary might suggest, but they are an indication of the very different possibilities which exist for thinking about childhood.

The globalisation of early childhood

In the North the institutional arrangements for young children – early childhood education and care – have become increasingly important, and are a subject for debate.

It is now fairly widely accepted, at least in the North, that governments have a role in promoting early childhood education and care. What governments do or don't do in relation to early education and care – funding, regulation, etc. – makes a real difference to the fabric of children's daily lives. Just as governments gradually took on board responsibility for schooling over the last century, now they are beginning to focus on children's experiences before school.

---

2 In South Africa, for example, primary schools routinely teach languages. At age eight my grandson was being taught in English, but required to learn Afrikaans and Zulu. His first question about moving to a school in the UK for a term was, 'What languages will they teach?'

All governments in the North have a national framework for the development and support of Early Childhood Education and Care (ECEC). The emphasis, the financing and the effectiveness with which ECEC is delivered vary considerably, even amongst rich nations but the commitment is unmistakable. The Organisation for Economic Co-operation and Development (OECD), a primary source of transnational policy and knowledge construction for the richest nations, suggests this investment in ECEC is for a number of reasons:

> Amongst the immediate factors turning governmental attention to ECEC issues are: the wish to increase women's labour market participation; to reconcile work and family responsibilities on a basis more equitable to women; to confront the demographic changes faced by OECD countries (in particular falling fertility rates and the general ageing of populations); and the need to address issues of child poverty and educational disadvantage. Because economic prosperity depends on maintaining a high employment/ population ratio, the wish to bring more women into the labour market has been a key driver of government interest in expanding ECEC services. European governments in particular, have put into place family and childcare policies to help couples have children and assist parents to combine work and family responsibilities ... Support for the view that early childhood education and care should be seen as a *public good* is growing and has received a strong impetus from the research of education economists. (2006:12)

In the South, too, the numbers of young children being cared for outside of the home appears to have grown exponentially, although robust statistical evidence is hard to come by (UNESCO, 2007). Almost every large city in the South now has extensive numbers of nurseries and crèches, although these are – except for the elite – of a very different standard from the North.

The demand for early childhood education and care in the South is partly to do with rural–urban migration, and increasing numbers of families (women) coming into cities to seek work and the consequent demand for childcare; and it is partly to do with changing official views about young children's needs, in particular their need for a good educational start, in order to mitigate school drop-out.

Yet although there is a good deal of rhetoric, much of it from external donors such as the World Bank, about the need for early childhood interventions (Garcia et al., 2008), the reality is that most provision in the South is provided by private entrepreneurs. People pay for what they can afford, and poor people who cannot afford to pay fees either receive a very poor service or none at all. Jody Heymann (2002), for example, undertook a large survey of the needs of working mothers across a number of countries in the South, and pointed out that up to 30% of working mothers leave their children in the care of siblings, or unattended, with the result that the accident rates for such children are shockingly high. The Association for the Development of Education in Africa (ADEA) points out that Early Child Development (ECD) is a very marginal activity.

> To date ECD has had low priority in government policies, ECD initiatives are limited and unevenly distributed, and there are wide differences in the quality of the initiatives. Most ECD programmes are developed and maintained by private sector, non-governmental organisations (NGOs) and international organisations. They suffer from inadequate funding and a lack of coherence, co-ordination, sustainability and long-term policies. This is particularly true in Africa, where scarce resources, especially for education, suggest that investment in ECD could endanger the commitment to other education sectors. (Association for the Development of Education Africa, 2005)

So, on the one hand, there is pressure to provide early childhood education and care, and, on the other, there are local traditions and contexts which suggest that models from the North may be inappropriate. The debate about the need for early childhood education and care generally draws on evidence from the North and ignores the circumstances of most children and the arrangements that are made for them. Yet the view of what constitutes good practice in the North is regarded as being a sound principle for export everywhere in the world. I recently carried out a review of the work of international donor agencies[3] in the field of early childhood. I undertook a web-based search of donor agencies including the World Bank, UNICEF, and related UN organisations, and international charities such as Bernard Van Leer and Save the Children which provide advocacy and support for early childhood. I compared their mission statements and visions, the range of their early childhood programmes, and their systems of accountability. What was striking was the similarity between the agencies' viewpoints and modes of operation, no matter which country they were operating in, and their reliance on the North American and, to a lesser extent, European early childhood literature in justifying initiatives in the South.[4]

The issue of knowledge transfer in education, and in particular the export and import of educational ideas from North to South has attracted considerable attention from scholars (Phillips and Ochs, 2004; Steiner-Khamsi, 2004; Steiner-Khamsi and Stolpe, 2006) although to date very little work has been done in the field of early childhood. Steiner-Khamsi argues that educational ideas are never

---

3 These are sometimes called 'global policy entrepreneurs' or 'global policy networks', putting forward 'travelling policies' – see Steiner-Khamsi (2004, 2006).

4 Penn, H. (2008) *Mapping Report for ISSA Strategic Plan 2009–2011*. This report was commissioned as an internal report for the International Step by Step Organization, and is not generally available, but is being rewritten and submitted as a paper for *Early Childhood Research Quarterly*.

straightforwardly transferred from one country to another, but there is always a mixture of adaptation, incorporation and resistance, according to local contexts. These local contexts are not 'untouched' relics of a traditional past, but are themselves the product of many past influences and current socio-demographic pressures. She uses the example of education in Mongolia to describe how educational reforms prescribed by the World Bank and other international agencies were nominally accepted because of the much needed money being offered, but the reforms were in fact subverted or not implemented. For example, she describes attempts by donors to introduce 'community participation' into schools, but there is no word in Mongolian for 'community'. The nearest translation was 'home-place' which rendered the planned interventions by donors meaningless. The reforms just petered out. Although donors are willing to export ideas, the process is rarely reciprocal, and local ideas are regarded as quaint rather than warranting serious attention.

My own experience is that many of the pre-school interventions sponsored by donors in ex-Soviet countries or countries within the orbit of the Soviet system like Mongolia were subverted because the Soviet system of kindergartens was so very much more comprehensive than anything that was offered in its place. Parents and staff were justifiably resentful of the reforms (parent and toddler groups, part-time provision, etc.) that were being introduced (Penn, 2005). More recently, I describe attempts by the World Bank to introduce early childhood initiatives in Namibia, which bordered on farce because the donors were unable (or unwilling) to comprehend the extent of inequality and poverty in the country, and assumed that a combination of private entrepreneurs and community action would provide a viable Euro-American style early childhood service (Penn, 2008).

Because globally imported initiatives and reforms mostly do not work, or do not work in the way that donors anticipate, the usual response is to blame the recipients. They 'lack capacity' or they are deemed too lazy or dishonest to undertake the work that is necessary. A detailed analysis of policy discourse, policy implementation or actual practice is rarely undertaken to explain the frequent lack of success or lack of sustainability of initiatives. As Popkewitz argues, a detailed examination of global knowledge transfer in education would incorporate a critical view of what knowledge exists on the topic (for example, is it as scientific and empirically based as its adherents claim); and 'how patterns of thought move through and are transmuted in different layers of the local and global systems' (Popkewitz, 2004: ix). From an early childhood perspective this would involve asking critical questions about practice; for instance, in the example cited above from South Africa, how do ideas about child-centred practice sit alongside ideas about learning self-restraint and respect? Or as Jones and Villar argue in relation to their work in Peru for the *Young Lives* project:

It is critical to unpack culturally specific understandings of core cultural concepts with which a research project is engaging (such as 'children' 'family' and 'work') and how these are subject to competing interpretations and reinterpretations in societies undergoing rapid social, political, economic and demographic transitions. (2008: 45)

Conclusion

This chapter has discussed the expectations and understandings about young children's lives and what they need and how they should be treated in different cultural contexts. It uses the example of the African concept of *ubuntu* to suggest that there are very different ways of bringing up children and very different values which underpin childrearing practices. Yet most of the academic and policy discussion that takes place in early childhood does so in a Euro-American context which is untypical of the situation of most children and does not recognise the range of variation which exists.

This lack of recognition of local context is important because when donors try to export ideas about early childhood (or education more generally) to countries in the South, they often fail. The chapter also discusses some of the ideas about how knowledge transfer takes place, how ideas – in particular, ideas about early childhood – get transferred and who by, and how the recipients incorporate and transform the projects that are often foisted upon them.

The issue of early childhood in the South is also important because of the very rapid urbanisation that is taking place in most countries of the world. Just as there has been a minor revolution about women's roles in the North, which has prompted the development of early childhood education and care as much as concerns about educational opportunity, so there is a rather different kind of minor revolution going on in the South. Life in the slums and poor quarters of big cities in the South is very problematic, and the kind of care and education offered to young children who live in potentially hostile environments is a matter of real concern for anyone concerned about childhood.

Questions and exercises

1 What do you think are the most important values in bringing up young children? Do you think they would be shared by everyone you know?
2 What difference do you think poverty makes to the way young children think of themselves?
3 Do you think young children in the South know about the lives children lead in the UK? If they do know, what would they think about the standards of provision that we have?

Further reading

LeVine and New's (2008) *Anthropology and Child Development* is a series of readings from classical anthropological studies that explore children and childrearing. It looks at standard child development issues – parenting, language acquisition and play – from mind-blowingly different perspectives from those that are conventionally understood in Euro-American texts. The authors' own overview is illuminating. The text by Garcia et al. (2008) *Africa's Future, Africa's Challenge: Early Childhood Care and Development in Sub-Saharan Africa* is an edited selection of articles from Africans and non-Africans about trying to develop early childhood education and care services where they have not been established before. It presents the rationales for introducing services and the discusses the difficulties in establishing them. The book illustrates – sometimes unwittingly – the pitfalls of exporting ideas about childhood from one continent to another.

PART TWO

THE DEVELOPING CHILD

This part of the book focuses on children's cognitive, social and emotional development as well as the acquisition of language and the developmental potential of play.

A consideration of the developing child necessarily encompasses an exploration of many different theories. Initially, some of these theories may appear contradictory. We need to recognise that theories may emerge from or reflect the particular interests of the theorist: consider for example the relationship between Piaget's theory and his early grounding in biology, or Vygotsky's theory and Marxism. In addition, the promotion or acceptance of theories at particular times in history can reflect the interests of dominant groups in society. However, the approach taken in this text is, in as far as it is possible, to consider and use different theoretical models in a complementary way, taking what each can offer to help build a holistic understanding of children's development.

A key theme underlying all the chapters in this part of the book is the role of children in their learning and development. Children are no longer viewed as passive beings who are moulded and shaped by those around them but are seen as being active in this process: rather than being passively 'socialised', they are actively 'self-socialising'. Thus the young child appears driven to learn the rules relating to particular cultural/social categories or groups and, at least initially, to fit in with those around her or him.

In Chapter 5, Ruth Ford develops these themes in her review of theories of cognitive development, asking questions such as: does children's cognitive development proceed gradually and incrementally or more abruptly through a series of stages? Do children learn independently or do they require assistance from others? Are improvements in children's thinking generic or 'domain specific'? In this new edition, the chapter also includes a substantial section on children's developing 'theory of mind'.

In Chapter 6, Tricia David turns to children's social, personal and emotional development, making clear that understandings about oneself and others are dependent on cognitive processes as well as social and emotional interactions. She shows the importance of 'attachment' and relationship not only in the development of identity, self-concept and resilience, but also in children's developing theory of mind.

In Chapter 7, Thea Cameron-Faulkner describes three approaches which have been adopted in the study of language development: behaviourist, formalist and more recently, constructivist. Within this approach children are again seen as active participants in their learning – this time, in relation to the acquisition of language. But, as Cameron-Faulkner points out, the significance of cultural context is also made clear, language acquisition being viewed as a specific form of cultural learning.

In Chapter 8, Justine Howard highlights the significance of play in early childhood. Howard outlines the numerous theories that have tried to explain why we play and indeed that have attempted to define this activity. She argues that in our attempt to understand play and to measure its developmental potential, we lost sight of its unique qualities. It is through an understanding of children's perspectives that we are able to re-connect with these qualities and recognise that, regardless of cultural context, play affords children the opportunity to learn and to heal.

Together these four chapters give us a picture of young children striving to make sense of the world around them, in particular the world of social interaction, and quickly becoming a part of it – influenced profoundly by their surroundings and by what happens to them, but also exerting their own influence on the world from their earliest days.

5

THINKING AND COGNITIVE DEVELOPMENT IN YOUNG CHILDREN

Ruth M. Ford

Contents:

- **Introduction**
- **Issues in cognitive development**
- **Theories of cognitive development**
- **An in-depth look at cognitive development in the social realm: children's acquisition of theory of mind**
- **Applied issues and future research directions**
- **Conclusion**

Introduction

The term *cognition* encompasses a range of mental processes, including perception, attention, language, reasoning, and memory. The term *cognitive development* thus refers broadly to the growth of children's cognition between birth and adolescence. Because cognitive development has such diverse aspects, it has not yet been explained fully by any single theory. This chapter gives an overview of some of the foremost accounts in the field, as well as providing an in-depth look at one widely researched topic in cognitive development, namely, theory of mind. The chapter begins by outlining some contentious issues in the study of cognitive development. It concludes by drawing attention to practical applications of cognitive developmental research and possible directions for future study.

Issues in cognitive development

Theories of cognitive development differ on a number of important issues. First, there is controversy regarding the relative contribution of nature versus nurture or heredity versus the environment. The question is whether children's development depends primarily on innate (i.e., genetically determined) abilities or on such environmental factors as family background and schooling. Second, the issue of continuity versus discontinuity concerns the trajectory of cognitive development. Although some theories perceive development as occurring smoothly and incrementally, others postulate the existence of abrupt transformations from lower to higher levels of functioning. Third, the issue of active versus passive development asks to what extent children initiate their learning. Notions about active development hold that children actively seek and construct knowledge as they attempt to make sense of their world. In contrast, notions about passive development suggest that children are inertly moulded by their experiences and heredity. Fourth, arguments about domain-general versus domain-specific development relate to the scope of cognitive growth. Domain-general theories assume that developments in children's thinking occur broadly across many areas of cognition whereas domain-specific theories assume that progress in one domain is largely dissociated from progress in others. Fifth, theories differ in their claims regarding the impact of the sociocultural context. Whereas some accounts view the child as being an independent learner, others postulate that cognitive development requires input from other people in the course of everyday social interactions. Finally, there is the problem of how change occurs. Rather than merely charting typical developmental progress and milestones, recent approaches to cognitive development seek to understand the precise mechanisms by which children learn.

Theories of cognitive development

Piaget's theory: the child as scientist

The study of cognitive development was initiated in the 1920s by Jean Piaget, a Swiss psychologist who carried out both large-scale studies of children's thinking and detailed examinations of the development of his own three children. Piaget's theory has been hugely influential, not only due to its pioneering nature but because it provided so many thought-provoking ideas that have continued to stimulate research programmes to the present day. In terms of central developmental issues, Piaget's theory acknowledges a contribution of nurture as well as nature to intellectual ability, describes both continuity and discontinuity in development, and stresses the active contribution of the child to its intellectual growth (e.g., Piaget, 1952; Piaget and Inhelder, 1969). Piaget originally trained in biology and philosophy and these orientations informed his approach to the study of psychology. His background in biology led to an interest in the relations between evolution and human cognitive development, prompting him to speculate that children are motivated to acquire knowledge because such behaviour is adaptive. His background in philosophy, particularly in logic, inspired him to search for internal consistency underlying children's errors in problem solving. Piaget's theory is described as *constructivist* in the sense that it depicts the child as actively constructing knowledge in reaction to their experiences (Slee and Shute, 2003). When Piaget's work began gaining attention during the 1960s, its impact was so great partly because it rejected ideas about passive, associative forms of learning (i.e., mechanistic or behaviourist models of learning) that had dominated psychology for the past 30 years. The essence of Piaget's theory is the notion of the 'child as scientist', carrying out simple tests to discover how the world works.

According to Piaget, continuity in development arises from three processes: assimilation, accommodation, and equilibration. *Assimilation* occurs when new experiences are integrated into existing knowledge, *accommodation* occurs when children modify their knowledge in response to new experiences that cannot be assimilated, and *equilibration* reflects the child's attempts to balance assimilation and accommodation to create stable understanding. Siegler et al. (2003) provide the hypothetical example of a pre-school child who believes that only animals are living things because only animals move in ways compatible with preserving their life. This child's ideas about life develop as she encounters new kinds of animals and assimilates these examples into her schema for living things. However, when she discovers that plants similarly move in ways that promote their survival, namely, towards sunlight, she experiences a state of disequilibrium in which she is unsure about how living and non-living things differ. After accommodating her knowledge structures to the new information about plants, she decides that since adaptive movement signifies life, plants as well as animals must be living things.

In Piaget's theory, cognitive development is additionally viewed as discontinuous such that children proceed through four discrete stages of ability. His theory assumes *epigenesis* in that later stages of development build on earlier achievements, furthermore, the stages are argued to be universal (true for all human cultures) and age-invariant (passed through in the same order by all children irrespective of their rate of progress). Crucially, the theory claims that patterns of thinking are qualitatively distinct at different stages and that development entails making an intellectual leap from one way of thinking about the world to a new, more advanced level of thinking. Thus, development does not merely involve an accumulation of skills and knowledge; a 12-year-old differs from a four-year-old not only quantitatively in terms of experience but also qualitatively in terms of thinking patterns.

The first stage of development is the *sensorimotor* stage, which lasts from birth to approximately two years of age. During this stage, infants are largely reflexive creatures whose thinking is dominated by immediate perceptual input. Through the mechanisms of assimilation, accommodation, and equilibration, infants construct progressively more sophisticated sensorimotor schemas (i.e., links between sensation and motor activity) that enable them to develop their notions of time, space, and causality. As they grow older, infants integrate simple reflexes such as gazing and grasping to achieve more advanced behaviours such as visually guided reaching, they attain an understanding that objects continue to exist even when they cannot be seen (the concept of object permanence), and they test ideas about cause and effect, for example, by shaking and biting a rattle to discover how to produce a noise.

By the time of their second birthday, most infants have entered the *pre-operational* stage of development. During this stage, lasting until approximately age seven years, children are capable of representing their experiences mentally using imagery and language. Their thinking is therefore described as reflective rather than merely reflexive. Piaget referred to children's newly developed representational capacity as the *symbolic function* and argued that it could be observed in both their deferred imitation and their frequent engagement in make-believe play. An example of make-believe play would be a three-year-old girl holding a banana to her ear and speaking into it as if it were a telephone. According to Piaget, such behaviour indicates that the child is capable of mentally representing the banana as something other than it really is. She thus understands and manipulates symbols of reality and not just reality itself. Once the symbolic function is in place, Piaget's theory suggests that subsequent cognitive development involves the acquisition of new modes of thinking, known as mental operations. Pre-operational children are misled by superficial appearances during problem solving because they lack important mental operations necessary for logical reasoning. For example, until they acquire 'reversibility', namely, the ability to mentally undo an action, children are unable to understand that the amount of liquid in a container does not change when it is poured into a container of a different shape (i.e., a failure of *conservation*). Three other important features of the pre-operational stage are *egocentricism*, the inability to take another person's point of view, *centration*, the tendency to focus attention on a single aspect of a problem at a time, and *animism*, the tendency to attribute life-like qualities and intentions to non-living things.

During the *concrete operational* stage, typically lasting from ages 7 to 12 years, children demonstrate the use of logic when dealing with problems involving concrete objects and events. Because they have acquired an understanding of reversibility, they succeed in solving conservation problems for number, volume, mass, and area. Children are also able for the first time to pass tests requiring *seriation* (i.e., the understanding of spatial and temporal sequences), *transitive inferences* (i.e., the mental rearrangement of a set of objects along a quantifiable dimension), and *class inclusion* (i.e., the manipulation of hierarchical part–whole relations). However, they do not yet show evidence of thinking in abstract or hypothetical terms and they cannot easily combine information systematically to solve a problem.

Finally, children enter the *formal operational* stage of development at approximately age 12. They can now consider abstract situations, formulate hypotheses, and test hypotheses in a scientific manner. For example, if given a pendulum with varying weights and lengths of string then formal operational children systematically manipulate the problem parameters to deduce what determines the rate of oscillation. Their ability to conceive of several possible realities also leads them to query the way society is structured and to ponder philosophical questions about truth, justice, and morality (Inhelder and Piaget, 1958).

Over the years, Piaget's theory has stimulated an enormous number of research studies. Many of these studies have concluded that Piaget underestimated young children's capabilities because he failed to take into account their memory and language limitations (Flavell, 1996; Schaffer, 2004). Whereas Piaget's basic findings in relation to the *sequence* of development have been extensively replicated, other research has challenged the fundamental assumptions of his theory on several grounds. The most contentious issues have been Piaget's notion of stages of development, his emphasis on domain-general reasoning abilities, and his neglect of the contribution of social interactions to children's thinking (Berk, 2003). These points have been addressed in turn by information-processing approaches, core-knowledge approaches, and sociocultural approaches to cognitive development.

Information-processing approaches: the child as a computational system

Information-processing theories reject Piaget's ideas about abrupt transformations in cognitive development and instead posit the gradual improvement of basic cognitive processes and memory capacities, an increase in knowledge, and the emergence of new learning strategies. In terms of core issues, information-processing approaches assume that development reflects both nature and nurture, is continuous rather than discontinuous, involves active planning and problem solving by the child, and that the mechanisms of change can be precisely specified.

Research within the information-processing framework has revealed both wide-ranging developments across the entire cognitive system and narrow forms of domain-specific learning (McShane, 1991). As children grow older they become more efficient at encoding information from the environment (e.g., Siegler, 1976), faster in their speed of mental processing (e.g., Kail, 1997), better able to use learning and memory strategies (e.g., Bjorklund et al.,1997), and more knowledgeable (e.g., Schneider and Pressley, 1997). From the information-processing perspective, such changes are sufficient to explain children's growing competencies on Piagetian tests without recourse to notions about the acquisition of mental operations.

Developmental improvements in information processing are likely to reflect both maturation and experience. Thus, superior learning and problem solving in older children relative to younger ones could be attributed either to the more efficient functioning of the brain's neurons with increasing age or to increments in relevant knowledge (Siegler et al., 2003). Certainly, knowledge acquisition is implicated in significant gains in memory capabilities during childhood. Both for children and adults, memory for new material is greatly enhanced when it can be related to what is already known (Chi, 1978). For example, young children become better at remembering novel events as they develop *scripts*, that is, mental representations of the usual sequence of activities for commonly experienced routines such as eating at a restaurant, attending a birthday party, or visiting the doctor (Fivush et al., 1992).

Recent years have seen a proliferation of information-processing theories of cognitive development. Whereas many such theories assume sequential processing of information, connectionist or neural-network models posit parallel processing in which different kinds of cognitive activity occur simultaneously. Connectionist models claim to mimic the physiological workings of the human brain, which are known to involve dense interconnected parallel-processing units (Elman et al., 1996). Another influential approach comes in the form of neo-Piagetian information-processing views, which seek to account for evidence of stage-like development in terms of age-related improvements in processing capacity (Case, 1985). Finally, dynamic systems theories reject ideas about linear causality (*x* causes *y*) and, instead, view development as a move towards greater complexity as mutually interdependent parts of the cognitive system co-operate in a non-linear fashion to produce new, emergent properties (Lewis, 2000; Thelen and Smith, 1994).

Core-knowledge theories: the child as a product of human evolution

Similar to both Piaget's and information-processing theories, core-knowledge theories assume that the child is an active agent in their own development who strives to learn. Uniquely, however, such approaches argue that children are born with learning abilities already in place that are specialised for particular domains of thought; that is, they emphasise the contribution to cognitive development of innate forms of knowledge that have arisen in response to human evolutionary history, without which it is presumed infants would have difficulty in beginning to make sense of the world. Innate knowledge is suggested to be crucial to the development of such skills as face recognition, semantic categorisation, and language. Importantly, core knowledge theorists assume that innate knowledge is domain specific rather than domain general, that is, restricted to particular, narrow areas of cognition (Carey and Spelke, 1994).

Core-knowledge theories are sometimes called *theory theories* because they argue that children's innate understanding in particular areas is organised in terms of naïve or informal theories (Wellman and Gelman, 1998). Naïve theories have been postulated to operate in the domains of physics, psychology, and biology (commonly known as *core domains*). For example, there is evidence that from a very early age children understand that the world contains physical objects that occupy space, move in response to external forces, and move continuously rather than discontinuously (Spelke, 1994), that people's behaviour is driven by their goals and desires (Wellman and Gelman, 1998), and that there are important differences between animals and inanimate objects (Springer and Keil, 1991). Evidence that young children have surprising competence in particular aspects of their cognitive development would not be predicted by a domain-general theory of cognitive development such as Piaget's.

According to theory approaches, cognitive development proceeds as the acquisition of new knowledge enables children to refine and extend their rudimentary theories to create better ones (Hatano and Inagaki, 1996). Notably, it has been postulated that learning can occur even in the absence of exposure to new information. Karmiloff-Smith (1992) posited a process of *representational redescription* by which existing knowledge is converted spontaneously to new and superior forms of knowledge (see also Mandler, 1992). According to her theory, knowledge is represented at both implicit (i.e., unaware) and explicit (i.e., aware) levels. Implicit knowledge is specific to particular parts of the cognitive system and is inaccessible to consciousness (for example, neonates' knowledge about physical objects). This knowledge is subsequently redescribed and made available to other parts of the cognitive system; eventually it reaches consciousness such that it can be verbalised and shared with others.

Core-knowledge theories form part of a larger class of theories in the rapidly growing field of evolutionary developmental psychology. As a whole, this approach seeks to explain how genes and the environment interact to produce development and the ways in which specific cognitive skills have developed in response to environmental pressures (Geary and Bjorklund, 2000). Evolutionary developmental psychology distinguishes between biologically primary abilities (i.e., cognitive skills determined by evolution, such as language) and biologically secondary abilities (i.e., cognitive skills determined by culture, such as reading). It is assumed that whereas the development of primary abilities requires little nurture from the environment, the development of secondary abilities draws on cognitive skills that evolved for other purposes and thus requires a higher level of external support (Bjorklund, 2000). Finally, the sub-domain of developmental cognitive neuroscience attempts to understand cognitive development in terms of brain structures and functions. For example, research in this tradition has implicated the maturation of the frontal lobes of the brain as underpinning age-related improvements in children's ability to curb their impulses (Dempster, 1993).

Sociocultural theories: the child as a social being

The theories reviewed so far have uniformly stressed children's active role in their own development as they identify problems and attempt to solve them independently. In contrast, sociocultural theories view development as taking place in a social context such that young children learn primarily through communicative interactions with other people (Bornstein and Bruner, 1989). Sociocultural perspectives share the notions of *guided participation*, referring to the way that adults assist children to achieve higher levels of skills than they would be capable of attaining on their own, and *cultural tools*, referring to language, other symbol systems, artefacts, skills and values that are important to a particular culture (Rogoff, 1990).

The sociocultural approach to understanding cognitive development was initiated by the Russian psychologist, Lev Vygotsky. Although Vygotsky was a contemporary of Piaget, his work received little attention in the Western world until it was translated into English as *Mind in Society* (Vygotsky, 1978). Vygotsky was intrigued by the idea that young children are born into a social world in which adults are motivated to help them learn. Whereas Piaget claimed that a child constructs knowledge by actively engaging with the environment, Vygotsky suggested that development arises from social interchanges and is thus a joint endeavour between the child and its caretakers. Moreover, whereas Piaget postulated the existence of qualitative stages in cognitive development, Vygotsky argued that social interactions produce continuous rather than discontinuous growth. Vygotsky's theory acknowledges the contribution of nature to development in the sense that infants are thought to enter the world equipped with basic cognitive functions such as the ability to attend and remember. Vygotsky argued that these basic abilities are transformed into higher mental functions by nurture in the form of social interactions and dialogues between a child and its parents, teachers, and other representatives of culture. He suggested that, through these interactions, children internalize increasingly mature and effective ways of thinking and problem solving (Vygotsky, 1978, 1981).

Vygotsky (1986) reasoned that social interactions benefit children's thinking due to the input of language. He argued that language enables thought and that progress in thinking is mediated by language. Vygotsky described three stages of language–thought development. In the first stage, called *external speech*, thinking comes from a source outside the child. For example, a father who is watching his young son scribbling might introduce the idea of representational drawing by asking, 'What are you drawing? Is it a dog?' In the second stage, called *private speech*, children talk to themselves as a way of directing their own thinking. Thus, while drawing the boy might verbally describe his progress by saying, 'This is my dog. Now I'm drawing his tail.' In the final stage, called *internal speech*, children have internalised their thought processes. At this stage of development the boy might think to himself,

'What will I draw? I know. I'll draw a picture of my dog.' Consistent with Vygotsky's views about the pivotal role of language in thinking, research has indicated that children who engage in private speech during problem solving achieve better outcomes than do children who remain silent (Berk, 1992).

Vygotsky also introduced the idea of the *zone of proximal development*. This refers to an area of functioning just beyond the child's current level to which they are capable of progressing given appropriate assistance from other people with greater knowledge. Vygotsky defined it as 'the distance between actual developmental level as determined by independent problem solving and the level of potential development through problem solving under adult guidance or in collaboration with more capable peers' (1978: 86). Vygotsky thus assumed that in most instances children's potential level of functioning exceeds their actual level of functioning.

Subsequent work in the Vygotskian tradition drew attention to the role of *intersubjectivity* in social interactions, that is, mutual understanding arising from joint attention to the same topic as well as sensitivity to the other person's point of view (Gauvain, 2001; Rogoff, 1990). It additionally described *social scaffolding*, that is, the process by which adults provide a temporary framework to support a child's thinking at a higher level than they can yet reach on their own (Wood et al., 1976). As an analogy, the child can be viewed as a building under construction. Scaffolding takes the form of explaining the goal of the task, demonstrating how the task should be done, and carrying out the more difficult aspects of the task. At first, children require extensive support to attain a higher level of thinking about a particular problem but, over time, they come to require less assistance until eventually they can complete the task on their own. Importantly, children who receive appropriate scaffolding show faster acquisition of new skills than do children who learn independently. Successful teachers are those who pitch their instructions and demonstrations at the right level to suit the child's current expertise; that is, they discover and operate in the child's zone of proximal development (Wood, 1998). The following example from Berk illustrates a social interchange between a mother and her three-year-old son as she attempts to help him solve a jigsaw puzzle while keeping her suggestions and prompts at an appropriate level of difficulty (2003: 258):

Sammy:	I can't get this one in. [Tries to insert a piece in the wrong place.]
Mother:	Which piece might go down here? [Points to the bottom of the puzzle.]
Sammy:	His shoes. [Looks for a piece resembling the shoes but tries the wrong one.]
Mother:	Well, what piece looks like this shape? [Pointing again.]
Sammy:	The brown one. [Fits it in; attempts another piece and looks at mother.]
Mother:	Try turning it just a little. [Gestures to show him.]
Sammy:	There! [He puts in several more pieces while his mother watches.]

Vygotsky's theory is an example of a *dialectical theory*; it emphasises the development of cognition under social influence. Other sociocultural approaches can be described as *contextualist*; they stress the wider influence of environmental contexts on development. Interest in contextualism was prompted by the publication of *The Ecology of Human Development*, by Urie Bronfenbrenner in 1979. Bronfenbrenner suggested that, 'the ecology of human development involves the scientific study of the progressive mutual accommodation between an active, growing human being and the changing properties of the immediate settings in which the developing person lives, as this process is affected by relations between these settings, and by the larger contexts in which the settings are embedded' (1979: 21). His approach therefore views cognitive development as proceeding within a nested series of contexts.

Bronfenbrenner (1979) distinguished between three main levels of the environment. First, the *microsystem* comprises the various settings in which the child directly participates, such as home, school, and neighbourhood. Second, the *exosystem* comprises systems that affect the child indirectly by virtue of their influence on microsystems. Such settings include the extended social network of the family and the media. Finally, the *macrosystem* comprises the cultural environment of the child, for example, characteristic of a particular socioeconomic or ethnic background. More recently, Bronfenbrenner (1986) incorporated the notion of the *chronosystem*. The chronosystem refers to influences on development that are specific to a particular historical period. For example, children growing up today differ from previous generations in their extensive exposure to television and computers. Importantly, Bronfenbrenner advocated a transactional view of development in that he believed children, caregivers, and the environment exert a mutual influence on one another (Bronfenbrenner and Morris, 1998; Sameroff et al., 1993). In this sense, the child is not a passive recipient of environmental forces but to some extent selects their experiences. For example, a child who is raised by parents who encourage reading might develop an enjoyment of literature that later leads them to seek out friends with similar interests.

An in-depth look at cognitive development in the social realm: children's acquisition of theory of mind

One of the most widely studied aspects of cognitive development over the last two decades has been theory of mind. The term *theory of mind* refers to the understanding that human behaviour is governed by a complex system of mental states, such as desires, knowledge, beliefs and emotions (Premack and Woodruff, 1978). Such understanding includes the realisation that mental states are internal and, thus, might not correspond with actual events (Wellman et al., 2001). Theory of mind enables us to make sense of what people say and do and thus is vital for successful social interaction. As adults, we are aware that other people may have a view of the world that differs from our own, or from reality. Because we appreciate that people's actions are driven by what they know, we realise that if a person is mistaken about the current state of affairs then they may take an erroneous action in pursuit of their goal (Wellman, 2002). The importance of theory of mind is reflected in our frequent use of mental-state terms in everyday language (e.g., John looked for his keys in his coat pocket because that is where he *thought* they were; John is opening the biscuit barrel because he *wants* a biscuit).

Young children appear to lack a fully fledged theory of mind, as evinced by their poor performance on tests of the understanding of false belief. False-belief tests gauge children's appreciation of the fact that people can possess and act on beliefs that do not reflect reality. One of the most commonly employed false-belief tasks is the unexpected transfer task, devised by Wimmer and Perner (1983). In the original version of this task, children watched a story conveyed by puppets. The story featured a little boy called Maxi who put his bar of chocolate in a blue cupboard in his kitchen and then left the scene. During his absence, Maxi's mother entered the kitchen and moved his chocolate bar to a green cupboard. Upon Maxi re-entering the kitchen, children were asked to predict where Maxi would look for his chocolate. Wimmer and Perner found that 58% of the children aged 4 to 5 years incorrectly responded that Maxi would look for the object in its actual location (i.e., the green cupboard), whereas 92% of the children aged 6 to 9 years correctly responded that Maxi would look for the object in its original location (i.e., the blue cupboard). Such findings have been widely replicated over the years using a variety of false-belief tests (review by Wellman et al., 2001), leading to the conclusion that children younger than 5–6 years have difficulty acknowledging the existence of mental states that are discordant with the real state of affairs. They therefore appear to lack a well developed theory of mind.

Investigations of children's theory of mind have raised the usual issues central to cognitive development. First, there is controversy regarding whether acquisition of theory of mind is continuous or stage-like. Based on the finding that the majority of typically developing children do not attain an understanding of false belief until some time between their fourth and fifth birthdays, some researchers have argued that there is a radical shift in the child's thought processes at around this age and that younger children fail to possess a representational understanding of mind (i.e., the *representational deficit view*; Astington, 2001; Perner, 1991). The opposing argument is that the rudiments of theory of mind are evident in infancy and develop gradually over the course of childhood. In support of the latter view, it has been demonstrated that children as young as 36 months of age can pass false-belief tests if critical aspects of such tests are made more salient. For example, Chandler et al. (1989) found that tasks framed in terms of explicit deception, and that involve the child in concocting the deceptive circumstances, reveal higher levels of competency. Given that children younger than four years can engage in pretence (Leslie, 1987) and identify a variety of basic mental states and emotions (Harris, 1989), many researchers prefer to postulate continuity in the development of theory-of-mind capabilities during early childhood.

Second, there is debate surrounding whether theory of mind relies on domain-specific cognitive processes or domain-general cognitive processes. Whereas domain-specific accounts assume the existence of a specialised brain or cognitive system devoted solely to theory-of-mind reasoning, domain-general accounts argue that theory-of-mind problems are solved by all-purpose cognitive mechanisms. Domain-specific accounts include the proposals that theory of mind depends on a dedicated cognitive module (*modular theory*; Scholl and Leslie, 1999) or, alternatively, a set of causal, explanatory rules pertaining uniquely to human behaviour (*theory theory*; Gopnik and Wellman, 1992). Regardless of whether there is an element of domain-specificity to theory of mind, a role of domain-general processes is suggested by evidence that young children's performance on false-belief tests is positively related to their working memory capacity and powers of inhibitory control. Such evidence implies that success on false-belief tests depends to some extent on children's ability to remember the sequence of events (Gordon and Olson, 1998) and to suppress their (salient) knowledge of current reality in order to respond to their (less salient) knowledge of past reality (Carlson and Moses, 2001).

Finally, research into theory of mind highlights issues of nature versus nurture. The view that there is a genetic component to theory of mind holds that children's mentalising abilities develop according to an innately determined timetable. In contrast, notions about nurture suggest that individual differences in theory-of-mind performance can largely be attributed to environmental factors (Hughes et al., 2005). A contribution of heredity to theory of mind is suggested by brain imaging studies with adult participants that implicate a specific network of brain areas (namely, the medial prefrontal cortex and temporal poles) as the neural substrate of theory-of-mind abilities (e.g., Frith and Frith, 2001). Nevertheless, environmental influences appear substantial, as indicated by speedier theory-of-mind development in children with older rather than younger siblings (Ruffman et al., 1998), and in children whose mothers engage more frequently in mental-state language (e.g., Ruffman et al., 2002). Conversely, theory-of-mind development is severely delayed in deaf children from hearing families who have restricted opportunities for conversation at home during the first few years of life (Peterson and Siegal, 1995). The finding that theory of mind fails to emerge normally in deaf children who are deprived of information about other people's mental activities provides strong evidence for an important contribution of nurture to the acquisition of theory of mind during early childhood.

Applied issues and future research directions

It is clear that theories of cognitive development have profound implications for the education of young children. Approaches to formal schooling have been heavily influenced by Piaget's theory, with its suggestion that allowing children to interact with the environment will facilitate their learning, its notion of cognitive *readiness* for determining when and what children should be taught, and its detailed analysis of children's emerging concepts about number and physical causality (Piaget, 1965, 1969). Additionally, information-processing theories have introduced microgenetic methods of exploring learning to educational research (Siegler, 2000), studies of core knowledge have provided important information regarding young children's ability to reason about unobservable causes of events (e.g., the role of germs in producing illness and the role of genes in biological inheritance; Solomon and Johnson, 2000), and discoveries within developmental cognitive neuroscience have indicated ways that stimulating specific brain regions by appropriate experiences during early childhood can improve aspects of academic learning (e.g., using music and arts training to enhance young children's performance in mathematics; Gardiner et al., 1996). Finally, sociocultural theories of cognitive development can be credited with drawing educators' attention to the importance of make-believe and socio-dramatic play in children's learning (Fromberg and Bergen, 1998) as well as prompting moves to encourage co-operative learning and peer tutoring in schools (Palincsar and Herrenkohl, 1999). Moreover, a growing awareness of the ecological context of development has led to efforts to involve members of the wider community in the educational system with the aim of developing a culture of learning both within and beyond the classroom (e.g., Brown, 1997).

Theories of cognitive development are relevant to the education of young children even before they start school. All contemporary theories are agreed that the environment, both physical and social, plays an important role in nurturing children's learning. They therefore imply that children's cognitive growth can be enhanced by enriching their pre-school experiences, for example, by increasing their access to books and toys, their opportunities for play, and their exposure to social interactions with more capable others. For example, studies in the sociocultural tradition have revealed that instructing parents in the use of specific conversational techniques with their young children can enhance pre-schoolers' language (e.g., Whitehurst et al., 1988), event memory (e.g., Boland et al., 2003), and problem-solving capabilities (e.g., Tzuriel, 1999). Such findings have implications for early intervention programmes targeting low-income families, many of which have high-lighted deficient verbal mediation within the parent–child dyad as a prime factor in children's poor school achievement (Duncan and Brooks-Gunn, 2000; NICHD Early Child Care Research Network, 2002).

In conclusion, the study of children's thinking and learning is a dynamic and evolving field that covers a diversity of topics. Not surprisingly, recent writings have emphasised the need for theoretical synthesis (Richardson, 1998; Parent et al., 2000). Bjorklund (2000) identified a growing recognition of the *joint* role of biological factors and the social/cultural context in children's development. These perspectives are no longer seen as mutually exclusive and attention has shifted towards the reciprocal transaction of a child's biological constitution and their environment, both physical and social (Lerner, 1998; Siegler, 2000). The challenge for future research is therefore to work within a theoretical framework that integrates these different perspectives on cognitive development.

Conclusion

In summary, theories of cognitive development grapple with issues of nature versus nurture, continuity versus discontinuity, active versus passive development, domain-general versus domain-specific learning, the role of the sociocultural context, and how change occurs. Pioneering studies by Piaget led him to propose that there are four distinct stages of cognitive development, with progress marked by the emergence of more advanced modes of thinking in each successive stage. Piaget viewed young children as amateur scientists who carry out simple experiments on their world to discover how it works. Subsequent investigation in the information-processing tradition suggested that development is continuous rather than stage-like and that it can be understood in terms of age-related improvements in processing mechanisms, memory capacity, and knowledge. Additionally, research into innate competences has indicated that infants are born possessing certain kinds of knowledge that facilitate their learning in particular core domains. Finally, the work of Vygotsky has implicated a contribution of social and cultural factors to children's learning. Vygotsky argued that cognitive development occurs within social interactions such that children are guided into increasingly mature ways of thinking by communicating with more capable others. All accounts have important insights to offer, and recent writings have emphasised the need for theoretical integration, particularly with the aim of explicating the reciprocal relations between biological and social influences on children's development.

Questions and exercises

1 Evaluate Piaget's contribution to contemporary theories of cognitive development.
2 Why do information-processing theorists claim that cognitive development is continuous rather than stage-like?
3 What are core domains of thought? Explain how core knowledge is thought to support children's early learning.
4 What are the key assumptions of the transactional approach to understanding the contributions of nature and nurture to cognitive development?
5 Give examples of ways in which parents can use guided participation and social scaffolding to facilitate their children's learning.
6 Evaluate evidence of domain-specific and domain-general contributions to children's developing theory of mind.

Further reading

Berk, *Child Development* (2003) is a comprehensive text about child development that relates theory to practice. Bjorklund, *Children's Thinking* (2000), reviews competing theories about cognitive development in relation to children's thinking, perception, language, and intelligence. Gauvain, *The Social Context of Cognitive Development* (2001), extends Vygotsky's ideas about the role of the sociocultural context in cognitive development by examining recent research into children's problem solving, attention, and memory. Miller, *Theories of Developmental Psychology* (2002), contains chapters summarising the developmental theories of Piaget and Vygotsky and their impact on current thinking about cognitive development. Schaffer, *Introducing Child Psychology* (2004), is an accessible introduction to the field of child psychology that is designed for readers with little background knowledge and charts both cognitive and social/emotional development. Siegler et al., *How Children Develop* (2003), is an introductory textbook about child psychology aimed at undergraduate students, including chapters on cognitive development that provide a good description of information-processing and core-knowledge approaches.

6

YOUNG CHILDREN'S SOCIAL AND EMOTIONAL DEVELOPMENT

Tricia David

Contents:

- **Introduction**
- **Born to be social**
- **So what is attachment?**
- **The bedrock of emotional development**
- **A growing sense of self: personal development**
- **Children with 'special needs'**
- **Mind-reading experts**
- **'Belonging'**
- **Conclusion**

Introduction

This chapter explains how emotional and social development form the bedrock of all areas of a child's development. It uses research evidence to highlight the crucial nature of close and loving relationships, as well as discussing the ways in which young children learn about themselves and how their social worlds 'work'. The importance of the relationships between children and their parents, with siblings and with friends is also covered.

Born to be social

From the moment of birth, babies are intensely interested in other people. In the first months of life they are trying to form close relationships and they are beginning to develop an individual sense of self. At the same time they are coming to know if those individual selves have any agency, or power, over their own lives. Babies' *attachments* at four months old are said to be good predictors of their attachments and their ability to regulate their emotions at a year old (Braungart-Rieker et al., 2001).

> In social interactions, the infant whose behavior succeeds in eliciting a positive and sensitive response from the parent feels encouraged to continue the behavior. During the first year, interaction patterns, coping experiences, and resulting views of self are the building blocks of the child's working models of self and relationships. (Davies, 1999: 147)

Understanding about oneself and others is dependent on social and emotional interactions in which cognitive processes come into play. This interweaving of all areas of development is now recognised. As Judy Dunn (1999) points out, in the past psychologists studied children's development in prescribed compartments but they are now aware of the need to explore the influence different areas have on each other. Human beings seem to be born to be social and human emotions are the most basic building blocks of their entire, holistic development, including the personal and social aspects.

Even in the first months of life, babies make distinctions between people/objects, self/other (Stern, 1985; Rosser, 1994). They appear to need to form *attachments* to the people who are familiar and significant to them (usually a parent or other relative at first). It is in the everyday interactions of being sensitively cared for that they begin to be aware of themselves and despite the fact that researchers a quarter of a century ago argued that children do not develop a sense of self (i.e., recognise themselves as separate people with an individual identity) until the second year, more recent research indicates that this amazing feat begins soon after birth (Bretherton et al., 1981; Odofsky, 1987; Sigelman and Rider, 2008). These first attachments provide a 'model' which will be drawn upon later in life. When adults – and older children – adjust their behaviour sensitively to what they perceive as the baby's needs and wishes, we say they are behaving *contingently*.

So what is attachment?

John Bowlby formulated the theory of attachment (Bowlby 1951, 1953, 1969, 1973, 1980) and his ideas were supported and developed by his colleagues (e.g., see Ainsworth, 1967; Robertson and Robertson, 1989). He proposed that attachment is an innate device intended to protect the immature offspring of a species by attracting adults who will ensure their survival. This idea fits with the observation that a newborn can be comforted by anyone but a slightly older baby prefers his/her primary attachment figure/s. Some researchers suggest attachment is universal, but others argue that it is expressed differently in different cultures (LeVine and Miller, 1990; Wang and Mallinckrodt, 2006). One important 'message' from recent research is the fact that babies can have a network of attachments made up of different members of 'the family' – all the familiar people with whom the baby has attachments (Forrest, 1997). These social experiences are influential in the process of achieving healthy social development (NICHD, 2006). It is when they reach three to six months of age that babies start making preferential attachments. They behave in ways that are designed to attract the person's attention – smiling, cooing, trying to make eye contact – when that person is near and they will be pacified by that person's voice, a look from them or the presentation of a toy, for example. Some of these preferred attachment figures will be the older children in a household. Different attachment figures will elicit different responses from a baby, for example, it may be that a young child starts to cry when collected from an early childhood education and care (ECEC) setting and this can be disconcerting to a 'new' parent. In fact the tears do not mean the baby is rejecting the parent, or that they do not feel contented at the setting. Passionate crying in such a circumstance can mean that this is the baby's preferred attachment figure and it may indicate the strength of the attachment (Watson, 1994; Davies, 1999).

Murray and Trevarthen (1985) showed that from two months of age, around the time they also engage in social smiling, infants are sensitive to *social contingency* (the mother's responsiveness to the infant's signals), especially to the timing of their mothers' emotional *attunement* in their two-way exchanges. These attuned exchanges indicate the development of *primary intersubjectivity* – the rudiments of turn taking, sensitive timing and responsiveness to the other's behaviour, especially facial expressions. Intersubjectivity is thought to be the foundation of early social interaction. Such early, playful interactions are called 'proto-conversations' and they gradually offer the young child opportunities for anticipating and predicting and they form the basis for social and cognitive advances that occur during the first year (Trevarthen and Aitken, 2001).

Naturally, attachments change over time (Dunn, 1993; Belsky et al., 1996). As Dunn's research shows, this is unsurprising, since even mothers can change their attitudes/approach towards their children at different ages, preferring particular phases of development. In addition, as Noriuchi et al. (2008) point out, changes in the mother's approach are likely to initiate particular behavioural responses from the infant which in turn will have an effect on the mother's emotions and her subsequent maternal behaviour.

Attachment theory has been used to encourage mothers to stay at home, rather than seek employment outside the home, and it has induced guilt in several generations of women, because it has been used politically at certain times, with warnings of dire consequences for babies – *maternal deprivation* – if their mothers are unavailable as primary attachment figures because they go out to work for long hours. Recent research demonstrates, however, that not only can babies form attachments to a number of people, it may be that they are better protected and better equipped to form subsequent relationships by having several primary attachment figures rather than the sometimes claustrophobic (and unnatural in human terms) relationship which can result from long hours spent in the company of only one adult, their mother. For example, in the event of the mother suffering from postnatal depression, the attachment process and the baby's emotional development are disrupted (Kumar, 1997; Cooper and Murray, 1998).

Bowlby (1988) himself stated that attachment research had shown up flaws in his theory and that instead of the idea of specific, crucial phases of development he had come to prefer a theory of developmental pathways. Despite these reservations, attachment remains a useful concept in trying to understand babies' need to relate positively to the people closest to them and in recognising the ways in which early interactions provide the building blocks for the sense of self and models for later social competence.

The bedrock of emotional development

According to Roberts (2002), Goldschmied and Jackson (2003) and Selleck and Griffin (1996), responsive, loving attention in the years between birth and three provide children with opportunities to develop a positive personal identity, self-concept and interdependent relationships. To achieve all these young children are said to need unconditional acceptance from the significant people in their lives. To such young children these people are important and powerful and they learn they are acceptable when one of these people smiles at them or comes in response to their call. This is how they learn to instigate pleasurable interactions and every interaction at this stage is a learning experience. A baby's first language is body language and they learn about themselves and their world through what they can feel, taste, hear, smell and see.

Babies and young children are also able to recognise mismatches between what they hear and a person's body language. Such incongruities confuse them. In the worst cases of insensitivity to babies, when abuse is being perpetrated, even very young children will try to make themselves acceptable by negating feelings of pain, anger and fear, by shutting down their emotions. This can have a negative effect on their emotional health and it can also impact on their physical growth and brain development.

Of course, even sensitive parents cannot respond to every cue from their children but we know from research (Aber and Allen, 1987; Lyons-Ruth and Zeanah, 1993) that babies who experience success in re-establishing contact with a key adult who was previously preoccupied gain a stronger sense of self-efficacy and a growing feeling of being successful. Additionally, emotionally sensitive parents and carers who encourage young children to explore and enjoy 'their world' find these children take greater pleasure in goal-directed task persistence, and as a result are socially and cognitively more competent in later life, whereas babies whose key adults constantly fail to support them can develop 'learned helplessness'.

So we can conclude that emotional well-being is the bedrock on which all later development depends. Happily, human brains and human beings generally are 'plastic' – they never stop learning and they can change, given the right conditions, as the research on resilience shows.

Children and adults who have factors in their lives enabling them to cope with any adverse circumstances which may beset them are said to be resilient. The research indicates that the factors relevant to this chapter which appear to foster resilience in children include: a positive disposition; a positive self-concept; good social skills; a balance between independence and interdependence; good relationships with other children; strong attachment relationships; competent parents who model competence for the child; household rules and parental monitoring; a stable relationship between parents; family expectations about positive social behaviour; supportive adults outside the family; family participation in a religious community; not being poor; positive alliances between local workers and the community; positive attitudes on the part of professionals; neighbourhood stability and policies which result in increased resources (Gilgun, 1996; Masten and Coatsworth, 1998; Davies, 1999; Breton, 2001; Chenoweth and Stehlik, 2001; Clark, 2001; Pedro-Carroll, 2001). Above all, according to Werner (1996), who studied a group of high-risk children through to adulthood, the most important 'ingredient' is a significant person in the child's life to whom that child and what they do 'matters'.

A growing sense of self: personal development

One of the most striking changes during the transition from babyhood to early childhood is a child's growing sense of self (Dunn, 1993). Individual children become aware of how others view them and, as emphasised earlier, it is usually the parent–child relationship that provides the basis for fostering a sense of self-competence and worth. Along with this growing sense of self, the child will be trying to gain a sense of independence, wishing to be seen as capable by others – and told so in words and actions when attempting to be independent (Karmiloff-Smith, 1994). These experiences enable the child to learn that they are a competent member of society and this promotes their ability to interact successfully with peers throughout middle childhood (Mikulincer and Shaver, 2007).

As Hutchins and Sims (1999) point out, children develop self-awareness and social awareness in conjunction with a sense of their own agency. When they have parents and practitioners who allow them to assert some power and control over their own lives, they learn to be self-regulating and autonomous.

By 18 to 24 months old, young children usually recognise themselves in mirrors, begin to use 'I', 'me' and 'mine' and use their own name. They also start to assert their own wishes. A few more months on and they begin to develop their gender identity, and to show awareness of racism in their society. Iram Siraj-Blatchford (2001) suggests strategies for dealing with discrimination, because 'A positive self-concept is necessary for healthy development and learning and includes feelings about gender, race, ability, culture and language. Positive self-esteem depends on whether children feel others accept them and see them as competent and worthwhile' (Siraj-Blatchford, 2001: 104).

Children with 'special needs'

Parents who have been informed soon after their baby's birth that their child has identifiable 'special needs' are often left to deal with powerful emotions which may impact upon the attachment process (Herbert, 1994; Herbert and Carpenter, 1994). According to Doyle (1997), despite the Children Act 1989, which required different professionals to work together more effectively in the 'best interests' of children, the UK still lags behind other countries in its ability to ensure this in practice. She maintains that research, training and resources in this area have been neglected and her view is supported by more recent research about multi-professionalism by Atkinson et al. (2002).

Disruption to the attachment process is also more likely if a baby needs in-patient hospitalisation or many visits in the first few weeks of life. Fenwick et al. (2008) refer to the significance of physical contact between mother and baby and where this is denied – for example, through restrictions in postnatal access – the impact that this can have on the attachment process. As Menzies Lyth (1995) emphasises, it is important that staff in institutions such as hospitals are aware of the potential effects of lack of continuity in early relationships and their key role in supporting parents. It is vitally important that medical staff understand the problems that mothers face when there is limited access to their baby, and also the importance of treating the mother and baby as a single entity (Erlandsson and Fagerberg, 2005).

Another group who require special support are children with autism, who appear aloof and indifferent and who do not seek out meaningful interactions with other children or with adults. This is because they do not perceive their world in the same way that other children do (Trevarthen et al., 1998).

Children born to parents who did not themselves experience warm and sensitive parenting, or who are experiencing high levels of stress, also tend to have attachment difficulties (Siegel, 1999; Steele et al., 1995) and babies described as irritable or difficult, whose parents (usually the mother), because of anxiety, respond aggressively rather than being able to calm them, tend to have low resilience later in life (Hagekull et al., 1993).

Mind-reading experts

Towards the end of their first year, most young children will begin to point to things and they will also be able to follow someone else's gaze when they are pointing. Such pointing activity involves referencing by looking back at the other person's face, to check they are looking at the same object, and this tells us that the child has some understanding about other people's viewpoints (Gopnik et al., 1999). Even babies younger than six months old have been observed using *social referencing* strategies, searching their parent's face for reassurance when something surprising and strange (to them) happens (Channel 4, 1992, and the allied text, Konner, 1991; for further information on social referencing see for example, Striano and Rochat, 1999; Moses et al., 2001; Clearfield et al. 2008).

During the second year, too, young children begin feigning crying (showing they are aware of its effect) and they are also more likely to make caring gestures when someone else is upset or hurt. They also begin to engage in pretend play with adults or other children. As Judy Dunn (1999) points out, being able to agree on what is happening in fantasy play, even for a short bout, shows they can take account of the play partner's thoughts, and by playing in this way children develop the ability to collaborate and develop narratives.

This is important, because, as Gopnik et al. (1999) remind us, one of the main tasks of childhood lies in understanding the difference between their own minds and those of others (see also Ereky-Stevens, 2008). Interactions with other young children, who will not make allowances for different views (or with the 'zany uncles', advocated by Urie Bronfenbrenner, who challenge through unconventional behaviour), are vital to the young child's developing brain, because parents and carers will often try to minimise such differences of opinion, scaffolding a child's attempts and looking for commonality. The challenges from other children, meanwhile, help them begin to understand that other people do not necessarily always think as they do and this is when their ability to 'mind-read' begins to come into play. Parents, grandparents, siblings, educators and others will then become subject to the child's attempts to manipulate them through this ability because they will know what makes them loved and acceptable to these important people. For example, Joe (four years) and Sam (three years) were playing with the large blocks in their nursery, building a space rocket, when Tom (three years) tried to join them. They rejected his involvement and started to make threatening gestures, Sam at one point even taking a swing at Tom – clearly intended to miss but nevertheless threatening – with a large torch in his hand. Few words had been exchanged and almost all the conflict was expressed through behaviour on the part of all three. However, after swinging the torch, Sam had caught the eye of a member of staff and he suddenly handed the torch to Tom, gesturing to him to join the play. Children use various cues, such as facial expressions, but also language, to read the minds of others and they usually try to be in the 'good books' of the people who matter to them.

When they are between the ages of two and three years, children's narratives through pretend play begin to proliferate (Bruner, 1990; Feldman, 1992). These narratives are at their most sophisticated when they are concerned with emotional events – particularly negative ones involving fear, anger or distress – and they are sequentially and causally accurate (Dunn, 1999). It has been suggested that this externalising of emotions through language supports the development of coping strategies and resilience (Lutz et al., 2007) while both Bruner and Feldman argue that narratives are used to generate a person's sense of self, to make sense of their lives and to explain the actions of ourselves and others.

'Belonging'

Wrapped up in the process of emotional, social and personal development is the child's sense of 'belonging'. Families today are very different from the families of even a generation ago, and as Jagger and Wright (1999: 3) point out, 'The family is neither a pan-human universal nor a stable or essential entity … Families and family relations are, like the term itself, flexible, fluid and contingent.' However, since research shows how important familiar, loving, significant people are to babies and young children, it is vital that, as a society, we explore ways of ensuring that they feel they are part of a 'family', however it is constituted.

Nancy Boyd Webb's (1984) research highlighted the ways in which certain behaviours gave children messages about themselves and their place in their 'family'. She observed 24 children aged under four, who had experienced multiple caring in their earliest years. She found that the most socially competent, confident and self-assured children had parents who 'bugged and nudged' them (to do, show or share something they had achieved to another of their significant adults); they had pet names, and they had rituals that the children had devised and which were respected (for example, 'He always has his "snuggly" and a cup of water at bedtimes'). (For the significance of family rituals see also Black and Lobo, 2008.)

While it does not appear to matter who does what, or whether one's parents are a cohabiting heterosexual couple, since what matters is the act of 'mothering/fathering/parenting', we live in a gendered society and research has often explored the roles taken up by mothers and fathers. Apparently, most fathers behave differently towards their children compared with the mothers. However, as Anderson (1996) points out, it can be the mother who acts as a gatekeeper, either including or excluding the father and thus encouraging or discouraging a meaningful relationship between a father and his child. According to Belsky (1996), fathers whose infants are securely attached to them are usually more extrovert and positive about their home lives than fathers whose children are insecurely attached to them. In fact, research by Fox et al. (1991) suggests that the strength of attachment to one parent is usually a good indicator of attachment to the other. Additionally, the relationship between a mother or father and their first-born appears to set the tone for the attachments of later offspring (Volling and Belsky, 1992; Brumbaugh and Fraley, 2006).

Young children's ambivalence towards new siblings is common (Dunn, 1984) but with parental support and encouragement they soon show that, even before they are three years old, they can adapt the way they talk and behave, for example, using terms of endearment towards a baby that a parent, grandparent or other significant adult has modelled. For Kieran, having new twin brothers when he himself was still not quite two years old could have been a tremendous upheaval. However, as a result of his parents' sensitive and loving approach to all their sons, Oliver and Sam quickly became family members, and sometimes when they cried, and Kieran's mum was preparing a bottle or food, he would suggest that he would like some music on so he could dance to cheer them up – and he did, because his brothers were entranced by this wonderful, agile and entertaining little person.

Of course, all siblings have their quarrels – and sometimes fights: the incidence of fighting between sisters and brothers is higher than that between friends outside the home, although the incidence for boys is roughly the same as that with peers. As Dunn (1984: 144) adds, 'It is because they understand their siblings so well, and because they feel so strongly about them, that their relationship is so significant and so revealing.'

For ECEC settings, the issues related to staff relationships with children and the difficulties of shifts, holidays and other complications require debate. Elfer et al. (2002) advocate the key worker system, to enable close relationships, which the babies and young children need, to develop. While Dahlberg et al. (1999) argue that one should not create 'false closeness'; they too advocate a concept of intensity of relationships with a small network of familiar adults and children, and Rutter (1995) has demonstrated the benefits to children of closeness and continuity.

Attendance at an ECEC setting affords babies and young children opportunities to make friends and to play with other children. Again, Judy Dunn (1993) tells us that young children's friendships are important to them and often children as young as four have friends they made when only two. Friends are also important when children move to a new ECEC setting or group (Howes, 1987). Those who, on transition, had a friend who moved setting with them fared much better in comparison with those who did not move with a friend, and Dunn (1993) found that they remembered that it was the presence of the friend that made them happy in a new setting.

Children's relationships with their friends were also the focus of research into whether the ways in which family members related to one another were reflected in interactions in nurseries. Importantly, children who enjoyed high levels of involvement with their mothers were more likely to be conciliatory and to compromise with friends. They also engaged in longer and more elaborate bouts of shared fantasy play and conversations (Dunn, 1993).

A similar effect was found when Howes and her colleagues (1994) explored children's relationships with their ECEC practitioners. Where the practitioners modelled socialisation the children seemed to be more accepting towards each other and when they felt secure in their setting they displayed complex play with other children, with whom they were also more gregarious than children who did not experience positive relationships with staff. Sally Lubeck's (1986) fine-grained account of two very different settings in an American city also showed the influence the style of interactions between staff and children, as well as those involving staff with other staff, can have on how children relate to one another and how this affects their learning. In one setting the staff related very much to individual children and there was little if any staff–staff interaction in the presence of children, while in the other group staff discussed problems together (modelling for the children) and they used a much higher level of group activities with the children. As a result, the children from each setting were losing out to some extent, since some had few opportunities to experience co-operation and interdependence, while those attending the other rarely experienced independence.

The New Zealand Ministry of Education (1996: 54) argues that all children need to have a feeling of belonging, because it 'contributes to inner well-being, security and identity. Children need to know that they are accepted for who they are. They should know that what they do can make a difference and that they can explore and try out new activities.' McGuire (1991) found that nursery staff in the UK often failed to give additional support to withdrawn children to help them become integrated into a group or to engage in play activities and Anning (1999) observed that three-year-olds struggling to make sense of themselves as members of a family and a group setting were given insufficient support in dealing with discontinuities between the two contexts.

Harris (1989) explains how different cultures build on what may be a universal, innate ability to recognise positive and negative emotional states. He also discusses the ways in which the emotions of guilt and shame are used to socialise children and different cultures use these to varying degrees. By the time they are two years old children are learning the 'scripts' assigned to different emotions by their family or community, that are learned to make one acceptable. Sometimes they will use 'transitional objects' to help them in this regulation of the emotions. These might be dummies, favourite soft toys, comforters that have been self-chosen.

Children who have warm, affectionate relationships with their parents have been found to be more likely to have high self-esteem, to be better socially adjusted and to achieve academically (Mortimer, 2001). Siegel argues that if parents – and one might surmise this could also apply to practitioners – did not enjoy warm, close relationships with their own parents, then encouraging them to reflect on their narratives of their own childhoods and to understand how they feel, can help them become more positive, so that they are able to engage in the loving, sensitive interactions which will benefit their children's emotional well-being and personal and social development.

Conclusion

The main points debated in this chapter have been as follows. Early relationships with sensitive, loving others form the model for later relationships; pleasurable interactions during the first two years provide the scripts which children adopt in their later friendships – i.e. adults and older children act as models. Children who, early in life, have been encouraged by emotionally sensitive parents and carers to explore and enjoy their world will take greater pleasure in goal-directed behaviour later in life and they will persist at difficult tasks; they will also be more competent socially and cognitively. Resilient people tend to have, or have had, at least one person in their life to whom they feel they (and what they do) matter. Staff in ECEC settings sometimes need to help children integrate into the group and they need to be aware of how friendships can help children cope with transitions. Most important, babies and young children need to experience unconditional acceptance, continuity of relationships – these can be with several key people – and to bask in interactions and play with those who love them.

Questions and exercises

1 Reflect on your own feelings as an adult, when thwarted, spurned or hurt. How do you react and why? What helps you cope? What prevents you from coping? What do you think both adults and children need if powerful feelings about negative experiences are not to overcome them and become destructive?

2 Think of an observation you have recorded (in your mind or on paper) of an incident in an ECEC setting when a child has been upset. How was it dealt with? Did the event or incident contribute to that child's, or other children's, learning about emotions, and if so, how? If you think the event was handled in a negative way, how would you like it to have been different?

3 What can be done to help shy or isolated children gain entry to a group?

Further reading

Dowling (2003), 'All about resilience', *Nursery World*, includes clear explanations about what we know from research about *resilience* and how to foster this important characteristic through our practice, in interactions with babies and young children. Roberts, *Developing Self-esteem in Young Children* (2002), deftly combines findings from research with insightful examples from real life. David et al., *Birth to Three Matters* (2003), a review of over 500 research references for the DfES project 'Birth to Three Matters', includes a chapter called 'A strong child', focusing mainly upon children's emotional and social development. However, the review also points out that children's development is not compartmentalised, it is interconnected. Gopnik et al., *How Babies Think* (1999), is first, a really good read – it provides a mass of neuroscientific research evidence in such an accessible way! Second, the authors give those of us in the ECEC field extra support in arguing for humane, loving and exciting contexts for babies and young children.

7

LANGUAGE DEVELOPMENT IN THE YOUNG CHILD

Thea Cameron-Faulkner

Contents:

- **Introduction**
- **Theoretical approaches to language development**
- **Language development across cultures**
- **Conclusion**

Introduction

For decades, researchers from a range of disciplines have been intrigued by the process of language development and the insight it can provide for our understanding of human cognition. The field of child language research is rich with competing theories, all of which aim to address the key question in the field: what are the processes and knowledge base that underlie the development of language in humans? In this chapter I will outline three approaches to the study of language development: the behaviourist approach, the formalist approach and the constructivist approach. While each of these labels subsumes a network of related theories the categorisation provides a useful starting point. Following the theoretical overview, the discussion will be widened to encompass cross-cultural aspects of language development and their impact on our understanding of the process in general.

Theoretical approaches to language development

In some ways the most logical place to start this discussion is by considering what kind of linguistic knowledge is ascribed to adults. By considering the type of knowledge a child must acquire we can then focus on the manner in which they traverse the path of development from preverbal infants to fully fledged members of their linguistic community.

The behaviourist approach

In the behaviourist tradition, most typically associated with Skinner (1957), language is situated within the behaviourist rubric of classical and operant conditioning, that is learning evoked through 'stimulus and response' and 'reward/punishment' processes. Classical conditioning is claimed to underlie the child ability to associate a stimulus (e.g., a noise or object) with an arbitrary verbal sign (i.e., a word or phrase). For example, consider a caregiver and child playing with a rattle. The child holds and shakes the rattle and looks towards the caregiver. The caregiver then comments on the object, 'Yes, it's a *rattle*. Do you like the *rattle*?' Over time the child begins to associate the form *rattle* with the object and acquires a new word form. Thus, the early stages of language development involve the child imitating a linguistic form presented in response to a particular stimulus.

The response of the caregiver to the child's utterances further shapes the child's linguistic system through the process of operant conditioning as forms eliciting 'rewards' are retained while forms resulting in 'punishment' are avoided. Thus, if the child produces a linguistic form that approximates a word and is appropriate in a given context, she or he will be rewarded in some way by the adult (e.g., a positive verbal response 'yes', the presentation of a requested item, or the continuation of a conversation). Conversely, if a child produces a form that does not represent the child's target language or is not produced in response to the appropriate stimulus then it is more likely that she or he will not be rewarded (e.g., the adult may ignore the utterance, ask for clarification, or fail to produce the item that the child attempted to request). So, from the traditional behaviourist perspective, language development was viewed as a process involving imitation of input forms and subsequent shaping of the linguistic system through feedback from more experienced conversational partners.

The formalist approach

Skinner's most famous critic, Noam Chomsky, launched a devastating attack on the behaviourist account to language development in his 1959 review of Skinner's book

Verbal Behavior (1957). Chomsky claimed that the behaviourist characterisation of language was too simplistic and did not capture the underlying complexities of linguistic knowledge. In his review Chomsky proposed that our knowledge of language was highly abstract, consisting of algebraic rules and abstract categories that no child could learn without considerable innate knowledge. Consequently, Chomsky claimed that humans must be endowed with a genetic blueprint of language, known as Universal Grammar (UG). It was claimed that the linguistic information contained within UG went beyond the concrete linguistic expressions produced in everyday speech and captured the underlying rules and regularities which shape all natural languages.

As with all dynamic approaches to theoretical issues, the formalist approach is continually evolving. One of the more recent approaches is the Principles and Parameters theory (e.g., Chomsky, 1995) in which UG is claimed to consist of two types of information: firstly, structural information which equips the child with a set of general linguistic principles, and secondly a set of parameters ('switches') which allow the child to 'set' certain aspects of their linguistic knowledge to particular values in response to their language of exposure. To take a concrete example, consider the variation in word order across languages. In English, verbs follow subjects as in (1):

1   It fell.

whereas in Irish subjects follow verbs (2):

2   Thit sí.
     Fell-it.
     'It fell.'

Through exposure to their target language the child would subconsciously switch the appropriate parameter in line with the word order patterns attested in their language and thus be said to have acquired the word order (and associated values known as 'headedness') of their native language. In this way the input a child receives acts as a trigger as opposed to the sole source of linguistic evidence available to the child.

Chomsky bolstered his linguistic theory by positing a number of claims pertaining to the linguistic input received by young children. Firstly, Chomsky claimed that the input children receive is degenerate, that is the language children hear contains incomplete utterances, grammatical errors, false starts and many other features of everyday informal speech (Chomsky, 1965). Therefore, if the child's only available source of linguistic knowledge is the ambient language then how could they be sure which utterances were grammatical and which were not? In addition to this,

Chomsky and other UG researchers claim that the input does not contain the wide range of structures necessary for a child to work out the underlying categories and rules of their target language:

> People attain knowledge of the structure of their language for which no evidence is available in the data to which they are exposed as children. (Hornstein and Lightfoot, 1981: 9)

Together these two claims are known as the Poverty of the Stimulus argument and are presented as a challenge to any approach to language development in which the input plays a central role.

Chomsky also claimed that children do not receive explicit feedback on the grammaticality of their utterances. For example, a child who produced errors related to negation (e.g., *I not do it*) would not be informed consistently of the correct form (i.e., *I didn't do it*). This claim is referred to as the 'no-negative evidence' problem and is widely upheld within the formalist tradition:

> I think that the assumption that negative evidence is not available to the child's learning mechanisms is warranted. There are, no doubt, cases in which parents correct their children (e.g., over-regularized affixing). However, there is anecdotal evidence that even in such cases, children are oblivious to such corrections. (Pinker, 1984: 29)

As Pinker points out, even when feedback is on offer there is evidence to suggest that this input is not always positively received as the well-quoted example from McNeill indicates:

Child: Nobody don't like me.

Mother: No, say 'Nobody likes me'

Child: Nobody don't like me.

(dialogue repeated eight times)

Mother: Now listen carefully, say 'Nobody likes me.'

Child: Oh! Nobody don't likes me.

(McNeill, 1966: 69)

In McNeill's example the mother attempts to correct the child's utterance but regardless of instruction the child continues to struggle with the grammaticality of the utterance.

Thus, formalists claim that children could not learn their target language from the input alone and thus must be genetically equipped with some form of linguistic knowledge. Within this framework then the child's task in acquiring their native tongue is to fine tune their innate linguistic knowledge in order to reflect the structural properties of their target language.

The 'no-negative evidence' argument and the 'Poverty of the Stimulus' argument are central to the formalist approach. However, not all researchers agree that children are bereft of feedback or indeed agree on what should be counted as feedback. A number of studies conducted in response to claims about no-negative evidence indicated that caregivers have a tendency to 'recast' their children's ungrammatical utterances as shown in (3) below:

3   Child: fix Lilly

    Mother: Oh…Lilly will fix it.

(Sokolov and Snow, 1994: 47)

In (3) the child produces an ungrammatical utterance and the mother reformulates the gist of the utterance into a grammatical form. The process of recasting can be viewed as a form of feedback; firstly, the recast indicates to the child that their utterance was ill-formed in some way, and secondly, the target form is presented in quick succession to the error. This implicit feedback appears to have a positive effect on linguistic development (e.g., Demetras et al., 1986; Bohannon and Stanowicz, 1988). There have also been challenges regarding Chomsky's claims about the linguistic input available to young children (i.e., the Poverty of the Stimulus) as researchers investigate the characteristics of Child Directed Speech (CDS) at a fine-grained level. In order to present these arguments I will now move on to discuss a contrasting view of language development broadly referred to in this chapter as the constructivist approach.

The constructivist approach

While researchers working within the formalist tradition focused on the acquisition of linguistic structure and the form of underlying linguistic knowledge, a growing body of developmental linguists and psychologists were shifting attention towards more semantically orientated theories (e.g., Bloom, 1970) and frameworks in which the social nature of language provided the backdrop to development (e.g., Bates and MacWhinney, 1982; Bruner, 1983; Braine, 1994; Ninio and Snow, 1999). The constructivist approach as described below is an umbrella term for a range of theories (e.g., social interactionist, usage-based, and connectionist) which share a common belief that linguistic knowledge is constructed by the child as opposed to being pre-given at birth. Constructivist theories challenge the formalist representation of linguistic knowledge and suggest that adult linguistic knowledge is shaped by experience, that is the language addressed to and used by individual speakers (e.g., Hopper and Thompson, 1984; Langacker, 1987; Bybee and Scheibman, 1999; Tomasello, 2000; Croft, 2001). Rather than viewing language as an abstract system of categories and rules, researchers working within constructivist approaches typically view language in terms of linguistic constructions which are tied to specific functions. Thus, in the words of the cognitive linguist Langacker, the grammatical systems of natural languages consist of 'a structured inventory of conventional linguistic units' (Langacker, 1991: 548). This characterisation of language is reflected in the work of many linguists who believe that much of the speech we produce is not stored in terms of abstract linguistic units but instead as 'chunks' of speech with a specific purpose. Coulmas states:

> A great deal of communicative activity consists of enacting routines making use of pre-fabricated linguistic units in a well-known and generally accepted manner. We greet and bid farewell to one another, introduce ourselves and others, apologize and express gratitude, buy groceries and order meals, exchange wishes, make requests, ask for advice or information, report on what we did, and announce what we are about to do. As similar speech situations recur, speakers make use of similar and sometimes identical expressions, which have proved to be functionally appropriate. Thus competent language use is always characterized by an equilibrium between the novel and the familiar. (Coulmas, 1981: 1)

This representation of language leads to very different claims regarding the type of knowledge the child has to learn and how they proceed in acquiring it. For example, Tomasello, Lieven and colleagues (e.g., Tomasello, 1992; Lieven et al., 1997; Dabrowska, 2000; Theakston et al., 2001; Lieven et al., 2003) claim that children rely heavily on lexically-based constructions in the early stages of language development (e.g., *It's a X, want Y*). These units are then stored and form the basis of the child's knowledge of their target language. As more units are stored the child subconsciously extracts the underlying structural patterns that form the fabric of their target language.

Critiques have suggested that constructivist accounts bear a strong resemblance to old fashioned behaviourism; that is, language develops through imitation of the input. However, the constructivist approach differs to behaviourism on two fundamental issues. Firstly, although it is claimed that children are learning from the input, their learning is not straightforward imitation but rather a specific form of cultural learning. As Tomasello states:

> Human children differ from their nearest primate relatives not only in having language but also in being able to imitatively learn other types of social conventions, to communicate with others declaratively, to use material symbols such as pictures and maps, to make and use intentionally defined tools with a history, to collaborate using complementary roles, to teach one another, and to create social institutions such as governments and money. This suggests a fairly general human ability to interact with conspecifics culturally, that is, to create material, symbolic, and institutional artefacts historically and to acquire their use ontogenetically. No other species on the planet has this same propensity for things cultural. (2003: 290)

In the approach to development captured in the above quote Tomasello situates language and its development in children as an intrinsic part of cultural behaviour. Secondly, children are not limited to input forms but instead move beyond the input by constructing a more schematic representation of language. Therefore, a child learning English will gradually formulate a schema for plural formation which will results in the production of NOUN+s schema. By using this schema a child will produce both correct forms (e.g., *cars, bikes, cakes*) but also from time to time use the schema erroneously (e.g., *sheeps, feets*). Thus, unlike a behaviourist account, the child is not simply mimicking the input but instead working from the bottom up by learning lexically-based constructions and then subconsciously working out the regularities between them.

Within the constructivist approach to language development the linguistic input that children receive is central to the developmental process. What then of the formalist claim that the input that children receive is 'impoverished'? Whether we believe that the language children hear is sufficient for language to develop or not very much depends on the nature of what we think it is that they are acquiring. If the child's task is to discover an abstract and highly rule governed system from the onset of language development then most researchers would agree that the language children typically hear does not contain the vast range of structure necessary for a child to know that '*he*' in (4a) could refer to Jay while in (4b) '*he*' could also refer to someone other than Jay:

4a   When Jay entered the room, he was wearing a yellow shirt.

4b   When he entered the room Jay was wearing a yellow shirt.

(Anderson and Lightfoot, 2002: 19)

However, if we claim that the child's task is to store units of speech and then use these as a basis to gradually extract the patterns of their language then research would indicate that the language children hear is well suited to the task. The specific nature of Child Directed Speech (CDS) has been well documented in language development literature. Typically the speech addressed to young children has a specific form of intonation, shorter sentence structure, restricted vocabulary and focuses on the here and now:

> The broad outlines of mothers' speech to children – that it is simple and redundant, that is contains many questions, many imperatives, few past tenses, few co- or sub-ordinations, and few dysfluencies, and that it is pitched higher and has an exaggerated intonation pattern – are quite well established. (Snow, 1977: 36)

All these adaptations appear well suited to gaining and maintaining the attention and understanding of young language learners. Studies also indicate that the structures used in CDS are highly repetitive and may thus facilitate the segmentation and abstraction of the lexically-based frames which dominate young children's early linguistic systems. For example, Cameron-Faulkner et al. (2003) conducted a lexically-based analysis of

CDS from 12 mothers. The results demonstrated a high degree of lexical specificity in the speech of the mothers with over half of the CDS sample consisting of a very limited number of lexically-based frames (e.g., *Are you...? Look at ..., It's a ..., What's that?*). Thus, the study indicated that rather than being degenerate the input addressed to nascent language learners may be well suited to the task at hand.

While studies of Child Directed Speech indicate the adult may adapt their speech to young children, there are limitations as much of this work is based on a specific sample of the population, namely caregivers living in Western industrialised countries. As a number of researchers have pointed out, CDS is not attested in all cultures. In the next section child language development is discussed within a cross-cultural perspective.

Language development across cultures

Cultural attitudes to language development differ worldwide. In the cultural context of Western, middle-class English-speaking communities, adults tend to employ some form of modified speech when talking to children, as mentioned in the previous section. However, as Lieven (1994) points out, this does not appear to be a universal phenomenon. In a number of cultures adults do not address children directly, for a variety of reasons. Heath (1983) presents an ethnographic study of two rural working-class communities ('Trackton' and 'Roadville') in the Piedmont, South Carolina. Trackton is a black working-class area in which the older generations engaged in farming, while Roadville (only a few miles down the road) was predominantly a white working-class area based around employment in the textile mills. Despite their close proximity, Heath's ethnographic study indicated clear differences within the cultures of the two communities and suggested that these differences are also manifested in caregivers' approach to language development:

In Roadville, Heath comments that:

> When the baby begins to respond verbally, to make sounds which adults can link to items in the environment, questions and statements are addressed to the baby, repeating or incorporating his 'word'. (Heath, 1983: 123)

While Heath comments that in Trackton:

> [caregivers] do not see babies or young children as suitable partners for regular conversations. For an adult to choose a preverbal infant over an adult as a conversational partner would be considered an affront and a strange behaviour as well. (Heath, 1983: 86)

Heath claims that in the Roadville community language is viewed as a skill that should be fostered and nurtured by caregivers. Adults modify their speech when addressing young children in order to accommodate the linguistic knowledge of their conversational partners. In contrast, according to Heath, the prevailing ethos in Trackton is that children should discover how the world works for themselves and that this ethos also extends to the acquisition of language. Children are required to find their own way of breaking into the linguistic system of their speech community. However, it is important to note the social environment of the Trackton children:

> Infants are held during their waking hours, occasionally while they sleep, and they usually sleep in the bed with parents until they are about 2 years of age. They are held, their faces fondled, their cheeks pinched, and they eat and sleep in the midst of human talk and noise from the television, stereo, and radio. Encapsulated in an almost totally human world, they are in the midst of constant human communication, verbal and non-verbal. They literally feel the body signals of shifts in emotion of those who hold them almost continuously; they are talked about and kept in the midst of talk about topics that range over any subject. (Heath, 1986: 112)

Thus, while the Trackton children may not have been addressed directly, they were continually exposed to their target language and to the routines and daily activities encoded by it.

Schieffelin (1994) also presents an ethnographic account of language socialisation but this time in amongst a very different population: the Kaluli community of Papua New Guinea. Schieffelin highlights the lack of Child Directed Speech attested in the community, but further comments that:

> However, this does not mean that Kaluli children grow up in an impoverished verbal environment and not learn how to speak. Quite the opposite is true. The verbal environment of the infant is rich and varied, and from the very beginning the infant is surrounded by adults and older children who spend a great deal of time talking to one another. (Schieffelin, 1994: 485)

The onset of language development is marked by the use of two key words by the child; 'mother' (no) and 'breast' (bo). After this point linguistic interaction between caregiver and child commences as the child is presented with eliciting 'ɛlɛma' (say like that) constructions such as (5) and (6). The ɛlɛma are used to inform the child of the appropriate linguistic conventions required within a given context and provide direct instruction to the young language learning child.

5   ni nuwe sukɛ! ɛlɛma.
     My grandmother picked! say like that

6   gi suwo?! ɛlɛma.
     Did you pick?! say like that

(Schieffelin, 1994: 486)

The ethnographic descriptions presented by Heath and Schieffelin are two of many studies which indicate that many children are exposed to language in an indirect way and thus 'tend to participate in communicative interactions in the role of overhearers of non-simplified conversations between others' (Ochs and Schieffelin, 1995: 78). There is a growing body of research that indicates children can and do learn aspects of language through overhearing speech as opposed to being addressed directly. For example, Akhtar et al. (2001) compared the ability of two-year-olds to acquire novel nouns and verbs when the items were presented direct and indirectly (i.e., with the children overhearing the words in question). The findings of the study indicated that children of around two-and-a-half found it just as easy to acquire the words in both conditions and thus that children can learn words which are not directly addressed to them (Akhtar et al., 2001). The results echoed the perceptions of the parents whose children were involved in the study:

> Many parents reported that their children knew many more words than they had been explicitly taught (including some words that parents would prefer their children had not learned). (Akhtar et al., 2001: 428)

Nevertheless, children from these communities still acquire their native tongue and in addition there is evidence to suggest that children from CDS and non-CDS cultures actually develop language on the same timescale (Ochs, 1985). Such communities are still underrepresented in the field of language development. However, it could be argued that in order to fully understand the process of language development it is not only the ranges of languages that needs to be widened with regard to analysis but also the cultural diversity in which children learn the language of their community.

Conclusion

In this chapter, three approaches to language development have been presented. Each approach is informed by a different set of assumptions regarding the nature of linguistic knowledge and as a consequence results in markedly distinct theories of language acquisition. The final section highlighted the cross-cultural differences with regard to linguistic input presented to young language learners and indicated that the characteristics of the linguistic environment reflect the cultural beliefs of the community with regard to the transmission of knowledge.

Questions and exercises

1. What skills do children bring to the language learning task?
2. To what extent does the presence of Child Directed Speech (CDS) facilitate language development.

3 How would the formalist and functionalist approaches account for atypical language learning populations?
4 What contribution could siblings play to the development of language?

Further reading

There are a range of child language textbooks on the market many of which present the major issues pertaining to language development from a theory neutral perspective (for example Hoff, *Language Development* (2008) and Berko Gleason, *The Development of Language* (2005). Lust *Child Language: Acquisition and Growth* (2006) presents a more formal linguistic approach to the study of language acquisition. For a thorough investigation of the usage based approach to language development the reader is directed towards Tomasello *Constructing a Language* (2003). In order to gain an insight into the debate between the innatist and non-innatist approaches to language development useful books are Pinker, *The Language Instinct* (1994) and Sampson, *Educating Eve: The 'Language Instinct' Debate* (2005).

8

PLAY AND DEVELOPMENT IN EARLY CHILDHOOD

Justine Howard

Contents:

- **Introduction**
- **Why do we play?**
- **What is play?**
- **How do children define play?**
- **Play and development**
- **Professional play practice**
- **Cultural differences in children's play**
- **Conclusion**

Introduction

The view that play is important, if not essential for children is something that is often assumed rather than demonstrated (Sutton-Smith, 1997). Play is 'all pervasive yet too vaguely acknowledged as a good thing' (Blenkin and Kelly, 1987: 37). Play scholars span many disciplines (e.g., philosophy, psychology, sociology and anthropology) and their work highlights play's complexity from a historical, cultural and developmental perspective. It would be impractical to attempt an overarching review within an introductory chapter. The purpose here is to highlight the significance of play in early childhood and the problems associated with its definition. In particular, it will draw attention to the value of eliciting children's own perceptions and emphasise how play's fundamental qualities separate it from other modes of action.

Why do we play?

There have been many attempts to organise accounts of why we play. Strategies range from the popular classical versus dynamic distinction used by Saracho (1991), to the exotic, cross disciplinary rhetorics of Sutton-Smith (1997). The well-used phrase derived from Greek philosophy that there is nothing new under the sun is almost certainly true for organising the literature surrounding play.

Hughes (1999) suggests play theories differ according to whether they emphasise physical, emotional or intellectual development. Earlier accounts focus on one of these domains, for example, philosophical ideas suggest physical reasons for play, psychoanalytic approaches see play as central to emotional health whilst constructivist theories consider intellectual development. More recently, however, there has been a move toward holistic theories that consider the underlying features of play and its significance across multiple domains.

Early ideas about play

Ellis (1973, cited in Saracho and Spodek, 1998) describes early accounts of play as armchair theories as they come from the philosophical tradition and are largely based on *ideas* about human existence rather than *supporting evidence*. Saracho (1991) presents these theories as competing pairs. Surplus energy versus relaxation, where play either consumes or creates energy, and recapitulation versus pre-exercise, where play either reflects evolutionary extinct behaviours or serves as practice for skills required in adult life (Howard, 2002). The regulatory function proposed by energy theorists is echoed in the arousal modulation of Berlyne (1969). Here children are motivated to play because it provides an optimum means of regulating environmental stimulation. An over-stimulating environment requires exploration (to reduce nervous activity) whereas an under-stimulating environment requires play (to increase nervous activity). The proposition that play allows children to practise essential social skills is an important feature of the bio-cultural approach. This suggests that increased anti-social behaviour in modern society may be a result of reduced free play opportunities and increased adult surveillance, disrupting the development of essential neural pathways and compromising social competence (Jarvis, 2007).

Developmental theories

Whereas philosophical accounts were primarily concerned with why play exists, developmental theories seek to detail the nature and function of this play.

The earliest developmental theories stem from the psychoanalysis of Sigmund Freud (1856–1939) and are concerned with the role of play for social and emotional development. Whilst many of Freud's ideas have been discredited, it is important to recognise the significance of his work, in particular for our appreciation of the unconscious mind and the impact of early experiences. Anna Freud (1968) developed her father's theory and maintained that during play children resolved anxiety and developed coping strategies for future use. Play afforded the opportunity to explore feelings that it would be inappropriate to tackle in everyday life. These ideas were further developed by Erikson (1977) who, in addition to the resolution of trauma, suggested that play provided an opportunity for learning about the self and others. In play children learned about their personality characteristics and the complexity of human relationships. Psychoanalysis continues to make an invaluable contribution to the growing professional fields of therapeutic play and playwork.

Constructivist accounts of play are embedded within broader theories of development and include the work of Piaget and Vygotsky. Piaget (1952) maintained that as a species we are motivated to learn in order to ensure that our mental representation of the world matches reality: this he described as equilibrium. To achieve equilibrium we are born with two mechanisms of change, assimilation and accommodation (described in Chapter 5). Of significance, is that Piaget saw play as largely assimilative, consolidating existing knowledge rather than being a principal mode of learning. His theory of play was strongly associated with his stage theory of development and he described play as reflecting increased cognitive ability. For Piaget, play was secondary to the business of learning and allowed children to perfect, rather than acquire, developing skills.

Vygotsky maintained that development was driven by our motivation toward social interaction. A central tenet of his work was the zone of proximal development (again see Chapter 5), and of significance was his proposition that play itself provides such a zone, where children are able to set their own challenges. Vygotsky argued that in play 'a child always behaves beyond his average age, above his daily behaviour' (1978: 102). This demonstrates his view of the child as both an independent and critically, a social learner. He was particularly interested in symbolism during imaginative play and it is argued that, for Vygotsky, the ability to allow one thing to stand for something else represents children's first experience with systems they will later apply in numeracy and literacy (Whitebread and Jameson, 2005).

Alternative theories describe the holistic value of play rather than focusing on one particular developmental domain. These accounts propose that the value of play lies in its ability to promote adaptive and flexible patterns of behaviour. Bruner (1974) and Sutton-Smith (1979) suggest that play supports behavioural flexibility by freeing children from external goals and opens children's eyes to cognitive alternatives. During play children mix and match behaviours and being in control of the activity minimises the potential to fail and allows them to experiment with combinations fluidly. The power of play to facilitate adaptive and flexible thought is supported by animal analysis of Fagan (1984) who demonstrated that rats who were exposed to enriched, playful environments during infancy showed greater behavioural flexibility. Studies of their brain activity revealed that those who were reared in playful environments had increased neural interconnectivity, indicated by the complex branching and density of synapses. It is suggested that the increase in neural activity occurs because play activity stimulates the production of proteins that are responsible for the growth of important nerve cells (Siviy, 1998).

What is play?

Holistic theories are exciting as they remind us that there is something unique about play that requires investigation if we are to fully understand its contribution to development. A fundamental problem, however, is agreeing on an operational definition of what play actually is. Providing a definition is important as it ensures we are all talking about the same thing. Attempts to define play can be grouped into those that consider categories, criteria and continuum.

Concordant with his theory of cognition, Piaget (1951) identified three types of play that reflected children's thinking ability: practice play, symbolic play, and games with rules (Howard 2002). These types of play were predominant at particular stages of development (e.g., practice play during the sensorimotor period) and were dependent on cognitive ability (e.g., symbolic play emerging with symbolic thought). Piaget's identification of early sensory play resonates in Elinor Goldschmied's work on heuristic play that describes infants' absorption with objects chosen for their sensory and non-prescriptive qualities (see Goldschmied and Jackson, 2003). The proposition that early sensory experience is important for the development of future play skills is a pivotal feature of Jennings' (1999) Embodiment, Projection and Role paradigm (EPR) in therapeutic play. Smilanksy (1968) argued that Piaget's typology did not account for certain forms of play and added a category for construction but for Piaget, this represented accommodative rather than assimilative activity. This highlights the issue of subjectivity, what is considered play by one person may not be considered play by another (Howard, 2002). Even the 15-category typology of Hughes (1996) may defy this neat categorisation, and all encompassing typologies, such as the ludic/epistemic distinction made by Hutt et al. (1989), may be too broad to be useful.

Criteria approaches suggest that for an activity to be defined as play it must demonstrate intrinsic motivation, positive affect, freedom from rules, non-literality and attention to means over ends (e.g., Rubin et al., 1983). However, there is debate amongst scholars as to the relative importance of each of these characteristics. Smith and Vollstedt (1985) presented adult raters with video clips of children at play and found that the most common indicators used were non-literality, flexibility and positive affect. Interestingly intrinsic motivation was not used by the raters despite it being a consistent feature of play within the literature. Smith and Vollstedt subsequently adopted these three principal criteria despite other theorists maintaining that play does not always appear enjoyable or involve pretence (Sutton-Smith and Kelly-Byrne, 1984). The usefulness of the criteria approach is further reduced when we consider that Smith and Vollstedt's adult raters felt that at least two characteristics had to be present before a play judgment was made. Might an activity still be play even though only one characteristic is observed?

Rather than using criteria to make an absolute decision as to whether an activity is or is not play, Pellegrini (1991) suggests that the number of criteria present can be used to place the play on a continuum. More criteria indicate a closer proximity to pure play. As with broad typologies, however, the value of this is questionable. Garvey (1991) presents a dynamic continuum and suggests that during an episode of play, children move in and out of the play frame using different modes of action. This movement in and out of the play frame highlights how difficult it is to make a decision as to whether or not activity is play regardless of whether we adopt a category, criteria or continuum approach as the situation is ever changing. Garvey's work is also interesting as it hints at the significance of play as an attitude or mode of action.

How do children define play?

Animal studies aside, most play research relates to children and it is surprising that only a limited amount of time has been spent investigating their views. As Takhvar comments:

> as play is mostly practiced during childhood, perhaps children themselves could provide a means to define this behaviour, or at least illuminate how far and to what extent they share adults' views. (1988: 238)

Play means different things to different people in different contexts (Guha, 1988; Howard, 2002). By focusing on theories and definitions of play that are the result of adult observations we have arguably been missing the affective elements that render it a powerful developmental media. Winnicott (1971) distinguishes the noun 'play' from the verb 'playing' and proposes that it is the noun, rather than the verb, that warrants investigation. This point is echoed by Lieberman (1977), who separates the behavioural elements of play from its quintessence: the quintessence of play being its essential and defining quality. Recently, there has been renewed interest in children's own perceptions of play in an effort to pinpoint what this illusive quality might be.

Interview studies have revealed that children categorise play according to activity type (e.g., role play, construction activities and outdoor play rather than writing, drawing or reading books), the level of control they are afforded and whether or not an adult is present (e.g., King, 1979; Karrby, 1989). Similarly, using the Activity Apperception Story Procedure (a photographic sorting task), Howard (2002) found that children used cues to categorise play-based on who was involved (adult or no adult presence), the activity type (e.g., sand and water versus writing and drawing), whether or not they choose to participate and, in addition, where an activity took place (table or floor). This work and that of Karrby (1989) also demonstrated that children developed these cues as a result of their experiences with both the physical and social environment.

Play and development

The difficulties associated with defining play coupled with the need to isolate play as a causal determinant has meant that empirical support for the developmental potential of play has been limited. Research includes observational, longitudinal and experimental studies, each with its own strengths and limitations.

In the field of language acquisition, observational studies show how children play with sounds, nonsensical rhyming patterns and the grammatical construction of sentences (Hughes, 1999). Whilst there are correlations between these acts of play and other skills, for example, children's rhyming ability and reading achievement (Athey, 1984, cited in Hughes, 1999), we cannot infer that this is a direct result of play. During physical play we observe children running, jumping, and riding bicycles. These children appear intrinsically motivated and seem to be having fun. There is no doubt that they are developing muscle control, co-ordination, balance and self-awareness but again this is not necessarily a result of the play. For instance, had the children been instructed to ride on the bicycles and in protest rode repetitively back and forth from one end of the yard to the other, the physicality of the activity would remain.

The impressive longitudinal Effective Provision of Preschool Education project (EPPE) reports that quality, play-based provision in the early years leads to superior social, emotional and cognitive development (Sylva et al., 2004). However, a quality environment is defined via indicators such as the nature of adult–child interaction, and it is questionable whether this is in keeping with the fundamental qualities of play as children often categorise play as being something that does not involve adult participation (e.g., King, 1979; Howard, 2002).

Experimental studies attempt to isolate play as a causal factor but even these do not escape criticism. The classic lure retrieval study by Sylva et al. (1976) is frequently cited as evidence for the relationship between play and problem solving. Children who were allowed to play with materials in a practise session performed better at retrieving an object with clamps and sticks than those who had not engaged in the play beforehand. This study (and others of a similar design) have been criticised, however, for failing to differentiate between play and initial exploration with materials (Sutton-Smith, 1997).

Understanding children's own perceptions of their play has led to significant advances in demonstrating the relationship between playfulness and development. The cues used by children to define play (location, choice and adult involvement) have been used to manipulate experimental conditions in studies designed to measure the impact of playful practice on various familiar problem solving tasks. These have consistently revealed that playful practice leads to significantly improved performance (Ramani 2005; Thomas et al., 2006).

Professional play practice

We have come to acknowledge that emotional health lies at the core of children's development and that play is a key way to support this (Howard and Prendiville, 2008). Policy relating to care and education emphasises the importance of well-being and many local authorities offer training courses for professionals to learn how to support children's emotional health. Although educational, recreational and therapeutic professionals may encounter play in different settings and experience different pressures in relation to the experiences provided, they are unified by the qualities of play that render it powerful. Rather than seeing play as being qualitatively different across contexts (e.g., play as pedagogy or play as therapy) it may be more useful to see this as a spectrum of practice. There is developmental, educational and therapeutic value in all of children's play although the emphasis placed on these values may differ according to context. The benefits children accrue in play will vary depending on the depth and nature of the relationships that develop, the child's circumstances and the skills and judgement utilised by the practitioner.

Therapeutic play

The therapeutic power of play is rooted in the psychoanalytic tradition and since the 1920s play has been used to help children express themselves more readily (Landreth, 2002). *Play therapists* harness play to resolve psychosocial difficulties and to make clinical decisions about children's therapeutic needs. They are often, but not always, trained in psychotherapy and their emphasis is on the development of a therapeutic relationship. *Developmental and therapeutic play specialists* use play to enhance children's holistic development, and they work with individuals and groups, facilitating play skills to promote well-being and resilience (Howard and Prendiville, 2008). Approaches can be directive, non-directive or integrative. In a directive approach the therapist offers interpretation as to the meaning of the play and may plan specific interventions based on this interpretation. The early psychoanalytic approaches of Anna Freud and Melanie Klein were consistent with this tradition and saw play as an information gathering opportunity. Non-directive approaches are characterised by the active role of the child who essentially leads the session. Carl Rogers instigated a move towards client-led therapies (Hughes, 1999) and this is extended in the work of Virginia Axline (1969), whose approach draws attention to the value of both the therapeutic relationship and the play process. As well as using selected toys, therapeutic play also involves puppetry, storytelling, art, music, drama and dance. This range of media ensures opportunities for multi-sensory experiences, symbolism and role play, all of which are fundamental to the EPR paradigm. This developmental approach to therapeutic play emphasises the successful negotiation of progressive play stages. The process begins with embodied sensory experiences, progresses to symbolism in projective play and cumulates in children's ability to enact roles. Each stage is important, providing 'intrinsic learnings…for life preparation' (Jennings, 1999: 55).

Playwork

The importance of play as a child-directed process and the sensitive nature of adult–child interaction in play are principles shared by therapeutic play and playwork. The parallels between the two professions are particularly evident within the psycholudic approach that draws together the key features of play activity that facilitate healing and development and proposes that, regardless of professional status (e.g., teacher, therapist or playworker), being involved with children during play immerses both the player and adult attendant into a space where healing and development are negotiated (Sturrock, 2003). Whilst playworkers are often associated with recreational play and out-of-school clubs, the range of employment is much wider than this, for example, playworkers may also work in a therapeutic context. Playworkers adhere to a set of principles that are founded on children's right to play and the belief that opportunities for self-directed play are fundamental to development. In particular, they are very aware of the impact adult presence can have on children's play and work hard to ensure that play opportunities remain child-directed. Playworkers understand and respond appropriately to children's play cues, creating stimulating and flexible opportunities that allow children to pursue their own agendas (Brown, 2003). Despite debates surrounding the principles of playwork compared to play in educational settings, many of these objectives are shared by teaching professionals but implementing a play-based approach in educational contexts has proven to be rather more problematic.

Play in early education

Piaget (1951), Vygostky (1978) and Bruner (1974) have played pivotal roles in the shaping and re-shaping of educational practices and we now acknowledge the importance of child-initiated activity and social interaction for learning and development. Whilst play is clearly embedded within current curriculum initiatives (ACCAC, 2004; DfES, 2007a) this is not that new. The Plowden Report (CACE) clearly advocated the importance of play as a 'principal means of learning in early childhood' (1967: 193) as did the curriculum guidance for the foundation stage (QCA, 2000). Despite this, observations of classroom practice demonstrated that play often tended to fulfil a subordinate role, secondary to principal classroom activity (Ofsted, 1993). The reasons for this have been researched widely. Bennett et al. (1997) propose that whilst teachers may advocate play, the uncertainty amongst scholars as to its value means that they lack the confidence to utilise it at classroom level. Other difficulties associated with implementing play-based curricula have included increased class size, pressure to account for and measure children's abilities, parental pressure toward the teaching of basic skills and a lack of understanding as to how to become involved in children's play (Sylva et al., 1992; Stipek and Byler 1997). Prendiville (2008) also found that some teachers were intolerant of the mess associated with some forms of play such as sand and water. Over-prescriptive curriculum guidelines and outcome measures have meant that, rather than using their professional skills, teachers have often felt that they have been driving a curriculum van (Edwards and Knight, 2000).

A re-conceptualisation of play that emphasises affective rather than behavioural qualities could ensure the success of curricula that centralise play. Research has shown that children's perceptions of play can be used diagnostically to plan a playful early years environment (Westcott and Howard, 2007). Understanding the cues children use to signal play as their mode of action allows teachers to create playful environments rather than activities that look like play and also understand how they can become accepted as co-operative play partners (Rich, 2002). These affective qualities empower practitioners and allow them to celebrate children's many ways of thinking, speaking and listening.

Cultural differences in children's play

Just as there are regional trends toward particular games *within* any given culture, there are also quantitative and qualitative differences in play *across* cultures. The unifying fact is that all children play. Hughes (1999) notes that the main conclusive evidence for cultural differences in children's play relates to competitive and co-operative play behaviour. Children within technologically advanced cultures are more likely to engage in competitive play and children from less affluent, underdeveloped countries in co-operative games where the emphasis is on sharing and collectivity. From a social constructivist perspective these differences are unsurprising and even before this theoretical approach gained momentum within the social sciences, Lieberman talked of parents and teachers as 'cultural surrogates' (1977: 99) representing the environment at large in encouraging or inhibiting children's play behaviours. Research into children's perceptions of play has demonstrated that children develop an understanding of what it means to play, based on cues from their environment and social interaction (Howard, 2002; Howard et al., 2006).

For play professionals there are many reasons why understanding cultural difference is important. In some cultures, dolls are not regarded positively for religious reasons and the act of dressing up can bring bad luck (Lindon, 2001). Children's play can be influenced by immediate experiences (such as parental separation, war or famine) but also by culturally dependent myth and legend (Jennings, 1999). These differences have implications for practice in therapeutic, educational and recreational play contexts. Whilst a common feature of good early years practice from a white Western view includes opportunities for children to engage in messy play (such as finger painting, clay, sand and water), David and Powell (2005) found that Chinese practitioners had great difficulty understanding the value of this, as it conflicted with their principles of orderliness and cleanliness. Children were afforded opportunities to be playful but these opportunities were different. Indeed, David and Powell note how Chinese practitioners frequently utilised children's natural propensity toward playfulness in their teaching.

It has often been wrongly assumed that the absence of a particular form of behaviour means that it is not essential for children's development. Whilst there are cultural differences in the nature of adult–child interaction during play, the types of play children engage in and the value placed on play for development (Roopnarine et al., 1998), there is little evidence that one particular practice is beneficial over another. Cross-cultural research into children's play warns us against the use of universal, observable behaviour as an indicator of developmental significance. Rather, we should seek to identify and explain the underlying qualities of this behaviour that render it important. It would seem that playfulness is the universal.

Conclusion

This chapter has considered theoretical perspectives as to why we play and the problems associated with defining this complex activity. It has shown how, in our quest to understand play and measure its developmental potential, we became distracted and lost sight of its unique qualities. Understanding children's perceptions draws us back to these qualities and reminds us that play is special. Play affords children the opportunity to learn and to heal and there is potential for these things to occur regardless of the context in which the play activity takes place. That is what makes play unique. Regardless of culture, in play children are afforded freedom. The freedom and choice in play promotes flexible and adaptive thinking and builds confidence, esteem and resilience.

Questions and exercises

1 Why are children's perceptions of play important?
2 What evidence is there for learning through play?
3 Why is an appreciation of cultural difference in play important?

Further reading

There are many general texts on play but I highly recommend the following, for their unique merit: Sue Jennings (1999) *Introduction to Developmental Play Therapy* provides a wonderful insight into therapeutic play, interwoven with beautiful case studies and powerful literary reference. Fraser Brown (2003) *Playwork: Theory and Practice* is remarkably complex, drawing on the literature from psychology, anthropology, sociology and education while Marjatta Kalliala (2006) text *Play Culture in a Changing World* offers a fresh and innovative consideration of play over time and across cultures. The latter is one of many insightful books from the *Debating Play* series edited by Tina Bruce, all of which are highly recommended.

PART THREE

POLICY AND PROVISION FOR YOUNG CHILDREN

In this part of the book the focus is on policy and provision in relation to the education, health and welfare of young children. Readers will find that a number of themes recur through the chapters that follow. Several of these are related to the general theme of difference and change over time and across cultures, which we noted in Part One. Here, however, we see how difference and change not only affect perceptions of children and childhood but also impinge on policy and practice. This is well illustrated in the contrasts made by several of our authors between 'medical' and 'social' models: for example, disability can be seen as an individual deficiency or as a problem of societal attitudes; ill-health can be viewed in terms of physical symptoms in need of treatment, or alternatively within a broader framework of social factors such as housing, poverty and diet.

The significance of changing perceptions and values is very apparent when we think about young children's education. More than one author shows how early years policy and practice in education have varied in different times and places, to an extent that compels us to consider how we understand childhood, the purposes of education, how children best learn, and what constitutes 'quality' of provision.

Two further elements of change over time feature in more than one chapter. One is a shift from family or community responsibility for children towards a greater degree of state responsibility and control. This trend is uneven, interrupted as it is from time to time by calls for greater parental or shared responsibility, and currently by a greater recognition of the need to take into account the views of parents. Nevertheless, the extent of official intervention, both in the lives of individual children and in the setting and monitoring of standards for all, seems to advance inexorably. This is evident in relation to all the services described in this section.

The other element of change which needs emphasis is the recognition that children's views and opinions also matter. Beginning in child welfare, but now also in health, education and other areas of policy, there is an increasing emphasis on hearing 'the child's voice' – even the voices of very young children. Increasingly, early years policy and practice is viewed not as something done *to* the child but as something done *with* the child. This is linked to our general theme of children's rights, which is discussed further in Chapter 10.

A final theme to which we draw attention, and one that runs powerfully through these chapters, is the need for integration of services dealing with young children's care, health, welfare and education. Several writers point to the dangerous fragmentation of services in the past and argue for the adoption of a more unified or 'holistic' approach. This, as we shall see later in this book, makes interagency collaboration extremely important. In fact it has been argued that to think in terms of 'children's services' and 'children's needs' at all militates against a holistic approach, and that we should rather think of 'children's spaces' in which children are enabled to develop their strengths (Moss and Petrie, 2002).

In Chapter 9, Sonia Jackson and Mary Fawcett review early years policy and services in the UK. They analyse the development of early years policy and the factors which have shaped it, concluding that there is still some way to go before all young children have access to high quality services appropriate to their age and family circumstances. Compared with other Western European countries, early years services in the UK have been under-funded and split between care and education, although since 1997 a radical transformation has been under way.

In Chapter 10, Nigel Thomas focuses on children's rights and the law relating to children. He provides an introduction to theories of children's rights and international instruments such as the United Nations Convention on the Rights of the Child, and then asks how these rights are expressed in law. Thomas argues that the history of childcare law is marked by an increasing emphasis on children's welfare, on mutual accountability between families and the state, and more recently on the child as a person with wishes and feelings, and with rights. Of particular significance in this context are the Children Act 1989, the incorporation into law of the European Convention on Human Rights, and more recently the introduction of Children's Commissioners in the four nations of the UK.

In Chapter 11, Iram Siraj-Blatchford notes that all children have a right to education which has the power to transform children's lives. Of course, as Siraj-Blatchford makes clear, education does not begin when children start school; rather, it begins at, or even before, birth. In this respect Siraj-Blatchford notes the significance of play but in exploring findings relating to the nature and impact of quality pre-school education, particularly for those children disadvantaged by poverty, challenges the belief that we should exclusively encourage 'free play'. Siraj-Blatchford agues instead that the role of the skilled and sensitive practitioner is vital.

In Chapter 12, Bob Sanders examines the role of social work services in providing support for children 'in need' and protection for those 'at risk'. He considers the circumstances of, and services for, children who are in need, who are looked after away from home (or adopted) and those at risk of abuse or neglect, focusing on how services in the UK have been influenced in recent years by countervailing trends of both diversification and integration, and changes in the fundamental principles underpinning the delivery of child and family services.

In Chapter 13, Liz Noblett makes clear from the outset that her focus is not on ill-health but rather on what helps a child to remain healthy and how external factors – environmental, economic and familial influences – can impact on the health and well-being of the child. Having considered how we might define child health and reviewed some policy frameworks, she examines some key and contentious issues – child poverty, immunisation and child obesity – before looking at the health and well-being of children living in special circumstances. A key message in this chapter is the importance of the context in which children spend their early years in relation to their health and well-being (in the broadest sense) in adult life.

In Chapter 14, Guy Roberts-Holmes argues that inclusion is primarily concerned with the politics of social justice. Holmes maintains that social justice is dependent on both national policies that reduce economic and social inequalities and respectful relationships created within early years settings – relationships which ensure that all children and their families feel accepted and valued. Having discussed barriers to inclusion, Roberts-Holmes turns to examples of policy that have supported inclusion as well as approaches and strategies (past and present) that have been used to support the establishment of inclusive practice within early years settings. Play is again a theme in this chapter: Roberts-Holmes argues that it is play that is central to an inclusive early years curriculum.

9

EARLY CHILDHOOD POLICY AND SERVICES

Sonia Jackson and Mary Fawcett

Contents:

- **Introduction**
- **Influences on early childhood policy**
- **Changing times**
- **Childcare for working parents**
- **Children's services from 2004**
- **Issues in childcare and early education**
- **Professional development and training**
- **Learning from other countries**
- **Conclusion**

Introduction

This chapter discusses the development of early years policy in the UK and the influences that have shaped it. Having reviewed the range of early childhood services, it concludes that, despite considerable progress, there is still some way to go before all young children have access to high quality services appropriate to their age and family circumstances. Comparisons with other Western European countries highlight the effect of years of political neglect and under-funding and the damaging split between care and education. Since coming to power in 1997 the Labour Government has been working on a radical transformation of early childhood services with a huge investment of public funding. Some of the issues raised by the rapid pace of these changes will be discussed in this chapter.

There are increasing signs of divergence between the four nations of the UK, and amidst the bewildering succession of new initiatives there is hardly time for one to be absorbed before it is overtaken by another. In the past the practice was for England to set the policy framework with the other countries following on later with minor adaptations but, since the introduction of devolved government in 1999, there is increasing divergence. The main focus in this chapter is on developments in England, referring to the rest of the UK, in particular Wales, when there are important differences. More detail about the other parts of the UK as well as the Republic of Ireland can be found in Clark and Waller (2007) *Early Childhood Education and Care*. However, because the picture is changing so rapidly at the time of writing, the best source for up-to-date information is the Internet, and a number of useful websites are listed at the end of the chapter.

Influences on early childhood policy

Early years policy in any country is shaped by a complex interaction of different factors. Despite many new initiatives, there are still, at the time of writing, striking historical continuities in early years policy and provision which continue to shape services today, for example the short hours of publicly-provided nursery education, early entry to primary school, the limitation of funded day care to 'deprived' areas or poor families and the low pay and inadequate training of the workforce.

Ideology

The strongly negative view of working mothers, prevalent throughout most of the twentieth century, had an ideological basis, which has been rather unfairly attributed to the influence of John Bowlby, who developed the concept of attachment (Bowlby, 1965). Bowlby made an enormous contribution to our understanding of childhood by drawing attention to the emotional needs of children, which until his pioneering work had been largely ignored. But his linking of early separation from mother with later delinquency and mental ill-health referred to much longer periods of separation, with unsatisfactory substitute care. However, his research as misinterpreted was widely used to support what became a fixed official orthodoxy, constantly repeated in official circulars and guidance (Jackson, 1993).

The report of the Plowden Committee on Children and their Primary Schools (Central Advisory Council for Education, 1967) set the pattern of nursery education to the end of the century and beyond. In contrast to other countries, almost all early years education in the UK is delivered in sessions lasting two-and-a-half hours, morning or afternoon, making it useless as a service for working mothers. Implementation of the Plowden Report recommendations had the perverse effect of ending most existing full-time nursery provision and making nursery education inaccessible to the most needy children whose mothers had no choice but to go out to work (Jackson and Jackson, 1979). The persistence of the Plowden philosophy in official circles was remarkable. As late as 1991 the Education Minister, Angela Rumbold, stated in a parliamentary debate, 'In no way should (nursery education) be regarded as a mechanism to enable women to work' (Moss and Penn, 1996). Even when a nursery school and day nursery existed on the same site, they were usually run completely separately, and the staff would often refer to 'education' or 'social services' children as if they were different beings (Ferri, 1981; Jackson, 1993).

Educational theories

Books about child development usually begin by expounding the views of the philosophers John Locke and Jean-Jacques Rousseau, to which many existing schools of pedagogical theory can be traced. Locke believed that a child's mind at birth was a 'tabula rasa', a blank slate; he thought that all human knowledge and abilities were acquired by learning through teaching and experience. Rousseau, on the other hand, thought that, given the right environment, the child's innate capacity would simply unfold through exploration, discovery and imagination (see Doddington and Hilton, 2007).

The nature–nurture debate, as it became known, is now considered rather irrelevant since contemporary advances in the study of very early brain development have shown that an infant is learning not only from the moment of birth but even while still in the womb (Gopnik et al., 1999; Selwyn, 2000; David et al., 2003) Genetic and environmental influences are so enmeshed that the attempt to ascribe any individual child's characteristics to one or the other is a fruitless exercise. Factors such as the mother's diet in pregnancy as well as more obvious negative influences such as drug addiction, alcohol misuse or smoking have been shown to have long-term effects which are difficult to disentangle either from genetic or postnatal environmental influences.

Few people would now dispute that children's earliest experiences have a profound, though not irreversible, influence on their ability to take advantage of opportunities to learn. But the persistence of two distinct schools of thought can still be seen by the contrasting approach to early education in the USA and European countries, with England as usual somewhere in between.

Cultural influences

One way of looking at these two views of childhood is suggested by Gunilla Hallden (1991). They are 'the child as project' and 'the child as being'. In the first view the child is seen in terms of the future, someone to be moulded by parents and society.

Parents set goals for their child and have a firm belief in expert knowledge as relayed by teachers and psychologists. The 'child as being' implies that the young child develops autonomously as an individual with his or her own driving force to learn and grow, needing adults as supporters not instructors.

Historical and cultural influences usually remain invisible but they are very important in understanding why things are the way they are. For example, the First World War (1939–45) had a different impact on countries that experienced it at first hand. One of the strengths of the much-admired Reggio Emilia early childhood service is the political support it has enjoyed. Mayor Bonacci explained to Gunilla Dahlberg that the fascist experience had taught them that people who conformed and obeyed were dangerous. In building a new society it was imperative to nurture and maintain a vision of children who can think and act for themselves (Dahlberg et al., 2007).

The Reggio Emilia perception of children sees them as powerful and competent from birth. This image of the child has led to a culture of adults listening to children, where adults are seen as co-constructors of knowledge with the children, where children are viewed as citizens now – not only in the future – and that ideas and feelings can be expressed and represented through the 'hundred languages of children' (Edwards et al., 1998). This view of childhood has strong affinities with the children's rights movement, which seeks to make a reality of Article 12 of the UN Convention on the Rights of the Child, setting out the principle that children have a right to be consulted on matters that concern them, but goes much further in asserting that children, however young, are entitled to be heard and listened to.

Evidence from research

As far back as the 1980s, analysis of data from the 1970 British Cohort Study (CHES) had quantified the benefits of pre-school education, especially for disadvantaged children (Osborn et al., 1984). However, the first large-scale research to have a major influence on policy was the EPPE project, based at the London University Institute of Education. EPPE (the Effective Provision of Pre-school Education) is a large-scale European longitudinal study investigating the effectiveness of pre-school education and care in terms of children's development. It is discussed at greater length by Iram Siraj-Blatchford in Chapter 11 of this book.

Changing times

The election of a Labour government in 1997 was a significant turning point. For the first time the state recognised a responsibility towards its youngest citizens and announced a National Childcare Strategy. This also introduced an important change in terminology, with the term 'childcare' (one word) largely replacing 'day care' in official documents. (Note that 'childcare' is one word; 'child care' usually refers to substitute care for children unable to live in their own families.) Another change in terminology is the now general use of the phrase 'early years' to cover the period from birth to six or in some cases up to eight. For a time the term 'educare' achieved some popularity, underlining the fact that, at least in the early years, care and education are inseparable. However, this never really caught on, and at the time of writing, the term most used seems to be 'early childhood education and care' (ECEC).

Government initiatives resulted in improved access to early years education over the next few years, supporting developments already in progress and stimulating new forms of provision. At the same time a falling child population created free places in infant schools, which in many areas were filled by admitting four-year-olds to full-time education. In Wales almost all four-year-olds were in school by the year 2000. At the time of writing (in 2008) the government funds part-time nursery places (12.5 hours a week) for all three- and four-year-olds in England whose parents want them, but there is considerable pressure on parents to send four-year-olds to full-time school as otherwise they risk not getting a place in the primary school of their choice. This is seen by many early years and child development experts as a negative development, as discussed later.

The Childcare Act 2006 was something of a landmark in early childhood services. It is the first ever piece of legislation to be exclusively concerned with early years and childcare. It is intended to take forward some of the key commitments from the Ten Year Childcare Strategy, published in December 2004, and is based on the five outcomes set out in *Every Child Matters* (see below), with special reference to early years care and education. The intention of the Act was clearly to bring early years within the mainstream of local authority provision but many of its provisions remain aspirational and fall far short of the universal full-time nursery education, with extended hours of childcare if needed, available to all children aged three to six years in Nordic countries and in many other parts of Europe.

Sure Start

For a few years the largest new component of Labour's Childcare Strategy was 'Sure Start', the first government programme ever to be targeted at the 0 to 3 age group. Originally set up as an independent agency, the ideas behind Sure Start were partly derived from the American Headstart programme, and partly from the Educational Priority Areas initiated by the Plowden Report (CACE, 1967). Sure Start is an area-based programme providing funds for a variety of different early education, childcare and family support services for children under four in the most disadvantaged areas. An important economic and political motive for the generous funding provided by the Treasury was to enable mothers, particularly single mothers, to work instead of being dependent on welfare payments, so that every Sure Start scheme had to include day care.

Sure Start has already been through many changes since it was set up but is generally regarded as one of the major successes of the Childcare Strategy. Evaluation has shown small but significant improvements in outcomes for children – for instance, in improved language development in two-year-olds and reduction in parental anxiety (Harris et al., 2003). The main criticism is that it reaches only a third of children in poverty and that services are still fragmented rather than joined up.

In England, Sure Start projects have been largely subsumed into the government's new vision of integrated children's services which include centres providing early education, childcare, health services, family support and help into employment in every community, but in the short term these will still be targeted at the most disadvantaged areas.

Childcare for working parents

A major weakness of all UK government policy statements on ECEC up to the present is that they often fail to differentiate between short-term sessional provision and full day care adapted to normal adult working hours. Both are described as childcare, although the practical implications for families are very different.

Day care

Despite Sure Start and the recent changes, the level of publicly-funded provision of childcare in the UK continues to be extremely low. Day care for children of working parents remains largely in the private sector, provided either by childminders or in childcare centres run for profit and increasingly by commercial chains. Private childcare centres largely serve families where both parents have professional jobs and the fees they charge often put them out of reach of ordinary families. Mothers with fewer educational qualifications are much more likely to work part-time and turn to relatives, especially grandmothers, for childcare. However, Brannen and Moss (2003), researching four-generation families, found that this supply of childcare was drying up, with grandparents increasingly unwilling to provide full-time day care on a regular basis.

The Day Care Trust's 2008 report on childcare costs notes that low income households spend 20% of their income on childcare compared with 8% on average spent by better-off families. There is a system of childcare tax credits to help low income families but it is not widely taken up and only covers part of the cost.

Playgroups

The playgroup movement started in the 1960s as a response to the acute shortage of nursery places for three- to four-year-olds. Intended as a temporary stopgap, it remained the major form of pre-school provision until schools began to admit four-year-olds and is still an important element in the patchwork of early years services. Though some pre-schools attain standards comparable to nursery schools and classes, the majority have to operate in unsuitable and often shared premises and staffing depends on the availability of women prepared to work for token pay or none. On the positive side, this often proved a valuable opportunity for women who had been out of paid employment for several years to acquire confidence and organisational skills. However, pre-schools now have considerable difficulty in finding suitable staff and volunteers, as women seek paid employment at an earlier stage in their children's lives.

Some writers have suggested that the growth of the playgroup movement, which had no parallel in other European countries, and the strength of the Pre-school Playgroups Association (PPA), now called the Pre-school Learning Alliance, enabled governments to ignore the campaign for nursery education. There was well-argued opposition in pre-school circles to the downward extension of the school starting age which meant that pre-schools lost the older age group and were obliged to accept two-year-olds to remain viable. In Wales the Welsh-medium playgroups (*Mudiad Ysgolion Meithrin*) have played an important role in promoting the language and were concerned that children might move into English-speaking primary schools before their speech was fully established. However, it seems more likely that the opposite effect has occurred, creating a growing demand for Welsh medium schools (Siencyn and Thomas, 2007).

In 1998 the government took the bold step of moving responsibility for all early years' services from the welfare (social services) into the education system. The government's strategy for extending nursery education now allows pre-schools to apply for education funding provided they meet Ofsted standards for the Early Years Foundation Stage.

Childminding

For children under three the most common form of out-of-home care, apart from playgroups and private day centres, is still childminding, known as family day care in most countries other than the UK. Childminding has a long history and has always been extensively used by poor working mothers, but its existence was not formally recognised in the UK until 1948 with the passing of the Nurseries and Childminders Regulation Act (amended in 1968). The Act made provision for registration of childminders and inspection of premises but was mainly concerned with physical safety.

Research during the 1970s uncovered some shocking conditions, especially among unregistered minders – rows of carry cots in a garage, toddlers spending long hours tied to push chairs, overcrowding, bare and unstimulating environments and minders unable to communicate with the children they were caring for (Jackson and Jackson, 1979). In 1976 the BBC ran a series of twenty short television programmes for childminders, accompanied by a handbook issued free to all registered minders through social services departments (Allen and Jackson, 1976). This was a breakthrough, presenting childminding as an important public service rather than a dubious back-street activity. The final programme in the series launched the National Childminding Association (NCMA), to which half of all registered minders now belong. NCMA receives a government grant, and provides training and support, with a strong commitment to raising standards of care and improving working conditions. NCMA developed the idea of childminding networks, designed to combat the isolation of childminders, which has always been a major problem in the UK. Other countries have systems for linking family day care workers to provide professional and mutual support and training. For example, in France day nurseries (*crèches collectives*) often have an attached group of home-based childcare workers (*crèches familiales*). The family day care workers have access to the facilities of the centre and their own co-ordinator, sometimes the deputy head of the nursery.

An important landmark for childminding was the belated recognition by the government that childminders are educators as well as carers. All registered childminders must now offer the Early Years Foundation Stage curriculum. Childminding has become one of the children's services overseen by Children's Trusts or Local Area Partnerships and is inspected by Ofsted. There continues to be a tension, however, between standards and costs. Childminding is no longer a cheap service for poor parents, and the fees asked by registered childminders are at a similar level to those charged by private day nurseries. The result is that a high proportion of mothers are obliged to give up work when they have a second or third child.

Children's services from 2004

The Laming report (2003) (see Chapter 12), together with early findings from the EPPE project (see Chapter 11), led to a new policy framework called *Every Child Matters*. The goals were not just to protect children from harm, but to stress their entitlement to five positive outcomes:

1 Being healthy – enjoying good physical and mental health and living a healthy lifestyle.
2 Staying safe – being protected from harm and neglect.
3 Enjoying and achieving – getting the most out of life and developing the skills for adulthood.
4 Making a positive contribution – being involved with the community and society and not engaging in anti-social or offending behaviour.

5   Economic well-being – not being prevented by economic disadvantage from achieving their full potential in life, and by implication being equipped by education to access satisfying employment and earn a good income.

This has led to a series of legislative and policy initiatives. From 2004 the ten-year strategy *Choice for Parents, the Best Start for Children* has been in place. Local authorities now have Local Area Partnerships or Children's Trusts charged with improving the outcomes for all children and narrowing the gap between those who achieve and those who do not. They aim to reach their goals through the development of integrated education, health and social care services with extended school hours, better support in the pre-school years, better qualified staff and targeted services. They have also set a target to eliminate child poverty by 2020, partly by increasing childcare provision and thus allowing women to work.

The last of these provisions is still in process of development, held back by the huge costs involved, so that availability of early years care and education remains largely dependent on the private and voluntary sector and depends on parents' own financial contributions.

Though the early years landscape is changing, the range of services is still diverse and uneven. Parents have access to Children's Information Services in most local authorities, but they are faced with a bewildering array of services and their so-called 'choice' may in practice be limited by cost, availability, transport difficulties and the needs of school-age children in the family. Full day care is rarely available at an affordable price, so that working parents often have to put together packages of care which result in children having a fragmented and confusing experience (Clark and Waller, 2007).

Establishing national standards

'In essence, the ten-year childcare strategy is designed to rationalise, redesign and re-badge the existing early years initiatives so that they fit within the *Every Child Matters* framework and become a coherent strategy for improving the quality of services' (Owen, cited in Pugh and Duffy, 2006). However, since the government has brought under one legislative umbrella all kinds of early years provision and is investing large sums of public money it needs to find a way of showing that this is of benefit to the nation. Ofsted now inspects all services and all children are assessed through the Early Years Foundation Stage Profile (www.standards.dfes.gov.uk).

Early Years Foundation Stage

In England, the Early Years Foundation Stage became a statutory requirement from September 2008 for every type of early childhood service, including childminders, to be enforced through inspections by Ofsted. It brings together *Birth to Three Matters* and the Foundation Stage Guidance and incorporates the *Every Child Matters* agenda. It sets out four themes and principles:

1 A unique child
2 Positive relationships
3 Enabling environments
4 Learning and development.

Within learning and development there are six areas:

1 Personal, social and emotional development
2 Communication, language and literacy
3 Problem solving, reasoning and numeracy
4 Knowledge and understanding of the world
5 Physical development
6 Creative development.

The new framework is generally regarded as an improvement on earlier policy documents in that it largely endorses a play-based, developmentally appropriate approach to childcare and education for children from birth to five. However, the British Association for Early Childhood Education (BAECE) and other groups have identified a serious problem with regard to some of the early learning goals. In particular, the two literacy goals have proved to be purely 'aspirational' for many children resulting in feelings of demoralisation and failure for teachers and creating a culture of deficiency and failure for young children. The Association spelt out these concerns in a letter to the Minister, Beverley Hughes, in March 2008, arguing that inappropriate pressures for formal skills too early affect the children's current well-being and their future motivation.

It seems curious that the first principle of the Early Years Foundation Stage emphasises the 'unique child' but the literacy goals and the prescription of one method, 'synthetic phonics', as the means of achieving them, seem not to value children's different pace of development, to respect their individual styles of learning or to take account of their pre-school and familial experiences. Liz Brooker's ethnographic study of a primary school reception class shows how this lack of awareness can translate into great difficulty for the child in adapting to the culture of the school and its implicit expectations about behaviour and adult–child communication (Brooker, 2002). Children from minority ethnic families may be particularly adversely affected. The emphasis in England on formal assessment and record keeping also reduces the time available for creative activities and conversation.

Early education in Wales has developed on very different lines. The consultation document on the early years curriculum for Wales opened with an extract from the poem 'Afon' by Gerallt Lloyd Owen in which the poet remembers early childhood as a magical time of exploration and discovery (David, 2001). The resulting Foundation Phase Framework for children aged three to seven years has been described by the First Minister, Rhodri Morgan, as a break with 125 years of British educational practice. Drawing on practice from, amongst others, Nordic countries, it adopts an active, play-based approach to learning in both indoor and outdoor environments, balancing teacher-led and child-initiated activities. Wales is no less committed to high standards than England, and, similarly to England, early years settings are now inspected by Estyn (equivalent to Ofsted) but because Key Stage tests have been discarded and league tables for primary schools are not published, teachers are under less pressure than in England to achieve curriculum goals tied to chronological age.

Wales was also the first UK country to appoint a Commissioner for Children and to adopt a rights-based policy. Although it has not followed England in joining up care and education formally, the Flying Start programme launched in 2005 lays a strong emphasis on integrating childcare, early learning, parenting and health services. The other main difference in Wales is, of course, the emphasis on bilingualism. This has many benefits, as pointed out by Siencyn and Thomas (2007) and the Welsh experience could be used with advantage by pre-schools in parts of England where a high proportion of children do not have English as their first language.

Children's centres

As already mentioned, an important element in the new landscape is children's centres built on the Early Excellence and family centre models (Whalley, 2000; Draper and Duffy, 2001). They are charged with incorporating high quality nursery education, some day care for children of working parents, integration of health and social services support with a strong ethos of partnership with parents. Although many exemplify good and innovative practice, they are still limited by the differing terms and conditions of employment for staff from different professional backgrounds, and by the very low level of training and qualifications (NVQ Level 2) required of those who work directly with young children (see below).

Issues in childcare and early education

Publicly funded childcare in Britain was traditionally seen as a welfare service, reserved for children with families under stress or who were judged incapable of caring for them well enough, a view reinforced by the Children Act 1989. The shrinking number of local authority day nurseries reserved their places for 'priority cases', resulting in a highly dysfunctional concentration of the most disadvantaged children in these settings (Goldschmied and Jackson, 2003) . While the Children Act 1989 did nothing to change this situation, the legislation of 2004 is attempting to alter the system of childcare in England fundamentally. However, the most recent (August 2008) review by Ofsted indicates that, as so often, children who are particularly vulnerable and most in need of high quality childcare are least likely to receive it. According to the review, between 2005 and 2008 the availability of good quality childcare by childminders has fallen, the incidence of inadequate childcare has risen and it is in areas with high levels of deprivation that the services are worst. This is unlikely to change unless the government is prepared to introduce much higher subsidies for placements with childminders, or to turn at least some family day care into a public, salaried service, following precedents in Sweden and New Zealand.

Professional development and training

The early years workforce in the UK has always been overwhelmingly dominated by poorly paid women with low levels of education and few career prospects. If the aspirations of the ten-year strategy, *Choice for Parents, the Best Start for Children* (2004), are to be achieved, there is no doubt that this needs to change, and the development of a highly skilled workforce is essential. The EPPE research has demonstrated, what was already well known in practice, that the standard of provision is dependent on the quality and professional development of the staff.

The underlying issues in the training, qualifications and workforce organisation are well set out by Owen (in Pugh and Duffy, 2006):

- Growing understanding, through research, of the needs of young children and families
- The continuing low status of staff
- Low levels of qualifications
- High rates of turnover
- Persistence of low standards in some provision
- How to deliver the *Every Child Matters* agenda
- How to realise the vision of an integrated workforce.

Unfortunately a large assortment of qualifications has evolved, unplanned, over the years. For example, in 2005 the Qualifications and Curriculum Authority website noted 77 different qualifications in child development. The situation now may be even more complex and certainly very confusing for people seeking the best career path in early years work.

A major innovative development in the early 1990s was the inception of Early Childhood Studies degrees (the first being at the University of Bristol). Among the goals was the raising of the status of the early years as an area of academic study which crossed academic disciplines. The intention was to give students a broad base from which to move into the various professions concerned with young children and families, such as education, social work, law and health. In this it foreshadowed the latest thinking embodied in integrated services.

National Vocational Qualifications date from the same period – aimed at those in work with experience but no formal qualifications. Though widely taken up there are continuing concerns. Candidates may move too quickly through the qualification leading to lower quality work (Owen, cited in Pugh and Duffy, 2006). The emphasis on learning and assessment on the job carries a danger of undervaluing the theoretical component and recycling bad practice. In addition, as already noted, the levels of qualification required for early years work remain very low (NVQ 2), especially compared with other parts of Europe where nursery settings normally employ qualified teachers.

More recently Early Years Foundation Degrees have been promoted for access to higher education for non-traditional students and in England the government has established a new qualification, the Early Years Professional status, and for those in managerial roles, a National Professional Qualification in Integrated Centre Leadership (NPQICL).

Two organisations initiated in 2005 are working on workforce issues for young children: the Skills Council for Social Care, Children and Young People (SCC) for the whole UK, and the Children, Young People and Families Workforce Development Council (CWDC) specifically for England. The goals of the new Integrated Qualifications Framework (IQF) are to create a set of approved qualifications for progression, continuous professional development and mobility between services.

The debate remains as to whether the goal should be a new role of 'social pedagogue' along the lines of the Scandinavian model or to work towards an early years qualified teacher model, as favoured by EPPE.

Learning from other countries

There is only space here to mention some of the main overseas influences on UK policy and practice.

The USA

The idea of Sure Start, initiated by the Treasury mainly as a way of reducing poverty by enabling mothers to get back into paid employment, originated in American programmes such as Headstart, Welfare to Work and 0–3, but has grown far beyond its original conception. The widely publicised High/Scope Program, also from America, in which children are encouraged to plan and review their activities, has contributed to a more structured approach to the early years curriculum (see also Chapter 11). American writers on early years generally stress the instrumental benefits of pre-school education, such as being prepared for formal schooling, being less likely to repeat grades, having less need for remedial or special education and scoring better on standardised tests (Zigler et al., 2006). This contrasts sharply with, for example, the Swedish approach, which places a high value on childhood in its own right.

New Zealand

A second influence, which can be seen in the attempts, especially in Wales and Scotland, to develop an early years curriculum that escapes from the narrow economic imperative of preparing children for later schooling and the world of work, comes from New Zealand. *Te Whariki* is a curriculum with its philosophical roots in Maori cultural perspectives, taking a holistic view of the child in the community. It sees the curriculum through the early years as a tapestry (the word Whariki means 'woven mat') rather than a ladder, with a strong emphasis on play and discovery, allowing children to learn and develop at their own pace. This philosophy relates back to Rousseau and long traditions of a European 'child-centred' ethos (Doddington and Hilton, 2007). It is explicitly bicultural and thus has particular relevance for Wales.

Although there have been difficulties, due to political changes, *Te Whariki* is still part of the officially recognised early years curriculum in New Zealand and has provided a model for other countries, including the UK (Carr and May, 2000). In contrast to England's assessment practice, the New Zealand concept of Narrative Assessment, *Kei Tua o te Pae* (see websites, p. 133) emphasises recording children's actual achievements through creating portfolios for each child. Wales is now working towards a similar approach, emphasising narrative assessment rather than the tick-box type of monitoring prevalent in England.

Italy: Reggio Emilia

A third strong influence on early years practice comes from Italy, in particular the city of Reggio Emilia, already mentioned earlier. Inspired by the thinking of the psychologist Loris Malaguzzi and guided by him, they designed an early childhood education system founded on the idea of the child as an active agent in his or her own learning, including the construction of the curriculum (Edwards et al., 1998; Dahlberg et al., 2007). Among the many innovative ideas and practices associated with the system is that of involving local artists, musicians and drama specialists in pre-school facilities. Many projects around the UK have been inspired by this approach (see for example Bancroft et al., 2008 and www.sightlines-initiative.com).

The Nordic countries

The Nordic countries, in particular Sweden, provide a gold standard for early years services, integrating employment legislation, childcare services, early education, family support services, training and curriculum development into a system which is designed with the well-being of the child as the most important consideration (Dahlberg et al., 2007).

Conclusion

After more than 30 years when the shape of early childhood services in the UK remained almost unchanged, 1997 marked a significant shift in government policy. For the first time the well-being of children under school age was recognised as a legitimate subject of public concern, not simply the responsibility of their own parents, and after 2003 the government was spurred to action through the Climbié tragedy.

From that date the main developments have been:

- A commitment to universally available educational provision for three- and four-year-olds albeit still on a part-time basis.
- Transfer of responsibility for early years to the Department for Children, Families and Schools. National standards for all forms of early years provision receiving state funding.
- Much more awareness of ethnic diversity and responsiveness to the needs of local communities.
- A growing extension of after-school provision for children of working mothers.
- Local Area Partnerships or Children's Trusts designed to achieve better integration of all services used by families with young children.
- New Children's Centres with a strong emphasis on partnership with parents to provide a model of good practice.
- Implementation of the new Early Years Foundation Stage with inspection by Ofsted, obligatory for all services (and parallel developments in other UK nations).

In England, every local authority has appointed a Director of Children's Services with a long-term aim of integrating all children's services. Sure Start Children's Centres are to be created in each of the 20% most deprived neighbourhoods in England, combining nursery education, family support, employment advice, childcare and health promotion on one site. (This may be a sign of a centralising tendency reasserting itself, in contrast to the original emphasis in Sure Start on local communities defining their own needs and designing services to meet them.)

Since its election in 1997 the Labour Government has committed billions of pounds to a major ambitious reform of early childhood services. The vision and the investment are greatly to be welcomed but, as discussed throughout this chapter, there are still serious weaknesses in the system which need to be addressed if the aspirations of *Every Child Matters* are to be realised.

Questions and exercises

1 Should full childcare be a universally available service?
2 Has a focus on early literacy undermined the importance of play?
3 What do we mean by quality? What characteristics of early years services are associated with good outcomes for children?
4 How can early years policies balance the needs of parents and the well-being of young children?
5 Are there important lessons to be learnt from policy and practice in other countries?

Further reading

The following texts are suggested: Brannen and Moss, *Rethinking Children's Care* (2003) ranges over the whole field of childcare, combining theoretical and historical perspectives with accessible accounts of empirical research; Clark and Waller (eds), *Early Childhood Education and Care: Policy and Practice* (2007) spells out in detail the different ways services for young children have developed in the four nations of the UK as well as in the Republic of Ireland; Goldschmied and Jackson, *People Under Three: Young Children in Day Care* (2003), one of the few texts to focus on the 0–3 age group, discusses management and organisation of nursery and childcare centres as well as day-to-day care and curriculum; the introductory chapter of Pugh and Duffy (eds), 2006 *Contemporary Issues in the Early Years* (4th edition, 2006) provides an excellent overview of policy and services in the UK at the time of writing.

Websites

British Association for Early Childhood Education: www.early-education.org.uk

ChildcareLink: www.childcarelink.gov.uk (funded by DCSF)

Children in Northern Ireland: www.ci-ni.org

Children in Scotland: www.childreninscotland.org.uk

Children in Wales: www.childreninwales.org.uk

Daycare Trust: www.daycaretrust.org.uk (UK National Childcare Campaign, good for statistics and reports)

Department for Children, Schools and Families: www.dcsf.gov.uk

Early Years Foundation Stage Curriculum: www.standards.dfes.gov.uk/eyfs

Effective Provision of Preschool Education (EPPE) Project: www.ioe.ac.uk/ecpe/eppe

Every Child Matters: www.everychildmatters.gov.uk

National Childminding Association: www.ncma.org.uk

National Children's Bureau: www.ncb.org.uk

National Day Nursery Association: www.ndna.org.uk

New Zealand's website on early education: www.educate.ece.govt.nz

Pre-school Learning Alliance (playgroups): www.pre-school.org.uk

10

CHILDREN'S RIGHTS AND THE LAW

Nigel Thomas

Contents:

- **Introduction**
- **Theories of rights**
- **Theories of children's rights**
- **Conventions of children's rights**
- **The United Nations Convention on the Rights of the Child (UNCRC)**
- **Participation rights**
- **Young children's rights**
- **How rights are expressed in law**
- **The development of legal provision for children**
- **The Children Act 1989**
- **The Human Rights Act 1998**
- **The Children Act 2004 and Children's Commissioners**
- **Conclusion**

Introduction

The aims of this chapter are to introduce some key ideas about children's rights, to show how these are expressed in international instruments such as the United Nations Convention on the Rights of the Child, and then to use this as a foundation to explore the law relating to children, particularly in England and Wales, and how it expresses – or fails to express – children's rights. The chapter concludes with some reflections on the new role of Children's Commissioner.

Theories of rights

According to *The Oxford English Dictionary*, a right is 'a justifiable claim, on legal or moral grounds, to have or obtain something, or to act in a certain way.' We can distinguish between legal rights, which are based in law and whose existence is therefore a question of fact, and moral rights, which are based in ethics and whose existence is a question of values. The idea of rights emerged in Western thought mainly from the seventeenth century, in contrast with the mediaeval idea of divine authority, with an appeal to nature as source of authority through the concept of 'natural rights'. Philosophers such as Hobbes, Locke and Rousseau developed ideas of liberty and the 'social contract', and Thomas Paine put forward *The Rights of Man* as an intellectual basis for democratic revolutions in America and France at the end of the eighteenth century. Other philosophers have been hostile to talk of rights (such as Bentham, who famously described it as 'nonsense on stilts').

A right is a claim, entitlement or demand. A right may be absolute – but is not necessarily so. Eleanor Roosevelt captured something of the distinctiveness of rights when she reportedly said 'A right is not something that somebody gives you; it is something that nobody can take away.' Dworkin (1978) put it another way when he argued, using the metaphor of a card game, that rights 'trump' other values and considerations. Rights are not the same as wants or needs: they have a *fundamental* quality that justifies the force attaching to them. Cranston (1967) and Worsfold (1974) propose three essential criteria for rights – they should be practicable (consistent with conceptions of justice), universal (in that they apply to everyone) and paramount (i.e., important enough to override other considerations).

A distinction is often made between liberty rights (e.g., the right not to be imprisoned without good cause) and welfare rights (such as the right to a home or to a basic income). Some theorists argue that only liberty rights make sense as real rights; others disagree. Justifications of rights may be based on 'will', and so linked with membership of a community of rational autonomous individuals, or on 'interest', and so on our membership of a community who share needs and interests. Those who favour a justification based on 'will' are likely to be more interested in liberty rights; those who accept a justification based on 'interest' may be prepared to consider welfare rights.

Whichever justification is favoured, rights always appear to be based on some idea of membership of a community. This raises questions about precisely who is included. A conception of rights that emphasises rationality and 'will' may exclude adults with severe learning disabilities, or young children, while a conception that emphasises our common needs and interests may be more inclusive. Some philosophers believe that animals can have rights too (e.g., Singer 1995); indeed, in 2007 the Spanish Parliament extended rights to certain animals.

Theories of children's rights

The phrase 'children's rights' is a slogan in search of definition. (Rodham, 1976)

Until the twentieth century, discussions of human rights made little if any reference to children, and the extent to which children can be bearers of rights has been much contested since then. Although campaigns to promote rights for children have gathered strength in the past hundred years, there has not always been agreement about what those rights are. A fundamental question is whether children are 'rights-bearers' in the same way as adults, or whether they are in need of special protection that justifies curtailing their freedom.

One way to look at it is this:

a) Children have certain kinds of rights because they are fundamentally the same as adults. This includes rights to make decisions about their own lives.
b) Children have other kinds of rights because they are more vulnerable and dependent than adults. This includes care and protection, and it may include some restrictions on their freedom; but these restrictions must be justified and proportionate.

Consistently with this view, children's rights are sometimes divided into 'participation' rights – entitling children to take part in social and political life – and 'provision' and 'protection' rights – ensuring that children grow up safe and healthy.

Theoretical objections to the promotion of children's rights take two main forms. One form objects to children having *welfare* and *protection* rights, on the grounds that children indeed ought to be looked after, but that it is misleading to express this in terms of 'rights', when it is more a question of adult obligations (e.g. O'Neill, 1992). The other form objects to children having *participation* rights, on the basis that children are not competent to exercise these rights, and must wait until they are adult (e.g., Purdy, 1992).

A strong statement of children's rights is that made by John Holt (1975), who argued 'that the rights, privileges, duties, responsibilities of adult citizens be made available to any young person, of whatever age, who wants to make use of them.' This would include not only the right to vote, but 'the right to be legally responsible for one's life and acts', 'the right to direct and manage one's own education', and the right 'to choose or make one's own home'.

Others are less radical. Archard (2004) distinguishes between the 'libertarian' and 'caretaker' interpretations of children's rights, with the libertarian approach favouring maximum freedom and equality with adults, while the caretaker faction is much more cautious and protective. Archard himself argues, while not accepting the libertarian case fully, that it is a good starting point as it challenges us to justify any restrictions on children's liberty rather than accepting all restrictions without question.

However, there is a growing consensus that children do have rights, and that these include at least some rights that equate to the 'liberty' or 'participation' rights of adults, as well as other rights that assure children care and protection as they grow up. This consensus is forcefully expressed in a series of international conventions and declarations, of which the best known and most important is the United Nations Convention on the Rights of the Child.

Conventions of children's rights

Among the foremost advocates of children's rights in the first half of the twentieth century were Eglantyne Jebb and Janusz Korczak. Korczak was a Polish paediatrician and pedagogue who ran child-centred orphanages, with children's parliaments and a children's newspaper (see Lifton, 1988). His commitment to children was such that in 1942 he chose to accompany his Jewish orphans to Treblinka rather than accept an offer of safety for himself. Jebb was the founder of Save the Children, set up mainly to assist child refugees in the aftermath of the First World War. In 1924 she persuaded the League of Nations in Geneva to adopt a Declaration of the Rights of the Child, by which:

> men and women of all nations, recognising that mankind owes to the child the best it has to give, declare and accept it as their duty that, beyond and above all considerations of race, nationality or creed:
>
> 1 The child must be given the means needed for its normal development, both materially and spiritually.
> 2 The child that is hungry should be fed; the child that is sick should be helped; the erring child should be reclaimed; and the orphan and the waif should be sheltered and succoured.
> 3 The child must be first to receive relief in times of distress.
> 4 The child must be put in a position to earn a livelihood and must be protected against every form of exploitation.
> 5 The child must be brought up in the consciousness that its best qualities are to be used in the service of its fellow men.

After the second World War the United Nations adopted a Declaration on the Rights of the Child in 1948, which was an amended version of Eglantyne Jebb's document, and then a more extensive Declaration of the Rights of the Child in 1959. In 1979, the 'International Year of the Child', Poland, inspired perhaps by the memory of Janusz Korczak, proposed in the United Nations the drafting of a Convention on the Rights of the Child, which would be a formal treaty and therefore binding on States that ratified it.

The United Nations Convention on the Rights of the Child (UNCRC)

The drafting of the new Convention was a long and complex process, and the result was much more detailed and extensive than earlier Declarations. It was adopted by the General Assembly of the United Nations in 1989 and over the next three years was ratified by almost every country in the world (the exceptions to date being the USA and Somalia). States that ratify the Convention have to report at regular intervals to the Committee on the Rights of the Child on their progress in implementing Convention rights.

The Convention obliges States to make children's best interests a primary consideration. The first 41 articles set out in detail children's rights to an identity and a family life, to education and health care, to protection from abuse and harm, and to participate fully in their cultures and communities. The remaining 13 articles specify the duties of States to publicise and implement the Convention, and the process for ratifying and amending it. The full text of the Convention can be seen at www.unicef.org/crc/.

Participation rights

Unlike earlier statements, the United Nations Convention on the Rights of the Child includes children's rights to participate in decision making. Article 12 of the Convention says that:

> States Parties shall assure to the child who is capable of forming his or her own views the right to express those views freely in all matters affecting the child, the views of the child being given due weight in accordance with the age and maturity of the child.

The following five Articles assert children's rights to freedom of expression, thought and assembly, privacy and access to information. In other words, children are seen as bearers of liberty rights as well as welfare rights.

In the period since 1989 there has been a dramatic increase in the attention paid to children's participation rights, especially by governments and non-governmental organisations. Laws and policies have been reframed to give expression to these rights, at least to some extent. As organisations working for children and young people have shifted the emphasis of their programmes to a 'rights-based' rather than a 'needs-based' approach, participation has become an increasingly prominent feature of that work; and newer organisations have been set up whose primary purpose is to promote participation, some of them led by children and young people. How much difference that participation has yet made to policies and services, or to the reality of children's lives, is not entirely clear.

Young children's rights

For students of early childhood the most important question is how these theories of children's rights apply to children in the earliest years. If one accepts that it makes sense to talk of 'rights' to care, to health, education and welfare, then it appears that such rights apply regardless of age; and younger children's greater vulnerability may mean that their entitlement has greater urgency. If one takes the view that rights have to be claimed by rational autonomous beings, then the door opens to questions about who has sufficient rationality to be included, and whether this is limited by age. If rights are something one grows into, when and how does this happen? If rights are something we have from birth, then how are those rights to be exercised by babies and toddlers, who may not know that they have them? A fundamental question is; are young children competent to exercise participation rights?

For a theoretical answer to that question, we can draw on arguments from psychology, and even more from sociology, about how competence is situated in context, achieved and negotiated (see Hutchby and Moran-Ellis, 1998). For a practical response, we should look at evidence from research which shows how very young children, even babies, can express views, preferences and wishes with subtlety, if they are communicated with sensitively, respectfully and imaginatively (see Alderson 1993; Clark and Moss, 2001; Clark et al., 2005). It is also valuable to consult the General Comment on implementing child rights in early childhood (United Nations Committee on the Rights of the Child, 2006).

How rights are expressed in law

There are many laws that have an impact on children – in fact, it could be said that all laws do, directly or indirectly. Certainly, laws governing such things as health, housing and welfare benefits have a major impact on children's lives, even though they do not directly govern what children do or how their parents look after them. Education and employment law have a much more direct effect on children, because they spell out who is expected to go to school and what kind of education they are to receive, or at what age and in what circumstances children may work for payment. Criminal justice law makes specific provision for children and how they should be treated if they are thought to have committed an offence.

However, the laws that have the most profound impact on individual children's lives, and that may affect all children including the very youngest, are the laws governing children's care and upbringing. It is these laws that will be the main focus of this chapter. The legislation of most concern to us will be the Children Act 1989, which is the main provision directly concerned with children's welfare in England and Wales. The Act sets out the framework for the relationship between children, parents and the state. It provides for the resolution of disputes between family members and defines the circumstances in which the state may intervene in family life. It lays down the powers and duties of local authorities to provide for children's welfare, and provides safeguards against poor care, whether it is provided by private individuals and organisations or by state agencies. The equivalent laws in other parts of the UK are the Children (Scotland) Act 1995 and the Children (Northern Ireland) Order 1995, which are based on the same guiding principles but also incorporate significant differences.

The development of legal provision for children

It could be said that until the nineteenth century a child was not a legal entity. No *statute law* (Acts of Parliament) referred specifically to children. The *common law* of 'wardship' was designed to provide for situations when a child of a noble or royal family – or more often his or her property – needed protection. The feudal theory was that the monarch owned all land and all allegiance, and individuals held property only by virtue of the king or queen's will. In 'wardship' the monarch took responsibility for a child and his or her inheritance, and in time the courts took on this role. A child without property or inheritance was of little interest to the legal system. Children enjoyed no special legal protection and had no rights to plead a case. The only other time the law became interested in them was when they stole or robbed, when the full weight of the law – including imprisonment and capital punishment – might fall upon them.

Laws to protect children developed in the mid-nineteenth century, beginning with factory legislation designed to prevent the worst excesses of exploitation in the industrial workplace, and leading to the highly novel idea that children should not be working at all. This was followed by laws prohibiting cruelty to children (which followed on from laws prohibiting cruelty to animals). This was an important development, because it meant a breach in the principle of family privacy and parental (or, more precisely, paternal) authority. Laws to provide for children's welfare followed much later, beginning with the introduction of state elementary education, then of compulsory health surveillance (following alarm at the poor condition of recruits to the army in the Boer War), and finally the extension of duties under the Poor Law to provide for destitute children.

On these foundations developed the modern law relating to children, through a series of landmark Acts of Parliament during the course of the twentieth century. The Children Act 1908 extended protection from cruelty and neglect. The Adoption Act 1926 created a legal institution of adoption for the first time. The Children Act 1933 established a juvenile court system, introduced a 'fit person order' where children could be removed from home without an offence being proved, and established a schedule of offences against children which is still in use today. The Children Act 1948, arguably the most important single piece of child welfare legislation to date, ended the Poor Law treatment of children, required local authorities to appoint Children's Officers, introduced the provision of care as a service to children and families rather than as a punishment, and improved the supervision of foster homes. The Children and Young Persons Act 1969 reformed the juvenile justice system on welfare principles (although it was never fully implemented) and established non-punitive grounds for children to be removed to local authority care. The Children Act 1975 introduced safeguards for children against abuse of parental rights, required children to be consulted about decisions in care, and modified adoption law.

Even from such a brief summary of the history of child welfare law, some consistent themes can be discerned. It appears that the history of child care legislation is characterised by an increasing emphasis on children's welfare, and a shift away from 'cruelty' to 'care' as the key operating concept. It is also characterised by an increase in mutual accountability between families and the state; the first stage in this was the breaking of the barrier against any intrusion into family privacy or parental authority, while the second stage was bringing parents back into the picture as participants in the decision to provide 'care'.

What is missing up to this point is any real voice for children themselves, who are conceived of as *done to* rather than *doing*. Not until the Children Act 1975 does the law consider child's wishes and feelings, and then only in a very limited way. It is only with the Children Act 1989 that the law begins to take children seriously as people with the right to a say in their own lives.

The Children Act 1989

Current legal provision in England and Wales is dominated by the Children Act 1989. Heralded by the Lord Chancellor as the greatest reform in child care law this century, it was more wide ranging than any previous legislation because it brought together the *public law*, governing state services to children and child protection, and the *private law*, governing family life and disputes over children's upbringing, in the same statutory framework. This made it possible for courts to make decisions about children in complex cases without the confusion that had often arisen in the past between public care issues and private or matrimonial issues. It also meant that where children were placed compulsorily in state care this was done under the same rules and principles in all cases. The Act reformed the way in which courts intervened in family disputes and the kind of decisions they could make. It also reformed the duties and powers of local authorities to children and families, and the way in which services were provided – especially when children were looked after away from home. Finally, it reformed the arrangements for regulation and inspection of all child care services.

The Children Act is divided into twelve parts. Part One sets out some over-arching principles for dealing with children's cases, often referred to as the 'welfare principles':

- That when a court is making a decision about the upbringing of a child it should treat the child's interests as paramount.
- That a court should assume that delay in resolving a case is against the child's interests.
- That a court should not make any order in respect of a child unless satisfied that to do so is better for the child than making another order, or no order at all.

In deciding what is in a child's interests the court must have regard to a set of eight factors often referred to as the 'welfare checklist' – the first of which is 'the ascertainable wishes and feelings of the child'.

Other important principles in the Act include:

- The concept of 'parental responsibility', which any legal parent has automatically and which others can acquire. Parental responsibility cannot be taken away from a parent except by the adoption of a child. Parents who separate or divorce are therefore expected to remain part of their child's life and share in their upbringing and in making decisions. Parents whose children go into care are also expected to remain involved in their lives.
- The 'presumption of contact' – i.e., the presumption that contact is normally in the interests of children and should be positively promoted when they are separated from a parent or other significant person.

Part Two provides for disputes between parents and other relatives to be settled under the above principles. The starting assumption is that children's upbringing will be a matter of agreement between those involved, without the need for court intervention. The days of automatic custody orders being made on divorce have ended – indeed there is no requirement for the court to 'be satisfied' as to the arrangements made between the parties. The court only becomes involved if the parties cannot agree and someone applies for an order to be made. The most common orders are *residence* orders and *contact* orders, which decide whom a child will live with and who will have contact with the child.

Part Three of the Act, which governs services to children and families, defines when a child is 'in need' and indicates the services to which they or their family are entitled (see Sanders, Chapter 12). These services may include 'accommodation' if, for example, the child's parents are temporarily or permanently unable to provide appropriate care. This normally requires the agreement of a parent (or the child if she or he is over 16 years). A child accommodated in this way is not 'in care' and the local authority does not have parental responsibility. They are, however, required to assess the child's needs, and agree a plan with the parents and child.

Part Four of the Act relates to 'care and supervision' of children. It sets out the circumstances in which children may be removed from their families or the powers of parents restricted, and the process by which this may be done. Applications may be made by the local authority or NSPCC. Parents and children have the right to oppose the order and be represented. A 'children's guardian' is appointed to safeguard the child's interests and advise the court. Before making an order the court must be satisfied that: the child is suffering or likely to suffer 'significant harm' if action is not taken. Once this is established, cases are dealt with under the 'welfare principles', and the court is obliged to do what is best for the child. This can include making a care order, which means that the child is committed to the care of the local authority, which then has parental responsibility.

All children who are either accommodated or subject to care orders are 'looked after' within the terms of the Act. Agencies have a duty to safeguard and promote the child's welfare, to consult the child and family before making decisions, to review the child's case at regular intervals and to hear any complaints and representations.

Part Five of the Act deals with protection of children. It provides orders which courts may make in order to protect children from significant harm, and sets out the duties of local authorities to investigate situations of risk. Other agencies have duties to assist the local authority with their enquiries – particularly housing, health and education authorities and the NSPCC. This provision is the basis for the 'child protection system', the apparatus of inter-agency work to protect children, including case conferences and child protection registers. This is a distinctively UK response to the problem of how to protect children from harm. Continental approaches tend to be based more on encouraging families to seek help on their own terms – for example, the 'confidential doctor' service in Belgium. In the UK, as in North America and Australasia, the emphasis is on investigation, often leading to legal action. Only in the UK is there a legal requirement on agencies to work together to investigate abuse, supported by government regulation and guidance which also requires agencies to work together to plan a response to child abuse.

More recently, and specifically in relation to children in the early years, the Childcare Act 2006 placed duties on English local authorities to improve the well-being of young children and reduce inequalities between them, in addition to a series of provisions requiring the provision of specific services (See also Chapter 9).

The Children Act 1989 and children's rights

The Children Act 1989 aims to strike a balance between the rights of children to autonomy and a voice, their right to care and protection, and the rights of parents to bring up their children in the way they see fit. The Act puts into effect some of the key provisions of the UNCRC: the right to live with his or her parents or at least to maintain contact with them; the right to protection from abuse and neglect; the right to suitable care if not able to live with the family. Other legislation in the UK gives some effect to other Convention rights, such as the right to a good education and to participation in recreation and culture, the disabled child's right to care and education to help lead a full and active life, and the right to social security and an adequate standard of living. In each case there are limits on how fully the rights are implemented, which have been well scrutinised in reports such as *Righting the Wrongs* (Save the Children, 2006).

The Article of the UNCRC that has perhaps attracted most attention is Article 12, which gives the child the right to express an opinion, and to have that opinion taken into account, in any judicial and administrative proceedings affecting them. The Children Act 1989 makes that right a reality at least for some children – those whose upbringing is being considered by a court, and those who are looked after by a local authority. It does not give the same right to children living in their own families. The Children (Scotland) Act 1995 does give parents a duty to take account of their children's wishes in making decisions affecting them, so that children in Scotland have more rights in this respect than those in England and Wales.

The Human Rights Act 1998

The European Convention on Human Rights was signed in 1950 by the Council of Europe (an organisation formed after the Second World War which has nothing to do with the European Union, and which now includes 47 states). The Convention was intended to ensure that the atrocities of the Nazi era could not be repeated. It has become the basis of much European law, under the direction of the European Commission on Human Rights and the European Court of Human Rights in Strasbourg. Human rights under the Convention include the right to life, liberty, fair treatment at law, privacy and respect for family life, freedom of thought, conscience and religion, freedom of expression, assembly and association, and the right to marry and found a family. The Convention prohibits torture, inhuman or degrading treatment, slavery, and also prohibits discrimination in enjoyment of all of the above rights.

By passing the Human Rights Act 1998, Parliament incorporated the European Convention into UK national law. The Act says that a court or tribunal determining any question in connection with a Convention right must take into account any judgment or decision of the European Court or Commission, and that as far as possible national law must be interpreted in a way which is compatible with the Convention. If national law is incompatible with the Convention, the court may make a 'declaration of incompatibility', and the government then has the power to amend the legislation by making an order.

The Human Rights Act also says that it is unlawful for a public authority to act in a way which is incompatible with a Convention right. A person may bring proceedings against a public authority which has acted unlawfully in this way; the court can order the authority to act differently, and may also award damages.

Although the Human Rights Act and the European Convention do not mention children directly, they are clearly included. Article 14 prohibits discrimination 'on any ground such as sex, race, colour, language, religion, political or other opinion, national or social origin, association with a national minority, property, birth or other status.' It does not specifically mention age, but there is nothing in the Convention to suggest that all rights do not apply equally to children. Although the Human Rights Act is less comprehensive than the UNCRC, it has more 'teeth' because it can be enforced by the courts.

The Children Act 2004 and Children's Commissioners

As Bob Sanders notes (Chapter 12), the Children Act 2004 contains a number of important reforms to provision for children. One of the key ones is the establishment of the Children's Commissioner for England. This long-overdue reform meant that now each part of the UK had a Children's Commissioner. The Children's Commissioner for Wales was the first to be appointed in 2001, followed by the Northern Ireland Commissioner for Children and Young People in 2002 and Scotland's Commissioner for Children and Young People in 2003. Children's Commissioners are there to promote and safeguard the rights of children and young people, and to be a voice and champion independent of Government. All the Commissioners have slightly different powers and duties, in particular the English Commissioner, whose duties are less firmly based on children's rights under the UNCRC and who can be required by Government to investigate particular matters. The Republic of Ireland also has a Children's Ombudsman, and the five Commissioners work together through the organisation known as BINOCC (British and Irish Network of Ombudsmen and Children's Commissioners).

It remains to be seen how successful the Children's Commissioners will be in advancing the rights and interests of children; however, their introduction arguably represents a major step forward in basing policy and services on children's rights and wishes, rather than simply on their needs as perceived by adults.

Conclusion

I hope that this chapter has served to introduce the theoretical basis for ideas about children's rights, and some of the ways in which they are contested, and has shown how the adoption of the United Nations Convention on the Rights of the Child was a key moment in the development and implementation of these ideas. We have seen that even young children have rights, and how UK law attempts, in a rather uneven way, to give expression to children's rights, including the right to take part in decisions. I hope that, in examining key provisions of the Children Act 1989, we have also learned something about the ways in which the law frames childcare policy, including the potential impact of the Human Rights Act 1998. Space has not permitted us to look in similar depth at other areas of law, or at the detailed provisions in Scotland and Northern Ireland, which in some respects are different from those in England and Wales. However, I hope this chapter will have served as an introduction to this field, and that the suggestions for further reading below will help those who wish to take the subject further. I have also included two case examples which readers may like to use in further study.

Questions and exercises

Example 1 – John

John's parents are separated and he lives with his mother. He wants to see his father but his mother is unwilling. She has been insulted and verbally abused by John's father in the past, he does not pay regular maintenance, and she does not see why he should visit John and take him out for treats when she is struggling to bring him up on a limited income.

1   What are the options for the parties in this case, and how could it be resolved using the Children Act 1989?
2   What is the relevance of the UNCRC and the Human Rights Act?

Example 2 – Helen

Helen is aged 16. She met a man of 30 when she was on holiday in Greece, and she wants to marry him. Her mother supports her plan, but her father is opposed.

1   What are the important issues in this case, and how could it be resolved using the Children Act 1989?
2   What is the relevance of the UNCRC and the Human Rights Act?

Further reading

On children's rights the most useful texts are probably Archard (2004), Alderson (2008), Franklin (2002) and also Flekkoy and Kaufman (1997). Muscroft (1999) is a useful commentary on the United Nations Convention on the Rights of the Child. Bainham (1998), Barton and Douglas (1995) and Fortin (1998) are excellent guides to the law relating to children and families and to children's rights. Hershman and McFarlane (2002) and Lowe (2002) are authoritative sources for the Children Act 1989. Stainton Rogers and Roche (1994) are good on the policy issues, and on the relationship between rights and welfare. The Children's Legal Centre and its monthly journal *Childright* are an excellent source of information on children's rights and the law (www.childrenslegalcentre.com/).

11

EARLY CHILDHOOD EDUCATION (ECE)

Iram Siraj-Blatchford

Contents:

- **Introduction**
- **An emergent curriculum**
- **Play and Early Childhood Education (ECE)**
- **Effective pedagogy and 'sustained shared thinking'**
- **International Early Childhood Education models**
- **Other common pedagogical models of ECE**
- **Conclusion**

Introduction

The United Nations Convention on the Rights of the Child (Article 29, 1) agreed that all children have a right to education:

1 States Parties agree that the education of the child shall be directed to:

   (a) The development of the child's personality, talents and mental and physical abilities to their fullest potential;

   (b) The development of respect for human rights and fundamental freedoms, and for the principles enshrined in the Charter of the United Nations;

   (c) The development of respect for the child's parents, his or her own cultural identity, language and values, for the national values of the country in which the child is living, the country from which he or she may originate, and for civilizations different from his or her own;

(d) The preparation of the child for responsible life in a free society, in the spirit of under-standing, peace, tolerance, equality of sexes, and friendship among all peoples, ethnic, national and religious groups and persons of indigenous origin;

(e) The development of respect for the natural environment. (UN, 1989)

The educational component of early years provision has the potential to transform a child's life and set them on a positive learning trajectory for life. A child's education doesn't miraculously begin when they start 'school', it is therefore important to recognise that these principles should extend to all children regardless of age. For many children in their earliest years parents provide a rich educational as well as physical and social environment in the home. Unfortunately research shows us that this is not the case for all children. For many children from families disadvantaged by poverty and/or a lack of cultural capital, the quality of the home learning environment is poor and educational provisions of their nursery or playgroup have a significant and long-term influence upon their abilities, learning and life chances (Schweinhart et al., 1993; Siraj-Blatchford and Sylva, 2004; Sylva et al., 2004; Schweinhart et al., 2005). Education begins at birth (some would argue, even earlier) and to understand the nature of education in the first five years of early childhood three concepts are particularly valuable: 'pedagogy', 'curriculum' and 'emergent development'. The first two of these originate in educational theory and the third is more often applied from developmental psychology. It is important for all those who work with young children to understand the transformative potential of good, early education.

An emergent curriculum

While curriculum may be considered to define the content or product of teaching, the word 'pedagogy' is used by educationalists to describe the form that the teaching takes or the processes that are involved. Pedagogy is defined here following Gage (1977, 1985) as 'the science of the art of teaching' and every capable early educator may certainly be considered to be a *practising artist*. The best early childhood educators creatively draw upon their knowledge of the interests and capabilities of the children in their care, and also upon a wide range of material, cultural and intellectual resources to provide the children with the most effective and rewarding stimulation and hands-on learning experiences possible on a day-to-day basis. And, just as a kind of scientific 'development' may be seen in the work of a great painter (Cezanne comes to mind as a really good example), the performance of an effective early childhood educator also develops as they continually reflect upon, critically evaluate and moderate their practice to achieve excellence. This requires a very good understanding of how children learn, the content of what they could learn – for example, including a good knowledge of the *Early Years Foundation Stage* in England (DfES, 2007b), the *Foundation Phase* in Wales (DCELLS, 2008) or the *Curriculum for Excellence* in Scotland (CRPB, 2006) – and the ability to assess, plan and use the child's social and cultural experiences to help them 'access' the curriculum.

In the context of early childhood education, the term curriculum may be defined broadly as 'all of those experiences, activities and events, whether direct or indirect, intended or otherwise, that occur within an environment designed to foster children's learning and development'.[1] Young children are actively observing and exploring all of the time, they learn from everything that happens in the environment around them. However implicit or *hidden* the curriculum may be in some childcare and education settings, the content of this learning (i.e., the 'curriculum') is thus always determined by the adults who care for them. The notion of a totally 'free' play environment is really a myth. The material resources (toys, furniture, props) that are selected and the activities, the social interactions, and the environments that we offer children, define both the opportunities and the limitations for their learning. The linguistic and cultural context in which children are immersed even more fundamentally influences what it is that they learn.

'Emergent development' is actually a philosophical notion that dates back to the very earliest writings in nineteenth-century psychology (Sawyer, 2003). In terms of child development, emergence may be considered to involve processes that occur over time that result in the development of higher order structures of the mind. These may relate to particular intellectual, social and cultural competencies and capabilities, and research has shown that in the early years they are initially developed in social interaction with babies and pre-schoolers, as well as the acquisition of a range of communication and collaboration skills in play (see Siraj-Blatchford, 2008).

But it is important to recognise that there is much more than any simple process of accumulation of skills involved in this. According to the principles of 'emergent development', the developmental structures that finally emerge are *irreducible* to their component parts. In fact, from the perspective of emergent development, it is considered impossible to deduce the child's development as a *whole* from any observations of their previously learnt behaviour or behaviours (Sawyer, 2003). This does not mean that we should not learn from our observations of children but that we accept there is a whole lot more going on than can be observed. Emergent development requires an emergent curriculum, that is, content which is experienced but not in the main directly or didactically taught.

---

1 Adapted from New Zealand Ministry of Education, 1996, p. 10.

'Emergent Literacy' was a term first applied in Marie Clay's doctoral dissertation (1966), and Whitehurst and Lonigan (1998) cite Sulzby (1989), Teale and Sulzby (1986) and Sulzby and Teal (1991) in defining the concept as:

> the skills, knowledge, and attitudes that are presumed to be developmental precursors to conventional forms of reading and writing ... [as well as] ... the environments that support these developments. (op cit: 849)

Clearly this definition may be applied much more widely, with 'Emergent Curriculum' practices and resources being applied to support young children in learning and experiencing the skills, knowledge and attitudes identified as developmental precursors to a much wider range of curriculum subject areas and communities of practice:[2]

> Rather than individual development being influenced by (and influencing) culture, from my perspective, people develop as they participate in and contribute to cultural activities that themselves develop with the involvement of people in successive generations. People of each generation, as they engage in sociocultural endeavors with other people, make use of and extend cultural tools and practices inherited from previous generations. As people develop through their shared use of cultural tools and practices, they simultaneously contribute to the transformation of cultural tools, practices, and institutions. (Rogoff, 2003: 52).

Often this is how young children are learning in the home, in contingent, embedded contexts that they and their family share, often made more explicit through interactions and making meaning with the child.

Play and Early Childhood Education

Rogoff and others (e.g., Maybin and Woodhead, 2003) have shown that a wide range of *playful activities* progressively engage children in the cultural life of adults and their communities (Rogoff et al., 1993; Rogoff, 2003). Play is also widely recognised as a leading context for the child's acquisition of communication and collaboration skills and if we apply our conception of 'emergence', then children's day-to-day learning through play may also be seen as contributing towards, but not itself constituting, the

---

2 While the subject of science has been studied in depth as a community of practice (Kuhn, 1970), the concept may be applied much more widely to include schools of art and other scholarly communities.

achievement of either a series, or continuous process, of irreducible restructurings of the young child's mind[3]:

> A child's play is not simply a reproduction of what (s)he has experienced, but a creative reworking of the impressions (s)he has acquired. (Vygotsky, 2004: 11)

For neo-Vygotskians, play is considered to be a 'leading activity' (Leontiev, 1981; Oerter, 1993) but it is important to recognise here that this doesn't mean that play should be considered to predominate in the life of young children, that play is the *only* way that young children learn, or that *all* kinds of play promote development or learning. Play provides an important *context* for learning and development, as Vygotsky put it:

> Only theories maintaining that a child does not have to satisfy the basic requirements of life, but can live in search of pleasure, could possibly suggest that a child's world is a play world. (1933: 1)

But:

> The child moves forward essentially through play activity. Only in this sense can play be termed a leading activity that determines the child's development. (1933: 1)

In terms of empirical progression we know from decades of research that play begins with solitary play and the child goes on to develop the capability to share, then to co-operate, and finally to collaborate in their play (Siraj-Blatchford, 2008). We also know that these developments open up much wider opportunities for learning. But solitary play, shared play, co-operative and collaborative play are not discrete 'stages' that the child works through. Even solitary play serves us well at times throughout our adult learning lives! In most theoretical accounts describing the ways in which these different forms of play open up the possibility of learning, the notion of emergent development is often implicit. For example, when describing play as a 'leading activity', it is only being suggested that it should be seen as a driving force in the child's development of new forms of motivation and action.

Effective Pedagogy and Sustained Shared Thinking

The Effective Provision of Pre-school Education (EPPE) research project (Siraj-Blatchford and Sylva, 2004) has provided a large-scale, longitudinal, mixed method research study that has followed the progress of over 3000 children, from age three

---

3 This may be seen as a 'renaissance' of the mind, and/or as a gestalt change.

to eleven. The children started in 141 pre-schools and then entered 800 primary schools across England. The study applied multi-level modelling to investigate the separate effects of personal and social and family background, the quality of the learning support provided in the home, and the quality of the learning environment provided by the children's pre- and primary schools, as well as the effectiveness of the pre-/primary schools. The study has shown that quality pre-school education (as assessed by standardised instruments such as the *Early Childhood Environment Rating Scale,* Harms et al., 1998; Sylva et al., 2006) can ameliorate the effects of disadvantage by increasing children's learning attainment thereby reducing the effects of social exclusion. High quality Early Childhood Education (ECE) can be a strong equaliser for the most disadvantaged children. While all children benefit from high quality ECE, some only get it through pre-school provision rather than in the home.

Sustained Shared Thinking (SST) was first identified in a qualitative analysis carried out in the *Researching Effective Pedagogy in the Early Years* (REPEY) project undertaken in association with the EPPE project (Siraj-Blatchford et al., 2002; 2003). The REPEY project was developed to identify the most effective pedagogical strategies that are applied in the early years settings to support the development of young children's skills, knowledge and attitudes, and ensure they made a good start at school. The qualitative case studies provided detailed accounts of the learning and teaching that was observed (400 hours of adult observations and 254 episodes of child observations) in 12 of the most effective settings identified by EPPE (from a national sample of 141 settings).

The transcriptions of episodes of SST were subsequently found to provide valuable (concrete) examples of the kind of effective pedagogy that were needed to develop practice. *Sustained Shared Thinking* thus featured in the *Key Elements of Effective Practice (KEEP)* (DfES, 2005) that was distributed to all English pre-school settings, and it has now been included in the national *Early Years Foundation Stage* (EYFS) a curriculum framework and guidance for England (DfES, 2007b).

The REPEY findings may be summarised as follows:

1 Adult initiated activity – Effective pedagogues model appropriate language, values and practices. They also encourage socio-dramatic play, and praise, encourage, ask questions, and interact verbally with children. Excellent settings tended to achieve a good balance between teacher-led and child-initiated interactions, play and activities. Two-thirds of activities were child-led but in excellent settings half of these were extended with appropriate, guided, cognitive challenge by the adults.

2 Child initiated but adult extended activities – This is a particular form of teacher/practitioner initiation that may also be applied in cases where the child initiated. The most effective settings were found to provide both teacher-initiated group work and freely chosen, yet potentially instructive play activities. 'Extension' was included in the definition of 'sustained shared thinking' (see below), and one of the implications clearly identified in the research was that effective pedagogues require a good knowledge and understanding of the curriculum, and of how child learn.

3   The provisions of differentiation and formative assessment – Effective pedagogues assessed children's performance to ensure the provision of challenging yet achievable experiences (i.e., within the Zone of Proximal Development, Vygotsky, 1978) and provide formative feedback. The most effective settings seemed to have shared educational aims with parents supported by regular communication; weekly or monthly dialogues were more effective than termly or annual meetings.

4   Attention to the relationships between children – Effective settings viewed cognitive and social development as complementary and they supported children in rationalising and talking through their conflicts and resolving problems for themselves with the help of adults. This was not the case where the adults dominated and told the children what to do.

5   Sustained shared thinking and open-ended questions – Adults and children in the excellent settings were more likely to engage at times in 'sustained shared thinking': episodes in which two or more individuals 'worked together' in an intellectual way to solve a problem, clarify a concept, evaluate activities or extend narratives, etc. During periods of sustained shared thinking (SST) both parties contributed to the thinking and developed and extended the discourse. Associated with SST was also the adult's skilled use of open-ended questioning. These are questions that could genuinely have more than one answer, e.g., 'What do you think?' 'What would you do?' (See Siraj-Blatchford and Manni, 2008 for the analysis of around 6,000 questions asked of children in 12 pre-schools).

In the UK context, such findings also challenge entrenched beliefs about the value of exclusively encouraging free play, and promoting a solely non-interventionist role for early childhood practitioners.

International Early Childhood Education (ECE) models

An 'ECE model' is an educational system that combines theory with practice. A number of such models may be identified in the UK and overseas that combine a theoretical knowledge base (that may reflect a particular philosophical orientation). The 'qualities' of several particularly popular and 'successful' international ECE models were identified in the *Start Strong Report* (OECD, 2004) and as Pramling et al. (2004) and Siraj-Blatchford (1999) have observed, a number of interesting commonalities can

Table 11.1   OECD Curriculum Outlines

	Teacher's initiating activities	Teachers extending activities	Differentiation and Formative Assessment	Relationships and conflict between children	Sustained Shared Thinking
EEL*	Introducing new activities	Enriching interventions	Observe children	Work out sustaining relations	Engagement
High Scope	Sharing control	Participation as partners	Plan, do, review	Adopt a problem solving approach	Authentic dialogue
Reggio Emilia	Development of short- and long-term projects	Sustaining the cognitive and social dynamics	Teachers first listen don't talk	Warm reciprocal relationships	Reciprocity of interactions
EPPE/ REPEY	*Correlations found with effective practice*	*Correlations found with effective practice*	*Correlations found with effective practice*	*Correlations found with effective practice*	*Correlations found with effective practice*

Note: 'Teacher' also refers to any other adult in early years settings
Source: OECD, 2004
*'Effective Early Learning' (EEL) (Pascal and Bertram, 1995), referred to as 'Experiential Education' (EXE) in Praming et al. (2004) taken from the work of Ferre Laevers.

be found between the most successful (widely replicated) ECE models developed in different countries. Similarly, if we consider the accounts of the three ECE models most clearly identifying their pedagogy in the *Starting Strong Report* (OECD, 2004), we can see that the particular strategies applied according to these accounts of the models (by Ferre Laevers, David Weikart and Carla Rinaldi) match very closely with the REPEY findings, and with additional evidence from the EPPE study (Siraj-Blatchford and Sylva, 2004) that show positive correlations as can be seen in Table 11.1.

In the UK, the Effective Early Learning (EEL) project has drawn upon work carried out by Ferre Laevers (1995) in Belgium to provide a professional development programme that is intended to evaluate and develop quality in early childhood settings (Pascal and Bertram, 1995, 1997). In EEL, effective learning is considered to involve an essentially symbiotic relationship characterised by the 'involvement' of the child and the 'engagement' of the teacher. An involved child is one who has focused their attention and is persistent, is intrinsically motivated, rarely distracted, fascinated and absorbed by their activity. An engaged adult is one who shows sensitivity, stimulation and yet grants enough autonomy for the child to make their own judgments and express their ideas.

Reggio Emilia is a district in Northern Italy where over the last 35 years, the municipality has developed an extensive network of early childhood services for children from birth to six, providing for over a third of children under three and nearly all children aged three to six. The city has become world famous for the pedagogical work in these services, attracting many visitors from all over the world (for further reading, see Edwards et al., 1993). The early childhood services in Reggio understand the young child to be a co-constructor of knowledge and identity, a unique, complex and individual subject, engaging with and making sense of the world from birth, but always doing this in relationship with others, both adults and other children. Reggio pre-schools employ specialist staff such as an atelierista, a person who runs the atelier, the school's art studio, and a pedagogista, who acts as a key worker providing support with documentation and individual planning for a group of children (often across a group of settings) and their families.

The High/Scope approach (Schweinhart et al., 2005), which has also gained considerable popularity in the UK, is based upon an approach originally developed from the practice of Sara Smilansky. The High/Scope daily routine consist of a cycle of a 'planning', 'doing' and 'reviewing'. During planning, children decide what activity they will engage in for the session. Once the 'do' part of the routine is complete, the children recall what they have done during review time. A setting organised to provide the High/Scope experience is divided into interest areas to promote active learning and specific kinds of play and the materials are accessible to the children to allow independence. The adult's role is to participate as a partner in the children's activities and there is an emphasis on positive interaction strategies, allowing children to share control and form authentic relationships with other children. In addition, the adult must support children's learning and extend it by helping children to find solutions to problems they encounter.

There is strength to be found in variety and as each of these models are culturally specific it would be a mistake to make any judgment between them. But as suggested above, there are commonalities that may be identified to inform the development of all provisions (Siraj-Blatchford, 1999). To take just one other significant example, the 'documentation' applied in Reggio Emilia and other ECE models provides a means by which children are encouraged to reflect upon their own work and that of their peers. They, therefore, 'become even more curious, interested, and confident as they contemplate the meaning of what they have achieved' (Malaguzzi, 1993: 63). When the children's efforts, intentions, and ideas are shown so clearly to be taken seriously by the adults this encourages the children to approach their work with greater responsibly, energy and commitment. Documentation also provides a basis for continuous planning based on the evaluation of work as it progresses; it provides a context for communicating with parents which often leads to them to become more involved in their child's education.

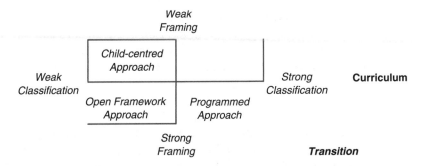

Figure 11.1   Pedagogy (Siraj-Blatchford, 2008)

High oblique Scope takes the emphasis on continuous planning and review that is found in Reggio a stage further, providing a more structured and institutionalised approach in the daily plan-do-review routines.

Other common pedagogical models of ECE

A typology of the most commonly applied models of early childhood education has been adapted from a model first developed by Weikart (2000), and is shown in Figure 11.1.

The major organising principles applied in the typology are pedagogy and curriculum (Bernstein, 1981) and the different forms of early childhood practice are distinguished by applying Bernstein's formulation of classification and framing. 'Classification' refers to the strength of the boundaries placed between 'curriculum subjects'; in the early years we might refer to these as *domains of learning*. Where the curriculum content is clearly defined in terms of school subjects we refer to that as *strong* classification. Framing is about who is in control: who it is that selects, sequences or paces the learning. When framing is weak the child has more apparent control, and when it is strong it is the adult or educator who is most clearly in control. So for example, a collaborative, progressive and permissive classroom illustrates weak framing and a traditional didactic one strong framing.

In the most extreme applications of the Child-centred approach in ECE, the teacher responds entirely to the individual child's interests and activities. More often, topic or project themes are adopted that have been chosen especially to appeal to the children's interests. The curriculum emphasis is on encouraging children's independence, their social and emotional growth, creativity and self-expression. The classroom or playroom environment is often rich in stimulus, permissive, and provides for open-ended exploration and discovery.

An Open Framework approach provides the educator with a strong pedagogic structure (or framework) that supports the child in their explorations and interactions with, and reflections upon, their learning environment. In this model, the curriculum classification is weaker as the child has a good deal of freedom to make choices between the various learning environments that are on offer. But the optional environments (e.g., sand, water, block play, puzzles) are often provided to achieve particular (usually cognitive or conceptual) curriculum aims, and these aims may be more or less acknowledged by the setting. In some settings children's choices are carefully monitored and a broad and balanced curriculum (including physical, creative, social and academic) is encouraged over the medium or long term.

The Programmed approach is highly teacher directed providing for little initiative on the part of the child. The rationale for this method is drawn significantly from theories of learning. This pedagogy is usually applied where curriculum objectives may be clearly (and objectively) classified and is likely to be most effective where learning involves the development of simple skills or memorisation. The curriculum content in Programmed approaches is often highly structured. This sort of programme has been shown to be detrimental to children's long-term development (Schweinhart and Weikart, 1997).

Some longitudinal studies have shown us that young children provided with Programmed Instruction sometimes do better than those provided with other forms of pedagogy in the short term (e.g., Karnes et al., 1983; Miller and Bizzell, 1983). But the studies also suggest that even when these effects are apparent, the gains are short lived, with all the significant differences having 'washed out' within a year of the provision ending. Programmed Instruction has also been found to result in children showing significantly increased stress/anxiety behaviours (Burts et al., 1990). A more recent and rigorous longitudinal study conducted by Schweinhart and Weikart (1997) showed little difference in the academic performance of young children provided with Programmed Instruction but significantly more emotional impairment and disturbance leading to special educational provision. More importantly, the Schweinhart and Weikart study showed that in later years the Programmed Instruction group experienced more suspensions from work and more than double the rate of arrests as either of the other two groups. In terms of serious crimes requiring a custodial sentence, 43% of the Programmed Instruction group gained a criminal record, compared with only 17% of the child-centred group and only 10% of the open framework group by the age of 25. Both the Schweinhart and Weikart (1997) study and the High/Scope Perry Pre-school study showed a significant difference in the percentage of young adults married and living with their spouses: while 31% of the Open Framework group and 18% of the Child-centred group were married at age 23, none of those experiencing Programmed Instruction was (Schweinhart and Weikart, 1997).

The England and Northern Ireland EPPE 3–11 has now identified similar patterns: children who attended medium and high quality pre-schools were found to have higher levels of 'Self-regulation' in Year 6 (age 11, end of primary school) than others. Children who attended high quality pre-schools were also found to display more 'pro-social' behaviour and were less likely to display 'hyperactivity' in Year 6 than children who had attended low and medium quality pre-schools (Sammons et al., 2007). EPPE also shows the importance of having professionals trained specifically in the teaching of young children: graduate teachers as managers of centres or higher proportions of graduate teachers were associated with better outcomes for children. Mixed teams of professionals which included teachers seem to work well (Sylva et al., 2004).

Conclusion

Of course, each of the approaches that are described here and in the *Starting Strong* report remain 'ideal types', and the practices in many settings will involve a combination of all of them. The challenge for early childhood educators is to provide a gradual and supportive transition as the children become more capable that stimulates learning and development while avoiding any risk of regression or failure. This transition is often reflected in changes in the strength of the classification and framing offered to children as they get older (as shown by the arrow in Figure. 11.1).

The EYFS guidance (DfES, 2007a) and the Foundation Phase (DCELLS, 2008) promote a pedagogy which involves negotiating and co-constructing the curriculum through playful processes of 'sustained shared thinking' (SST) that may be initiated by either the adult or the child. The question of who initiates this SST is actually less relevant as long as both parties are committed to playing an equal part in determining its focus and direction (its co-construction) in 'collaborative free flow'. In a sense, 'initiation' is taken in turns as different material and symbolic resources are drawn upon, and each play is extended as a more or less unique improvisation. As children develop the capability and are motivated to play with peers, the curriculum guidance in the UK encourages us to continue to provide children with a rich range of experiences and resources to draw upon in collaborative play and to support them in developing a greater awareness of their development and learning. Ultimately, in school, young children take pleasure in learning for its own sake and restrict their play to scheduled playtimes, more disciplined creative activities, and their involvement in a variety of games with more formal rules.

Longitudinal studies from America provided early evidence of the effectiveness of pre-school education. The High/Scope Perry Pre-school evaluation showed the substantial benefits that were to be gained through pre-schooling for children brought up in low-income households and at high risk of school failure. Many studies have also shown that social and motivational elements of pre-school programmes are as important as academic outcomes. Early childhood education really matters.

Questions and exercises

1 Why is ECE important in the quest for equality of opportunity?
2 What are the key components of quality programmes?
3 What kinds of professionals are required to support the best outcomes for children? What are the obstacles to this being achieved?
4 What do we know from research about the benefits of ECE?

Further reading

Two publications provide the most comprehensive synthesis of the theory and evidence related to early childhood education currently available. Both of these are US publications, the first comes from the National Research Council and Institute of Medicine: *From Neurons to Neighbourhoods: The Science of Early Childhood Development* (2000), and the second is Bowman et al. (2001) *Eager to Learn*. The *Effective Provision of Pre-School Education (EPPE)* has had a considerable impact on government policy and provided the first robust evidence of the positive effects of pre-school education in the UK. EPPE has shown that high quality pre-school education can help reduce social exclusion and has the potential to break cycles of educational disadvantage. *EPPE Technical Paper 10* (Siraj-Blatchford et al., 2003) provides case study illustrations of good pre-school practices identified through EPPE. In the *Team Around the Child: Multi-agency Working in the Early Years*, I have a chapter that makes the case for integrating education with care in the early years (Siraj-Blatchford, et al., 2007), and my paper, 'Creativity, communication and collaboration: the identification of pedagogic progression in sustained shared thinking' (Siraj-Blatchford, 2007) presents a conceptual model to support further development of good practice in early childhood education.

12

CHILD WELFARE AND CHILD PROTECTION

Bob Sanders

Contents:

- **Introduction**
- **Devolution and child and family policy**
- **Victoria Climbié and Laming Report**
- **Every Child Matters**
- **Integrated children's services**
- **Children in need, children with a disability, and family support**
- **Looking after children and adoption**
- **Safeguarding children from abuse and neglect**
- **Conclusion**

Introduction

This chapter focuses on child welfare and child protection in the UK as influenced in recent years by countervailing trends of both diversification and integration. Even since 2004, there have been significant changes in the fundamental principles underpinning the delivery of child and family services. The chapter will consider the circumstances of, and services for, children who are in need, who are looked after away from home (or adopted) and those at risk of abuse or neglect.

Devolution and child and family policy

As noted by Sanders and Pope (2008) it is no longer possible to speak of a single social policy for the UK as the impact of political devolution (1 July 1999) has created significantly greater internal autonomy. This has meant for example, in Wales, that the National Assembly for Wales, a newly established representative body, is allowed a significant control over how money designated for Wales by Parliament is disbursed in Wales.

The implication of this for the professional practitioner is that one needs to be aware of the application and remit of policies. This chapter will focus on England and Wales, and clarify for the reader whether the provisions described apply in England, Wales, or both. As one might imagine, this has made the task, both for the author and the reader, more complex than it might have been even as recently as five years ago.

The Children Act 2004 is an example of legislation highlighting this emergent differentiation. Sections 1–4 deal with the Children's Commissioner for England; section 5 deals with the functions of the Children's Commissioner for Wales (the two have different remits). Sections 10–12 are about children's services in England; section 25 outlines similar provisions, but with significant differences, for children's services in Wales. Likewise, different sections of the Act deal separately for the provisions in England and Wales of databases, local safeguarding children's boards, children and young people's plans, new designated roles, the Child and Family Court Advisory Service (CAFCASS), and private fostering. In addition to the ways in which the law now distinguishes between Wales and England, there are now provisions for 'legislative competence', areas which are designated as being those in which Wales may make primary legislation. One such area is in relation to 'vulnerable children'.

In Wales, unlike in England, social policy for children is formally based on the United Nations Convention on the Rights of the Child:

> The Welsh Assembly Government has adopted the UN Convention on the Rights of the Child as the basis of all our work for children and young people in Wales. (Welsh Assembly Government, 2004: 28).

These Convention rights have been translated into seven core aims underlining policy in Wales, which are 'to ensure that all children and young people:

- have a flying start in life;
- have a comprehensive range of education and learning opportunities;
- enjoy the best possible health and are free from abuse, victimisation and exploitation;
- have access to play, leisure, sporting and cultural activities;
- are listened to, treated with respect, and have their race and cultural identity recognised;
- have a safe home and a community which supports physical and emotional wellbeing; and
- are not disadvantaged by poverty. (Welsh Assembly Government, 2004: 28)

Child policy in Wales can be classified in accordance with which of these policy aims it is trying to achieve, as has been demonstrated by Butler (2007).

Having considered the trend towards diversification, let us now consider the trend towards integration.

Victoria Climbié and the Laming Report

On 25 February 2000, Victoria Climbié (8 years 3½ months) died in a London hospital as a result of sustained abuse and maltreatment perpetrated by her great aunt and the aunt's boyfriend. Victoria, a child from the Ivory Coast, was brought to London after a five months' stay in France, on 24 April 1999. Less than one year later she was dead. During this time, the treatment that she received at the hands of her carers was no less than ongoing torture:

> Victoria spent much of her last days … living and sleeping in a bath in an unheated bathroom, bound hand and foot inside a bin bag, lying in her own urine and faeces. It is not surprising then that towards the end of her short life, Victoria was stooped like an old lady and could walk only with great difficulty.

… and

> At the post-mortem examination, Dr Carey recorded evidence of no fewer than 128 separate injuries to Victoria's body, saying, 'There really is not anywhere that is spared – there is scarring all over the body. (Laming, 2003: 2)

The death of a child at the hands of carers is not new. Approximately 50–100 children are killed in the UK every year by those responsible for them (HM Government, 2003). However, this case caused particular concern:

> But Victoria's case was altogether different. Victoria was not hidden away. It is deeply disturbing that during the days and months following her initial contact … Victoria was known to no less than two further housing authorities, four social services departments, two child protection teams of the Metropolitan Police Service (MPS), a specialist centre managed by the NSPCC, and she was admitted to two different hospitals because of suspected deliberate harm. The dreadful reality was that these services knew little or nothing more about Victoria at the end of the process than they did when she was first referred. (Laming, 2003: 3)

However, at no time did Victoria ever successfully cross the threshold from being considered as a 'child in need' (below) to being defined as a child 'at risk of significant harm', despite her circumstances being considered by various agencies. Much of the concern focused on why this failed to happen.

The report contained 108 recommendations with varying timescales for implementation (three months, six months, two years). Recommendations included reviewing the law on private fostering (Victoria's legal status) the amalgamation of government guidance (*Working Together* and the *Assessment Framework*), sharing of information between agencies even when child protection is not a concern, government guidance on data protection, the replacement of the child protection register and the establishment of a national children's database.

Although individual shortcomings were identified, the report was mostly critical of management systems and in particular the interface between services for children who are in need and those who are at risk of significant harm. Overall, the Laming Report recommendations were largely implemented through the devices of three government actions: *Every Child Matters,* the Integrated Children's System, and the Children Act 2004.

Every Child Matters

This document, which applies only in England, but with the Scottish Parliament and the Welsh Assembly committed to pursuing similar lines, is more than just a 'green paper'; it is a policy agenda setting out the government's position on the principles to underpin future services for children. Five very important key outcomes were identified for the well-being of children and young people:

1   Being healthy
2   Staying safe
3   Enjoying and achieving
4   Making a positive contribution
5   Economic well-being.

The government committed itself to a system in which:

> child protection services are not separate from support for families, but are part of the spectrum of services provided to help and support children and families. (HM Government, 2003: 64)

It sought views on a number of issues including the following:

- An independent commissioner for England
- The establishment of children's trusts (uniting local health, education and social services)
- The appointment of a local children's director
- The replacement of ACPCs with local children's safeguarding boards
- Every child to be given a unique ID number

- Joint training and protocols for childcare professionals to promote interprofessional working
- More family support services.

Unlike the long list of prior child fatality inquiries since the Maria Colwell report (DHSS, 1974), the Laming Report set out to spearhead a major transformation of children's services, the like of which had not been seen since 1948.

Integrated children's services

In order to maximise efforts to ensure better working together at various levels the government implemented a major new strategy, illustrated in Figure 12.1.

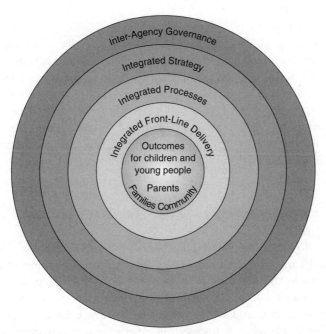

Figure 12.1   Every Child Matters: Change for Children (from www.everychildmatters. gov.uk/aims/strategicoverview/?assetdocument&id=21444)

Inter-agency governance

The local authority children's services director will have a key role in facilitating this, and a vital component of this will be replacing the non-statutory Area Child

Protection Committees with a new, statutory body, the local safeguarding children boards whose remit will be broader than child protection.

Integrated strategy

The children's services authority will have responsibility to produce a three-year children and young people's plan which will be genuinely inter-agency, and will involve children, young people and parents, and will link into the new annual improvement plan. The strategy also mandates joint inspection of children's services authority, and the development of integrated front line services.

Integrated processes

The central mechanism here is the establishment of the common assessment framework (CAF), a tool designed to: 'reduce duplication of assessment, produce a shared language across agencies and improve referral between agencies' (HM Government, 2008). An important feature here are the steps taken to promote information sharing between agencies. The reliance on electronic means of entering and retrieving information about children and families, within clearly specified protocols for sharing and divulging information between agencies and professionals, is a central component of this.

Integrated front-line delivery

The aim here is to remove agency and discipline as the basis for the provision of service to children and families, and instead to aim for a relative dissolution of these rather rigid boundaries to provide a more seamless service. Co-locating different services (e.g., within schools) and the establishment of multidisciplinary teams to provide children's services are both endorsed as ways to achieve this. Ultimately it is to be hoped that the children and families themselves will experience more integrated services.

Children in need, children with a disability, and family support

Despite the operation of these new mechanisms for integrating all services for children (those in need, those at risk of abuse, those who may be of concern for other reasons), the Children Act 1989 still remains the basis for providing children's services (with certain Children Act 2004 modifications).

In general, families who require support ought to be able to receive it without stigma: however, there is a threshold for entitlement to local authority support. In England and Wales this threshold is section 17 of the Children Act 1989, which defines when a child is 'in need'. The vast majority of children in the community will not be 'in need', being a child in need is not necessarily a permanent state of affairs, and not all children who need services in the ordinary way will be considered as 'in need' for the purposes of the Act. Even many children who have special education needs may not be defined as children 'in need' of local authority social services (although arguably such children will be more likely to receive a seamless service through the provision of the integrated children's system). The intention in defining 'need' in this way is to provide a means to target limited resources at those children who *most* need services.

In general terms the local authority is *required* to 'to safeguard and promote the welfare of children within their area who are in need', and to 'promote the upbringing of such children by their families, by providing a range and level of services appropriate to those children's needs'. These services may be provided to the child directly or to the child's family.

In practice, the principal services provided for children in need and their families are the services of social workers, access to support groups of various kinds, day care and family centres, and foster care and residential care for those who need it. There are a number of ways that professionals can assist children in need and their families. They may provide advice, guidance and counselling. They may provide advocacy on behalf of clients with agencies providing income support, housing, health, and education services. They may in exceptional circumstances provide direct financial assistance to families.

The Children Act for the first time introduced an expectation on local authorities to provide *family centres* as appropriate for children in their communities. These centres, frequently provided by large voluntary bodies (e.g., Barnardo's, NCH) in partnership with the local authority have now become the mainstay of family support provision.

Children with a disability

Disabled children are defined as children 'in need' for the purposes of local authority services. There is more than one way of thinking about disability. Increasingly in social work the *social model* is the one used to understand and respond to the significance of disability in the lives of children and their families. This is frequently considered in contradistinction to the *medical model,* a positivist approach which treats disability as a disease requiring diagnosis, treatment and prognosis. However, the application of the medical model to disability is often criticised for its failure to recognise the constraining processes within society which not only make the condition of disablement worse than it might otherwise be, but can actually be said to be the origin of the restrictions that one experiences in terms of the failure to fully participate in society.

A view frequently expressed in connection with disabled children is that they are children first, and disabled second. The significance of this is clear when we face situations in which the child's needs arising from a disability are in conflict with the ordinary needs that all children have. An example of this was the former practice of placing children with severe learning difficulties in long-stay hospitals. It was believed that the need for a family life experience with opportunities for attachment and bonding, which all children have, was less important than the need for highly trained specialist care arising from the child's special needs.

Looking after children and adoption

The Children Act 1989 brought significant changes in the way we think about children in the care system. Among these was the concept of 'looked after', which includes children who are 'accommodated' under voluntary arrangements and children who are 'in care' under compulsory provisions. Children may be looked after in a variety of settings by a range of agencies. These include foster family placements provided by the local authority or by private or voluntary agencies, foster placement with relatives of the child, residential care of various kinds, and sometimes supported lodgings for older children. In addition some children formally in care are supported to live at home with their own families.

Whether a child is looked after on a voluntary or compulsory basis, there are legal requirements concerning the arrangements to be made. The agency has a duty to safeguard and promote the child's welfare and a responsibility to accommodate and maintain the child. The agency must give 'due consideration' to the wishes and feelings of the child and the family. It should arrange for the child to be looked after near his or her home, and for siblings to be accommodated together, whenever appropriate. The particular needs of disabled children should be catered for, and the placing agency must give consideration to the child's religious persuasion, racial origin, and cultural and linguistic background.

Regulations require written plans for the child, in advance of the placement, or in an emergency, as soon as possible afterwards. These should include the immediate and long-term plans for the child; the expected duration of the placement; arrangements for contact; the child's state of health and health care needs; arrangements for the child's education; and whether an independent visitor should be appointed. The child should be medically examined and the child's plans and progress should be reviewed at specified intervals. Reviews should include consultation and participation by the child and family, and the child's rights should be explained to her or him.

Contact with family and friends is very important when a child is living apart from family, home, and community. Regular contact is associated with a successful placement and successful return home, and legislation strongly emphasises the importance of family contact. Planning for the child's eventual return home, or if necessary for a move to a permanent substitute family, should be a part of every review.

A particularly important concept to be developed in looking after children in recent years is that of the *corporate parent*. This term has been developed to remind agencies that the responsibility for looking after a child is not just the responsibility of the social worker, care service providers and social services, but rests with the local authority as a whole.

Theoretical foundations underpinning looking after children

It is important for those working with looked after children to have a strong theoretical foundation to their work. Thomas (2005) discusses a number of these. Understanding child development theory is clearly most important, and within this, it can be argued that *attachment* theory will feature particularly for at least two reasons. First, looked after children will be experiencing separation, and attachment theory indicates that separation, depending upon a wide array of factors, can be damaging. Contact (discussed above) is one way of mitigating the potentially damaging effects of separation. Second, many, if not most, looked after children will have had pre-care experiences that have compromised their ability to form positive, secure attachments, and instead have rather insecure attachments or may even be in that very small group of children who are non-attached. The evaluation of a child's past, current, and likely future attachments is an essential part of the assessment.

However, damaging experiences are not the end of the story, and one of the very important things that we have learned in recent years is that the impact of early adverse experience is not linear, that is, the more bad things happen to a child in early life, the more negative consequences there are in later life. *Resilience* thinking (Rutter, 1985; Mrazek and Mrazek, 1987; Fonagy et al., 1994; Herrenkohl et al., 1994) has helped us to understand that there are a wide array of factors, within the child, within the family and within the community (Daniel et al., 1999) that influence the impact of adversity and trauma on the lives of children. We have reached a stage where we can possibly learn more from studying children who are successful and have reasonably positive outcomes despite having severely harsh childhoods than we can from further detailed study of the manifold ways in which children are harmed by adversity in their lives. We can try to learn how to help children have the types of outcomes that the more resilient children have. However, one of the difficulties here is that some of the factors identified that may promote resilience are those over which we have no control (e.g., gender of the child). Nevertheless, there remain many factors (e.g., the availability of a 'mentor') where informed practice can make a difference.

Seeing the child in his or her wider social and societal context has become very important in recent years. The Assessment Framework (DoH et al., 2000, now integrated into the Common Assessment Framework) placed considerable emphasis on the child's social context as one of three sides of the assessment triangle. Bronfenbrenner (1979), an *ecological systems* theorist, has been particularly influential. Direct work techniques with looked after children have, for example, frequently included the use of an ecomap, a visual representation for both the child and worker of the child's social network, and the quality of the relationships between the child and other people. It is also very important to see the child holistically, in other words, to not to focus on one aspect of a child's situation to the exclusion of others. The UK would appear to do this less well when compared with other European countries, as is argued by Petrie et al. (2006) in their endorsement of a pedagogical approach to working with children in care.

Hearing the *voice of the looked after child* when making and reviewing the arrangements has become very important. This important advance in thinking about looked after children was strongly influenced by the Children Act 1989, but has more recently been significantly enhanced by two developments, the introduction of Independent Reviewing Officers (IRO), and the availability of advocacy services for looked after children who wish to make representation (as implemented in the Adoption of Children Act 2002). In terms of the IRO's role, guidance (DfES, 2004: 28) states:

> IRO should ensure that the right steps have been taken so that the child can make a meaningful contribution to their review. If the child is able and willing to speak for themselves at the meeting, the IRO as chair should facilitate this.

As argued by Williams (2008) a focus on the rights of children (as contained within both the United Nations Convention on the Rights of the Child and the European Convention on Human Rights) should help us to resolve tensions, conflicts and apparent contradictions when trying to apply legal frameworks to children.

Health and education of looked after children

There has been considerable research into poor health and education outcomes for looked after children. The policy context in relation to health has attempted to broaden the concept – getting away from the previous focus on the 'medical' dimension by conceptualising health as more than the mere absence of illness and by focusing on mental as well as physical health. There has been an effort to motivate and engage children and young people in promoting healthier lifestyles generally.

The emphasis on children's mental health fits in well with the government's recent strategy to develop better child and adolescent mental health services (CAMHS) generally throughout the UK (NHS Health Advisory Service, 1995; National Assembly for Wales, 2001; DoH, 2004). It also acknowledges the particular mental health difficulties of children in the care system (from experiences both before and during the care episode). Previously seriously disturbed children in the looked after system had difficulty accessing CAMHS help because they did not fulfil diagnostic criteria (that is, having a formally recognised mental illness) to receive a service. Today there are different local arrangements in place which attempt to link CAMHS services with services for looked after children.

There are long-standing concerns about the very poor educational achievements of looked after children. A significant debate which has emerged is the extent to which this is largely due to educational disadvantage *before* the children came into the care system (Cocker and Allain, 2008). For example, we know that family socio-economic status (SES) is 'a fairly good predictor of children's academic achievement (Meadows, 1993: 304) and that social class begins to divide children's academic attainment between the ages of three and five (Sutton Trust, 2007). Given that the circumstances of children who come into the looked after system are extremely disadvantaged, (Bebbington and Miles, 1989) it is reasonable to conclude that it is unfair and unwise to compare educational outcomes of children who are looked after with educational outcomes for children generally. They will, of course, be lower. What is unclear, even now, is what is the relative contribution of each, socio-economic class and looked after status, to this educational disadvantage?

Leaving care

Not only are looked after children disadvantaged by their pre-care and care experiences, they are further disadvantaged by their post-care experiences. Stein and Carey (1986) highlighted the very difficult circumstances of care leavers and noted how those experiences compared extremely unfavourably with children leaving their families for independent living. Care leavers left younger and had fewer financial resources and support mechanisms to fall back on.

Despite previous legislation (dating back to 1980!), it seems not to have been until there was legislation specifically designated for care leavers, the Children (Leaving Care) Act 2000, that real action began to be taken. Stein (2006) highlights the vulnerability of care leavers and classifies them into three groups, 'moving on', 'surviving' and 'victims' depending upon their experiences during care, prior to leaving care, and after leaving care. He argues for the experience of leaving care to be as 'normative' as possible, in other words, similar to the experience of a non-looked after child leaving his or her family.

Adoption

Adoption, first introduced in 1926, has remained the only means possible whereby the parental responsibility for a child is completely and irreversibly transferred from one set of parents to another. For this reason, an Adoption Order is only made after the most serious and careful consideration. In recent years, adoption has come to be seen as a means of securing permanence for children who might otherwise remain in care for many years without a family. Children who have been adopted from care are no longer 'looked after' by the local authority, but given the trends in adoption over the last three decades, most children will have been looked after for a period prior to being adopted.

Over the last 35 years, the overall numbers of children being adopted in England and Wales have declined from 21,500 (in 1971) to 4,980 (in 2006). Within those decreasing numbers, the proportion of adoptions which are of children under one year has also been declining – only 197 (in 2006). This is far fewer than the numbers of couples unable to have children of their own who would like to adopt.

Under the Adoption and Children Act 2002 all local authorities are required to provide adoption services (either directly or through others) for:

- Children who may be adopted, their parents and guardians
- Persons wishing to adopt a child
- Adopted persons, their parents, natural parents and former guardians.

This includes making arrangements for the adoption of children and providing adoption support services. Non-statutory agencies can also provide adoption services, and local authorities are expected to work in partnership with them.

Adoption is a controversial topic about which many people have strong views. Issues such as trans-racial adoptions, inter-country adoptions, openness in adoption, post-adoption services, applicants being overweight or smokers, upper age limits of applicants, have at different times all been the focus of considerable media attention – often concluding that social workers and adoption agencies are being unfair or 'politically correct'. However, the standards applied to adoption in the UK are second to none in the world, and it is only through keeping a clear focus on adoption as a service designed to meet the needs of the child, and not the needs of adults wishing to have children (important as those needs may be), that such standards have been able to be maintained.

Safeguarding children from abuse and neglect

A fundamental premise of child protection work in the UK is that children are best protected when agencies involved work well together. It follows that children are less well protected where there is disharmony, poor communication or even hostility between agencies. In the wake of a series of child tragedies in which children have been killed by their parents or carers, over the last 35 years an elaborate system has been developed enabling agencies and departments to work together at different levels: the national level, the local level, and the level of the individual case.

However, with devolution, using Wales as an example (Williams, 2007), it remains to be seen how far Welsh policy to protect children will diverge from policy in England. A possible concern will be whether children will be better or worse protected depending upon which part of the UK they live in, and that will need to be closely monitored.

The recent national policy emphasis on integrating children who are in need with children who are at risk from abuse and neglect does not mean that the child protection system can be dismantled. The duty placed upon local authorities (in England and Wales) to investigate concerns about the possibility of abuse under section 47 of Children Act 1989 remains. What is required is for local authorities to integrate their responsibilities under section 47 coherently with their responsibilities to children in need (under section 17) as well as keeping in mind the general welfare of *all* children within their area under the five key principles above (seven in Wales).

This integrationist philosophy in child protection was given added impetus with the Laming Inquiry into the death of Victoria Climbié (2003) and the subsequent government agenda.

> Effective measures to safeguard children are those that also promote their welfare. They should not be seen in isolation from the wider range of support and services already provided and available to meet the needs of children and families. (HM Government, 2006: 33)

Within every local authority area there is required to be a Local Safeguarding Children Board (LSCB) – statutory bodies replacing the non-statutory Area Child Protection Committees. However, in both England and Wales, LSCB priority will remain to protect children from harm, ensuring that this area of work is well covered, before considering their wider remits to *all* children. This is expressed slightly differently in the two guidance documents setting out the roles and functions of the LSCBs:

In England (HM Government, 2006: 76):

> 3.10 Safeguarding and promoting the welfare of children includes protecting children from harm. Ensuring that work to protect children is properly co-ordinated and effective remains a key goal of LSCBs, and they should not focus on their wider role if the standard of this core business is inadequate. However, when this core business is secure, LSCBs should go beyond it to work to their wider remit, which includes preventative work to avoid harm being suffered in the first place.

In Wales, (Welsh Assembly Government, 2004: 119) the phrasing is slightly different:

4.15 The focus for Safeguarding Boards should remain the protection of children from abuse and neglect. Policies and practice should therefore be primarily targeted at those children who are suffering, or at risk of suffering significant harm.

4.16 Ensuring that effective policies and working practices are in place to protect children and that they are properly co-ordinated remains a key role for Safeguarding Boards. Only when these are in place should Boards look to their wider remit of safeguarding and promoting the welfare of all children.

At the level of the individual case the key provision is the *child protection conference*. It is here that the individual circumstances of particular children are considered; usually at an initial child protection conference followed if necessary by review conferences. Whenever a case involves suspected harm in relation to a child or children, a decision will be made, following in most cases an investigation–planning strategy discussion, about convening a child protection conference. The conference aims to bring together information concerning the child and carers, to assess the future likelihood of significant harm, and to make a plan to promote the child's welfare. Someone independent of the management of the case chairs the conference. A range of professionals are invited to attend: social worker, health visitor, teacher, police, paediatrician and so on. Parents are normally invited, although in some circumstances, in accordance with specified criteria, they may be excluded from part or all of the meeting. Depending upon age and understanding children may be invited to attend, although this is still quite rare; other ways may be found to convey the child's views to the conference (e.g., via an advocate or professional speaking on their behalf, or via videotape, audiotape or letter). However, the conference should be appraised of the child's views on his or her circumstances and the concerns.

In the past the decision to be made by the conference was whether or not to add the child's name to the child protection register. Under the new, bifurcated arrangements, child protection registers continue in Wales, but not in England. However, in both cases, the details will be entered onto the electronic Integrated Children's System (ICS) and the essential feature of there being a consensus about the concern for the child is that there should be a child protection plan. This feature is extremely important as it has been long recognised that the plan is all important in addressing the issues of concern, not mere registration in itself. However, the conference cannot override agencies in their individual responsibilities for children.

In both England and Wales, following inclusion in the ICS, there should be a key worker appointed and arrangements made for a core group to implement and monitor the plan between review conferences. Parents are normally part of the core group, and occasionally children may be included. In these ways the conference is responsible for co-ordinating inter-agency work to reduce the risk to the child.

Most children involved in child protection are not the subject of court applications for care orders (although it is likely true that most children involved in care applications are involved in child protection proceedings). There are many complex issues involved where children are involved in care proceedings, but an important recent policy change has been the introduction of *concurrent planning*. In order to avoid delay, where there are care proceedings in respect of a child (a longstanding concern of the judicial system) the local authority is required to make simultaneous plans for both the child's eventual reunion to his or her own family, or placement with a permanent substitute family. Thus, if return home should fail, then an alternative plan is already reasonably well advanced.

Conclusion

There are at the present time in the UK very strong unifying and diversifying forces at work in child welfare. The unifying forces are largely derived from a small number of cases causing serious concerns, and aim to promote a standardised approach to ensure that the failures of inter-agency working, so often seen as the primary cause of major concerns, are addressed at all levels. The latest case of concern, that of Victoria Climbié, addressed these issues at the highest governmental levels (whereas many of the previous concerns merely focused on the local inter-agency working arrangements). The diversifying trends on the other hands reflect different political priorities. Wales has different needs from England. The impact of devolution has been to allow and encourage the four UK nations to find unique solutions to their unique problems. The extent to which this may, however, result in some children being less well protected (or supported) in some parts of the UK than in others is a potential danger that must be monitored in order to be prevented.

Questions and exercises

Arrange to interview a childcare social worker in a child and family team, or a project worker in a voluntary organisation family support project (for example, a family centre). Ask the social worker/project worker:

1   What is the worker trying to achieve in work undertaken with children and families?
2   What are the obstacles to achieving the agency's objectives?
3   How are the agency and worker addressing those obstacles?

Further reading

Colton et al. (2001), Butler and Roberts (2003) and Brandon et al. (1998) are all useful texts guiding social workers in their practice with children and families. Parton (2006) offers a very good overview of recent trends in safeguarding children. Hendrick (2005) offers an overview of various aspects of child welfare, highlighting some of the contradictory views of children and childhood contained within it. Beckett (2007) offers an authoritative view on contemporary child protection.

13

CHILD HEALTH

Liz Noblett

Contents:

- **What is health?**
- **The politics of child health**
- **Child health programmes**
- **Child poverty**
- **Immunisation**
- **Child obesity**
- **Children in special circumstances**
- **Conclusion**

Introduction

In 2006, for the first time, child mortality rates fell below 10 million (UNICEF, 2007). It seems startling that such an immense loss of life should be deemed a success but as in the 1960s the rate was around 20 million deaths per year, perhaps there is some cause for celebration.

As a number of researchers have indicated (e.g., Belli et al., 2005), there appears to be a clear relationship between child health and the economy: poverty of health in childhood leads to economic poverty in adulthood. The converse is also true: investment in a children's health leads to improved economic outcomes for adults. However, child health is not simply about shoring up the economic security of a nation but is firmly entrenched within the United Nations Convention on the Rights of the Child (UNCRC), the first international agreement that put children at the forefront of political thinking. As a result, children have the right to good healthcare so as to enable them to achieve their true potential as adults.

This chapter aims to explore the many and varied factors which influence child health. It is not a chapter about *ill* health, there are many more appropriate text books where the interested reader can discover more about the many illness and diseases that can blight childhood. It is rather an investigation into what helps a child to remain healthy and how external factors can impact on the health and well-being of childhood. Environmental, economic and familial influences will be discussed and their effect on child health determined.

What is health?

The most frequently quoted definition of health was produced by the World Health Organisation (WHO) in 1948. Despite its age, the theory that 'health is a state of complete physical, mental and social well-being and not merely the absence of disease and infirmity' (WHO, 1948) provides us with a useful starting point.

It may be argued, however, that the standpoint of the WHO cited above is static and rather impersonal and also rather meaningless to children. In a study reported by Chapman et al. (2000), young children defined health as being 'a good diet', 'exercise' and 'keeping clean'. It seems that these children focused on external influences rather than any internal feelings of being healthy. Similarly, the National Children's Bureau has suggested that children view health as a 'reflection of their lifestyle and wellbeing' (2005: 18). Therefore, it could be argued that what constitutes 'child health' is subjective and shaped by knowledge, experience and expectations.

In the UK, social class differentials in health appear to be growing (Bradshaw and Mayhew, 2005). The link between socio-economic disadvantage and children's health has been identified in particular areas: low birth weight; not being breastfed; low immunisation uptake; higher rate of both accidental and non-accidental injuries; developmental delay; behavioural problems and a higher representation in the child protection system (Bradshaw and Mayhew, 2005; Hall and Elliman, 2006). With evidence that poor health rises with increased poverty one is reminded of the 'Inverse Care Law' which states that where health need is the highest, provision is at its lowest (Hart, 1971).

The politics of child health

Since devolution, the responsibility for child health has been ceded from central government to the four constituent countries of the UK. This has led to each country developing its own approach to health in general and to child health in particular.

Whilst some components of child health provision remain UK-wide – for example, the Immunisation Programme – other aspects, such as the development of National Service Frameworks, have been left to individual countries to determine. As a result, political priorities for spending the 'health care pound' have led to huge discrepancies in service provision, including provision related to child health. For example, in England there has been a disinvestment in the health visiting service leading to frozen vacancies and caseloads well above the recommended 1: 300 (CPHVA/UNITE 2008). Conversely, in Wales, the Assembly Government has invested millions into the early intervention programme 'Flying Start', a scheme which aims to make a real difference to the health and well-being of children and their families.

With such vast differences across the UK it becomes difficult to compare the health of children on a 'like by like' basis. It also means that when one is writing about child health, it is important to identify clearly the area of the UK under consideration. It seems clear that the suggestion made by Baistow (1995: 24) that 'notions of child health are constructed out of essentially politically motivated considerations' applies to the state of child health today.

National Service Frameworks and child health programmes

England and Wales have developed specific National Service Frameworks (NSF) for children, young people and maternity services in order to help deliver the National Health Service (NHS) Plan (Department of Health, 2000). The NSF aims to drive up quality and to reduce variations in service delivery. It is delivered as a partnership between 'social care', 'education' and 'health', with links to the voluntary sector and parents. The overarching aim is that:

> All children and young people achieve optimum health and wellbeing and are supported in fulfilling their potential. (Welsh Assembly Government, 2005: 1)

In order to achieve this aim, a key component of the NSF is the directive that all children and their families should have access to a child health programme that provides both universal and targeted health promotion. The NSF directive together with the publication of the fourth edition of *Health for All Children* (Hall and Elliman, 2006) has led England, Scotland and Northern Ireland to establish national programmes. At the time of writing, Wales has yet to develop a country-wide child health programme although most counties have now implemented their own interpretation of the NHS directive.

So why target children and their families with health promotion messages? The Ottawa Charter of 1986 describes health promotion as 'the process of enabling people to increase control over, and improve their health' (WHO, 1986: 1). While it is clearly very hard for babies to influence their environment in relation to a healthy lifestyle, it is vital that there is a system in place that follows children through from the earliest maternity care to the age at which they leave school. A good child health programme must allow children gradually to begin to make their own health choices based on informed knowledge.

In order to successfully develop and deliver a child health programme three challenges must be met:

1 The need to promote health and development
2 The need to facilitate the early detection of diseases and disorders
3 The need to move to a public health approach to prevention and community development.

(Hall and Elliman, 2006)

To respond to these challenges a change in focus is required. Health promotion cannot be viewed as an activity that is passive, something that is enforced upon others. Rather, parents and children must be viewed as strong and competent partners: relationships formed with families must therefore be based on 'partnership' rather than 'supervision' (Hall and Elliman, 2006). This brings to mind the idea of the 'team around the child': professionals from various agencies working together. This strengthening of relationships can only be beneficial to children as professionals can spend time talking to parents about what is most important to the family (French, 2007). A good quality child health programme must also be based on the model of progressive universalism: that is, a programme which offers 'a range of preventative and early intervention services for different levels of risk and protective factors' (DOH, 2008: 11). Therefore, although the programmes themselves are universal in that they are available for all families to access, it is implicit in their design that some families will have greater need than others.

The challenge of identifying disease and disorder in early childhood demands that a systematic approach is taken in order to deliver a programme of health surveillance which can determine whether children are at risk of, or are already suffering from, a particular condition. It is important to acknowledge that surveillance is not about a one-off contact with families but about the collection of relevant data from a variety of sources over time (Baird et al., 2001). The requirement to compile information from many professionals highlights the need for all those who work with young children and their parents to have a thorough understanding of child health and development. Early Years professionals must also ensure that they are fully aware of the processes and procedures that are in operation in their area of work.

Child health programmes, although predominately the remit of health professionals such as health visitors and school health nurses, also rely on the involvement of all those who work in the 'team around the child' (McCullough, 2007). While interagency and multidisciplinary work can be challenging (see Chapter 17), the sharing of knowledge about individual children can ensure that life trajectories are positively influenced.

Child poverty

It has long been recognised that there is a link between poverty and child health (for example, Hart, 1971; Hall and Elliman, 2006). UNICEF (2005) claim that half of all children living in the 'developing world' are living in poverty. The UK remains a relatively poor performer in the poverty tables in comparison with other so-called 'developed countries', despite evidence that child poverty is beginning to decline (Bradshaw and Mayhew, 2005). However, it has been noted that as yet there is no common approach to measuring child poverty (Minujin et al., 2006). What is more important, perhaps, is to determine how poverty influences health and welfare and to determine which interventions can best ameliorate any negative effects.

It is apparent that economic poverty has a greater impact in those countries, where unlike the UK, health care is not free at the point of delivery. For example, a study carried out in New Zealand (Baker, 2002) found that parents adopted a 'wait and see' approach prior to seeking medical attention for their children. One mother in this study wondered whether she 'could get him better by lunchtime' to avoid paying consultation fees to a medical practitioner to whom she already owed a large some of money. A consultation may also lead to charges for a prescription or for further treatment. It appeared from the participants' responses that despite recognising illness in their children and caring about them, seeking appropriate health care was prohibitively expensive.

Economic poverty is also more likely to be experienced by lone parent families: Bradshaw and Mayhew (2005) report that 52% of children living with a lone parent are poor. Poverty may have an impact on family relationships. It has been reported, for example, that low income mothers appear to be less responsive to their children and that it is this lack of maternal responsiveness which has an adverse impact on children (Evans et al., 2008).

One of the key themes of childhood poverty is that of social exclusion and the concept of an 'underclass' that is somehow separate from society (Welshman, 2006). This separation leads children to suffer from a poverty of experience, which may just be as detrimental as the economic poverty which is at its root cause. Children may experience a feeling of shame that they are unable to dress like their peers or indeed to partake in activities such as school trips or family holidays (Bradshaw and Mayhew, 2005).

Another field in which there appears to be an over representation of impoverished children is child protection. An American study found that poverty and economic status led to child neglect, regardless of the quality of parenting (Shook Slack et al., 2004). However, researchers in Australia suggest that rather than poverty leading to child abuse, 'a complex process leading to poverty outcomes in adult life can stem from experiences of abuse and adversity in childhood' (Frederick and Goddard 2007: 323). This revealing study concluded that child abuse results from 'a complex interaction of individual, social and environmental influences' (2007: 338). It should be emphasised, however, that while there may be links between poverty and child abuse, the vast majority of families in economic distress do not intentionally abuse their children (Shook Slack et al., 2004; Bradshaw and Mayhew, 2005; Frederick and Goddard, 2007;).

There is wide ranging evidence to suggest that children living in poverty can develop into adults who have poorer physical, mental and psychological health than their more affluent peers (Hall and Elliman, 2006). If childhood is to be viewed as a foundation for individual development (Yaqub, 2002) then it is unsurprising that during this influential time in lifespan development poverty may have a negative impact which continues into adulthood. However, Yaqub (2002) issues caveats that 'certain types of damage can – *but not always* – result from childhood poverty and some – *but not all* – damage may be permanent. It is essential that early years practitioners do not make negative assumptions about those who are already struggling with disadvantage.

It is also clear from the vast body of literature devoted to child poverty that professionals engaging with families living in poverty must take a 'multi-layered' approach. Advocacy for parents is essential in order to ensure that maximum economic aid is accessed. However, a community-based approach is also necessary to reach families most in need. The ultimate aim must be a reduction in the negative outcomes associated with growing up in poverty. The idea of progressive universalism, noted above, is a reversal of the 'Inverse Care Law' (Hart, 1971) where those in greater need receive the lesser service. Hart's article denigrating the Inverse Care Law may have appeared in the *Lancet* almost 40 years ago but unfortunately it still rings true today.

Immunisation

A key component of any child health programme is the delivery of immunisations to the population. As Hall and Elliman (2006) state:

> After clean water and safe sewage disposal this (immunisation) is the most effective of all preventative health care measures.

Smallpox was a major killer prior to the invention of the vaccination. At the end of the nineteenth century smallpox caused one fifth of all deaths in Glasgow with nine out of ten victims being under the age of five (DOH, 1996). This devastating disease which left those lucky enough to survive severely scarred was the first disease to be vanquished by the newly invented vaccination. Edward Jenner, a country doctor, demonstrated that inoculation with the pus from cow pox blisters immunised against smallpox, the human equivalent of the disease. That Jenner carried out his experiments by purposefully infecting a young child now seems highly unethical but was, for its time, an acceptable methodology. The cow pox pus was obtained from the blisters on the hand of a milkmaid. The cow, Blossom, was immortalised in the name that Jenner gave to his new invention. The word vaccination comes from the Greek for cow – vacca.

The Vaccination Act of 1853 made vaccination compulsory for all infants in the first three months of life with defaulting parents at risk of fines or even imprisonment. Despite the success of the vaccination the public responded with the establishment of the Anti-Compulsory Vaccination League. Political cartoons of the day showed illustrations of people with cow parts growing out of their anatomies. In 1948 compulsion was withdrawn and by 1980 the World Health Assembly accepted that smallpox has been eradicated. Thus, the only vaccination to have been made compulsory by law finally brought to an end the reign of terror of the smallpox disease.

Today in the UK parents have the right to determine whether or not to immunise children against an ever-increasing list of infectious diseases. Just like the population in the nineteenth century, some parents are distrustful of the Immunisation Programme and refuse to vaccinate their children. Adverse publicity, in particular concerning the Measles Mumps and Rubella (MMR) vaccine, was sparked off by the publication of an article in 1998 which suggested a link between the MMR vaccine and autism. Despite positive evidence to the contrary, there was a reduction in uptake from nine out of ten children in 1997 to eight out of ten children in 2003 (Bradshaw and Mayhew, 2005). This fall in uptake has inevitably led to an increase in the incidents of these far from harmless diseases.

The MMR debate has led to the suggestion that the government should once more legislate to ensure that parents are compelled to immunise their children. It has been suggested that some public interventions must be enforced 'because the public cannot be trusted to comply unless there is a degree of compulsion' (Issacs et al., 2004: 393). The removal of parental choice is unlikely to prove prudent politically and it is difficult to believe that a government would risk votes. However, other European countries have made the Immunisation Programme compulsory. Indeed in France, completion of the programme is linked to Child Benefit payments.

One of the underlying tensions here is that health professionals tend to make decisions based on what they feel is best for *all* children, whilst parents tend to make decisions on what they feel is best for their own child. Further, unlike usual medical procedures which are administered to someone who is already ill, vaccination requires that a well child undergoes an unpleasant procedure for an unseen benefit (MacIntyre and Leask, 2003). In the UK, parents fears about immunisations may have been exacerbated by a concern that General Practitioners are paid to reach particular targets for the administration of the Immunisation Programme (General Medical

Council, 2003). As a result, some parents have questioned whether the advice given by them was impartial (Lewendon and Maconachie, 2002).

If professionals are to discuss the safety and efficacy of vaccinations, they must have access to accurate information so that they can respond appropriately to parental concerns (MacIntyre and Leask, 2003). These professionals must be skilled in communicating the issues without emotion, bias or technical language (MacDonald, 2007). This is extremely important as: 'It is every child's right to be protected against infectious diseases. No child should be denied immunisation without serious thought as to the consequences both for the individual and the community' (Department of Health, 1996: 19).

Child obesity

Child obesity is an area of growing public health concern across the Western world and beyond. Indeed, based on findings from national surveys going back over the past twenty years, Matyka and Malik (2008) refer to an 'obesity epidemic'. They claim that by 2010 more than one million children in the UK will be obese if no new action is taken by the medical community. Recently released figures from the Child Growth Foundation (2008) reveal that around one in four five-year-olds in the UK are overweight or obese. It is not yet clear what adult health problems obese children go on to develop but overweight children do tend to become obese adults (Bradshaw and Mayhew, 2005). There are certainly concerns that the rise in the number of obese children worldwide may lead to a reversal in the gains in longevity made over the past one hundred years (Ibid).

In the UK, the issue of childhood obesity has led both to government concern and a media storm (Marshall et al., 2007). As is often the case, the big question seems to be: 'Who should we blame for this latest public health disaster?' For some, poor quality school meal provision is a prime target, while for others the blame is laid solely at the feet of parents. However, like every other aspect of child health, obesity has many causes and assigning the blame without correctly identifying potential interventions is inappropriate.

According to the WHO (2006) obesity is caused by 'an energy imbalance between calories consumed and calories expended'. However, this simple explanation of a complex condition does not adequately identify the reasons why so many children are becoming obese. Numerous explanations have been offered. For example, the 'National Obesity Forum' website suggests that a mother's diet during the ante-natal period predisposes the unborn child to obesity. However, one must consider whether this is due to nature or nurture. Does the mother-to-be who eats unhealthy food during her pregnancy then proceed to feed her child on that same unhealthy diet? Or is the child destined to become obese regardless of his dietary intake?

Young (2005) maintains that childhood obesity is the result of a 'complex inter-action of genetic, environmental and behavioural factors' (2005: 165). One such fac-tor may be television viewing. Jordan and Robinson (2008), for example, cite studies which indicate that as the number of hours spent in front of the television rises so too does the risk of becoming overweight. As children in the USA can spend as many as five hours per day using screen media (Jordan and Robinson, 2008) this is of extreme concern. These data may relate to American children but there is no rea-son to believe that children in the UK are any less vulnerable to excess television use.

Linked to television usage is the idea that the marketing of high fat, salt and sug-ary (HFSS) foods in advertisements screened during children's programming increases 'pester power', with children demanding that their parents buy them unhealthy snacks. A study conducted in New Zealand (Marshall et al., 2007) found that children in the focus groups made clear that the adverts for HFSS food were appealing to them and also made them feel hungry. However, children were found to underestimate their 'power' in persuading their parents to purchase these snacks!

Whatever the causes of obesity are, it is clear that evidence-based interventions are required in order to attempt to defuse this public health time bomb. Part of the UK government's response has been to issue a National Institute of Clinical Excellence (NICE) Guideline for Obesity (NICE, 2006). Published in 2006, the document pro-vides a framework for health professionals to provide interventions to children and their families.

One such intervention is the 'Fighting Fit Tots' pilot programme run in Lambeth as part of the Sure Start initiative. The eleven-week course was for toddlers whose weight placed them on or above the 91st centile (that is, in the heaviest 10% of the population, adjusted for age) and who had at least one parent who was obese. In their report of this course, Wolman et al. (2008) claimed some success, albeit through parental self-reporting. However, Matyka and Malik maintain that despite a growing body of studies relating to childhood obesity, there are, as yet, no 'really effective interventions to provide significant, long term weight loss' (2008: 181).

It is certain that the problem of childhood obesity is not going to disappear and education aimed at children and their families together with non-contradictory advertising and public health messages (Mikhailovich and Morrison, 2007) may be part of the solution.

Children in special circumstances

There are some groups of children who are particularly vulnerable in terms of health and well-being. Child asylum seekers, alone and often unable to communicate with officials, are an extreme example of this group. In order to be officially recognised as a refugee a child must be judged to have left his or her country, 'owing to a well founded fear of being persecuted for reason of race, religion, nationality, membership of a particular social group or political opinion' (Home Office,1999: Section 11).The assumption is, therefore, that a child has already suffered enormously prior to their arrival in the UK. This is well illustrated in the words of one child refugee who stated: 'I was running away from death' (Thomas et al., 2004). Indeed Thomas et al. (2004) found that some form of violence was the primary reason for flight with 32% of children in their study reporting rape – half of these reporting multiple rapes. Carrying the memories of such traumas it is of no surprise that these children have unique difficulties on entrance to the UK. Many children suffer from Post Traumatic Stress Disorder and may even develop physical illnesses in response to these stresses.

There are other health issues which may need consideration when working with child asylum seekers. Children may present with unfamiliar diseases. Without any previous health surveillance, undiagnosed conditions may be present. Some children may have no idea of how old they are and as malnutrition can have a devastating effect on growth and development, making accurate assessments of chronological age almost impossible. Further, young girls may present with Female Genital Mutilation (FGM) requiring a very sensitive response from her carers. Whatever ethnocentric view we might hold, it is vital to remember that in some cultures FGM is deemed essential in order to ensure a daughter's marriage prospects.

A proportion of refugee children seeking asylum have lived in war torn areas. In 1995, one in every 200 people in the world had been displaced by war or by political oppression (Mandalakas, 2001) and with continuing armed conflict the world over there is no reason to suggest that this number has been reduced. The experience of conflict affects children in a number of ways. For example, these children are less likely to develop a sense of trust. The malnutrition which is a common side effect of war can have a negative impact on cognitive and behavioural functioning throughout childhood which can lead to an increased incidence of psychiatric illness in adulthood (Galler and Barrett, 2001). Malnutrition in the very early years of childhood can also lead to developmental delay, speech and language delay and decreased cognitive functioning. Children malnourished in early childhood display a higher incidence of Attention Deficit Disorder and have irreversibly reduced head circumferences (Kuh et al., 2002).

Adults working with children who are refugees should ensure that they are aware of the many problems faced by those who have lived through such traumatic times at such an influential stage in their development. These children may have left behind families and all reminders of their previous lives and cultures. The almost inevitable behavioural problems that occur should be dealt with sensitively. It is also vital to bear in mind that Article 22 of the UNCRC states that children who enter the country as refugees should have the same rights as those who are born here. However, children who are asylum seekers are not entitled to welfare foods and vitamins, including formula milk, nor are they entitled to a Disability Living Allowance.

Refugee parents may not claim Child Benefit, nor do they receive maternity payments (Home Office, 1999). In this respect it would seem that, within the UK at least, Article 22 is not being met.

Children living in drug-abusing families

In the UK, two to three per cent of all children under the age of 16 are living with a parent who is abusing substances (Advisory Council on the Misuse of Drugs, 2003). During periods of stability – when parents are either drug free or controlling their intake – the impact on family functioning may be minimal. However, any escalation of drug use can undermine this stability. Parental focus often moves from caring for their children to the compulsion to obtain and use illicit drugs. This may lead to lapses in hygiene and inconsistent regard for child safety. The parental preoccupation with sating their own addiction leads to an abandonment of their children. Drug use can compromise a parent's ability to be warm and emotionally responsive to their children and maternal abuse of drugs such as PCP, cocaine and opiates has been linked to insecure and disorganised attachment (Goodman et al., 1999) again causing long lasting damage to the child that may continue to adult life.

Parental drug use often involves families in the child protection system: indeed parental drug and alcohol abuse remains the most likely reason for children to be received into the care system (Barnard and McKeganey, 2004). However, whether it is the drug use *per se* or the disadvantaged circumstances which go hand-in-hand with the problems of addiction that most compromises parenting is not known (Mayes, 1995, cited by National Research Council and Institute of Medicine, 2000). What is certain, is that children of drug abusers are more likely to experience permanent separation from their biological parents than any other group (Barnard and McKeganey, 2004).

Gypsy Traveller children

The Housing Act 2004 describes Gypsies as 'persons of a nomadic nature whatever their race or origin' (Office of the Deputy Prime Minister, 2006: 5). However, this definition is concerned with habitual lifestyle rather than ethnicity. With current difficulties in living a nomadic life, many Gypsies are confined to specific sites and their identity is acquired from their ethnicity.

The Gypsy population appears to have disproportionate health difficulties. These health problems are evident even before birth. A survey carried out by Linthwaite et al. (1983) of 263 mothers identified a stillbirth rate nine times greater than the population as a whole. These findings were supported by a later study which discovered that the perinatal mortality rate in the Gypsy population of 28 per 1000 compared with a rate of 10 per 1000 in the general population (Barry et al., 1989).

Surviving the neonatal period does not ensure good health. Kemp (2003) discovered a higher incidence of Accident and Emergency (A & E) department attendance by children living on a local public site, even when compared to a control group of children from the area scoring highly on deprivation indices. However, this high use of A & E resources may be linked to the difficulties that some Gypsy families experience in registering with a General Practitioner (GP). Indeed, Feder et al. (1989) found that 10% of GPs surveyed would refuse to register a Gypsy in their practice.

The health of Gypsy children is affected by many factors. Frequently sites have very poor amenities with a lack of basic facilities. The children appear to be more prone to accidents and as previously mentioned access to preventative health care may be limited. There are high levels of consanguinity, which can cause a higher than average number of birth defects. One study noted that 38% of children were born to parents who are related (Gordon et al., 1991) while Barry and Kirke (1997) found rates of 19% within the Gypsy community compared with 0.16% in the settled community. Notwithstanding the health risks that such high levels of consanguinity can represent, judgmental attitudes of professionals can prevent the establishment of positive and therapeutic relationships with the families.

When considering how best to improve the health and well-being of children in the Gypsy community it is important to bear in mind that initial access to the community can prove difficult due to the distrust of 'outsider'. Low adult literacy rates mean that written materials are largely irrelevant. However, there have been successful interventions: for example, linking a lay volunteer mother with a Gypsy mother. This project demonstrated improved outcomes which were beneficial to both baby and the family (Fitzpatrick et al., 1997). This study emphasises the need for professionals working with children from the Gypsy community to ensure that they understand their traditions and particular needs in the same way as they would when dealing with any other ethnic group.

Conclusion

The Ottawa Charter 1986 states that 'health is a resource for living, not the object of living. It is a positive concept emphasising social and personal resources as well as physical capabilities' (p. 1). Children themselves relate being healthy to themes such as 'achievement' and 'being involved' (Blair et al., 2003). We have seen that child health is influenced by a variety of factors and there is growing evidence to suggest that communities, relationships and the environment are all important determinants of health (Hall and Elliman, 2006).

Child health and well-being require the commitment of both individuals and organisations; it is, however, the family context of early life that sets the trajectory into adulthood (Wadsworth and Butterworth, 2006). Child health care in the UK has moved from an initial focus on illness and death to a concept of social medicine with the creation of preventive and interventionist activities (Baistow, 1995). The emphasis now is on developing sound evidence-based practice which ensures that the ultimate aim of child health policy, practice and provision is that individuals are able to achieve their true potential at maturity. As Hutchinson (cited by Baistow, 1995) asserted in 1940: 'survival beyond infancy, or an apparent absence of disease are no longer sufficient indicators of child health or predictors of adult health.'

Questions and exercises

1   How would you define health and is this definition based on personal experiences?
2   How do the family and the greater community affect child health?
3   Is the Immunisation Programme 'too important' to leave to parental choice?
4   Is child obesity an issue for child protection?

Further reading

Blair et al. (2003) *Child Public Health*, although written from a medical perspective, contains a useful history of child health within the UK, together with exemplars for practice. Bradshaw and Mayhew (2005) *The Well-being of Children in the UK* (2nd edition) is an excellent resource, providing epidemiological data covering all aspects of childhood. Another text written for health professionals – Hall and Elliman (2006) *Health for All Children* (4th edition, revised) – forms the basis for child health programmes. It is an invaluable tool for anyone working in the field of Early Childhood.

14

INCLUSIVE POLICY AND PRACTICE

Guy Roberts-Holmes

Contents:

- **Introduction**
- **The social model of inclusion**
- **Inequality and poverty as barriers to early years inclusion**
- **Sure Start: increasing early years inclusion through policy**
- **Play as an inclusive approach in the early years**
- **Multi-culturalism and anti-racism**
- **Anti-discriminatory legislation**
- **Practitioner reflection for inclusive practice.**
- **Conclusion**

Introduction

Inclusion is primarily concerned with the politics of social justice. Social justice within early childhood education and care is dependent firstly upon national policies which redistribute wealth across communities and secondly respectful relationships within an early years setting. At a national level socially inclusive policies attempt to promote social justice through the reduction of financial and social inequalities. The Nordic countries' (Norway, Sweden and Denmark) policy of a high tax system, for example, ensures the redistribution of wealth across all communities enabling the provision of high quality universal childcare and education for *all* children and their families (Dahlberg and Moss, 2005).

At an institutional level inclusion refers to children, families and staff feeling that they are accepted and valued. Early years staff must work towards respectful relationships which value all children and their families. Inclusion in early years settings involves increasing the participation of children and families in play and learning (Booth et al., 2006). Barriers to inclusion may be inadvert discriminatory attitudes and practices such as sexism, racism and 'disablism'. An inappropriate emphasis on subject-based learning may also provide barriers to young children's participation. Inclusive practice depends upon staff working with families and children to develop 'a culture of participative collaboration' (Booth et al., 2006: 3). Such a collaborative culture values and respects children's important play and learning experiences that they bring from home.

Inclusion is a much broader concept than a narrow focus upon those children labelled as 'SEN' (Special Educational Needs), important though this is (Jones, 2004). Indeed diversity and difference in an early years setting needs to seen as 'a rich resource to be utilised for the benefit of all rather than as a problem to be overcome' (Booth et al., 2006: 10). Inclusion demands that early years staff are ever vigilant and responsive to the diversity of children and families in their communities. Issues of inclusion and exclusion are constantly shifting and early years staff need to be critically reflective of how they might meet new challenges. For example, recently Islamophobia has seen a significant rise in some UK communities (Pew Survey of Global Attitudes, 2008).

The social model of inclusion

This chapter is informed by a 'social' rather than a 'medical' model of inclusion. The medical model of inclusion focuses upon the individual child and is normally expressed in terms of a child's individual 'needs' or deficit. Within this medical model of inclusion children may be assigned specific labels leading to 'special' and/or segregated and exclusionary provision. In contrast to this individualistic model the social model of inclusion sees difference as being socially constructed. The key to the social model of inclusion is that 'special needs' and disabilities are seen as being *created* by discriminatory attitudes, actions, cultures, and policies (Booth, et al., 2006: 5). Rather than the special need or disability being the problem, the focus of attention is shifted to the discriminatory attitudes. For example, instead of asking whether a disabled child can participate in a mainstream setting, the question should be how can the early years provision be organised in such a way that makes the educational development of *all* children possible (Jones, 2004). This inclusive model is premised upon the vision of an inclusive society of which early years education and care is a part. Hence, when discussing inclusion, this chapter uses the concept of barriers to play, learning and participation, rather than the concept of Special Educational Needs or 'SEN'.

Inequality and poverty as barriers to early years inclusion

At its heart social inclusion is about a reduction of social and economic inequalities (Nutbrown and Clough, 2006). Thus, when analysing issues of inclusion in early childhood it is essential to understand the wider socio-economic and political contexts in which early years settings operate. Inclusion is concerned with the issues of pluralism, diversity and difference and democracy. Social inclusion is also about a reduction in discrimination based upon differences in gender, class, disability, sexuality and age. Therefore, early childhood inclusion has the potential to question, disrupt and challenge traditional power hierarchies within society (Booth and Smith, 2002; Nutbrown and Clough 2006; Robinson and Diaz, 2006).

Within nearly all European countries social inclusion is a central goal of early years education and care policy documents (OECD, 2006). For example, the UK government has described inclusion as 'the keystone' to good practice (DfES, 1998a: 8). Despite some limited success in reducing child poverty in the UK, recent research suggests that child poverty is now on the increase again, with approximately 3.9 million children (one-third) living in poverty (Joseph Rowntree Foundation, 2008). Child poverty matters because it creates a series of barriers to young children's inclusion. These barriers include higher child mortality rates; child abuse; child homelessness; child mental health problems; anti-social behaviour; and poor educational achievement (Bradshaw, 2001; Preston, 2008). In addition, recent research has noted 'a very sharp rise' in the association between educational attainment and poverty (Blanden and Machin, 2007: 19). Hansen and Joshi (2007) have shown that children's attainment is already structured by social class (in other words parental income) at 22 months and this gets more extreme as the child gets older. By the age of three, children from poor families are lagging a full year behind their wealthier contemporaries in terms of cognitive development, social skills and school readiness.

It is important to note that there is nothing 'natural' about the historically high rates of child poverty within the UK. For example, the Nordic countries have very much lower rates of child poverty brought about through decades of sustained financially inclusive policies (Bennett, 2008). On a global scale, millions of young children in the majority world are excluded from basic health care and early education due to poverty (Penn, 2005).

Sure Start: increasing early years inclusion through policy

In England, the UK Government embarked upon Sure Start (DfES, 1998a) as a way of combating poverty and social exclusion amongst young children and families.

Sure Start was designed to deliver a whole range of services to all pre-school children and their families. Sure Start was informed by the EPPE project (Sylva et al., 2003: 5) which stated that 'pre-school can play an important part in combating social exclusion and promoting inclusion by offering disadvantaged children, in particular, a better start to primary school.'

Through the National Childcare Strategy (DfES 1998a), New Labour was committed to affordable and accessible childcare. This was to be achieved through a plethora of initiatives, such as Sure Start in England, particularly directed at disadvantaged areas and lower income families. However, Penn (2007: 196) notes that 'Sure Start has made little or no difference to mothers' employment rates, and therefore to poverty levels'. The Daycare Trust (2008) has noted that despite significant increases in children attending Sure Start projects and Children's Centres, 70% of parents reported a lack of affordable childcare in the last 12 months. For many poorer parents, even with tax credits, finding suitable and affordable childcare for children is difficult because of the 'shockingly high costs of childcare in Britain' (Daycare Trust, 2008: 6). Thus, childcare costs for UK parents of young children can be exclusionary, especially for children under three years old. Dahlberg and Moss point out that 'the Swedish welfare state, with its strongly redistributive regime of high tax levels and universal and generous benefits and services, has been rather successful both in preventing poverty in the first place and in providing accessible and affordable pre-schools to all families who want them' (Dahlberg and Moss, 2005: 42). Over 80% of Swedish pre-schools are provided by local authorities and the remainder, although independent, are publicly funded.

One of the reasons for high childcare costs in the UK is the seven-fold increase in corporate private childcare since 1997 (Penn, 2007). Large nationwide (and international) nursery chains such as Stepping Stones, Nord Anglia, Leapfrog, Jigsaw, Asquith Court, and the Nursery Years Group dominate this growing market (Ball and Vincent, 2001). Currently 58% of Children's Centres pre-schools in England are owned and managed by the private sector and the government 'encourages Sure Start Children's Centres to involve private service providers' (Written Answers, 2007). There is evidence to suggest that such privatisation of early childhood services can lead to increased and exclusionary fees (Penn, 2007). Thus, the development of the privatised childcare market tends to run counter to the government's rhetoric of increasing social inclusion.

Referring to this tension between market led childcare provision and the aspirations of social inclusion, Booth et al. state:

> It is hard to reconcile inclusion as the 'keystone' of government early years policy with policies which encourage competition between settings and parents to shop around to find a setting they prefer, which may be outside of their immediate area. (2006: 14)

Thus, the aspirations of high quality early years settings for all young children are problematic within an increasingly privatised sector. The irony is that increased childcare costs may sometimes exclude the most vulnerable families and young children who are in most need of high quality pre-school education and care.

Play as an inclusive approach in the early years

A tension for early years practitioners is that between the current discourses and practices associated with raising attainment on the one hand and inclusion on the other. Within the attainment discourse, there is a potential danger that the child is assessed and monitored according to a barrage of normalised standards and targets (Nutbrown and Clough, 2006). If a child falls outside these 'norms' then he or she is deemed problematic and is 'pathologised' (Jones, 2004). This contradicts an inclusive philosophy in which difference is seen as contributing to the learning of all. It is sometimes hard for early years practitioners to reconcile these competing discourses.

Play is at the core of an appropriate and respectful curriculum for young children in an early years setting (Moyles, 2005). Play should be valued for its own sake not as something that can be controlled and measured. In England, despite the Early Years Foundation Stage stating that 'play underpins the delivery of all the EYFS' (DCSF, 2008: 8), the Assessment Profile focuses early years' practitioners' attention on targets and individual achievement. Similarly, in Wales, despite its rhetoric of being play focused, the Early Years Foundation Phase is assessment-driven (WAG, 2008). An outcomes-driven curriculum may be perceived to be at odds with a play-based curriculum. Too great an emphasis upon early assessment can be a barrier to young children's inclusion and participation (BERA EYSIG, 2003: 14). Such attention to targets and individual achievement is not the experience in all countries. Denmark, for example, has a minimally prescribed curriculum with an emphasis upon playing and social development (OECD, 2006) whilst New Zealand's *Te Whariki* encourages an holistic approach (Nutbrown and Clough, 2006).

Multiculturalism and anti-racism

Within early childhood, traditional power hierarchies have tended to be located within white, Western, middle-class values. It is claimed that these values have effectively silenced and marginalised minority economic and sociocultural groups (Robinson and Diaz, 2006). Within early childhood education and care there have been various responses and resistances to this. One such movement was the multi-culturalist curriculum of the 1970s and 1980s. The multi-cultural curriculum attempted primarily to educate children about ethnicity and differ-ence. The multi-cultural curriculum was underpinned by the belief that if children knew and understood about different ethnic traditions, religious beliefs and festivals, then they would not hold prejudiced stereotypical views. However, such a multi-culturalist curriculum was superficial and trivialised power relationships, such as racism, between different ethnic groups. The multi-cultural approach began to be derided as a 'somas, saris and steelbands' curriculum (Donald and Rattansi, 1992).

The anti-bias movement (Derman-Sparks, 1989) in the late 1980s and 1990s arose out of dissatisfaction with the multi-culturalist curriculum. The anti-bias curriculum is an activist approach which its proponents claim challenges forms of prejudice such as racism, sexism, ableism/disablism, ageism and homophobia. Dahlberg et al. (1999) argue that without such political reflection and action, early childhood institutions may inadvertently perpetuate the 'normalising' discourses of racism, sexism and dis-ablism, that tend to be found within everyday society. Thus, subconsciously held ideas concerning sexism, racism and/or disablism need to be reflected upon and challenged. The anti-bias movement attempted to actively educate children with an understanding that social problems were based upon issues of power. The anti-bias curriculum also aimed to equip children with strategies to combat bias and improve social conditions for all.

The anti-bias curriculum may be useful at challenging stereotypes held by young children. Research indicates that by the time children enter primary schooling their perceptions of difference tend to conform to and perpetuate those stereotypes and prejudices that dominant in the wider society. Roberts-Holmes (2004) has shown that very young children are aware of ethnicity through their drawing of different hair types while Connolly (1998) demonstrates that young boys and girls are highly competent at negotiating and reworking racialised and sexualised discourses. In a similar manner, Walkerdine (1990) notes in her research that four-year-old boys were capable of exercising sexist power over their female teachers by positioning them within the 'woman as sex object' discourse. Thus, early childhood education and care needs continuously to challenge not only the stereotypes that children bring with them but also the ongoing forms of prejudice and discrimination that children actively create in their social worlds.

Such research adds weight to post-structuralist constructions of childhood, which argues that young children hold power and agency in their narratives and lives (Robinson and Diaz, 2006). Such understandings have encouraged researchers to pay attention to the ways in which children can play an active role in the perpetuation of social inequalities with each other and with adults. Additionally, children are growing up in a world where they have access to technological advances such as the Internet, film and television that have blurred the distinctions between adults and children. Consequently, children are arguably more knowledgeable and less naïve than earlier generations (Buckingham, 2000). Therefore, children are interested in and have a right to be included in discussions concerning broader social inclusion and political issues. Within any discussion of inclusion it is important to understand that children are socially competent and actively involved in the negotiation of their social worlds. Accepting young children's social competency and agency offers an important way forward for early childhood practitioners who wish to engage in critical inclusive professional development.

Anti-discriminatory legislation

Early years practitioners need to be aware of the Single Equality Bill (Home Office, 2006). This Bill combines all of the equality enactments within the UK and provides comparable protections across all equality strands. Those explicitly mentioned include age; disability; gender; race; religion or belief; and sexual orientation. The Bill is intended to simplify the law by bringing together existing anti-discrimination legislation. Thus, the new Equality Bill will up-date and streamline the Sex Discrimation Act (1975); the Race Relations Act (1976); and the Disability Discrimation Act (1995). Legislation such as the Equality Bill are vitally important in raising awareness and challenging attitudes within early years settings. However, legislation can only go so far in motivating people to shift their attitudes. Reflective practice is necessary to make significant and lasting change towards inclusive practice in early years settings.

Practitioner reflection for inclusive practice

There is no doubt that UK early years' policies such as *Birth to Three Matters* (Sure Start, 2002) and the Children Act 2004 have significantly raised practitioners' awareness and understanding of the importance of inclusion. These UK-wide policies spoke with increasing intensity of young children's needs and the importance of multi-agency, 'joined up services' and the importance of early education and care provision. In the light of such intense early years policy development, Nutbrown and Clough (2006) talked to early years practitioners about their understandings of early years inclusion. Despite the policy emphasis upon broad-based inclusion for all children found within the policies, roughly half the practitioners gave responses which could be classified as 'narrow' definitions. These practitioners defined 'inclusion' as an issue solely relating to children with special educational needs or learning difficulties. However, for Booth such a narrow position regarding inclusion is problematic:

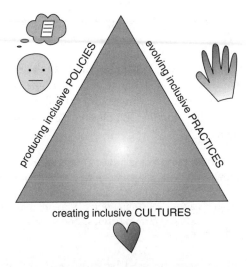

Figure 14.1   Index dimensions (Booth et al., 2006: 2)

> Some continue to want to make inclusion primarily about 'special needs education' or the inclusion of young children with impairments but that position seems absurd ... if inclusion is about the development of comprehensive community education and about prioritising community over individualism beyond education, then the history of inclusion is the history of these struggles for an education system which serves the interests of communities and which does not exclude anyone within those communities. (2004: 64)

This universal community wide approach to inclusion is reflected in the following practitioner's broad understanding of inclusion:

> For us inclusion is accepting each child as an individual – this applies to travelling children, refugees, families in poverty, families from minority religious and cultural groups as well as children with learning difficulties. Inclusion means ensuring everyone works together in the child's best interests to enable them to reach their full potential. (Sue, nursery school head teacher, in Nutbrown and Clough, 2006: 42)

Among some early years practitioners there is considerable anxiety and lack of confidence in their own abilities and knowledge concerning inclusion (Nutbrown and Clough, 2006). Such confidence can, in part, be developed through whole institutional reflective staff development. The Index for Inclusion (Booth et al., 2006) was issued to all early years and childcare settings in the UK and is a useful document to initiate such reflective discussion. Within the Index, reflection of the above issues involves critically examining the cultures, policies and practices of an early years setting as set out in Figure 14.1.

The start of this critically reflective process is the understanding and creation of inclusive cultures: this lies along the bottom of the triangle. This reflective development of shared inclusive values and collaborative relationships can lead to changes that in turn produce inclusive policies within settings. Collaboratively owned policies can then evolve into inclusive practices. Discussion can lead to a transformation of practitioner understanding:

> I learned loads just by reading through the Index – thinking about the questions posed under the different dimensions – there's so much to think about – mind blowing! It's a process that's never actually finished – but it feels very good. It is really about developing relationships – that's what it's about – valuing people enough to make relationships with them and then find ways of working in that richness of diversity. (Janie, nursery teacher, in Nutbrown and Clough, 2006: 123)

The Index contains materials to be used by early years practitioners which focus upon: building community; establishing inclusive values; and orchestrating play and learning. Within the Index there are approximately 50 series of questions. Staff decide what their priorities are and focus discussion upon the relevant series of questions. For example, the following questions from the Index focus practitioners' minds upon collaborating with parents and carers and thus building an inclusive culture with parents/carers in a setting:

a) Do parents/carers and practitioners respect each other whatever their status or whether or not they are in paid work?

b) Do practitioners attempt to form strong links with fathers as well as mothers?

c) Is respect shown for all families, including lone parents/carers, same sex parents/carers, dual and multiple heritage families, large and small families?

d) Are particular efforts made to build strong links with the carers of 'looked after children'?

e) Are all parents/carers well informed about policies and activities?

f) Are all parents/carers involved in decisions about the setting?

g) Do all parents/carers feel that their concerns are taken seriously?

h) Are the fears that some parents/carers have about meeting practitioners recognised and steps taken to overcome them?

i) Is there a variety of opportunities for parents/carers to become involved?

j) Are the different contributions that parents/carers can make equally appreciated?

k) Is there a variety of occasions when parents/carers can discuss their children with practitioners, with and without the children present?

l) Do practitioners value the knowledge that parents/carers have about their children?

m) Are there regular opportunities for parents/carers and practitioners to share ideas about how their children communicate, play and learn in the setting and at home?

n) Are there regular opportunities for parents/carers to share ideas about how children's lay and learning can be encouraged?

o)   Do parents/carers and practitioners have a shared understanding about ways of responding to babies' and children's emotions?

p)   Do practitioners inform parents/carers about any significant events occurring for a child or baby during the day?

q)   Do practitioners and parents/carers share a home-setting record?

r)   Do parents/carers and practitioners collaborate over issues of hygiene, such as head lice, washing and bathing?

(Booth et al., 2006: 54).

Other sets of questions focus upon:

- Practitioners working well together
- Children helping each other
- Ensuring that practitioners link what happens in the setting to children's lives at home; establishing that expectations are high for all children
- That the setting helps children to feel good about themselves.

Working with the Index is not always easy. One practitioner commented that 'it was painful at times. I had to confront and admit some personal prejudices' (Sue, early years nursery nurse, in Nutbrown and Clough, 2006: 45). Practitioners felt that they could only address their prejudices in 'safe' circumstances with other practitioners who were also seeking to be more inclusive in their practices. Through developing a shared dialogue, inadvertent discrimination in an early years setting can be challenged.

Conclusion

The quality of inclusive provision in early years settings is linked to the quality of staff that work in them (Sylva et al., 2003). In contrast to the well-qualified and rel-atively well-paid pedagogues in the Nordic countries, in England the early years workforce is generally under qualified and poorly paid (Miller, 2008). It could be argued that further 'professionalisation' and its concomitant remuneration, is central to developing high quality early years inclusive practice.

In the UK, major policy developments such as *Birth to Three Matters* (Sure Start, 2002); The Children Act 2004 and Sure Start initiatives have impacted on inclu-sive practices and, in specific communities, have brought about high levels of resources. These policies have all acknowledged the importance of early interven-tion to address social exclusion. In the communities where funding has been forthcoming these programmes have addressed a range of inclusive educational, medical, economic and social issues (Nutbrown and Clough, 2006). However, despite recent increases, levels of UK pre-school provision are still much lower than in the Nordic countries. The UK still spends only about 0.4% of GDP on early years provision whereas Sweden spends approximately eight times that amount (Dahlberg and Moss, 2005; OECD, 2006). In the UK childcare is 'a private responsibility exercised through the purchase of private services' in the market place whereas in Sweden there is an entitlement to a state funded pre-school for all children from 12 months upwards (Dahlberg and Moss, 2005: 132). Additionally, Sweden has a strong system of parental leave (including paternity leave) on 80% of normal earnings. There is no doubt that if such a universal entitlement to education and care for all UK pre-school children and their families existed this would help to make inclusion much more of a reality for communities than it currently is. This universal entitlement is fundamentally based upon the politics and principles of inclusion and citizenship as found in the pre-schools of Reggio Emilia in Northern Italy.

Questions and exercises

1   How 'inclusive' are you? Do you believe that everyone should be included in main-stream early years education settings and no child should be excluded – for what-ever reason? Or do you believe that *some* children may necessarily need to be *segregated* from mainstream settings on some occasions?
2   What are the most important aspects of your identity? What more could be done to reflect these aspects of your identity in the institution where you work?
3   To what extent does the early childhood institutional environment reflect the diver-sity of the children's and families identities?
4   What are the most important factors to consider when devising an inclusive prac-tice policy for an early years provision?

Further reading

Tony Booth et al. *Index for Inclusion* (2006) is a valuable set of materials, devised by a multidisciplinary team of professionals, parents, children and disabled people, that guides pre-schools through stages to develop an inclusive environment for all. Caroline Jones *Supporting Inclusion in the Early Years* (2004) is a good introduction to the debates surrounding the inclusion of Special Educational Needs (SEN) children.

Websites

The Alliance for Inclusive Education: www.allfie.org.uk

Centre for Studies on Inclusive Education: www.csie.org.uk

The Equality and Human Rights Commission: www.equalityhumanrights.com

The Working Group Against Racism in Children's Resources: www.wgarcr.org.uk

PART FOUR

DEVELOPING EFFECTIVE PRACTICE

This final part of the book looks at some of the ways in which we can put our understanding of early childhood into practice, and at some of the practical issues that arise in working with young children. The chapters that follow address these themes in different ways and on different levels. Although the focus is on practice, theory still features very strongly. We referred in our initial introduction to Schön (1983) and the 'reflective practitioner'. The reflective practitioner develops his or her theories in practice, by thinking and reflecting on work in progress, and by testing different approaches to see how they work in particular situations. However, she or he does this on the basis of the theories and knowledge that have been developed by others – both other practitioners and academic researchers. The final chapters in this book in their several ways all deal with this relationship between theoretical knowledge and what makes for effective and ethical practice.

In Chapter 15, Bob Sanders presents a model of child observation for students and practitioners. He gives advice on practical arrangements and draws attention to important ethical issues, such as consent. Sanders goes on to explain how the material from their child observation can be used by students and practitioners to extend their understanding of child development.

In Chapter 16, Alison Clark's focus is on research 'with' rather than 'on' children: that is, research in which children are viewed as active participants in the research process. Clark notes that there are particular challenges for those wanting to undertake research of this kind with young children, particularly those relating to language and power. Clark provides two case studies of research studies which set out to listen to children's perspectives before commenting on the impact this kind of research has for the roles adopted by adults and children.

In Chapter 17, Bob Sanders introduces some models of interagency and multidisciplinary working, and shows how they can help to promote effective collaboration in practice with children and families. Sanders looks closely at the advantages and the disadvantages of working together, and at some of the organisational and other barriers to good inter-professional working.

Finally, in Chapter 18, Carol Aubrey discusses effective leadership in early years settings, focusing on the ways in which early childhood leaders may have an impact on worthwhile outcomes for young children. Aubrey begins by examining existing literature before drawing upon research she and her colleagues undertook with early childhood leaders who were willing to explore their own leadership practice. Aubrey draws from this some emergent themes and emphasises, in particular, the current lack of opportunity for continuing professional development in relation to early childhood leadership.

15

CHILD OBSERVATION

Bob Sanders

Contents:

- **Introduction**
- **Setting up and undertaking a child study**
- **Learning from the child study**
- **Conclusion**

Introduction

There are a variety of models of child observation (Fawcett, 1996). Observation may be of the setting, of an individual child, or of a group of children. The focus in this chapter is on observation of an individual child. The aim is to provide the student with an opportunity to link theory and practice in child development.

Some models of child observation make use of a systematic scoring system that records predefined behaviours (e.g., number and targets of verbal communications, patterns of interactions with siblings, frequency of aggressive and prosocial behaviours etc). Observers work with a grid that lists the relevant behaviours and at the end of the observation session the totals of the different types of observed behaviours are recorded. Such models are frequently used by researchers seeking to translate behaviour into data to be analysed.

In another model (Tavistock) observations are followed by extensive and detailed 'process recordings' and the observer is invited to reflect on personal factors within him- or herself that contribute to the observation (Bridge and Miles, 1997). This model highlights observation as an active process of selection and interpretation, rather than as a passive process of recording; one in which we learn not only about the child, but about ourselves. In this model we consider the impact of what we observe on ourselves – our identification with the child's anxiety, our anger or sadness when the child is ignored, hurt or treated with a lack of dignity and respect. Such a model may open channels to reflection on how one's own childhood experiences link to what is being observed. One learns about child development through reflecting on one's own childhood, the childhood of the child being observed, and the relationship between the two. Needless to say, such a model requires a relatively small group in which an atmosphere of trust has been created, before people may be comfortable enough to share.

The model set forth in this chapter is an adaptation of the Tavistock model, but with a more academic emphasis. It relies on a similar methodology of detailed post-observation recording, but uses the observation to understand theories of child development. Within this overall aim, there are three main objectives for the observer:

1   To become familiar with theories of child development and to understand better how children develop, with the emphasis on social, emotional and identity development.
2   To understand the distinctions between observation, evaluation and assessment.
3   To develop an understanding of how contextual factors such as class, gender, race, culture, language and poverty influence child development.

Setting up and undertaking a child study

This child study model requires a minimum of six observations of a child in a pre-school setting – normally arranged with support from a tutor. During the first observation the observer is confronted with an array of behaviour; a good observer will come away with a rich palette of behaviours the child is capable of producing but there will be no sense of which behaviours are typical or atypical for that particular child. During the second observation, the observer is again confronted with an array of behaviours but this time should be able to note which behaviours occurred in only one session and which occurred in both sessions. In other words, the observer is beginning to weave a *pattern* out of the individual units of observed behaviour. But even two is too few: there may be a significance in which behaviour appeared in one or other session; some behaviours may be typical of a particular child but not observed on every occasion; some behaviours may be new, others disappearing. The third observation should begin to give the careful observer a good sense of which behaviours are highly characteristic of this child; which are less frequent, and which are unusual.

It is important that the observer notes behaviours which do *not* occur, as well as those that do. For example, it might be expected that if a child is in the vicinity of another child who is distressed, perhaps because of some slight injury, that the child would engage in some type of prosocial behaviour such as comforting, distracting, or bringing the distress to the attention of a carer. A child who is impervious to the distress of other children may thus display significant 'non-behaviour'.

After the third observation, the observer may begin to develop implicit hypotheses about what the child is like, which types of behaviours might be expected, and which not. The next three sessions enable the observer to test these hypotheses, as well as drawing a richer picture of the child's repertoire by remaining open to new behaviours. By six weeks, the observer should have a good idea of who this child is. The emphasis in ordinary child observation should be on ordinary behaviour; the student should not be actively engaged in looking for pathology or disturbance. The goal should be to achieve a reasonable understanding of who this child is.

Setting up the child study

In this model, the observer is responsible for identifying a target child (aged 1–5) for the study. The tutor does not arrange placements; however, the programme can facilitate the process of negotiating access by students. Letters are sent to local providers of day care and nursery schooling via the local education authority, social services and voluntary organisations such as the Preschool Playgroups Association (and, in Wales, Mudiad Ysgolion Meithrin), informing them of the purpose of the child study and the names of the students who will be undertaking it. The regional office of the National Care Standards Commission is also notified. Second, the observer is given a signed letter of introduction to use when negotiating agreement to observe a child. These steps are taken to create confidence for professionals approached by students that the request is bona fide. It is unfortunate that those who wish to harm children frequently use professional roles as a means to gain access to children and Early Childhood Studies programmes must take precautions not to be used in this way. Police checks are likely to be considered necessary.

The target child should *not* be a child in the observer's family or immediate social network because this can result in uncomfortable complications. For example, students undertaking observations of children frequently become aware that the care provided for children in many settings is less than ideal. The most likely settings to find a child to observe are nursery classes, nursery schools, day nurseries and playgroups but observations can also be undertaken of children in a family centre or with a registered childminder. If the opportunity arises, it may be helpful for group learning if some students can observe children of ethnic minority background, with special needs, or those whose first language is not English (including Welsh-speaking children).

Having identified a setting, the observer then needs to establish contact and explain the request. Initial contact would be with the playgroup or nursery supervisor. In a school setting it would be appropriate to go through the school headteacher. Sometimes writing in advance will enable the supervisor or headteacher to think ahead about the proposal, although this may need to be balanced against the need for fairly quick action.

In addition to the agreement of the pre-school supervisor or nursery teacher, observation of the child can only be undertaken with the agreement of the parent or carer, or person with parental responsibility. There should normally be direct contact with the parent or carer at this stage, although in exceptional cases an observation can proceed with the assurance from the programme supervisor that the parents have consented. The supervisor and parent or carer will need to be assured that information obtained in the study is confidential and will only be shared with others for purposes of learning. All written material will need to be anonymised. Identifying information should not be included, for example, where a parent has a very specific type of employment that would identify him or her.

The child should be told that he or she is going to be observed. Usually this can be in the form of something like: 'I am here to learn how children play and I would like to watch you at play.' This can be in advance, or at the time of the first observation (in advance is preferable). This is not the same as asking the child for consent, as usually children of such an age would be too young to give informed consent, but if the child indicates that she or he is unhappy with being watched, then one should not coax or persuade, but should identify another child for the observation. Mostly children are quite agreeable. Occasionally one learns that a student has not told the child about the observation, and then it is necessary to remind the student that the child will be aware of being watched (no matter how discreet the student may try to be) and that if not given a proper reason which makes sense, they may create fantasies about why they are being watched. This can cause unnecessary worries for the child.

The supervisor and parent or carer should be made aware that the observations are for the student's own learning about child development. Sometimes people may expect the student to provide information about the child, and it is therefore necessary to clarify that it is *not* an assessment. As observation notes are descriptive rather than evaluative, it should not be a problem if parents want to see them. However, it is for the student to decide whether or not to share notes with the parent or carer.

Before the first observation, the following information is needed:

1 About the child – sex, age, date of birth, ethnicity, position in family, physical appearance, personality, relationships with adults and other children, preferred activities.
2 About the family – age and occupation of mother and father and other significant relatives in the home (siblings, grandparents, etc.).

3   About the group setting – type, size, physical conditions, aims, training and attitudes of supervisor and other staff, how the provision fits into the local and national context.

Undertaking the child study

Six one-hour observations should be undertaken. If time and circumstances permit, more may be undertaken. However, observations should not extend beyond an hour; an hour is long enough for sustained concentration and observation. After each session, a full chronological recording should be made of everything observed during the session. This should include what the child does, where the child goes, how long the child spends on different activities, who the child speaks to and interacts with in other ways, etc. Such detailed recording is normally quite time-consuming. Usually, the writing up afterwards will take at least *twice* as long as the time spent observing. It is important to plan for this time; it is no good leaving it for a few days and then expecting the recall of detail to be still there. Do not take contemporaneous notes during the observation sessions because that can distract from observing what is actually happening. If notes are taken, they should be brief.

In this model of observation, rather than attend to the whole range of children's development, the observer is particularly asked to tune into three particular aspects: identity, emotional development, and social development. Therefore, in addition to the descriptive account of the sequence of events, it will be helpful to incorporate observations concerning the child's expression of self, his or her social interactions (including both verbal and non-verbal communication), and any indications of his or her emotional state. The observer should try to be aware of any selective attachments the child has; to whom is the child primarily attached, and how does he or she cope with their absence? One should try to recall and record what is said by the child to whom, and by others to the child, as an indication of social interaction. In all observations one should be alert to class, language, culture, race, and gender influences. After each observation is transcribed, take a moment to reflect on the relevance of theory and research to what has been observed.

Being an observer is a difficult role to undertake, and the observer should make every effort to stay in that role, avoiding interaction as far as possible unless it is necessary for reasons of the child's safety or well-being. *You should not be left in a position of being responsible for the child; primary carers or staff should always be present.* Interactions initiated by the child or other children should be gently discouraged, if necessary by responding in a way that does not invite further interaction but without being brusque, dismissive or unnecessarily abrupt.

If parents, staff or other adults try to interact with the observer during the observation, it may be necessary to remind them of the purpose of the exercise. No matter how much one clarifies the nature of the observation, and attempts to keep one's focus on the child, it frequently happens that those responsible for caring for the child show concern about being watched. They may attempt to engage the observer in conversation about the child; they may ask questions or make statements that show their concern that they themselves are being evaluated! This is understandable because being watched by somebody with whom one has no interaction can cause us to feel threatened and stimulate fantasies about what the other person thinks. One response is to try to pull the observer out of role by engaging them in social interaction. The observer may find it very difficult to stay in role and may have to resist social pressures.

There are also internal pressures. Many students, because of their fondness for children, find it very difficult to be in the presence of children without wanting to get down on the floor and interact. Some actually do get down and play with the children, attempting to engage in 'participant observation' but don't reveal it to the tutor! One of the things that students learn is how much they see as non-participant observers that the carers and staff do not, despite carer and staff efforts to be observant. It is being in the role of a non-interacting observer that enables this to happen.

Sometimes students ask whether the presence of the observer alters the dynamics and therefore creates artificiality in the observation. The answer is of course, yes, the presence of the observer does affect the dynamics. You are watching people who are being watched and who are aware of being watched. There is no attempt to claim objectivity in the observation process. It is not the same, nor is it intended to be the same, as having a video camera installed and watching the child through closed circuit television. Likewise, observation not only affects the person being observed, it also has an impact on the observer. You will often see things that invoke personal memories, or strong attitudes about the way children are or should be treated. This is all part of the process of observation.

The student is encouraged to use 'level of detail' as a criterion for the success of observation. Longer and more detailed notes of observations are more useful in revealing who the child is than brief notes hastily assembled afterwards. The more one sees of what is happening before ones eyes, the better informed will be the evaluations and conclusions that may eventually be based on those observations. A very good example of detailed observation is provided by O'Hagan (2006) in his description of the emotional indicators in children. Consider this description of an interaction between two children, Hemlata (age 6) outside the house, and Misha (the target child, age 21 months, inside the house):

When Hemlata reaches the window, she bends down and scoops two handfuls of snow from the grass. She holds them up to Misha; they form a little miniature mountain of snow stretched across the palms of her hands. Misha and her mum smile. Then Hemlata does something unexpected: she draws both arms back and throws the contents straight at Misha. Misha is a little startled. She sees the snow coming at her and disintegrating into hundreds of pieces, and amazingly, making no noise as it crashed into the window. Misha stiffens a little against her mother. She then relaxes and scrutinizes the consequences of her sister's action. (O'Hagan, 2006: 86)

Consider how much more detail there is than might be contained in a simple sentence, 'Her sister threw some snow at the window, and Misha recoiled a bit.'

Learning from the child study

In the model described here, child observation is combined with a series of lectures on theories of child development and a series of seminars in which students reflect on their observations. In these seminars each student presents at least one of their observations to the rest of the class, who are expected to contribute their own ideas to help understand the behaviour of the child who is being presented. Students have a collective responsibility for their own learning, and in particular for drawing on relevant theory to help understand the child's behaviour.

In the Swansea programme the focus of discussion in the seminars has included the following themes.

Approval seeking

Children can often be seen engaging in behaviour that they know will be approved of by adult caretakers. If they don't spontaneously get it, they will sometimes approach the carer to ensure that they have been noticed:

George (fictitious name), after seeing the teacher congratulate another child on her hard work, brings his drawing up to the teacher to see. 'Well, I worked hard too!' he says.

Attachment

There are at least two ways in which the issue of attachment emerges in the child studies. First, it emerges in the children's attachment to their primary caretaker, usually a parent. This may be observed in how children separate from, or are reunited with, their primary carers at the beginning and end of the day. Sometimes students will vary the time of their observation on occasion in order to be able to observe how the child deals with these events. These separations and reunions mirror the three-minute episodes in Ainsworth et al.'s (1978) 'strange situation' procedure designed to measure attachment. An important consideration for those children showing some level of distress at the separation is how long does it take for the child to develop a sense that reunions follow the separations, and a sense that the place where the child is being left is not quite so threatening as might have been imagined on the first day.

The attachment to the primary carer can also be seen in the way children recreate within the setting play, stories, and events which recapture for them the absent parent:

> Gemma was seen to start a flying game. It emerged that her father has his own plane.

A second sense in which attachment emerges is in the way in which children become attached to their temporary carers in the classroom or nursery. In time children build up very strong bonds, which are linked to their initial insecurity and become more apparent whenever anxiety is heightened:

> Alice was noted to be very 'clingy with the teacher'.

> Sharon appears to be very aware of the teacher all the time.

> Alun showed a look of concern when the teacher left the room.

Continuity of behaviour

Another important theme arising is continuity in children's behaviour. This arises in two senses: (a) continuity between how the child behaves at home and in the out-of-home setting and (b) continuity between how the child behaves at different times. This usually will be related to concepts of identity and consideration of the relationship between psychological and social identity – between an inner sense of self as continuous and a sense of self derived from social context which may be experienced somewhat differently in the various settings where a child may be:

> The observer noted a 'difference between how he is described by his parents (boisterous and outgoing) and how he appears to be in the group (reserved, almost isolated); in this session, he behaved differently; today, he has been quite aggressive …'

> The observer refers to speculation as to why Sharon might have been so different today; comparison was made with how she had been on previous occasion (quiet).

Dominance

A frequently seen aspect of children's interactions are the means they use to achieve dominance. James (1998) suggests that in children's play there are universal themes relating to children constructing and reconstructing power relations between people. Children adopt devices to get other children to comply with their wishes, and on occasion to avoid having to comply with the wishes of others. One strategy is to enforce recognised authority, exemplified by children who try to play the role of helper to those in charge; often such children's interactions with the staff tend to reinforce those roles. In other situations, children may simply try to bully others to comply. In pre-school situations, overt bullying is much less likely to go unnoticed by staff than in school; but there are covert means that children adopt to gain the compliance of others.

> Emma tells girl to wash herself; Emma is in control and in charge; She … takes over, and counts out the pieces … 'You can have these.' Emma thumps Rebecca on the arm quite violently and then walks away; Emma hits Rebecca and tells her to play properly.

> Anna shouted across the room to a little girl to get on with her work; bossing the others around … wagging her finger at the other girls.

Gender

It is inevitable that at some point seminar discussions will focus on gender. There are contentious and complex issues one needs to address. One is the balance between 'nature' and 'nurture' in determining gender characteristics; students sometimes overestimate the effect of genetics and underestimate the influence of environment. Even when the influence of environment is appreciated, one may struggle to see how in relation to the observed child the influence of other children and adults often serves to reinforce stereotypes about the ways in which boys and girls are supposed to behave. Statham (1986) notes how parents who strive to bring their children up with non-sexist values find much of their work is undone when children's social worlds expand with their entry into school – likewise with pre-school:

> Alex was seen as odd because he likes dressing up in girls' clothes when they have the drama session.

The following extract reminds us that this is an age when strong gender association patterns emerge. In part this may be because of common interests; in part it may be for other reasons:

> Boys go to the lego/popoid play area, and the girls go the stick-and-paste area.

> Jane gets on with the other girls in the class, but not so much with the other boys; they shout a lot; she is in the playhouse with four other girls.

> Maria and Sharon return to the home area to tidy it.

> Alice (NG): playing in an all girl group; one of the boys is the doctor … The other girl is the patient and Alice is a nurse.

Physical behaviour

Children are often much more physical than adults, and one may tune into the things that children do that would be frowned upon if done by an adult. For example:

> Emma scratches herself a lot; she has a habit of sticking her hands down the back of her tights.

> Megan plays with her hair a lot; scratches herself; during the story she is fidgety, and sticks her fingers in her mouth.

Sarah sitting cross legged on the floor, playing with her hair ... Sometimes during the session she leans on her knees and elbows ... Later she sits on a chair with one legged crossed over the other in a way that [Observer] considers to appear very grown up.

Observer role

The importance of making the child aware of the observation has already been noted. In some cases students, supported by staff, have thought it better not to inform the child. As often as not the child can work out what is happening; the child enters a distinctive relationship with the observer – the watcher and the watched:

> Alun was not told that he in particular would be observed; selected by teacher for the observation 'as an interesting specimen'.

> Teacher did not tell Megan that she in particular was being observed, although the class were told; Megan comes over to talk to [Observer]; she smiles at Megan.

> A girl comes up to Emma and tells her that the observer is watching her; they both look in the direction of observer.

Sometimes children may play a game, putting themselves in places where they cannot be seen and then looking to see if the observer is still watching, as if to say 'you can't see me now ... now you can'. As previously noted, there are forces that work to pull one out of the observer role, both from staff and from other children:

> Alex looks at observer, which is the first sign he shows of being aware of her; another child comes and stares at [Observer] which distracted her to the extent of losing concentration on Alex.

Prosocial behaviour

Examples of children demonstrating concern for others can be frequent even in a short period of observation. It is important to be aware of this, in order to counter-act a tendency to emphasise negative and disruptive behaviour rather than behaviour that serves to promote social interaction, facilitation and support:

Sarah showed a new child who was just up from the nursery class how to play with trains.

Greg draws the teacher's attention to a little girl who has a runny nose, and the teacher tends to it.

Billy appears concerned when John fell over and hurt himself.

Peer relationships and friendships

Observations of social interactions are an important feature of child study and sometimes a cause of concern for carers or observers. Sometimes a child's lack of relationships may be of concern; sometimes carers may be concerned about particular associations:

Billy has a very close friend John; they are together during registration; 'like being attached by a string'; why do the leaders want to separate Billy and John?

Carl's verbal interactions with other children were very low; 95% of the time playing on his own; he doesn't have a best friend, but he is quite close to the male carer; he watches the children playing, but does not get involved ... [Observer] wondered whether he should be interacting more with the other children.

Alex was quite introverted and did not interact well; he has no mate in class. He is involved with one boy and they are play-wrestling.

Sarah gives a lot of attention to her friend; she has friends but not one particular friend in the class; hasn't sat next to the same girl twice throughout the sessions.

Paul has a relationship with another child (Ellen) which the teachers are trying to discourage; they are trying to keep Paul and Ellen apart.

Socialisation

Evidence usually emerges in observation about how children are socialised to behave 'correctly'. Values of courtesy, tidiness and self-control begin at home and are generally continued within the out-of-home setting. One sees various indicators of the way children are taught 'proper' behaviour. It is sometimes interesting as well to look for children who are 'over-socialised', who have integrated so strongly the messages of self-control that they have sacrificed their spontaneity, individuality, and rebelliousness. The 'self' here has become submerged under an idealised notion of 'proper' behaviour. Idealised notions of self can be a source of considerable psychological stress in adults. One may find oneself hoping that the child will show some sign of breaking out of the constraints that bind her. These observations can lead to very interesting discussions about different conceptions concerning the 'true' nature of children (e.g., innately good, in need of drawing out versus innately wild, in need of controlling). This may also lead to discussion of the application of external controls leading to the internalisation of controls, and the development of fears about what might happen if things get out of control. Several children's books are very relevant to this theme: for instance *Super Dooper Jezebel* by Tony Ross, and *Where the Wild Things Are* by Maurice Sendak.

> Barry was very concerned about mess – glue.
>
> Pamela tells girl to wash herself; she then bangs two figures on the floor 'Stop it you two! Behave!'
>
> Alice was clearly shocked by the new girl's tantrum.
>
> Emily is not naughty or disobedient.

Other themes

These are some of the main themes that have emerged from observations, showing how they can provide students with a strong foundation from which to discuss and learn about issues in child development. Some other issues that have cropped up are: the types of play that children engage in; children being disciplined and how; the exertion of adult authority; how much of what is observed is down to temperament, character, or personality. This is not an exhaustive list of the potential material that might emerge from child observations. The range of themes and issues is as varied and wide-ranging as are children themselves.

Conclusion

Child observation as a method has been found to be an effective means to facilitate student learning. In this chapter I have described the value of the approach in relation to integrating child development theory with the observed behaviour of the child. The chapter described how to set up and undertake the observation, and discussed some of the themes that have emerged from observations previously undertaken by students. The developmental focus of this particular approach has been on the social, emotional and identity dimensions of children's growth and development.

Questions and exercises

1   It is suggested in this chapter that very young children cannot give 'informed consent' to being the subject of observation. What do you understand by 'informed consent' in this context? Do you think that children should be asked to agree to being observed? Can you think of difficulties, other than those described here, that

might arise if the observation is undertaken without informing and seeking the approval of the child?

2   Many of the comments made in the chapter about the children being observed are *normative* – children are described as showing some behaviour more or less than they 'should'. Do our values and assumptions get in the way of seeing children objectively, or do they help in giving us a focus?

3   The following is from O'Hagan 'Imagine you are an infant aged 20 months. Attempt to describe what it is like to be taken to a swimming pool for the first time. What do you develop in terms of your own developing perception (tactility, space, permanency of objects/bodies, etc.), attention and intelligence? (2006: 93).

Further reading

Clearly there are too many texts and journals that deal with child development to begin to list them here. You are advised to ensure you have access to a good overview child developmental text (for example, Helen Bee, *The Developing Child*, in the latest edition, as it is frequently revised and updated).

Crain (1992) is a useful outline of a number of theoretical approaches to understanding how children develop. Barnes (1995) is one of a series of Open University texts that are a very useful source of information on how children develop and is especially relevant for the themes developed in this approach to child observation. Beaty (1998) is a very useful book for highlighting the link between what one may observe in young children and theoretical considerations. Durkin (1996) is also good for its focus on the less tangible aspects of children's development, in particular their social development.

You may find it useful as well to look at some of the literature on the process of child observation. Fawcett (1996) provides an overview of the different methods of child observation. Bridge and Miles (1997) give examples of observations undertaken by students using the Tavistock approach.

16

UNDERTAKING RESEARCH WITH CHILDREN

Alison Clark

Contents:

- **Introduction**
- **Research 'with' not 'on' children**
- **Research with young children**
- **Case studies**
- **Roles in research**
- **Conclusion**

Introduction

This chapter sets out to provide an introduction to undertaking research with children and, in particular, young children under five years old. The focus will be on qualitative research methods. The chapter will discuss some of the characteristics of research 'with' rather than 'on' children. This will be followed by a brief exploration of a number of challenges and possibilities of carrying out research with young children. A chapter of this length cannot provide a comprehensive investigation of this important subject. Rather, it is intended as a pointer to a number of key issues which can be followed up in volumes dedicated to research methodology with children (e.g., Grieg and Taylor, 1999; Lewis et al., 2004; Christensen and James, 2008) and to individual research studies referred to in the text.

Research 'with' not 'on' children

Continuing interest in the sociology of childhood (see Chapter 3) has led to an increasing number of research studies which seek to understand children's own experiences of their everyday lives (e.g., Thomas and O'Kane, 1998; Candappa, 2002). This research paradigm focuses on research 'with' rather than 'on' children (Fraser, 2004). The differences are rooted in how children are viewed in the research process. Do researchers view children as passive research objects on whom research is carried out or as active participants in the research process, sharing in what is being studied, the control of research tools and in what happens next as a result of the research?

At the beginning of their book on research with children, Christensen and James (2008) explore a range of views about children which have been adopted by developmental psychologists. Within this discipline, Christensen and James identify the 'closely observed child' and the 'test tube child' (2008). The closely observed child might be the focus of intense observation in the same way as a wildlife documenter might observe animals from a hide:

> Observers may be found backed up against the corner of a classroom or playground trying to ignore children's invitations to join in the game, kidding themselves they can appear as a metaphoric fly on the wall. (2008)

A researcher setting out to observe three- and four-year-olds would probably encounter particular difficulties in trying to convince an enquiring group of young children that the researcher was in fact 'not there'. This particular form of non-participant observation is only one of a number of ways in which to undertake observations of children. Different approaches to observation will be discussed later in this chapter.

Christensen and James also illustrate their second category, the test–tube child, in which children are placed under a research 'spotlight' under laboratory conditions. They encapsulate this way of viewing children in research by referring to a photograph of the developmental psychologist, Arnold Gessell, undertaking research on a baby. The young child is seated within a glass dome. Gessell is standing in front of the child, dressed in his white laboratory coat. The photograph shows two other adults within the frame: a note taker and a cameraman (in addition to the photographer who captured this image). Two of the questions to be asked in interpreting such a scene might be: whose world is being explored here? Who is on strange territory, the researcher or the child?

Research which sets out to undertake research 'with' rather than 'on' children might, by contrast, be identified as research in which the *researcher* sets out to understand more about children's worlds by entering unfamiliar territory. This can involve learning directly from children on their own 'home ground' which may include a range of environments including a nursery (e.g., Clark and Moss, 2001; 2005), a residential children's home (Emond, 2005) or a local neighbourhood (e.g., Hart, 1979; Percy-Smith, 2002).

Research with young children

There are particular challenges for those who are setting out to involve young children in research. This section will examine some of these challenges. The issues discussed are not unique concerns to the field of early childhood research. There are many other research groups whose ways of communicating challenge research strategies based on the written communication. One such example is non-literate communities in the Majority World (see, for example, Holland and Blackburn, 1998). However, the factors discussed below can be accentuated in the case of young children, particularly if the research participants are pre-verbal or have limited apparent verbal skills.

Languages

Establishing modes of communication between the researcher and the research participant is central to many qualitative research studies (Fraser, 2004; Christensen and James, 2008). Carrying out an interview, for example, relies on the researcher being able to express her questions in a way which conveys her meaning clearly without forcing a hoped-for response (Hatch, 1990). Misunderstandings can abound whatever the age group of the participant but there are particular complexities related to the thinking and language skills of young children.

The following is an example of misunderstanding taken from a research study with a group of three- to five-year-olds about their outdoor play space (Clark, 2005; Clark and Moss, 2005). The researcher was interviewing a group of children whilst they were all sitting outside in a play house:

> The question was: 'What is missing outside at [your preschool]?' Some of the children's responses were more literal than anticipated. Children … answered 'the window'. The perspex was missing because a vandal had broken the pane and it had been removed.
> (Clark and Moss, 2005: 102)

This was a sensible answer in the context in which the researcher had asked the question but was a very different response than was anticipated. The research question appeared simple but was in fact asking the children to understand the term 'missing' in a particular way: 'In view of your experience of this and other play spaces what resources or opportunities should be added to this pre-school's outdoor space?' (Clark and Moss, 2005: 102).

This last example illustrates the link between language and context in establishing meaningful communication between young children and researchers. A child who appears to be 'non-verbal' or using few words in the research environment may in fact be talkative at home or in another setting (see, for example, Wells, 1986). This may especially be the case for children for whom English is an additional language (see, for example, Brooker, 2002). Cousins (1999) in her research which focused on listening to four-year-olds, discusses several examples where the children's spoken contributions to the research were influenced by where the conversations took place. She describes a four-year-old boy, Dean, who had not talked to anybody during his first two weeks in his reception class:

> By chance, I watched him in the playground and saw Dean bend down and peep through the railings to look longingly at his old nursery. The children were just going out for a walk and I could see big tears rolling silently down his cheeks. (1999: 25)

Cousins asked Dean if he would like to visit his old nursery and with the permission of his teacher the researcher and child made a visit together:

> The change in Dean when we stepped through the nursery door was instantaneous and I captured it all on my mini-tape recorder.

> The children were still out having their walk, so Dean rushed round and round the nursery touching familiar toys and looking in cupboards and on shelves. He talked non-stop and when he spotted the indoor pond full of fish and tadpoles he remembered all the details of going to collect them and building the pond with his nursery nurse…. (1999: 25)

These examples highlight the importance of considering how language is used, and the context in which it is used, to enable young children to be involved in research (see Morrow and Richards, 1996, for a discussion of the importance of context when conducting research with older children). This leads to the question of whether babies and older non-verbal children can be active participants in research rather than passive research objects. An important starting point in such cases is to begin by establishing the modes of communication used by each individual child, whether this is a baby or an older child with disabilities. This tuning in to each child's preferred ways of communicating may require considerable effort, patience and imagination on the part of the researcher (see, for example, Davis et al., 2000).

These concerns draw attention to the importance of respect within the research relationship between the researcher and the research participant. This notion of respect is one of the characteristics of research which sets out to work 'with' rather than 'on' children.

Power

Research can be understood in many ways. One interpretation is to see research as being about the revealing and handling of knowledge which in turn has an impact on the creators, gatherers and distributors of that knowledge. Research involving young children has the added complication of involving a generational imbalance of power between adult and child (Alderson and Morrow, 2004; Robinson and Kellett, 2004). When a researcher walks into a setting to begin a study she carries the twin advantage of being an adult and a 'knowledge collector': the bearer, perhaps, of a notebook or lap top and audio recorder. This impression can be heightened, the younger the age group of the research participants. Awareness of the power divide can be the starting point for efforts to attempt to lessen these gaps in order for more honest communication to take place (see below). However, adult researchers still remain the most powerful players in the research process. This highlights the importance of considering the ethical implications of undertaking research with young children. Alderson and Morrow (2004) identify ten topics to consider in ethical research which includes a focus on the purpose of research, considering questions of privacy and confidentiality, consent and the impact of research on children (2004: 137–42).

Case studies

This next section draws on examples of two research studies with young children. The studies illustrate different ways of engaging with the challenges of language and power posed by undertaking research with young children. Both studies seek to listen to young children's perspectives about their everyday lives. The first carried out by a Danish researcher, Hanne Warming, explores participant observation as a means of listening to young children (Warming, 2005). The second study involving the Mosaic approach (e.g., Clark and Moss, 2001; Clark, 2004; Clark and Moss, 2005) uses participatory, visual methods to involve young children in the process of building a new nursery (Clark, 2008).

Case study one: participant observation

Observation can cover a range of different approaches to research ranging from a detached 'invisible' observer described earlier to a 'total immersion' strategy whereby the observer seeks to join in or participate in the lives of those being observed. Warming describes the aim of 'participant observation' as to 'learn about "the other" by participating in their everyday life' (2005: 51). This is one of a number of interpretations of 'participant observation' (Adler and Adler, 1987; Atkinson and Hammersley, 1998).

The aim of Warming's study was to find out from young children about what an ideal life in early childhood provision would look like. She decided in this study to choose participant observation as the research method which fitted her research aims:

> Participant observation would allow me to study children's interactions with each other, with pedagogues and with the physical surroundings, whereas interviews would only allow me to study narratives about these interactions, producing a construction of children's cognitive perceptions of *det gode børneliv* contextualised by the interview process itself. (2005: 54)

The study carried out in a *børnehave* or kindergarten in Denmark involved Warming joining in the children's everyday lives. Warming explains:

> This participant role means the researcher makes an effort to participate in the children's everyday life in the kindergarten, and as far as possible in a way like the children do: play with the children, submit to the authority of the adult carers, abdicating from one's own adult authority as well as from one's own adult privileges. (2005: 59)

This approach can been seen as choosing to take a 'least adult' role (Corsaro, 1985; Mandell, 1991a; Thorne, 1993; Mayall, 2000). This is one way of engaging with the question of power in relation to undertaking research with young children. However, as Warming states, the differences between adults and children cannot be removed but perhaps reconsidered and renegotiated through this research approach.

Spending time in the research setting immersed in the everyday routines of the young children's lives revealed several different sources of information for piecing together what were the significant ingredients of a 'good life' for the children in the setting. These pieces relied on different languages or modes of communication. Several sources of research material emerged from listening to children's talk with each other and their pedagogues together with conversations with the researcher. However, how children moved around the space and expressed their feelings through a range of non-verbal communication also formed a rich source of information. Warming describes this as 'listening with all the senses' (2005: 55). Participant observation thus provided more than one method for engaging with the research question.

Listening to young children through participant observation can be seen as one way of addressing the questions of power and language discussed. Warming presents the case for listening through participant observation as a form of giving voice to young children's perspectives in contrast to listening as a way of understanding:

> Giving voice involves listening, whereas listening does not necessarily involve giving voice. Listening as a tool requires hearing and interpreting what you hear, whereas giving voice further requires 'loyal' facilitation and representation, making common cause with children. (2005: 53)

Case study two: the Mosaic approach

This second case study illustrates another possible research strategy for undertaking research with young children. The Mosaic approach is a framework for viewing young children as competent, active explorers of their environment. It has been developed by Alison Clark and Peter Moss as a research tool for listening to young children's perspectives (see Clark and Moss, 2001; Clark, 2004; Clark and Moss, 2005). The approach has since been adopted by other researchers and practitioners in the UK and abroad (e.g., see Einarrsdottir, 2005). There are links between this approach and the idea of 'documentation' promoted in the pre-schools of Reggio Emila in Northern Italy (Clark, 2005: 29–49).

The Mosaic approach is based on the following view or understanding of children and childhood:

- Young children as 'experts in their own lives' (Langsted, 1994)
- Young children as skilful communicators
- Young children as rights holders
- Young children as meaning-makers (Clark and Moss, 2005: 5–8).

The Mosaic approach (see Figure 16.1) uses several different ways of listening to young children – the tools of observation and interviewing together with participatory tools. These are tools in which the children are actively involved in expressing their perspectives. These include using cameras to take their own photographs, making books of their images, taking adults on tours and recording the tours themselves, making maps and responding to images of other spaces (the magic carpet). The approach is designed to be flexible to allow for other methods to be used according to individual children's strengths or needs. The emphasis is placed on the researcher adjusting to the modes of communication preferred by the children rather than those in which the researcher is most comfortable.

The adoption of digital photography as one of the research tools controlled by the children is one example of how young children have been 'placed in the driving seat'. During the first study in which the Mosaic approach was developed during 1999 and 2000, children took their photographs using single-use cameras. However, by the third study which began in 2004 many of the young children involved became more confident in using the digital camera and photo printer than the researcher! The introduction of visual methods, using both types of camera, opened up different possibilities for young children to document their experiences. Part of the value appears to relate to the cultural status of photographs :

Cameras offer young children the opportunity to produce a product in which they can take pride. Children who have seen members of their family taking photographs, pored over family albums or looked at photographs in books and comics, know that photographs have a value in the 'adult world'. This is not always the case for children's own drawings and paintings. (Clark and Moss, 2001: 24)

One of the research tools in the Mosaic approach is map-making using children's own photographs and drawings (see, e.g., Clark and Moss, 2001: 28–31; Clark and Moss, 2005: 39–43). This documentation can make children's perspectives visible in a way which can open up conversations with peers, practitioners, researchers and parents. The following example is taken from the Spaces to Play project, the second study undertaken by the authors of the Mosaic approach to involve young children in the redesign of an outdoor play space (Clark, 2005; Clark and Moss, 2005; Clark, 2007). Two three-year-olds, Ruth and Jim had been engaged in leading the researcher on a tour of their play space whilst they recorded the tour with photographs. Ruth and Jim met shortly after the tour to make a map using their chosen images and drawings. During this activity a visitor came to see the study in action:

Ruth:	This is a very pretty map.
Researcher:	It's a very pretty map. You know, it tells me such a lot about outside. Shall we see what Gina can see on our map? Gina, what do you think about our outside…
Gina:	I can see that Ruth and Jim have very special things outside. I can see that you chose the prams and the buggies, and I can even see you in the picture so I know you like playing with those things, maybe. And, Jim, your favourite thing … I think you're favourite thing outside might be the train. Yes? And can we have a picture of you outside with the train.
Ruth:	What do I like?
Gina:	You tell me what you like. Do you like Heather [member of staff] with the climbing frame?
Ruth:	No, I like going on.
Gina:	Oh, you like going on the climbing frame.

(Extract from Clark, 2005: 43–4)

Ruth relished the opportunity to be in control of the conversation and the meaning-making. She had been the one to ask the visitor for her interpretation of what she saw and took delight in contradicting the adult's interpretation. The power differences between adults and children are not removed by conducting research with children in this way but spaces are created within the research encounters which enable children to demonstrate their expertise.

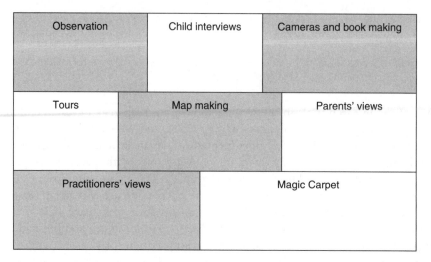

Figure 16.1   An example of methods brought together in the Mosaic approach
Source: Clark, 2005

Roles in research

This final section raises some questions about the roles of children and adults when research is undertaken with children. If the roles which children play within research are expanded there is a subsequent impact on the role of the researcher, other adults and at times, the research audience.

The roles of children in research

The case studies above illustrate some ways in which children can be active partici-pants during fieldwork. Alderson and Morrow (2004) have been among those to raise the question of how children, including young children, can be actively involved before and after fieldwork takes place – in setting the research agenda and in the analysis, writing up and dissemination. Kellett's work on children as researchers (e.g., Kellett, 2005) has raised new possibilities for how children can take responsi-bility throughout the research process. When the research participants are under five the term 'children as co-researchers' may be interpreted differently. The aim would not be to make young children into mini-adult researchers but to reinterpret the role in ways which demonstrated young children's competencies. In terms of setting research agendas, it is far easier for young children to influence the topic explored in an action research model of research in which the local knowledge of adults and children is valued (see, e.g., Reason and Bradbury, 2006).

There perhaps needs to be a note of caution here: that is, in assuming that every child will want to be engaged with research. As Roberts remarks:

> It cannot be taken for granted that more listening means more hearing or that the cost benefits to children of participating in research on questions which they may or may not have a stake is worth the candle. (2000: 229)

This warning applies whatever the age of children involved. A research study may not be of particular interest to individual children or may be seen as an invasion of their time. Roberts continues:

> we need to be clear when it is appropriate for us to ask young people to donate time – one of their few resources – to researchers and when it is not. (2000: 257)

Role of the researcher

Undertaking research with young children can release researchers from some responsibilities but at the same time add new dimensions to their role. A researcher who shares power with children is relinquishing the need to 'know all the answers'. This can be a relief: research seen in this way is not about gathering further evidence of what is known but expecting new ways of understanding to emerge. The role of 'adult as enquirer' may be at odds with the role children expect of adults. If the research context is one which highlights the role of adults as experts then this contrast may be marked. This may be the case for many children who take part in research in educational and health settings if the adults in these institutions are normally seen as the 'experts'.

A further freedom for researchers may emerge through the use of a wider range of 'languages' within the research process. Visual methods, for example, described in the second case study above, may open up new modes for communication for the researcher as well as for the research participants (see Pink, 2007; Thomson, 2008). This may lead to alternative approaches for researchers to record their research experience and to disseminate their findings.

But undertaking research with young children places different ethical responsibilities on researchers (e.g., see Farrell, 2005; Harcourt and Conroy, 2005). One particular concern when working with young children rests on how research findings are disseminated. Sharing conference platforms with young children may not be an appropriate use of their skills and time. However, this increases the importance of the researcher's role as mediator of the children's experiences.

Role of practitioners and parents

Research with young children needs to be viewed in context. Young children spend the majority of their time with adults and therefore research which seeks to understand their lives will also encounter adults, whether they are family members, practitioners or friends. There is a particular advantage in involving parents and practitioners in research with the youngest children, those under three, as their knowledge of the fine details of children's lives will add important perspectives to research undertaken (e.g., see the case study of Toni, age 22 months in Clark and Moss, 2001: 38–41).

Research into the everyday lives of young children in early childhood environments raises questions about the experiences of practitioners. These spaces are shared spaces in which adults and children spend many hours each week together. One possibility is that the principles which can be applied for engaging with young children in participatory research can also be explored with practitioners. Such ideas have been investigated in a three-year study, Living Spaces, which set out to involve young children and adults in the design and review of a nursery and Children's Centre (Clark, 2008). Here the visual, participatory methods have supported teachers, early years professionals, health workers and students to explore: 'What does it mean to be in this place?' This perhaps indicates that rather than discussing the need for child-friendly methods it is more a question of seeking 'participant-friendly methods' which enable participants of different ages and abilities to communicate their perspectives (Fraser, 2004: 25).

Conclusion

This chapter has considered some of the ways in which children and in particular young children, can be involved in research. It has highlighted two areas, in particular, which need to be addressed in undertaking research with young children, those of language and power. These in turn raise issues concerning the ethics of research. Once children are involved in research the roles of adults are changed in some way, whether they are acting as researchers, practitioners or as a research audience. This is one indication of why developments in this area may have wide implications for the undertaking of social research in general. Early childhood researchers, practitioners and students have important contributions to make to these debates.

Questions and exercises

1   How can researchers 'play to the strengths' of young children in developing methods which enable young children to communicate their views and experiences?

2   What research strategies would you suggest to take into account the power divide between researchers and young children?

3   What possible disadvantages for young children can you see if more research is conducted which elicits their views and experiences?

Further reading

Lewis et al. (2004), *The Reality of Research with Children and Young People* is an accessible volume which seeks to ground discussions about how to carry out research with children and young people with specific case studies written by researchers. Each chapter is accompanied by a short reflective commentary. *Spaces to Play: More Listening to Young Children Using the Mosaic Approach* (Clark and Moss, 2005) is a short volume which offers a way in to undertaking research with young children. The process of using a multi-method approach is demonstrated from the initial design stages of a project through to how to document research findings. The final section discusses ethical and methodological questions arising from this study about conducting research with young children.

17

INTER-AGENCY AND MULTIDISCIPLINARY WORKING

Bob Sanders

Contents:

- **Introduction**
- **Definitions and terminology**
- **Antecedents of inter-agency and multidisciplinary working**
- **Advantages and disadvantages of working together collaboratively**
- **Barriers to inter-agency and multidisciplinary working**
- **Dimensions of multidisciplinary teams**
- **Working together in children's services**
- **Evaluation of working together in children's services**
- **Conclusion**

Introduction

This chapter looks at theoretical concepts underpinning inter–professional working, and considers how they relate to provisions for joint working in services for children and families. It concludes with an evaluation of inter-agency working in children's services. But first let us consider the justification for collaborative working. At first, this might seem self-evident, in the light of both the more obvious benefits and the very strong emphasis in government policy on agencies crossing organisational and professional divides to communicate more effectively and develop joint working arrangements. However, it is useful to remember that there is a cost to collaboration.

Table 17.1 Terminology (from Rawson, 1994)

Problematic Association	Grouping	Focus of Operations
inter	professional	work
multi	occupational	teamwork
trans	disciplinary	collaboration
	sectoral	co-operation
	agency	integration

In this chapter the advantages and disadvantages of collaborative working are discussed. One might think it strange to think of disadvantages to collaboration, and yet it is important because workers may have a sense of having given up something (e.g., autonomy of action, independence of thinking, in some cases professional status, the relative comfort of working with exclusively like-minded people) in order to work effectively across agencies, or as different disciplines within multidisciplinary teams. It is important the worker understands that what is given up is worth what is gained.

Definitions and terminology

What exactly do we mean by words such as 'inter-agency' and 'multidisciplinary'? There is the potential for confusion. Rawson (1994) describes terms associated with three aspects of these interrelated concepts: the problematic associations (how individuals are connected), the grouping (the nature of the groups to which the individuals belong), and the focus of operations (the nature of the collaborative work in which the people are engaged). Each of these has various terms linked to it (see Table 17.1).

According to Rawson, 'Any permutation from the list is possible and has indeed been used in the literature.' Using just these examples described above, there are 75 different ways, derivable from the Table, to describe the process of different people working together. This suggests the question: Are there 75 different variants of working together, or are we talking about the same mechanism underlying collaborative processes? To what extent are these 75 combinations the same or different? 'Inter-professional work' is arguably the phrasing with greatest utility. Øvretveit et al. (1997) adopt the terminology 'interprofessional working', defining it as 'how two or more people from different professions communicate and cooperate to achieve a common goal'. 'Multi-professionalism' (David, 1994) and 'multi-professional communication' (Glenny and Roaf, 2008) are also used.

By considering the subtle differences of etymology it would appear that there are significant differences between the variants, and even if there are not so many as 75 separate concepts they are not simply different aspects of the same concept.

Antecedents of inter-agency and multidisciplinary working

A powerful driving force behind collaboration has been the continual emphasis in the last 30 years on working together in child protection. However, it is important to remember that other areas of public services (and even other areas of work with children) have placed considerable emphasis on collaboration.

The development of inter-agency working in child protection can be seen as a watershed of inter-agency working. Government guidance issued in April 1974 following the Inquiry and subsequent report into the death of Maria Colwell (Department of Health and Social Security, 1974) led to the setting up of Area Review Committees (predecessors of Area Child Protection Committees). By 1976 all areas in England and Wales had established Area Review Committees, child protection registers and case conference systems. Failures of agencies to co-ordinate their efforts continued to be seen as a significant contributing factor in the death of children through abuse (see Sanders et al., 1999). Leathard, in relation to the Inquiry into the circumstances surrounding the death of Jasmine Beckford, notes that there were '37 different individuals and agencies who, not for want of trying, failed to coordinate their work on child protection' (1994: 11). Therefore, working collaboratively continued to be a child protection theme, both in terms of government guidance and in primary legislation. Following from the post-Climbié government strategies to resolve residual difficulties in inter-agency working in child protection (see Chapter 12), it is interesting to note that there were calls at the time for there to be a dedicated national child protection service to ensure co-ordination of services for abused children at every level (Kendall and Harker, 2002). It was suggested that this would apparently eliminate the 'families' uncertainties whether social services were investigating them or supporting them' (2002: 17) .

Advantages and disadvantages of working together collaboratively

A lesson to be learned from the 1980s is that inter-agency working is not easy, and not self evidently useful.

(Department of Health, 1989: 41)

Professionally, we now operate in context in which working together collaboratively has become a principle so firmly entrenched in government philosophy ('joined up thinking') that it is sometimes difficult to acknowledge that there can be disadvantages to working together collaboratively. And yet, in order to engender commitment to inter-professional working, one must be aware of the down side. An 'eyes wide open' approach is always to be preferred to an approach in which one adopts the dictates of government rhetoric in an undigested and unanalysed manner.

Let us first consider the *advantages* of working together. Many of the arguments in favour stem from cost–benefit considerations; the reasons for its endorsement by government, concerned to deliver the best service at the lowest cost, will be obvious. Working together is seen, for example, as entailing a more efficient use of staff, providing more effective service provision, and enabling professional and lay people to achieve their objectives more fully and economically. From the perspective of the worker, if they can get a full picture of a situation (assessment) by drawing on the contributions of different workers to an overall assessment, this will save effort, and depending upon the nature of the information, may also be more reliable. For example, consider an assessment of a child with learning and physical disabilities being undertaken by a social worker. The worker is likely to need information on the child's educational and medical needs. This information is best obtained from those with specialist knowledge in such areas, rather than by the worker attempting to gain such information directly without the benefit of specialist training.

For the agency, there are a number of dangers to be avoided if workers from different services are operating jointly. The main two in terms of service delivery are *service gaps* and *duplication of service*. People who need services may fall between the activities of different agencies because the agencies either do not know of their existence or are not aware that other agencies are not providing the services. Failure of agencies to communicate with other agencies about families they are working with may lead to the family not receiving much needed services from those agencies. This is variously described as 'falling through the net', 'slipping through the cracks', or other metaphors.

On the other hand, different agencies may be providing a similar or even identical service to a single family. In this case failure to communicate between agencies contributes to a waste of resources. One family may be being provided with the same or similar service twice, whilst another family is not receiving a service at all or experiencing long delays before a service can be provided. This is clearly not cost effective for the agency, who will be intent on delivering the most efficient service.

We have discussed how effective working together may help the worker and the agency, but how will it help the service user? Clearly it will be of benefit to the service user to be on the receiving end of a service that is effectively delivered, avoiding both service gaps and duplication of services. They are more likely, within resource constraints, to get the service needed. And of course more effective use of existing resources should mean more resources available for service delivery. On a more pragmatic level, however, many service users become bewildered by the host of professionals involved in their lives (sometimes with reasonable justification because of the different services required) and find it particularly taxing when they are required to provide the same answers to the same questions to different agencies.

Finally, there is the *jig-saw* metaphor which has become established within child protection. Fatality inquiries have revealed that in many cases, whilst many of the agencies involved had a piece of the puzzle, no single agency had the necessary overview. This is why the child protection conference and the role of the key worker in child protection are so important (although clearly still not foolproof). The child protection conference provides an opportunity for all those involved with the child and family to come together to share the information they have. The agencies are contributing their pieces of the puzzle to the overall picture. The role of the key worker is to act as a focal point for all of the agencies involved to provide information, and to disseminate that information when it is received. The key worker is the individual who should have the overall picture and at various stages updates the different agencies so that they too have a better overall picture of the situation.

It is possible however to overemphasise the significance of omissions in inter-professional communications to child abuse fatalities. In networks as large as those surrounding children at risk of abuse (e.g., the previously noted 37 individuals and agencies involved in the case of Jasmine Beckford), it is almost inevitable that there will be gaps. To date there have been no fatality inquiries that have compared the pattern of inter-agency communication surrounding the fatally abused child with those patterns surrounding another child, or other children, in the same child protection system who have not been fatally abused. If, as suggested here, gaps in communication may be an inevitable feature of communication in such large and complex networks, then it may be unjustified to conclude that gaps in communication are significant factors contributing to the child's death. They may always be present, and yet their significance may seem magnified when examined retrospectively. That being said, there is clearly a benefit to maximising the effectiveness of inter-agency communication surrounding children who are at risk of abuse; indeed, the 'green paper' *Every Child Matters* (HM Government 2003), noted previously, set out proposals for removing some of the constraints on inter-professional communications concerning children who are, or may possibly be, at risk of abuse. There are now much clearer policies and explicit protocols in both England (DfES, 2006) and Wales (Welsh Assembly Government (WAG), 2006, Chapter 14: 295–310) on the arrangements for information sharing in connection with safeguarding children. Roaf (2002) (among many others) has identified the confidentiality policies of agencies as a major barrier to working together. The thrust of government policy has been specifically to clarify information sharing in the grey area between a child being in need where there are clearly no safeguarding concerns (where parental consent should invariably be sought for agencies to exchange information) and those situations where a child needs safeguarding (in which case, although parental consent to agency exchange should usually, but not invariably be sought, if the parents withhold consent, then agencies should and must override that consent, and share information. The Welsh guidance addresses this grey area by saying:

> It is also increasingly recognised in practice that a failure to share information, even at a level of a 'niggling worry', may have serious consequences for the welfare of a child or young person, or for others. Often it is not until information is shared and understood, that a clearer picture emerges, which may confirm or allay concerns about a child or young person's safety and welfare. (WAG, 2006: 297)

Now let us consider some of the *disadvantages* of working together. First, it is not necessarily easy. Wanting it is one thing but achieving it may be another. There are barriers to inter-agency and multidisciplinary working; and, whilst they are not necessarily insurmountable obstacles, some of the barriers do present very real challenges. Some of these will be discussed more fully in the next section.

Second, although inter-professional working can be cost-effective, there *are* costs associated with it. It takes time to liaise, consult, co-ordinate and collaborate. If a busy worker has to get on the phone to a number of different agencies to find out what they know about a child's situation, or to provide information about the latest developments in a particular child's case, this uses the worker's time; time taken away from direct contact with service users. Administrative and communication costs may also be high. Consider, for example, the cost of a child protection conference which may have 15 or so professionals in attendance for at least one and a half hours, some of whom may have travelled a considerable distance to attend. The cost in terms of staff time and expenses is considerable. Such meetings must be accountable for the balance between their cost and their necessity (in terms of the potential consequence(s) of not meeting to share information and concerns).

Third, collective decision making, can make workers feel deskilled. The reduction in autonomy consequent on inter-agency working – even if actual decision making continues to be devolved to agencies, as it is in child protection conferences – can lead workers to feel unable to make decisions without involving other agencies. For many, this may be perceived as undermining professional judgment and autonomy, which is not conducive to good inter-professional working.

Fourth, as noted by Glenny and Roaf (2008) *collaborative inertia* can be produced, whereby the costs of achieving collaboration and the efforts to achieve it, are not in the end justified by the gains from it, thus paving the way for frustration and disappointment.

Finally, whereas Thompson (2002) noted that role blurring can be a hindrance to achieving effective inter-agency working, we can also consider it as a potential negative outcome of a policy context that operates as if the only way to achieve true inter-agency working is in the establishment of multi-agency teams. As noted by Sayer:

> One of the interesting debates about multi-professional, inter-agency work is whether the individual professionals will retain their individual identity. (2008: 205)

Barriers to inter-agency and multidisciplinary working

In his work on primary health care teams Øvretveit (1990) describes barriers to effectiveness and efficiency – 'lack of time owing to pressure of work; large team numbers; different patient populations; unclear roles; and different policies between practitioners and different management structures' (cited in Leathard, 1994: 13). In a later work Øvretveit et al. (1997) consider the inherent problems in multidisciplinary working: understanding the purpose of inter-professional practice, understanding the roles of others, professional rivalry (a point noted by Roaf, 2002), exclusion of significant others (non-professionals), ownership of resources, discrimination and racism, and making sure that assessment is effective. Thompson (2002) describes 'helps' and 'hindrances' to the process of working together. Under hindrances he includes stereotypes, hidden agendas, differences in values, lack of trust, inappropriate use of language (jargon), lack of understanding of roles, and blurring of roles. Sanders et al. (1997) described two factors that influence the ability of different agencies to work together on Area Child Protection Committees: first, the extent of match between the child protection agenda of the agency and the agenda of the Area Child Protection Committee, and second, the extent of devolution of decision making within the agency. Barriers to joint working were created by the interests of the agency being remote from the child protection agenda, and by agencies being relatively autonomous in the extent that they could (or were seen to be able to) decide for themselves how far they would go along with locally-agreed procedures.

What other obstacles may arise when agencies, and workers within agencies, attempt to work together? For one thing, the professions they come from are frequently unalike in many ways. There may be different leadership styles, a factor encountered by Sanders et al. (1996) when comparing police involvement in child protection with that of other agencies. The professional groups may have different language and values; use of 'jargon' facilitates communication within a professional or occupational group, but is likely to have the opposite effect on communication outside the group. The professional groups may have profoundly different training backgrounds. The positivist model of knowledge serving as a foundation within the medical model, which places a great emphasis on objectivity, contrasts strongly with a postmodern understanding of knowledge, in which power is seen as an important influence on the subjective experience of knowledge, which may be found in a more socially-oriented knowledge base. Inequalities in status and pay between different professional groups may also be a barrier to effective working; and these may be related to levels of management support and accountability. Higher status professions are able to function more autonomously; a factor which caused considerable concern amongst those interviewed by Sanders et al. (1997).

These factors may also relate to lack of clarity about *roles*. Successive volumes of *Working Together* in child protection (Department of Health and Social Security, 1988; Home Office et al., 1991; Department of Health et al., 1999; National Assembly for Wales, 2000; Department for Education and Skills, 2006; Welsh Assembly Government, 2006) have stressed the importance of clarity of roles in child protection. A further factor may be negative perceptions about other roles. In the 1970s, at the time of the Maria Colwell Inquiry (Department of Health and Social Security, 1974) there was considerable mutual distrust between the police and social workers. Over the 30 years since, although there are still some frictions between the two, the situation has vastly improved. For this to happen, both services have had to go through significant changes, not only in relation to child protection (Sanders et al., 1996). During the same period of time when police were having a greater involvement in social issues as part of their everyday practice, social workers were taking on more of a policing role in their approach to child welfare. Whilst this may contain internal issues for both occupations, the greater degree of like-mindedness is no doubt a major contributing factor to the increased ability to co-operate between the two groups.

Dimensions of multidisciplinary teams

Øvretveit et al. (1997) offer a framework for understanding multidisciplinary teams (a concept which we can for our purposes take to include those 'teams' that might be formed by separate agencies working together). Youth Offending Teams (YOTs), established under the Crime and Disorder Act 1998, and Child and Adolescent Mental Health Services (CAMHS) teams are both good examples in children's services. Øvretveit et al. (1997) propose four significant dimensions of how such teams might differ from each other: degree of integration, membership of a permanent work group, process (the client 'pathway' through the team), and management (how the team is led and how practitioners are managed). We shall consider each of these in turn.

Degree of integration

If we define integration as the extent to which the team influences the decisions of its members, there is a continuum along which teams can be located. At one end is the 'loose-knit' team in which the membership changes and is voluntary. At the other end is the 'closely integrated' team, in which the work of the team is governed by team policy and team decisions, and the group is jointly accountable for its service to the service users. A distinction can also be made between the 'co-ordinated profession team' (CPT) and the 'collective responsibility team' (CRT). In the former the professional services are separately organised and accountable, although there are joint meetings to take on work and for other liaison purposes. In the latter there is a collective accountability on the part of the members of the group to use collective resources to meet the needs of service users.

Membership of a permanent work group

There are four aspects of membership which Øvretveit et al. (1997) consider to be significant influences on the nature of the work group: whether members are *core or associate* members, the *professional mix* within the team, the *personal mix* within the team, and the *roles* of the members. Being a *core* member of a team can mean being full-time, governed by team policy, managed by a single team leader, and having voting rights within the team. In contrast, being an *associate* member can mean being part-time, not being governed by team policy, managed by individuals outside of the team and not having voting rights on team decisions. The *professional mix* of the team refers to which professions and staff are included in the team and how many of each there should be. *Personal mix* refers to the personal attributes that individuals bring to the team. Membership *roles* refers to the work that members do and the autonomy they have within those roles. It may also relate to the types of informal roles that people take up when working within organisations.

Process – client 'pathway' through the team

This is one of the more difficult concepts of Øvretveit et al.'s framework, and one which benefits from the use of visual aids which they provide. They describe ten stages in the client pathway, which in general, all clients will pass through:

1 Referral sources
2 Reception
3 Acceptance for assessment
4 Allocation for assessment
5 Assessment
6 Acceptance for longer-term care
7 Allocation for longer-term care
8 Intervention and/or monitoring
9 Review
10 Closure.

Using this model they describe six common types of team process, on a continuum which reflects more and more of the decision making being done by the team at different stages in the process.

Management – how the team is led and how practitioners are managed

A very important aspect of how any team operates is its management. Øvretveit et al. suggest that there are two particular challenges to creating management structures in multidisciplinary teams. Firstly, there is the task of establishing management which allows members from different professions appropriate autonomy. Secondly, there is a need to establish responsibility for managing the total resources of the team. This includes assessing needs and making sure that members' time is efficiently used. Øvretveit et al. describe the key management tasks as drafting job descriptions, appointing staff, introducing the person to the job, assigning work, reviewing work, performance appraisal and objective-setting, ensuring practice quality, training and professional development, and disciplinary action.

In order to fulfil the role of management within the team, supervision is required, but there are different meanings attached to the concept. Supervision can mean *clinical advice* from a more experienced colleague. In this case the practitioner remains accountable, and the adviser has no accountability for the quality of the work done. *Clinical supervision* is undertaken by a senior staff member who is accountable for the quality of the supervisee's work. With *management monitoring* the role is to ensure that the worker adheres to agency procedures, but the manager is not normally accountable for clinical decisions. Finally, in *full management* the manager assumes responsibility for both the clinical and the organisational components of the role. They note that someone from a different profession could in principle undertake any of these four types of supervision.

Following these considerations of management and supervision, Øvretveit et al. describe five types of management structure for teams. In the *profession-managed structure* practitioners are managed within their professions by line managers who undertake all of the key management tasks described above. In the *single-manager structure* all practitioners, regardless of the professional discipline from which they come, are managed by a single manager who undertakes all eight key tasks in relation to all team members. This model is more common in the USA, Australia and the rest of Europe than it is in the UK. The *joint management structure* is a mixture of the previous two models: there is a central team co-ordinator and professional supervisors; the two types of supervisor have to clarify who is responsible for which key tasks, but all team members are employees. In the *team manager-contracted structure* the team is co-ordinated by a manager who has a budget and who contracts-in the services of different professionals to the team. Finally, there is a *hybrid management structure* based on characteristics of the other four models.

Working together in children's services

Joint working in children's services is achieved primarily through what Hallett and Birchall (1992) describe, in relation to child protection, as 'mandated co-ordination'. This entails agencies being 'directed or required to co-ordinate their activities by those in superordinate positions' (1992: 32). At the most superordinate level this requirement is contained within legislation. For example, in relation to children in need, section 27 of the Children Act 1989 provides that a local authority may request help from the local education authority, housing, the health authority, and indeed from any other local authority, when exercising any of its functions in relation to such children and their families. Likewise, section 47 of the Children Act places a duty on the same agencies to help a local authority with its enquiries in cases involving child protection. In addition, we have seen that both education and health authorities are involved in the process of looking after children, by contributing to the plans that are made for such children, and the periodic reviews of those plans. This has broadened the conception of responsibility for vulnerable children and it is common now to hear people talking of 'corporate parenting', a concept indicating that the responsibility for vulnerable children in the community is no longer the sole concern of the social services department.

A further vehicle for promoting inter-agency and inter-professional working in children's services in England and Wales has been the advent of *Children's Services Plans*. These are required to be developed by local authorities to ensure that local services for children are co-ordinated and comprehensive. Plans should identify the need for services locally and the services provided or planned to meet them. This should include family support services for children in need, child protection, and adoption services, and should encompass services provided both by the independent (private and voluntary) sector and by the statutory sector. Plans should address the needs of children in particular circumstances; for example, children under eight, children with disabilities or with mental health problems, young carers, looked after children, young runaways, young people leaving care and young people in conflict with the law.

Inter-agency and interdisciplinary work in assessment is at the heart of the *Framework for the Assessment of Children in Need and their Families* (Department of Health et al. 2000, National Assembly for Wales, 2000). The *Framework* applies both to children who are in need generally, and to children who may be in need because of risk of abuse or neglect. It is based upon a number of underpinning principles. Assessments should be child-centred, rooted in child development and ecological in their approach. They should ensure equality of opportunity, be based on working in partnership with children and families, and build on strengths as well as identifying difficulties. They should be multi-agency in their approach to assessment and service provision. The *Framework* prescribes three dimensions of the assessment: the child's developmental needs, parents' or caregivers' capacity to meet those needs, and wider family and environmental factors. Each of these is subdivided into component categories of the assessment.

In relation to inter-agency working, the *Framework* advises that it is essential to be clear about the purpose and anticipated outputs from the assessment, the legislative basis for the assessment; and the protocols and procedures to be followed. There should be no confusion about which agency, team or professional has lead responsibility for collecting information, analysing the results, constructing a plan and taking it forward. It is vital to be clear about the respective roles of the different professionals involved. Consideration must be given to the way in which information will be shared across professional boundaries and within agencies and be recorded. In a time of increasing awareness of the need to be exceedingly vigilant in the security of the data held by public bodies, this can present considerable challenges. Finally, consideration should be given as to how the child and members of the child's family will be involved in the assessment.

Finally, it should be noted that there is a sense in which the government has changed strategy to improve inter-agency working from one in which there was an emphasis on local and small scale projects devoted to enhancing co-ordination, collaboration, sharing. As noted by Roaf:

> Inter-agency practice is now developing rapidly in response to the setting up of large scale government supported initiatives. (2002:6)

Evaluation of working together in children's services

Earlier studies (Department of Health, 1993; Audit Commission, 1994; Colton et al., 1995; Social Services Inspectorate, 1996) found shortcomings in the ability of agencies to work collaboratively and effectively. Inter-agency working had been patchy and within the overall services for children there was an overemphasis on child protection, to the detriment of family support services. The Audit Commission suggested that *need* should form the focus of services.

Horwath and Morrison (2007) discuss 'the frameworks, challenges, and implications involved in the move to higher levels of collaboration, in particular the shift from coalition to integrated services for children vulnerable to abuse'. They note five levels of working together, communication, co-operation, co-ordination, coalition and integration. They note in particular how the mandate of government policy from one source may place agencies in conflict with other mandated governmental priorities thus creating conflict and confusion. Drawing on previous research, they suggest that in the period of transition within organisations children at risk may be put even further at risk, and that the process of managing change is as important as the goals, governances and structures that are put in place.

It should be noted that there are virtually no empirical studies that evaluate the relative merits of working together in one way with those of working together in another way in terms of beneficial outcomes for service users. There are even few studies evaluating the effectiveness of working together with the effectiveness of not working together. In connection with elderly people, for example, Brown et al. (2003: 85) suggest, 'Although it is perceived wisdom that joint working must be beneficial, there is, even at this stage, little evidence to support that notion', and in their empirical study found that 'the degree of "integration" seen within … co-located health and social care teams does not appear to be sufficiently well developed to have had an impact upon the clinical outcomes for the patients/service users.' And returning to children, Horwath and Morrison note:

> However, it remains the case that 'partnership' is still seen more as a means to promote interprofessional working rather than a way of placing service users at the centre of agencies' attention, as the primary stakeholder for collaboration. (2007: 61)

An exception to this lack of research into the effectiveness of multi-professional communication is the working relationship between Education and Social Services described in Glenny and Roaf (2008). They discuss three studies looking at strategies to go from 'downstream' (post-event intervention) to 'upstream' services (prevention) in helping schools and social services develop a more co-ordinated response to those youngsters who had difficulties that were not yet severe enough to be referred to the social services for a full-blown service. Some of the key issues they note associated with success are the development of a problem solving culture and the importance of relationships in the field.

Conclusion

This chapter began by examining the vexed question of the terminology used to describe the process of workers in different disciplines and different agencies working collaboratively, as a starting point to consider whether it is a single concept or a range of concepts being discussed. The chapter examined the advantages and disadvantages, with a view to ensuring the student is aware that there are costs to working collaboratively, and these costs must be justified by the hoped-for improved outcomes of better co-operation. Identification of obstacles to collaborative working, precede a discussion of the dimensions of inter–agency and multidisciplinary working. The ability of agencies to overcome obstacles is the focus of the final section on evaluating collaborative working.

Questions and exercises

1   We have all worked in teams at one point or another in our lives. Consider some of the teams you have worked in. What made those teams work well together? What stopped those teams from working effectively?

2   John (9 years) has mobility problems, is hyperactive, and has moderate learning difficulties. He has an older brother (13) and a younger sister (6), and lives with his two parents. His speech is very difficult to understand (which may in part be due to a slight hearing impairment). He is unable to use full sentences in his speech and he tends to use single words to indicate his needs. With intensive support he has been able to be maintained in his local primary school, but parents and professionals are very doubtful about his ability to cope with the requirements in secondary school. In addition, his parents find it increasingly difficult to care for him without assistance, and would like to arrange respite care. List as many professionals as you can think of who might need to be involved with John. How can this be co-ordinated so that the parents, and those who will provide future services for John are not overwhelmed?

Further reading

Whilst Øvretveit et al. (1997) are particularly good on conceptual models for understanding the varieties of ways in which working together can be achieved, Roaf (2002) and Glenny and Roaf (2008) are excellent sources for empirical studies of how working together can be practised.

18

EFFECTIVE EARLY CHILDHOOD LEADERSHIP

Carol Aubrey

Contents:

- **Introduction**
- **Context**
- **Theoretical perspectives**
- **Research on leadership in early childhood**
- **A case study of early childhood leadership**
- **Practitioners' views about early childhood leadership**
- **Views and perceptions of individual leaders and staff groups**
- **A typical 'day in the life' or leadership in action**
- **Making sense of leaders' work**
- **Mentoring as a leadership strategy**
- **Conclusion**

Introduction

This chapter concerns effective early childhood leadership. It will focus on the role that early childhood leaders play in the improvement of outcomes for very young children (e.g., Department for Education and Skills, 2003; The Children Act 2004) that include being healthy, staying safe, enjoying and achieving. It will not linger on generic leadership and management skills but will attempt to identify ways that early childhood leaders may have an impact on worthwhile outcomes for children. As Robinson (2006) indicates, educational leadership research has produced limited evidence about the links between leadership and learning and, to date, even that evidence is very inconclusive. She argues that educational leadership should be grounded in the best evidence about effective teaching that has a positive impact (or in the case of early childhood leadership, ensuring that children also stay healthy, safe and secure). The next step, she maintains, is a backward mapping process in specifying the processes and policies; in this case, within the early years setting that facilitates these conditions. The challenge is to strengthen those conditions that enable the setting to function effectively and weaken the impact of those conditions that inhibit or prevent the setting from functioning effectively.

This chapter will examine what existing early childhood leadership literature reveals. It will draw upon early childhood leadership research carried out by the writer and colleagues with early childhood leaders, willing to explore their own leadership and interrogate their own leadership practice. The chapter will end with an exploration of some emergent themes that may shed further light on effective early childhood leadership practice.

Context

Broad trends and influences on early childhood leadership can be discerned globally. These include a focus on the health, safety and emotional well-being of young children and families at risk, with corresponding efforts to integrate services for them and their families for which few professionals have received training to deliver. Drawing together services of education, health and social care means that provision, previously organised by a variety of agencies, is now linked up to work together for children and families. It brings a raft of new challenges for the professionals concerned that includes restructuring the way their organisations respond and hence creates a changed professional environment in which to work, without there necessarily being enhanced resources to support the new co-ordinated working practices that they are engaged in. Changes in the family structure also influence the provision of education, health and social welfare services by professionals. The decline of the extended family with its associated care and support mechanisms, the breakdown of the nuclear family, the increase of one-parent families and single people living alone also carry major implications for professionals providing services to families and family members. Since most children still live with their families, however constituted, at least for the first 16 years of life and often longer, any intervention related to a child's well-being inevitably includes attention to the well-being of their carers, whoever these may be.

The effects of poverty have an impact and are associated with unemployment, poor housing and an inadequate diet, as well as educational disadvantage. The challenge of poverty is exacerbated by increasing population mobility within and across countries that also increase demands on professionals, especially when home language, culture and religion differ from the local community. This takes place in a context of rising public expectations for improved care and workforce reform and a shift on the one hand, to greater flexible and community-based services but on the other, to increased 'managerialism' and accountability that redistributes professional boundaries and responsibilities. The context within which practitioners work becomes more complex just as the problems that young children and families present increase in complexity. As a result collaboration and interdisciplinary teamwork between professions worldwide becomes more and more important in the promotion of education, health and social welfare.

Theoretical perspectives

Recent comparative perspectives on early childhood leadership in five countries, Australia, Finland, England, Russia and the USA, have attempted to extend theoretical discussion about early childhood leadership in relation to a broad context and culture (Hujala and Puroila, 1998; Nivala and Hujala, 2000). Nivala (2000) advocates a context model founded in Bronfenbrenner's (1979) ecological theory that focuses upon the operating environments of leadership that range from the closest circle to the leader, *microsystem* or immediate environments of family, neighbourhood early childcare environment and peer group, to the *macrosystem* or larger sociocultural and economic context. Between these lie the *mesosystem* or connections between immediate environments, such as the child's home and the surrounding environment and the *exosystem* or external environmental settings that exert an indirect affect on leadership. Each system contains roles, norms and rules that can powerfully shape behaviour. For instance, an inner-city childcare organisation may experience environment privations that a more affluent childcare institution does not. This allows the examination of influences on early childhood leadership at a number of levels from family membership to political and economic structures.

Bennis (1999: 71) describes a world in which political and technological complexity and change encourage collaboration and teamwork and has called for an end to traditional leadership. A contracting world in which technological and political complexities increase at an accelerating rate offers fewer and fewer fora in which individual action and top-down leadership is sufficient. In his view, effective change is derived from a workforce in creative alliance with top leadership, evolving into federations, networks, clusters and cross-functional teams. In this context, a new kind of alliance between leaders and followers is required and a new indirect form of influence for leaders to be effective. Rost (1991, 1993) locates leadership within a dynamic relationship among a group of people, leaders and collaborators working together to generate change, with influence flowing in both directions. On this basis,

Gronn (2000) has argued that the focus of leadership should be followership, followers' minds and social networks. Spillane et al. (2001) have created a framework for considering effective leadership by considering not just the tasks completed and actions taken but also the influence of other people and the interactions within an organisation. This perspective is 'distributed' and focuses on the processes of leadership as a complex relationship operating in a specific social and situational context. Given the world of social, economic and technological change in which early childhood leaders operate, in which traditional family forms and work life, including institutional arrangements made for early childhood and social relationships within institutions have been unsettled, these models of leadership and change have much to offer. Waniganayake (2000) has already proposed a distributed early childhood leadership model where organisational learning is at the centre and there is the possibility of multiple leaders or specialists within one early childhood centre. For leadership to work within the organisational context, it is argued that a more participatory and decentralised approach is required.

Research on leadership in early childhood

A review of existing early childhood leadership was carried out by Muijs et al. (2004). This revealed a lack of early childhood literature that identified what effective leadership practice was in terms of processes and outcomes within the field of early childhood education and care. Literature in the field was not found to be well informed by theory or much linked to key concepts in educational, public sector or business leadership. Research was dominated by a relatively small number of researchers (for instance, Bloom, 1997, 2000; Rodd, 1996, 1997, 1999, 2006) though since that time interest has burgeoned in England (see, e.g., Moyles, 2006; Siraj-Blatchford and Manni, 2006; Aubrey, 2007; Jones and Pound, 2008).

The review indicated that there was some evidence suggesting that early childhood programmes had both short- and long-term benefits in terms of higher academic achievements, lower levels of grade retention, higher graduation rates and lower levels of delinquency in later life. A US review by Stipek and Ogana (2000), for instance, emphasised that children who had attended higher-quality early childhood centres showed better academic outcomes, more positive student–teacher relationships, better behaviour and increased social skills. A key element of quality provision was identified as leadership, in the context of a language-rich environment, sensitive teachers, child-focused communication with the child's home, higher levels of teacher–carer education, smaller child–adult ratios and lower staff turnover. An Australian study by Hayden (1997) found that a high-quality work environment was associated with lower levels of staff turnover, higher scores on child development and social and emotional skills. A US evaluation of *Head Start* programmes also suggested that leadership was found to exert a powerful influence on the effectiveness of programme implementation. Committed, competent and respected leadership was associated with successful programmes, whilst leaders who were less experienced, committed and involved, less skilful at training and supervising staff, and less effective at working with schools and community were associated with less successful programmes. The relationship of leadership to centre quality has been highlighted by a range of studies.

A number of studies have examined the roles and characteristics of effective early childhood leaders, but there appear to have been few case studies of effective leaders or quantitative analyses that linked inputs, procedures and processes to outputs and outcomes. The review revealed that to date there was little high-quality information that helped to identify the ways that effective leaders influenced those working in direct line with children to raise outcomes for children. It was concluded that theoretically-based studies allowing different models and characteristics to be empirically tested were long overdue.

A case study of early childhood leadership

In order to investigate further the views, experiences and practices of English early childhood leaders, the author and colleagues talked to a group of 25 local leaders selected on the basis of their effective practice (Aubrey, 2007). These leaders were asked to answer five key questions:

The first question was – what does leadership mean in your setting? Here the leaders stressed having a clear vision and working towards it. This meant to them having an awareness of the wider social, political and educational context. It entailed raising the profile of early education and care and developing a shared philosophy. Fundamental to this was a recognition of its multidisciplinary nature, valuing learning and having a commitment to ongoing professional development.

Second – what factors contributed to the effectiveness of this role? Promoting early years across a range of professional agencies was regarded as prerequisite, with a firm commitment to working towards specific outcomes. Again, commitment to ongoing professional development and support for staff was thought to contribute to effective leadership.

Third – what factors hindered effectiveness in this role? It was felt that the state of change and development over a number of years had created a real lack of clarity about the early childhood stage. This was coupled with a general lack of knowledge about childhood at all levels, a lack of status, a lack of resources in terms of staffing, time, materials and lack of professional development. In turn, it could lead to a sense of isolation and low levels of responsibility.

Fourth – what were the training needs? The need for more general accreditation of early childhood leadership and management at varying levels and with appropriate funding was identified.

Fifth – how could capacity be built in the field? Again, the need for national acknowledgement and recognition of the need for accreditation and training for early childhood leadership was emphasised and an identified funding stream for training and training the trainers stressed. It was clear that these leaders felt that there were distinct training and development needs in the sector. This sentiment resonated through their responses. Valuing learning was at the core, with a commitment to working towards specific outcomes and promoting early years across a range of agencies.

There was reference not only to 'direction' and 'vision' but also to the 'ability to inspire', 'to motivate', 'to enthuse' and 'empower'. Indeed, being able to articulate a personal value system and create unity of vision was an enduring feature of reported approaches to early childhood leadership. As Flintham (2003: 1) has indicated, an institution 'cannot move forward without a clear vision of where its leaders want it to reach ... hope is what drives the institution forward towards achieving its vision, whilst allowing it to remain true to its values whatever the external pressures.'

Flintham's study of 25 serving head teachers indicated that the successful head teacher acted as a 'wellspring of values and vision' and an external 'reservoir of hope' for the institution. Colleagues looked to the head to provide spiritual and moral leadership, the necessary coherence and unity of vision and to maintain its underpinning integrity of values. All the heads in the study were able to articulate an individual personal value system that underpinned their approach to leadership or an internal reservoir of hope from which these values and vision flowed. Fullan (2001) noted, too, moral purpose was a component of effective leadership required to achieve a culture of change.

In the same vein, aspiring to make a difference to the lives of children, their families and communities and integrity of values ran through the early childhood leaders' conversations, from the start. Asked what advice they would give to other leaders, one of our leaders said: 'We need passionate people working in integrated centres. I think that we have to inspire others. I think that we do have to champion this work.'

Twelve leaders and exemplar settings continued to work with us in investigating the full range of early childhood provision that included three private nursery and day care settings; two voluntary family centres; four nursery and reception classes in infant and primary schools (foundation stage units, for children aged three to five years); three integrated children's centres providing a range of services for children, birth to four years, their families and community.

Practitioners' views about early childhood leadership

One hundred and ninety-four practitioners responded to our preliminary survey of views that included the majority of leaders and middle leaders and a range of practitioners working in and around the centres concerned. In terms of demographics, the workforce was mainly female (four males responded), aged between 20 and 48 years old. The majority had at least a diploma in nursery nursing. Respondents in foundation stage units and integrated centres predominantly had a first degree or postgraduate qualification, whilst private and voluntary day care workers were more likely to have on-the-job National Vocational Qualifications (NVQs) at level 2 and 3. Two-thirds had original training that covered the period from birth upwards, whilst disproportionately respondents from foundation units had not trained to work with very young children.

In terms of roles and responsibilities, there was high agreement that the most important aspect of the leader's role was to deliver a quality service. By contrast, nobody ranked first an 'entrepreneurial approach, mindful of competition with others'.

With respect to personal characteristics of effective leaders, a more sophisticated analysis of responses suggested that respondents with postgraduate qualifications tended to favour warmth, rationality, knowledgeability, assertiveness, goal orientation, coaching, mentoring and guiding that we described as *leaders as guides*. Those with NVQs tended to favour vision, warmth, professional confidence, systematic planning, proactivity and empowerment that we described as *leaders as motivators*. Those with so-called 'other' qualifications who had been trained for professions other than education, such as the library service, health-related professions, play leadership or social work tended to favour systematic planning, risk-taking, influence, proactivity, vision and empowerment, that we described as *leaders as strategists*. Finally, those with postgraduate qualifications were also likely to favour influence, authority, economic competitiveness, business awareness and risk-taking that we described as *business oriented*.

Whilst there was some overlap between these categories there was at least some indication that leaders with different qualifications, coming from different professional heritages and working in different types of setting regarded a *different* set of characteristics and emphases as important to effective leadership. Given different job descriptions and role specifications among the range of leaders, this was hardly surprising. It does, however, indicate the existence of many different types of early childhood leader and the need for a 'best fit' approach that is derived from organisational development theory (e.g., Handy, 1993) and that takes account of leader, followers, task and environment. It may also go some way to understanding participants' response to the question – who makes the decisions? Major differences were found in the weight given to 'all staff', 'appropriate individuals', 'children' and 'parents'. Middle and senior management was regarded as virtually unimportant and the child was reported overall as having least input. Given the current emphasis on children's participation and voice, this finding was surprising, though private and voluntary providers were more likely to say decisions were made by children 'all the time' that might reflect a stronger emphasis on 'client' expectations. Integrated centre leaders were more likely to say that parents made decisions 'all of the time', in line with original programme practice that they should be locally driven and responsive to the needs of families.

Views and perceptions of individual leaders and staff groups

Consistent with the views of our original 25 leaders, survey respondents confirmed the value of learning and quality provision but held differing views about what constituted effective leadership according to their own qualifications and experience and about who made decisions within their organisation. A mixed view and hence possible ambivalence towards the role of entrepreneurial and business skills also emerged. These findings indicated some areas to pursue in in-depth interviews with leaders and staff.

Perceptions and definitions of early childhood leadership were wide-ranging and diverse. The role of previous experience, role models and academic study were all identified by leaders as important and a variety of training models considered that included peer mentoring, developing critical friends and paired visits to peers' settings. Staff groups collectively reported no experience of leadership training but mentioned the influence on them of role models and the more ad hoc picking up of 'nuggets of what people said'. Leaders acknowledged that general leadership theory and principles were common across sectors but what was distinctive about early childhood leadership was its female leadership, its emotional involvement and its caring. That is not to say that males do not make effective leaders but rather, as Blackmore (1989) has emphasised, organisational theorists have characterised leadership by masculine traits of aggression, competition and independence, whilst Shakeshaft (1989) in the USA revealed women's leadership as focused on collaboration, power-sharing, caring and relationships. Shakeshaft also noted women leaders were consultative, creating a nurturing and non-hierarchical culture that reflected Gilligan's (1982) 'ethic of caring'. Court (1994), in the New Zealand context, described women in leadership positions who 'empowered' or shared power with others and created organisational cultures based on collaboration, communication and shared decision making. In England, Hall (1996) identified an organisational culture created by women school leaders as one of trust, openness and commitment. In terms of our own respondents, staff inevitably stressed the leadership qualities that impacted on them as followers and leaders commented on the role of followers in shaping their practice.

In terms of roles and responsibilities, high-quality education and care and children's achievements were emphasised by leaders and staff alike. Views of leaders and staff on business and entrepreneurial skills were again mixed but the interview data uncovered a deep unease being felt about 'for profit' motives in a sector that was so poorly paid. One respondent stated: 'I came from the private sector because I did not like the idea of making a profit ... exploiting those on low wages.' In terms of decision making, there was recognition of 'top-down' local authority decision making but nevertheless retention of a collaborative culture within the organisation. Overall, respondents felt that their organisations were hierarchically organised at the strategic level but collaborative at the operational level.

A typical 'day in the life' or leadership in action

A typical 'day-in-the-life' was consistent with leaders' previous reports and included rich and varied activities. Leaders working in foundation-stage units had very demanding roles, balancing teaching, administration and pedagogical leadership. Leaders observed in private and voluntary organisations were more likely to lack administrative support and to be preoccupied with low-level administrative tasks. Leaders in integrated centres were seen working on complex and large-scale projects that might entail substantial financial and administrative responsibility for new buildings, developing new policy through consultation with the public, private and voluntary sector that represented a variety of professional groups. At the same time, there was a blurring of distinctions between private, voluntary and state, as new children's centres were being formed and extended schooling was developed. This meant that leaders were finding themselves taking on new major operational tasks, calling for financial and administrative or technical expertise that they must learn 'on the job'.

Robinson's earlier advice to employ backward mapping that involved working backwards from positive impacts on children to tease out leader influence provided a useful frame for examining observed practice. This revealed the high-intensity of foundation-stage leaders' roles in working both directly with children and with professionals and para-professionals that they worked alongside. This was exemplified by one leader observed to remain at school for a parents' meeting and return home at 9pm to telephone two recently employed newly qualified teachers. She later wrote in her diary record, 'Went to bed at twelve, an early night tonight.' The same intensity of focus on quality teaching was observed in those children's centre leaders, state, voluntary and private, who were observed to coach staff in planning, teaching and profiling of young children's work, supporting and challenging their practice in order to raise the quality of provision provided. The strong focus of attention was observed to be on play, learning and childcare experiences with a range of other indirect activities being carried out around core services of support for families and communities.

There was laughter when leaders shared their own video highlights. They exclaimed at their evident tiredness, the long hours and the intensity of their work, what Evans et al. (1994) first termed the 'culture of over-conscientiousness' of early childhood practitioners. They applauded their capacity to deliver the new childcare strategy. They celebrated their ability to 'hold focus' in spite of underlying emotions and uncertainties and indeed, were willing to articulate their feelings of inadequacy at times as well as their outstripping in expertise their own line-managers in the local authorities.

The need for and celebration of 'upskilling' in the workforce was very apparent in the displays of newly-acquired NVQs, the welcoming and greeting of new staff. These all marked the new pathways into the early childhood workforce. Leaders exclaimed at the lack of leadership training available, accentuating the gap in training opportunity between those least and most qualified. Indeed, the need for new skills, knowledge and understanding across the sector was a feature of the video footage. The scale of workforce reorganisation highlighted by the video recordings, the reported low status accorded to early childhood work and the variability of qualifications across the sector identified by the survey findings, threw into relief the lack of opportunity for early childhood leadership training.

Making sense of leaders' work

The video-clips reflected the range of activity that leaders had reported and the palpable sense of change and development within the sector. Leaders shared their practice with one another and were able to describe what they did as well as marvel at it, as outside observers. But after considering its strengths and weakness, the opportunities and threats they turned to the researchers and asked them what *they* thought about their practice. Identifying and explaining differences in practice was hard though the researchers continued to attempt to offer observations on the practice they witnessed. One way of attempting to understand the observed differences in practice was to quantify the relative amounts of time and emphasis being placed on leading, managing and administration. Another was to identify the extent to which leaders had direct or indirect engagement with young children, families and community.

Huffington (2004) noted that the massive effect of internal and external change alters the psychological contract between organisation and staff that held the organisation together in common purpose, vision, direction and loyalty. This notion of the 'psychological contract' had much in common with the metaphor of 'reservoirs of hope' mentioned earlier. Rice (1958) talked about the task that the system had been created to perform and Miller and Rice (1967) about the 'primary task' in relation to the priority it has been given over other tasks and the success with which this is performed. Miller and Rice (1967) regarded this as a means of exploring the ordering of multiple activities in the system where these existed, and a way to explore or compare different organisations with similar or different tasks. Lawrence and Robinson (1975) developed the concept further, distinguishing:

- The 'normative' primary task that those working in the organisation are expected to pursue;
- The 'existential' primary task that staff believe that they are carrying out; and
- The 'phenomenal' task that staff carry out, whether or not they are aware of it.

Obholzer and Miller (2004) considered that there had to be ongoing debate within the organisation about the primary task, in relation to goals, direction and functioning. Where the primary task was clear, as was the case in the foundation-stage units, debate was minimal. If it was more complicated, as in the case of the integrated centres, there was more to debate. Hoyle (2004) noted that the best position to be in was where the normative task and the existential task of an organisation were in alignment; that is, where staff identified with and believed in the task that they were employed to carry out. Discomfort over entrepreneurial skills, for example, was experienced in the context of 'for profit' motives, whereas staff regarded their role as one of caring and nurturing.

A core task of leadership is keeping the primary task in people's minds and continuously reviewing it, as well as modifying it in the light of changing circumstances. Where the task is clear, as in engaging children in enjoying and achieving in educational terms, there is little room for disagreement or purposelessness. Where the task is more complex, as in the case of integrated centre leadership, balancing many different outcomes and achieving of purposefulness is through other staff, there was likely to be a need for considerably greater effort being placed on maintaining common goals, direction and functioning. The leader has the job of reassuring staff that the primary task remains manageable despite changes in the outside world. At the same time, the visions, values, activities and outcomes need to be emphasised in communication with the external world of stakeholders in the family, neighbourhood and wider community.

Mentoring as a leadership strategy

Only one leader in our study was in the position of having a mentor and thus used to 'reflecting on action' or learning from experience (Schön, 1983, 1987). Bloom (1997: 32) described the professional development and careers of 20 early childhood directors as 'navigating the rapids'. She likened becoming a director or leader to improvisation, pointing out that career stage leaders might lack insight on their career motivations or a career plan that would help them to fulfil career goals. Bloom identified three stages of leadership as beginning director, competent director and master director. The beginning director may experience concern about personal adequacy to handle the demands of the job and about the quality and impact of their programme or primary task. Many but not all directors she interviewed described their work as survival focused and preoccupied with meeting the demands of the job. The competent director emerged after between one and four years, as struggling shifted to juggling, raised above meeting basic internal and external expectations to managing them better. The master director reached a higher level of reflection and competence, 'the metacognitive ability to stand back and reflect on *how* they are doing it *when* they are doing it' (Bloom, 1997: 36). Master directors also emphasised the importance of role models and mentors.

Throughout this chapter, the lack of opportunity for continuing professional development for leadership has been stressed. In this context, seeking ways to support new leaders through their leadership journeys or career cycles is important. A more experienced peer can often take on the role of coach in order to help new leaders develop their capability and to reach their potential. Thomson (2006: 62) has described the cycle as: establishing rapport, setting direction and prioritising initial needs, making progress, and moving on or reviewing what has been learned.

This serves to stimulate reflection, review and refinement of professional experience and makes a valuable contribution that a master early childhood leader can make to those coming newly into post. Rodd (1996, 2006) has advocated that leadership could and should be taught to aspiring and actual leaders. Ebbeck and Waniganayake (2000) suggested a collective model of mentoring, where a whole group is mentored, to offer an alternative approach. They maintained that the collective model of mentoring was more powerful in establishing group relationships, commitments to learn and new understandings and knowledge. In the light of discussion of the primary task in the previous section, it helps to build a common culture and a learning community within the organisation.

Conclusion

Ebbeck and Waniganiyake (2000: 28) considered that definitions of early childhood leadership lacked clarity, coherence and comprehensiveness due to a 'failure to take into account the circumstances and the consequent evolution of roles and responsibilities'. They called for a paradigm shift and a reconceptualisation of early childhood leadership within what they described as a 'distributive' model. By contrast, Robinson (2006) argued that we need theories of leadership that are firmly grounded in knowledge of the conditions that teachers (and carers) need to promote their children's learning (health, well-being and safety). As she noted, the question of whether or not the qualities of good leadership identified by such theories are the same as those identified by generic theories and models was an interesting one that will not be answered until research on leadership and research on effective teaching (caring and protecting) are more closely aligned.

Question and exercises

1 Moral leadership

Consider and outline the story of an incident about your setting/organisation when it was under stress.

1 Can you identify an individual personal value or belief system underpinning your approach (your leader's approach) in dealing with this?
2 What did you (your leader) do?
3 In what ways (if at all) did you (your leader) provide internal and external 'reservoirs of hope'?

2 Primary task

Think of the range of different tasks that you carry out in an average day in your organisational setting and identify what would be regarded as the primary task.

1 What would an observer see if you were watched whilst carrying out this task?
2 To what extent do you believe that this task really matters/is important?
3 To what extent does what you believe about the task, match your organisation's mission, goals and values?

Note that these activities work equally well whether you are an early childhood student and your organisation is a college or university setting or if you are already a professional working in children's services.

Further reading

If you want to find out more about different concepts and characteristics of early childhood leadership as well as the roles and responsibilities you might want to look at Carol Aubrey's text *Leading and Managing in the Early Years* (2007). A research-based resource pack based on this work, entitled *Reflecting on Early Childhood Leadership,* with further activities and a DVD of early childhood leaders in action can by obtained from Anne Nelson at The British Association for Early Childhood Education (Early Education), 136 Cavell Street, London, E1 2JA.

REFERENCES

Abbott, S. and Hobby, L. (2005) 'Poverty and health: primary care patients living at the interface', *Health Education Journal*, 64 (4): 363–71.

Aber, J.L. and Allen, J.P. (1987) 'Effects of maltreatment on young children's socio-emotional development: an attachment theory perspective', *Developmental Psychology*, 23: 406–14.

Abrams, R. (1996) *Woman in a Man's World*. London: Methuen.

ACCAC (2004) *The Foundation Phase – A Draft Framework for Children's Learning*. Cardiff: Qualifications, Curriculum and Assessment Authority for Wales.

Adler, P. and Adler, P. (1987) *Membership Roles in Field Research: Qualitative Research Methods Series* (Vol.6). Thousand Oaks, CA: Sage.

Advisory Council on the Misuse of Drugs (2003) *Hidden Harm Report*. London: HMSO.

African Charter on the Rights and Welfare of the Child. OAU Doc. CAB/LEG/ 24.9/49 (1990), entered into force 29 November, 1999. Available at: www.africa-union.org/root/au/Documents/Treaties/treaties.htm (accessed 11 December 2008).

Ainsworth, M. (1967) *Infancy in Uganda: Infant Care and the Growth of Love*. Baltimore, MD: Johns Hopkins University Press.

Ainsworth, M., Blehar, M., Waters, E. and Wall, S. (1978) *Patterns of Attachment: A Psychological Study of the Strange Situation*. Hillsdale, NJ: Lawrence Erlbaum.

Akhtar, N., Jipson, J. and Callanan, M. (2001) 'Learning words through overhearing', *Child Development*, 72: 416–30.

Alanen, L. and Mayall, B. (2001) *Conceptualising Child–Adult Relations*. London: Routledge Falmer.

Alderson, P. (1993) *Children's Consent to Surgery*. Buckingham: Open University Press.

Alderson, P. (2008) *Young Children's Rights: Exploring Beliefs, Principles and Practice* (2nd edition). London: Jessica Kingsley Publishers.

Alderson, P. and Morrow, V. (2004) *Ethics, Social Research and Consulting with Children and Young People*. London: Barnardo's.

Allen, D. and Jackson, S. (1976) *Other People's Children*. London: BBC Publications.

Anderson, A.M. (1996) 'Factors influencing the father–infant relationship', *Journal of Family Nursing*, 2 (3): 306–24.

Anderson, S. and Lightfoot, D. (2002) *The Language Organ: Linguistics as Cognitive Psychology*. Cambridge: Cambridge University Press.

Anning, A. (1999) 'The Influence of Socio-cultural Context on Young Children's Meaning Making'. Paper given at the BERA (British Educational Research Association) Conference, Sussex University, England, 2–5 September.

Anning A., Cottrell, D.M., Frost, N., Green, J. and Robinson, M. (2006) *Developing Multiprofessional Teamwork for the Early Years for Integrated Children's Services*. Maidenhead: Open University.

Applebaum, B. (1996) 'Moral paralysis and the ethnocentric fallacy', *Journal of Moral Education*, 25 (2): 185–99.

Archard, D. (2004) *Children: Rights and Childhood* (2nd edition). London: Routledge.

Ariés, P. (1962) *Centuries of Childhood*. London: Jonathan Cape.

Association for the Development of Education in Africa (ADEA) (2005) *Working Group on Early Childhood Development*. Available at www.adeanet.org/2adeaPortal/adea/workgroup/en_wgecd.html (accessed 27 February 2009).

Astington, J. (2001) 'The future of theory-of-mind research: understanding motivational states, the role of language, and real-world consequences', *Child Development*, 72: 685–7.

Atkinson, M., Wilkin, A., Stott, A., Doherty, P. and Kinder, K. (2002) *Multi-agency Working: A Detailed Study*. Slough: NFER.

Atkinson, P. and Hammersley, M. (1998) 'Ethnography and participant observation and interviewing', in N. Denzin and Y. Lincoln, (eds), *Strategies of Qualitative Inquiry*. Thousand Oaks, CA: Sage. pp. 110–13.

Aubrey, C. (2007) *Leading and Managing in the Early Years*. London: Sage Publications.

Audit Commission (1994) *Seen But Not Heard: Coordinating Community Child Health and Social Services for Children in Need – Detailed Evidence and Guidelines for Managers and Practitioners*. London: HMSO.

Axline, V. (1969) *Play Therapy*. New York: Ballentine Books.

Bainham, A. (1998) *Children: The Modern Law* (2nd edition). Bristol: Family Law.

Baird, G., Charman, T., Cox, A., Baron-Cohen, S., Swettenham, J., Wheelwright, S. and Drew, A. (2001) 'Screening and surveillance for autism and pervasive developmental disorders', *Archive of Diseases in Childhood*, 84: 468–75.

Baistow, K. (1995) 'From sickly survival to realisation of potential: child health as a social project in twentieth century England', *Children & Society*, 9 (1): 20–35.

Baker, M. (2002) 'Child poverty, maternal health and social benefits', *Current Sociology*, 50: 823–38.

Ball, S. and Vincent, C. (2001) 'A market in love? Choosing pre-school childcare', *British Educational Research Journal*, 27 (5): 633–51.

Ball, S. and Vincent, C. (2005) 'The "childcare champion"? New Labour, social justice and the childcare market', *British Educational Research Journal*, 31 (5): 557–70.

Bancroft, S., Fawcett, M. and Hay, P. (2008) *Researching Children Researching the World: 5×5×5=creativity*. Stoke-on-Trent: Trentham Books.

Barnard, M. and McKaganey, N. (2004) 'The impact of parental problem drug use on children: what is the problem and what can be done to help?' *Addiction*, 99 (5): 552–9.

Barnes, P. (1995) *Personal, Social and Emotional Development of Children*. Oxford/ Milton Keynes: Blackwell/Open University.

Barrett, J. (1998) 'New knowledge and research in child development', *Child and Family Social Work*, 3 (4): 267–76.

Barrett, S. (1996) *Anthropology: A Student's Guide to Theory and Method*. Toronto, Canada: University of Toronto Press.

Barry, J., Herity, B., and Solan, J. (1989) *The Travellers Health Status Study: Vital Statistics of Travelling People*. 1987. Dublin: Health Research Board.

Barry, J. and Kirke, P. (1997) 'Congenital abnormalities in the Irish traveller community', *Irish Medical Journal*, 90 (6): 233–4.

Barton, C. and Douglas, G. (1995) *Law and Parenthood*. London: Butterworth.

Bates, E. and MacWhinney, B. (1982) 'A functionalist approach to grammatical development', in E. Wanner and L. Gleitman (eds), *Language Acquisition: The State of the Art*. Cambridge: Cambridge University Press.

Bean, P. and Melville, J. (1990) *Lost Children of the Empire: The Untold Story of Britain's Migrants*. London: Unwin Hyman.

Beaty, J. (1998) *Observing Development of the Young Child* (4th edition). London: Prentice-Hall International.

Bebbington, A. and Miles, J. (1989) 'The background of children who enter Local Authority care', *British Journal of Social Work*, 19 (5): 349–68.

Beckett, C. (2007) *Child Protection: An Introduction* (2nd edition). London: Sage.

Bee, H. (1997) *The Developing Child* (8th edition). New York: Longman.

Belli, P.C., Bustreo, F. and Preker, A. (2005) 'Investing in children's health: what are the economic benefits?', *Bulletin of the World Health Organisation*, 83: 777–84.

Belsky, J. (1996) 'Parent, infant and social-contextual antecedents of father–son attachment security', *Developmental Psychology*, 32 (5): 905–13.

Belsky, J. (2001) 'Developmental risks (still) associated with early child care' (Emanuel Miller Lecture), *Journal of Child Psychology and Psychiatry*, 42 (7): 845–59.

Belsky, J., Campbell, S.B., Cohn, J.F. and Moore, G. (1996) 'Instability of infant–parent attachment security', *Developmental Psychology*, 32: 921–4.

Bennett, J. (2008) '*Public Policy and Early Childhood Systems in Europe*', Paper given at 18th Annual EECERA (European Early Childhood Education Research Association) Conference, Stavangar, Norway, 3–6 September 2008.

Bennett, N., Wood, E. and Rogers, S. (1997) *Teaching through Play: Teachers' Thinking and Classroom Practice*. Buckingham: Open University Press.

Bennis, W. (1999) 'The end of leadership: exemplary leadership is impossible without full inclusion, initiatives and co-operation of followers', *Organizational Dynamics*, 28 (1): 71–9.

BERA (British Educational Research Association) Early Years Special Interest Group (2003) *Early Years Research: Pedagogy, Curriculum and Adult Roles, Training and Professionalism*. Southwell, Notts: BERA.

Berk, L.E. (1992) 'Children's private speech: an overview of theory and the status of research', in R.M. Diaz and L.E. Berk (eds), *Private Speech: From Social Interaction to Self-regulation*. Hillsdale, NJ: Erlbaum.

Berk, L.E. (2003) *Child Development* (6th edition). Boston, MA: Allyn and Bacon.

Berko Gleason, J. (2005) *The Development of Language*. Boston: Pearson Education Inc.

Berlyne, D.E. (1969) 'Laughter, humour and play', in G. Lindzey and E. Aronson (eds), *Handbook of Social Psychology*. Reading, MA: Addison-Wesley.

Bernstein, B. (1981) 'Codes, modalities and the process of cultural reproduction: a model', *Language and Society*, 10: 327–63.

Bjorklund, D.F. (2000) *Children's Thinking: Developmental Function and Individual Differences* (3rd edition). Belmont, CA: Wadsworth.

Bjorklund, D.F., Miller, P.H., Coyle, T.R. and Slawinsky, J.L. (1997) 'Instructing children to use memory strategies: evidence of utilization deficiencies in memory training studies', *Developmental Review*, 17: 411–42.

Black, K. and Lobo, M. (2008) 'A conceptual review of family resilience factors', *Journal of Family Nursing*, 14 (1): 33–55.

Blackmore, J. (1989) 'Educational leadership: a feminist critique and reconstruction', in J. Smyth (ed.), *Critical Perspectives on Educational Leadership*. London: Falmer Press.

Blair, M., Crowther, R., Waterson, T. and Stewart-Brown, S. (2003) *Child Public Health*. Oxford: Oxford University Press.

Blanden, J. and Machin, S. (2007) *Recent Changes in Intergenerational Mobility in the UK: Report for the Sutton Trust*, December 2007, p.18. Available at: www.econ.surrey.ac.uk (accessed 14 March 2008).

Blenkin, G. and Kelly, A. (1987) *The Primary Curriculum*. London: Harper & Row.

Bloch, C. (2007) 'Foreign language learning in South Africa early childhood education', in M. Cochran and R. New (eds), *Encyclopedia of Early Childhood Education*, Vol.4: 1224–26.

Bloom, L. (1970) *Language Development: Form and Function in Emerging Grammars*. Cambridge, MA: MIT Press.

Bloom, P.J. (1997) 'Navigating the rapids: directors reflect on their career and professional development', *Young Children*, 52 (7): 32–8.

Bloom, P.J. (2000) 'How do we define director confidence?', *Childcare Information Exchange*, 138: 13–18.

Bohannon, N. and Stanowicz, L. (1988) 'The issue of negative evidence: adult responses to children's language errors', *Developmental Psychology*, 24: 684–9.

Boland, A.M., Haden, C.A. and Ornstein, P.A. (2003) 'Boosting children's memory by training mothers in the use of an elaborative conversational style as an event unfolds', *Journal of Cognition and Development*, 4: 39–65.

Booth, T. (2000) 'Reflection', in P. Clough and J. Corbett (eds), *Theories of Inclusive Education*. London: PCP/Sage.

Booth, T., Ainscow, M., Kingston, D. (2006) *Index for Inclusion: Developing Learning, Participation and Play in Early Years and Childcare.* Bristol: Centre for Studies on Inclusive Education.

Booth, T. and Smith, R. (2002) 'Sustaining inclusive education development: learning about barriers and resources in a London borough'. Revision of paper presented at the British Educational Research Association Annual Conference, University of Exeter, 12–14 September.

Bornstein, M.H. and Bruner, J.S. (eds) (1989) *Interaction in Human Development.* Hillsdale, NJ: Erlbaum.

Bossard, J. and Boll, E. (1966) *The Sociology of Child Development.* New York: Harper & Row.

Bourdieu, P. (1992) *The Logic of Practice.* Cambridge: Polity.

Boushel, M., Fawcett, M. and Selwyn, J. (eds) (2000) *Focus on Early Childhood: Principles and Realities.* Oxford: Blackwell.

Bowlby, J. (1951) *Maternal Care and Mental Health. Report to the World Health Organisation.* Geneva: World Health Organisation.

Bowlby, J. (1953, 1965) *Child Care and the Growth of Love.* Harmondsworth: Penguin.

Bowlby, J. (1969) *Attachment and Loss I, Attachment.* New York: Basic Books.

Bowlby, J. (1973) *Attachment and Loss II, Separation.* New York: Basic Books.

Bowlby, J. (1980) *Attachment and Loss III, Loss.* New York: Basic Books.

Bowlby, J. (1988) 'Developmental psychiatry comes of age', *American Journal of Psychiatry,* 145: 1–10.

Bowman, B., Donovan, S. and Burns, S. (eds) (2001) *Eager to Learn: Educating our Preschoolers.* Washington, DC: National Academy Press.

Boyd Webb, N. (1984) *Preschool Children with Working Parents: An Analysis of Attachment.* New York: University Press of America.

Bradshaw, J. (ed.) (2001) *Poverty: The Outcomes for Children.* London: Family Policy Studies Centre.

Bradshaw, J. and Mayhew, E. (eds) (2005) *The Well-being of Children in the UK* (2nd edition). London: Save the Children.

Braine, M. (1994) 'Is nativism sufficient?', *Journal of Child Language,* 21: 9–31.

Brandon, M., Schofield, G. and Trinder, L. (1998) *Social Work with Children.* London: Macmillan.

Brannen, J., Heptinstall, E. and Bhopal, K. (2001) *Connecting Children: Care and Family Life.* London: Routledge Falmer.

Brannen, J. and Moss, P. (2003) *Rethinking Children's Care.* Buckingham: Open University Press.

Braungart-Rieker, J.M., Garwood, M.M., Powers, B.P. and Wang, X. (2001) 'Parental sensitivity, infant affect, and affect regulation: predictors of later attachment', *Child Development,* 72 (1): 252–70.

Bretherton, I., McNew, S. and Beegley-Smith, M. (1981) 'Early person knowledge as expressed in gestural and verbal communication: when do infants acquire a "theory of mind?"', in M.E. Lamb and L.R. Sherrod (eds), *Infant Social Cognition*. Hillsdale, NJ: Erlbaum.

Breton, M. (2001) 'Neighbourhood resiliency', *Journal of Community Practice*, 9 (12): 21–36.

Bridge, G. and Miles, G. (1997) *On the Outside Looking In: Collected Essays on Young Child Observation in Social Work Training*. London: CCETSW.

Bronfenbrenner, U. (1979) *The Ecology of Human Development*. Cambridge, MA: Harvard University Press.

Bronfenbrenner, U. (1986) 'Ecology of the family as a context for human development: research perspectives', *Developmental Psychology*, 22: 723–42.

Bronfenbrenner, U. and Morris, P.A. (1998) 'The ecology of developmental processes', in W. Damon (Series ed.) and R.M. Lerner (Vol. ed.), *Handbook of Child Psychology: Vol. 1. Theoretical Models of Human Development* (5th edition). New York: Wiley. pp. 993–1028.

Brooker, L. (2002) *Starting School – Young Children's Learning Cultures*. Buckingham: Open University Press.

Brown, A.L. (1997) 'Transforming schools into communities of thinking and learning about serious matters', *American Psychologist*, 52: 300–413.

Brown, F. (2003) *Playwork: Theory and Practice*. Buckingham: Open University Press.

Brown, L., Tucker, C. and Domokos, T. (2003) 'Evaluating the impact of integrated health and social care teams on older people living in the community', *Health and Social Care in the Community*, 11 (2): 85–94.

Brumbaugh, C.C. and Fraley, R.C. (2006) 'Transference and attachment: how do attachment patterns get carried forward from one relationship to the next?', *Personality and Social Psychology Bulletin*, 32 (4): 552–60.

Bruner, J. (1960) *The Process of Education*. Cambridge, MA: Harvard University Press.

Bruner, J. (1966) *Towards a Theory of Instruction*. Cambridge, MA: Harvard University Press.

Bruner, J. (1972) 'Functions of play', in J. Bruner, A. Jolly and K. Sylva (eds), *Play and its Role in Evolution and Development*. Harmondsworth: Penguin Books.

Bruner, J. (1974) 'Child's play', *New Scientist*, 62: 126–8.

Bruner, J. (1983) *Child's Talk: Learning to Use Language*. Oxford: Oxford University Press.

Bruner, J. (1986) *Actual Minds, Possible Words*. Cambridge, MA: Harvard University Press.

Bruner, J. (1990) *Acts of Meaning*. Cambridge, MA: Harvard University Press.

Bruner, J. (2000) 'Foreword', in J. DeLoache and A. Gottlieb (eds), *A World of Babies: Imagined Childcare Guides for Seven Societies*. Cambridge: Cambridge University Press.

Bryant, B., Harris, M. and Newton, D. (1980) *Children and Minders*. Oxford: Oxford Pre-school Research Project.

Buckingham, D. (2000) *After the Death of Childhood: Growing Up in the Age of Electronic Media*. Cambridge: Polity.

Burts, D., Hart, C., Charlesworth, R. and Kirk, L. (1990) 'A comparison of frequency of stress behaviours observed in kindergarten children in classrooms with developmentally appropriate versus developmentally inappropriate instructional practices', *Early Childhood Research Quarterly*, 5: 407–23.

Butler, I. (2007) Children's Policy in Wales', in C. Williams (ed.), *Social Policy for Social Welfare Practice in a Devolved Wales*. Birmingham: BASW/Venture Press.

Butler, I. and Roberts, G. (2003) *Social Work with Children and Families* (2nd edition). London: Jessica Kingsley.

Bybee, J. and Scheibman, J. (1999) 'The effect of usage on degrees of constituency: the reduction of don't in English', *Linguistics*, 37: 575–96.

Cameron-Faulkner, T., Lieven, E. and Tomasello, M. (2003) 'A construction based analysis of child directed speech', *Cognitive Science*, 27: 843–73.

Candappa, M. (2002) 'Human rights and refugee children in the UK', in B. Franklin (ed.), *A New Handbook of Children's Rights*. London: Routledge Falmer.

Carey, S. and Spelke, E.S. (1994) 'Domain-specific knowledge and conceptual change', in L.S. Hirschfeld and S.A. Gelman (eds), *Mapping the Mind: Domain Specificity in Cognition and Culture*. Cambridge: Cambridge University Press.

Carlson, S. and Moses, L. (2001) 'Individual differences in inhibitory control and children's theory of mind', *Child Development*, 72: 1032–53.

Carr, M. and May, H. (2000) 'Te Whariki: curriculum voices', in H. Penn (ed.), *Early Childhood Services: Theory, Policy and Practice*. Buckingham: Open University Press.

Case, R. (1985) *Intellectual Development: Birth to Adulthood*. New York: Academic Press.

Central Advisory Council for Education (CACE) (1967) *The Plowden Report: Children and their Primary Schools*. Central Advisory Council for England. London: HMSO.

Cerezo, M.A., Pons-Salvador, G. and Trenado, R.M. (2008) 'Mother–infant interaction and children's socio-emotional development with high- and low-risk mothers', *Infant Behavior & Development*, 31(4): 578–89.

Chandler, M., Fritz, A.S. and Hala, S. (1989) 'Small-scale deceit: deception as a marker of 2-, 3-, and 4-year-olds' early theories of mind', *Child Development*, 60: 1263–77.

Chapman, N., Emerson, S., Gough, J., Mepani, B. and Read, N. (2000) *Views of Health Report 1: Report Based on Consultations with Groups of Children and Young People in London*. London: Save the Children.

Chenoweth, L. and Stehlik, D. (2001) 'Building resilient communities: social work practice and rural Queensland', *Australian Social Work*, 54 (2): 47–54.

Chi, M.T.H. (1978) 'Knowledge structure and memory development', in R. Siegler (ed.), *Children's Thinking: What Develops?* Hillsdale, NJ: Erlbaum.

Child Growth Foundation (2008) *An Approach to Primary Prevention of Obesity in Children and Adolescents*. Available at: www.childgrowthfoundation.co.uk (accessed 1 October 2008).

Children Act 2004. London: The Stationery Office.

Chomsky, N. (1959) 'A review of B.F. Skinner's "Verbal Behavior"', *Language,* 35: 26–58.

Chomsky, N. (1965) *Aspects of the Theory of Syntax.* Cambridge, MA: MIT Press.

Chomsky, N. (1995) *The Minimalist Program.* Cambridge, MA: MIT Press.

Christensen, P. and James, A. (eds) (2008) *Research with Children* (2nd edition). London: Routledge Falmer.

Clark, A. (2004) 'The Mosaic approach and research with young children', in V. Lewis, M. Kellett, C. Robinson, S. Fraser and S. Ding (eds), *The Reality of Research with Children and Young People.* London: Sage.

Clark, A. (2005) 'Ways of seeing: using the Mosaic approach to listen to young children's perspectives', in A. Clark, P. Moss and A.T. Kjørholt (eds), *Beyond Listening: Children's Perspectives, on Early Childhood Services.* Bristol: Policy Press.

Clark, A. (2007) 'View from inside the shed: young children's perspectives of the outdoor environment', *Education 3–13,* 13 (4): 349–63.

Clark, A. (2008) *Early Childhood Spaces: Involving Young Children and Practitioners in the Design Process. Working paper 45.* The Hague: Bernard van Leer Foundation.

Clark, A., Kjørholt, A.T. and Moss, P. (2005) *Beyond Listening: Children's Perspectives on Early Childhood Services.* Bristol: Policy Press.

Clark, A. and Moss, P. (2001) *Listening to Young Children: The Mosaic Approach.* London: National Children's Bureau.

Clark, A. and Moss, P. (2005) *Spaces to Play: More Listening to Young Children Using the Mosaic Approach.* London: National Children's Bureau.

Clark, M.M. and Waller, T. (eds) (2007) *Early Childhood Education and Care: Policy and Practice.* London: Sage.

Clarke, A. (2001) 'Early adversity and adoptive solutions', *Adoption and Fostering,* 25 (1): 24–32.

Clay, M.M. (1966) 'Emergent reading behavior'. Unpublished doctoral dissertation, University of Auckland, New Zealand.

Clearfield, M.W., Osborne, C.N. and Mullen, M. (2008) 'Learning by looking: infants' social looking behavior across the transition from crawling to walking', *Journal of Experimental Child Psychology,* 100: 297–307.

Cocker, C. and Allain, L. (2008) *Social Work with Looked After Children.* Exeter: Learning Matters.

Colton, M., Drury, C. and Williams, M. (1995) *Children in Need.* Aldershot: Avebury.

Colton, M., Sanders, R. and Williams, M. (2001) *An Introduction to Working with Children: A Guide for Social Workers.* Basingstoke, Hampshire: Palgrave.

Connolly, P. (1998) *Racism, Gender Identities and Young Children: Social Relations in a Multi-Ethnic, Inner-City Primary School.* London: Routledge.

Cooper, P.J. and Murray, L. (1998) 'Fortnightly review: postnatal depression', *British Medical Journal,* 316 (7148): 1884–6.

Corsaro, W. (1985) *Friendship and Peer Culture in the Early Years.* Norwood, NJ: Ablex.

Corsaro, W. (1997) *The Sociology of Childhood.* London and Pine Forge, CA: Sage.

Coulmas, F. (ed.) (1981) *Conversational Routine*. The Hague: Mouton.

Court, M. (1994) *Women Transforming Leadership*. Palmerston North, New Zealand: ERDC Press.

Cousins, J. (1999) *Listening to Four-year-olds*. London: National Early Years Network.

CPHVA/UNITE (2008) *Annual Report 2007/2008*. London: CPHVA.

Crain, W. (1992) *Theories of Development: Concepts and Applications* (3rd edition). Englewood Cliffs, NJ: Prentice Hall.

Cranston, M. (1967) 'Human rights, real and supposed', in D.D. Raphael (ed.), *Political Theory and the Rights of Man*. Bloomington, IN: Indiana University Press.

Croft, W. (2001) *Radical Construction Grammar: Syntactic Theory in Typological Perspective*. Oxford: Oxford University Press.

Cunningham, H. (2006) *The Invention of Childhood*. London: BBC Books.

Curriculum Review Programme Board (CRPB) (2006) *A Curriculum for Excellence: Progress and Proposals*. Edinburgh: Scottish Executive.

Curtis, H. and Sanderson, M. (2004) *The Unsung Sixties: Memoirs of Social Innovation*. London: Whiting & Birch.

Dabrowska, E. (2000) 'From formula to schema: The acquisition of English questions'. *Cognitive Linguistics*, 11: 1–20.

Dahlberg, G. and Moss, P. (2005) *Ethics and Politics in Early Childhood Education*. London and New York: RoutledgeFalmer.

Dahlberg, G., Moss, P. and Pence, A. (1999, 2007) *Beyond Quality in Early Childhood Education and Care: Languages of Evaluation* (2nd edition). London: Routledge.

Daniel, B., Wassell, S. and Gilligan, R. (1999) *Child Development for Child Care and Protection Workers*. London: Jessica Kingsley.

David, T. (1994) (ed.) *Working Together for Young Children: Multi-professionalism in Action*. London: Routledge.

David, T. (2001) 'Curriculum in the early years', in G. Pugh (ed.), *Contemporary Issues in the Early Years: Working Collaboratively for Children*. London: Paul Chapman.

David, T., Goouch, K., Powell, S. and Abbott, L. (2003) *Birth to Three Matters: A Review of the Literature* (DFES Research report No. 444). London: Department for Education and Skills.

David, T. and Powell, S. (2005) 'Play in the early years; the influence of cultural difference', in J. Moyles (ed.), *The Excellence of Play*. Buckingham: Open University Press.

Davies, D. (1999) *Child Development: A Practitioner's Guide*. New York: Guilford Press.

Davis, J., Watson, N. and Cunningham–Burley, S. (2000) 'Learning the lives of disabled children: developing a reflexive approach', in P. Christensen and A. James (eds), *Research with Children: Perspectives and Practices*. London: Falmer Press.

Daycare Trust (2008) *Childcare Costs Survey*. Available at: www.daycaretrust.org.uk/mod/fileman/files/Cost_survey2008.pdf (accessed 12 March 2008).

de Gaay Fortman, B. (2003) 'Poverty as global failure', *Development Issues*, 5 (1): 16–17.

DeMause, L. (1974) *The History of Childhood*. London: Souvenir Press.

Demetras, M., Post, K. and Snow, C. (1986) 'Feedback to first language learners', *Journal of Child Language*, 13: 275–92.

Dempster, F.N. (1993) 'Resistance to interference: developmental changes in a basic processing mechanism', in M.L. Howe and R. Pasnak (eds), *Emerging Themes in Cognitive Development. Vol. 1: Foundations*. New York: Springer-Verlag.

Department for Children, Education, Lifelong Learning and Skills (DCELLS) (2008) *Framework for Children's Learning for 3- to 7-year-olds in Wales*. Cardiff: Welsh Assembly Government.

Department for Children, Schools and Families (DCSF) (2008) *Practice Guidance for the Early Years Foundation Stage: Setting the Standards for Learning, Development and Care for Children from Birth to Five*. London: HMSO.

Department for Education and Skills (DfES) (1998a) *National Childcare Strategy*. London: HMSO.

Department for Education and Skills (DfES) (1998b) *Sure Start*. London: HMSO.

Department for Education and Skills (DfES) (2003) *Every Child Matters*. Green Paper. London: DfES.

Department for Education and Skills (DfES) (2004) *Independent Reviewing Officers Guidance Adoption and Children Act 2002*. London: The Stationery Office.

Department for Education and Skills (DfES) (2005) *Primary National Strategy Key Elements of Effective Practice (KEEP)*. London: DfES/Sure Start.

Department for Education and Skills (DfES) (2006) *Information Sharing: Practitioners' Guide – Integrated Working to Improve Outcomes for Children and Young People*. Availbale at: www.everychildmatters.gov.uk/informationsharing (accessed 11 August 2008).

Department for Education and Skills (DfES) (2007a) *Practice Guidance for the Early Years Foundation Stage*. Nottingham: DfES Publications. Available at: www.standards.dfes.gov.uk/eyfs/ (accessed 6 March 2009).

Department for Education and Skills (DfES) (2007b) *The Early Years Foundation Stage*. Nottingham: DfES Publications.

Department of Health (1989) *A Study of Enquiry Reports 1980–1989*. London: HMSO.

Department of Health (1993) *Children Act Report 1992*. London: HMSO.

Department of Health (1996) *The Green Book*. London: HMSO.

Department of Health (2000) *The NHS Plan*. London: HMSO.

Department of Health (2004) *National Service Framework for Children, Young People and Maternity Services: The Mental Health and Psychological Wellbeing of Children and Young People*. London: HMSO.

Department of Health (2008) *Child Health Promotion Programme*. London: HMSO.

Department of Health and Social Security (1974) *Report of the Committee of Inquiry into the Care and Supervision Provided in Relation to Maria Colwell*. London: HMSO.

Department of Health and Social Security (1988) *Working Together: A Guide to Arrangements for Inter-agency Co-operation for the Protection of Children from Abuse.* London: HMSO.

Department of Health, Department for Education and Employment, Home Office (2000) *Framework for the Assessment of Children in Need and Their Families.* London: The Stationery Office.

Department of Health, Home Office, Department for Education and Employment (1999) *Working Together to Safeguard Children.* London: HMSO.

Derman-Sparks, L. (1989) *Anti-Bias Curriculum: Tools for Empowering Young Children.* New York, NY: National Association for the Education of Young Children.

Deven, F. and Moss, P. (2002) 'Leave arrangements for parents: overview and future outlook', *Community, Work and Family,* 5: 237–55.

Dingwall, R. and McIntosh, J. (1978) 'Teamwork in theory and practice', in R. Dingwall and J. McIntosh (eds), *Readings in the Sociology of Nursing.* Edinburgh: Churchill Livingstone.

Doddington, C. and Hilton, M. (2007) *Child-centred Education: Reviving the Creative Tradition.* London: Sage.

Donald, J. and Rattansi, A. (1992) *Race, Culture and Difference.* Milton Keynes: Open University.

Dowling, M. (2003) 'All about resilience', *Nursery World,* 103 (3891): 15–22.

Doyle, B. (1997) 'Transdisciplinary approaches to working with families', in B. Carpenter (ed.), *Families in Context: Emerging Trends in Family Support and Early Intervention.* London: David Fulton.

Draper, L. and Duffy, B. (2001) 'Working with parents', in G. Pugh (ed.), *Contemporary Issues in the Early Years.* London: Paul Chapman Publishers.

Drew, A. (2001) 'Screening and surveillance for autism and persuasive developmental disorders', *Archive of Diseases in Childhood,* 84: 468–75.

Duncan, G.J. and Brooks-Gunn, J. (2000) 'Family poverty, welfare reform, and child development', *Child Development,* 71: 188–96.

Dunn, J. (1984) *Sisters and Brothers.* London: Fontana.

Dunn, J. (1993) *Young Children's Close Relationships: Beyond Attachment.* Newbury Park, CA: Sage.

Dunn, J. (1999) 'Mind reading and social relationships', in M. Bennett (ed.), *Developmental Psychology.* London: Taylor & Francis.

Durkin, K. (1996) *Developmental Social Psychology.* Oxford: Blackwell.

Dworkin, R. (1978) 'Liberalism', in S. Hampshire (ed.), *Public and Private Morality.* Cambridge: Cambridge University Press.

Dyhouse, C. (1989) *Feminism and the Family in England,* 1880–1939. Oxford: Blackwell.

Ebbeck, M. and Waniganayake, M. (2000) *Early Childhood Professionals: Leading Today and Tomorrow.* Eastgardens, NSW: McLennan and Petty.

Edwards, A. and Knight, P. (2000) *Effective Early Years Education – Teaching Young Children.* Buckingham: Open University Press.

Edwards, C., Gandini, L. and Forman, G. (1993) *The Hundred Languages of Children: The Reggio Emilia Approach to Early Childhood Education.* Norwood, NJ: Ablex Publishing.

Edwards, C., Gandini, L. and Forman, G. (1998) *The Hundred Languages of Children – Advanced Reflections.* Greenwich, CT: Ablex Publishing.

Einarrsdottir, J. (2005) 'Playschool in pictures: children's photographs as a research method', *Early Childhood Development and Care,* 175 (6): 523–42.

Elfer, P., Goldschmied, E. and Selleck, D. (2002) *Key Persons in Nurseries: Building Relationships for Quality Provision.* London: NEYN.

Elkin, F. (1960) *The Child and Society: The Process of Socialisation.* New York: Random House.

Elkind, D. (1987) *Miseducation: Pre-schoolers at Risk.* New York: Knopf.

Elman, J.L., Bates, E.A., Johnson, M.H., Karmiloff-Smith, A., Parisi, D. and Plunkett, K. (1996) *Rethinking Innateness: A Connectionist Perspective on Development.* Cambridge, MA: MIT Press.

Emond, R. (2005) 'Ethnographic research methods with children and young people', in S. Greene and D. Hogan (eds), *Researching Children's Experience: Approaches and Methods.* London: Sage.

Englander, D. and O'Day, R. (1995) *Retrieved Riches: Social Investigation in Britain, 1840–1914.* Aldershot: Scolar Press for the Open University.

Ereky-Stevens, K. (2008) 'Associations between mothers' sensitivity to their infants' internal states and children's later understanding of mind and emotion', *Infant and Child Development,* article in press.

Erikson, E. (1977) *Toys and Reasons: Stages in the Ritualisation of Experience.* New York: Norton.

Erlandsson, K. and Fagerberg, I. (2005) 'Mothers' lived experiences of co-care and part-care after birth, and their strong desire to be close to their baby', *Midwifery,* 21: 131–8.

Evans, G., Boxhill, L. and Pinkara, M. (2008) 'Poverty and maternal responsiveness: the role of maternal stress and social resources', *International Journal of Behavioural Development,* 32: 232–7.

Evans, L., Packwood, A., Neill, St. J. and Campbell, R.J. (1994) *The Meaning of Infant Teachers' Work.* London: Routledge.

Fagan, R.M. (1984) 'Play and behavioural flexibility', in P.K. Smith (ed.), *Play in Animals and Humans.* Oxford: Basil Blackwell.

Farrell, A. (2005) *Ethical Research with Children.* Maidenhead: Open University Press.

Fass, P. (2007) *Children of a New World: Society, Culture and Globalization.* New York: New York University Press.

Fawcett, M. (1996) *Learning Through Child Observation.* London: Jessica Kingsley.

Fawcett, M. (forthcoming 2009) *Learning Through Child Observation* (2nd edition). London: Jessica Kingsley Publishers.

Feder, G., Salkind, M.R. and Sweeny, O. (1989) 'Traveller–Gypsies and general practitioners in East London: the role of the traveller health visitor', *Health Trends*, 21: 93–4.

Feldman, C. (1992) 'The new theory of theory of mind', *Human Development*, 35 (22): 107–17.

Fenwick, J., Barclay, L. and Schmied, V. (2008) 'Craving closeness: a grounded theory analysis of women's experiences of mothering in the Special Care Nursery', *Women and Birth*, 21: 71–85.

Ferri, E. (1981) *Combined Nursery Centres*. London: National Children's Bureau.

Ferri, E., Birchall, D., Gingell, V. and Gipps, C. (1981) *Combined Nursery Centres: A New Approach to Education and Day Care*. London: Macmillan.

Fitzpatrick, P., Molloy, B. and Johnson, Z. (1997) 'Community mothers' programme: extension to the travelling community in Ireland', *Journal of Epidemiology and Child Health*, 51 (3): 203–303.

Fivush, R., Kuebli, J. and Clubb, P.A. (1992) 'The structure of events and event representations: a developmental analysis', *Child Development*, 63: 188–201.

Flavell, J. (1996) 'Piaget's legacy', *Psychological Science*, 7: 200–3.

Flekkoy, M. and Kaufman, N. (1997) *The Participation Rights of the Child: Rights and Responsibilities in Family and Society*, London: Jessica Kingsley.

Flintham, A. (2003) *Reservoirs of Hope: Spiritual and Moral Leadership in Headteachers*. Nottingham: National College of School Leadership.

Foley, P., Roche, J. and Tucker, S. (eds) (2001) *Children in Society: Contemporary Theory, Policy and Practice*. Basingstoke: Palgrave.

Fonagy, P., Steele, M., Steele, H., Higgit, A. and Target, M. (1994) 'The theory and practice of resilience', *Journal of Child Psychology and Psychiatry*, 35 (2): 231–57.

Forrest, G. (ed.) (1997) *Bonding and Attachment: Current Issues in Research and Practice. Occasional Paper 14*. London: Association of Child Psychology and Psychiatry.

Fortin, J. (1998) *Children's Rights and the Developing Law*. London: Butterworth.

Fox, N.A., Kimmerley, N.L. and Schafer, W.D. (1991) 'Attachment to mother/attachment to father: a meta-analysis', *Child Development*, 62: 210–25.

Franklin, B. (2002) (ed.) *The New Handbook of Children's Rights*. London: Routledge.

Fraser, S. (2004) 'Situating empirical research', in S. Fraser, V. Lewis, S. Ding, M. Kellett and C. Robinson (eds), *Doing Research with Children and Young People*. London: Sage.

Frederick, J. and Goddard, C. (2007) 'Exploring the relationship between poverty, childhood adversity and child abuse from the perspective of adulthood', *Child Abuse Review*, 16: 323–41.

French, J. (2007) *Multi-agency Working: The Historical Background in The Team Around the Child*. Stoke on Trent: Trentham Books.

Freud, A. (1968) *The Psychoanalytic Treatment of Children*. New York: International Universities Press.

Frith, U. and Frith, C. (2001) 'The biological basis of social interaction', *Current Directions in Psychological Science*, 10: 151–5.

Fromberg, D.P. and Bergen, D. (1998) *Play from Birth to Twelve and Beyond: Contexts, Perspectives and Meanings*. New York: Garland.

Fukuyama, F. (1992) *The End of History and the Last Man*. New York: Free Press.

Fullan, M. (2001) *Leading in a Culture of Change*. San Francisco, CA: Jossey-Bass.

Gage, N. (1977) *The Scientific Basis for the Art of Teaching*. New York: Teachers College Press.

Gage, N. (1985) *Hard Gains in the Soft Science: The Case of Pedagogy*. Bloomington, IN: Phi Delta Kappa CEDR Monograph.

Galler, J. and Barrett, L. (2001) 'Children and famine: long term impact on health', *Ambulatory Child Health*, 7: 85–95.

Garcia, M., Pence, A. and Evans, E. (eds) (2008) *Africa's Future, Africa's Challenge: Early Childhood Care and Development in Sub-Saharan Africa*. Washington: World Bank.

Gardiner, M.F., Fox, A., Knowles, F. and Jeffrey, D. (1996) 'Learning improved by arts training', *Nature*, 381: 284.

Gardner, K. and Lewis, D. (1996) *Anthropology, Development and the Post-Modern Challenge*. London: Pluto Press.

Garvey, C. (1991) *Play* (2nd edition). London: Fontana.

Gauvain, M. (2001) *The Social Context of Cognitive Development*. New York: Guilford Press.

Geary, D.C. and Bjorklund, D.F. (2000) 'Evolutionary developmental psychology', *Child Development*, 71: 57–65.

Geertz, C. (1973) *The Interpretation of Cultures*. London: Fontana.

General Medical Council (2003) *Target Payments for Preventative Health Measures*. Available at: www.gmc-uk.co.uk (accessed 26 September 2008).

Giddens, A. (1993) *Sociology*. Cambridge: Polity Press.

Gilgun, J.F. (1996) 'Human development and adversity in ecological perspective, Part I: A conceptual framework', *Families and Society*, 77 (7): 395–402.

Gilligan, C. (1982) *In a Different Voice: Psychological Theory and Women's Development*. Cambridge, MA: Harvard University Press.

Glenny, G. and Roaf, C. (2008) *Multiprofessional Communication: Making Systems Work for Children*. Buckingham: Open University Press.

Goldschmied, E. and Jackson, S. (2003) *People under Three: Young Children in Day Care*. London: Routledge.

Goodman, G., Hans, S.L. and Cox, S.M. (1999) 'Attachment behaviour and its antecedents in off-spring born to methadone-maintained women', *Journal of Clinical Child Psychology*, 28: 58–69.

Goody, J. (1982) *Cooking, Cuisine and Class*. Cambridge: Cambridge University Press.

Gopnik, A., Melzoff, A. and Kuhl, P. (1999) *How Babies Think: The Science of Childhood*. London: Weidenfeld & Nicolson.

Gopnik, A. and Wellman, H. (1992) 'Why the child's theory of mind is really a theory', *Mind and Language*, 7: 145–71.

Gordon, A. and Olson, D.R. (1998) 'The relation between the acquisition of a theory of mind and the capacity to hold in mind', *Journal of Experimental Child Psychology*, 68: 70–83.

Gordon, M., Gorman D.R., Hasham, S. and Stewart, D.Q. (1991) 'The health of travellers' children in Northern Ireland', *Public Health,* 105 (5): 387–91.

Gottleib, A. (2004) *The Afterlife Is Where We Come From: The Culture of Infancy in West Africa.* Chicago: University of Chicago Press.

Greene, S. and Hogan, D. (eds) *Researching Children's Experience: Approaches and Methods.* London: Sage.

Greig, A. and Taylor, J. (1999) *Doing Research with Children.* London: Sage.

Gronn, P.C. (2000) 'A realistic study of leadership', *The Practicing Administrator,* 22 (1): 24–7.

Guardian (2001) 'UK "most racist" in Europe on refugees', 3 April.

Guha, M. (1988) 'Play in School', in G. Blenkin and A. Kelly (eds), *Early Childhood Education.* London: Paul Chapman.

Hagekull, B., Stenberg, G. and Bohlin, G. (1993) 'Infant–mother social referencing interactions: description and antecedents in maternal sensitivity and infant irritability', *Early Development and Parenting,* 2 (3): 183–91.

Hall, D.M.B. and Elliman, D. (2006) *Health for all Children* (4th edition) (revised). Oxford: OUP.

Hall, S. (1992) 'The question of cultural identity', in S. Hall, D. Held and T. McGrew (eds), *Modernity and Its Features.* Cambridge: Polity Press.

Hall, V. (1996) *Dancing on the Glass Ceiling: A Study of Women Managers in Education.* London: Paul Chapman.

Hallden, G. (1991) 'The child as project and the child as being: parents' ideas as frames of reference', *Children and Society,* 5 (4): 334–46.

Hallett, C. and Birchall, E. (1992) *Coordination and Child Protection: A Review of the Literature.* London: HMSO.

Handy, C. (1993) *Understanding Organisations* (4th edition). London: Penguin.

Hansen, K. and Joshi, H. (2007) *Millennium Cohort Study Second Survey: A User's Guide to Initial Findings.* London: Centre for Longitudinal Studies, Institute of Education, University of London.

Harcourt, D. and Conroy, H. (2005) 'Informed assent: ethics and processes when researching with young children', *Early Child Development and Care,* 175 (6): 567–77.

Harker, L. (2006) *Delivering on Child Poverty: What Would It Take? A Report for the Department for Work and Pensions.* London: TSO.

Harkness, S. and Super, C.M. (1994) 'The developmental niche: a theoretical framework for analyzing the household production of health', *Social Science and Medicine,* 38 (2): 217–26.

Harms, T., Clifford, R.M. and Cryer, D. (1998) *Early Childhood Environmental Rating Scale* (revised edition) (ECERS-R). New York: Teachers College Press.

Harris, F., Law, J. and Kermani, S. (2003) *The Second Implementation of the Sure Start Language Measure*. London: City University. Available at: www.surestart.gov.uk (accessed 6 March 2009).

Harris, P. (1989) *Children and Emotion: The Development of Psychological Understanding*. Oxford: Blackwell.

Harris, P., Johnson, C., Hutton, D., Andrews, G. and Cooke, T. (1989) 'Young children's theory of mind and emotion', *Cognition and Emotion*, 3: 379–400.

Hart, J.T. (1971) 'The inverse care law', *The Lancet*, 405–12.

Hart, R. (1979) *Children's Experience of Place*. New York: Irvington Publishers.

Harwood, R., Miller, J. and Lucca Irizarry, N. (1995) *Culture and Attachment: Perceptions of the Child in Context*. New York: Guilford Press.

Hatano, G. and Inagaki, K. (1996) 'Cognitive and cultural factors in the acquisition of intuitive biology', in D.R. Olson and N. Torrance (eds), *Handbook of Education and Human Development: New Models of Learning, Teaching and Schooling*. Cambridge: Blackwell.

Hatch, J. (1990) 'Young children as informants in classroom studies', *Early Childhood Research Quarterly*, 5: 251–64.

Hayden, J. (1997) 'Directors of early childhood services: experience, preparedness and selection', *Australian Research in Early Childhood*, 8 (1): 49–67.

Hearnshaw, L.S. (1979) *Cyril Burt, Psychologist*. London: Hodder & Stoughton.

Heath, S.B. (1983) *Ways with Words*. Cambridge: Cambridge University Press.

Heath, S.B. (1986) 'What no bedtime story means: narrative skills at home and school', in B. Schieffelin and E. Ochs (eds), *Language Socialization Across Cultures*. Cambridge: Cambridge University Press.

Hendrick, H. (1994) *Child Welfare: England, 1872–1989*. London: Routledge.

Hendrick, H. (ed.) (2005) *Child Welfare and Social Policy. An Essential Reader*. Bristol: Policy Press.

Herbert, E. (1994) 'Becoming a special family', in T. David (ed.), *Working Together for Young Children*. London: Routledge.

Herbert, E. and Carpenter, B. (1994) 'Fathers – the secondary partners: professional perceptions and a father's reflections', *Children and Society*, 8 (1): 31–41.

Her Majesty's Government (2003) *Every Child Matters* (Cmnd 5860). London: The Stationery Office.

Her Majesty's Government (2006) *Working Together to Safeguard Children: A Guide to Inter-agency Working to Safeguard and Promote the Welfare of Children*. London: TSO.

Her Majesty's Government (2008) *Every Child Matters*. Available at: www.every childmatters.gov.uk/aims/strategicoverview/integratedprocesses/ (accessed 5 December 2008).

Her Majesty's Treasury (HMT) (2004) *Choice for Parents, the Best Start for Children: A Ten Year Strategy for Childcare*. London: The Stationery Office.

Herrenkohl, E.C., Herrenkohl, R.C. and Egolf, B. (1994) 'Resilient early school-age children from maltreating homes: outcomes in late adolescence', *American Journal of Orthopsychiatry*, 64 (2): 301–9.

Hershman, D. and McFarlane, A. (2002) *Children Act Handbook*. Bristol: Family Law.

Heward, C. (1988) *Making a Man of Him: Parents and their Sons' Education at an English Public School, 1929–1950*. London: Routledge.

Heymann, J. (2002) Social transformations and their implications for the Global demand for ECCE. *UNESCO Policy Brief 8.* Available at: www.unesco.org/education/ecf/briefs (accessed 6 March 2009).

Heywood, C. (2001) *A History of Childhood: Children and Childhood in the West from Medieval to Modern Times*. Cambridge: Polity Press.

Hill, M. and Tisdall, K. (1997) *Children and Society*. Harlow: Longman.

Hirst, P.Q. and Thompson, G. (1996) *Globalization in Question: The International Economy and the Possibilities of Governance*. Cambridge: Polity Press.

Hodgkin, R. (1994) 'Cultural relativism and the UN Convention on the Rights of the Child', *Children and Society*, 8 (4): 296–9.

Hoff, E. (2008) *Language Development* (4th edition). Belmont, CA: Wadsworth Publishing.

Holland, J. and Blackburn, J. (eds) (1998) *Whose Voice? Participatory Research and Policy Change*. London: Intermediate Technology Publications.

Holloway, S. and Valentine, G. (2000) *Children's Geographies: Playing, Living, Learning*. London: Routledge.

Holt, J. (1975) *Escape from Childhood: The Needs and Rights of Children*. New York: Penguin.

Home Office (1999) *The Immigration and Asylum Act 1999*. London: HMSO.

Home Office (2006) *Single Equality Bill*. London: HMSO.

Home Office, Department of Health, Department of Education and Science, and Welsh Office (1991) *Working Together Under the Children Act 1989: A Guide to Inter-agency Co-operation for the Protection of Children from Abuse*. London: HMSO.

Hopper, P. and Thompson, S. (1984) 'The discourse basis for lexical categories in universal grammar', *Language*, 60: 703–52.

Horn, P. (1994) *Children's Work and Welfare, 1780–1890*. Cambridge: Cambridge University Press.

Hornstein, D., and Lightfoot, N. (1981) *Explanations in Linguistics*. London: Longman.

Horwath, J. and Morrison, T. (2007) 'Collaboration, integration and change in children's services: critical issues and key ingredients', *Child Abuse and Neglect,* 31: 55–69.

Howard, J. (2002) 'Eliciting young children's perceptions of play, work and learning using the activity apperception story procedure', *Early Child Development and Care*, 127: 489–502.

Howard, J., Jenvey, V. and Hill, C. (2006) 'Children's categorisation of play and learning based on social context', *Early Child Development and Care*, 176: 379–93.

Howard, J. and Prendiville, E. (2008) 'Developmental and therapeutic play', *Ip-Dip: For Professionals in Play*, 5: 16–17.

Howes, C. (1987) 'Peer interaction of young children', *Monographs of the Society for Research in Child Development*, No. 217, 53: 1.

Howes, C., Hamilton, C.E. and Matheson, C.C. (1994) 'Maternal, teacher and child care history correlates of children's relationships with peers', *Child Development*, 65 (1): 264–73.

Hoyle, I. (2004) 'From sycophant to saboteur – responses to organisational change', in C. Huffington, D. Armstrong, W. Halton, I. Hoyle and J. Pooley (eds), *Working Below the Surface: The Emotional Life of Organisations*. London: Karnac.

Huffington, C. (2004) 'What women leaders can tell us', in C. Huffington, D. Armstrong, W. Halton, I. Hoyle and J. Pooley (eds), *Working Below the Surface: The Emotional Life of Organisations*. London: Karnac.

Hughes, B. (1996) *A Playworker's Taxonomy of Play Types*. London: Playlink.

Hughes, C., Jaffee, S., Happe, F., Taylor, A., Caspi, A. and Moffitt, T. (2005) 'Origins of individual differences in theory of mind: from nature to nurture?', *Child Development*, 76: 356–70.

Hughes, F. (1999) *Children, Play and Development*. Boston, MA: Allyn and Bacon.

Hujala, E. and Puroila, A.-M. (eds) (1998) *Towards Understanding Leadership In Early Childhood Context: Cross-cultural Perspectives*. Oulu, Finland: Oulu University Press.

Hutchby, I. and Moran-Ellis, J. (eds) (1998) *Children and Social Competence: Arenas of Action*. London: Falmer.

Hutchins, T. and Sims, M. (1999) *Program Planning for Infants and Toddlers: An Ecological Approach*. London: Prentice Hall.

Hutt, S.J., Tyler, S., Hutt, C. and Christopherson, H. (1989) *Play, Exploration and Learning*. London: Routledge.

Inhelder, B., and Piaget, J. (1958) *The Growth of Logical Thinking from Childhood to Adolescence: An Essay on the Construction of Formal Operational Structures*. New York: Basic Books.

Issacs, D., Kilham, H.A. and Marshall, H., (2004) 'Should routine childhood immunisations be compulsory?', *Journal of Paediatric Child Health*, 40: 392–6.

Jackson, B. and Jackson, S. (1979) *Childminder: A Study in Action Research*. London: Routledge.

Jackson, S. (1992) '"Benign or sinister"? Parental responsibility in Great Britain', in P. Close (ed.), *The State and Caring*. Basingstoke: Macmillan.

Jackson, S. (1993) 'Under-fives: thirty years of no progress?' in G. Pugh (ed.), *Thirty Years of Change for Children*. London: National Children's Bureau.

Jagger, G. and Wright, C. (eds) (1999) *Changing Family Values*. London: Routledge.

James, A. (1998) 'Play in childhood: an anthropological perspective', *Child and Adolescent Mental Health*, 3 (3): 104–9.

James, A., Jenks, C. and Prout, A. (1998) *Theorizing Childhood*. Cambridge: Polity Press.

James, A. and Prout, A. (eds) (1990, 1997) *Constructing and Reconstructing Childhood: Contemporary Issues in the Sociological Study of Childhood*. London: Falmer Press.

James, A. and Prout, A. (1996) 'Strategies and structures: towards a new perspective on children's experiences of family life', in J. Brannen and M. O'Brien (eds), *Children in Families: Research and Policy*. London: Falmer.

Jarvis, P. (2007) 'Monsters, magic and Mr Psycho: rough and tumble play in the early years of a primary school, a biocultural approach', *Early Years*, 27: 171–88.

Jenks, C. (1996) (revised 2005) *Childhood*. London: Routledge.

Jennings, S. (1999) *Introduction to Developmental Play Therapy*. London: Jessica Kingsley.

Jones, C. (2004) *Supporting Inclusion in the Early Years*. Maidenhead: Open University Press.

Jones, C. and Pound, L. (2008) *Leadership and Management in the Early Years: From Principles to Practice*. Maidenhead: Open University Press.

Jones, N. with Vilar, E. (2008) 'Situating children in international development policy: challenges involved in successful evidence-informed policy making', *Evidence and Policy*, 4 (1): 31–51.

Jordan, A. and Robinson, T. (2008) 'Children, television viewing and weight status: summary and recommendations from an expert panel meeting', *The ANNALS of the American Academy of Political and Social Science,* 615: 119–32.

Joseph Rowntree Foundation (2008) – Ref 2244 *A Minimum Income Standard for Britain: What People Think*. Available at: www.jrf.org.uk/publications/minimum-income-standard-britain-what-people-think (accessed 6 March 2009).

Kağitçibaşi, Ç. (1996) *Family and Human Development Across Cultures*. Mahwah, NJ: Lawrence Erlbaum.

Kail, R. (1997) 'Processing time, imagery, and spatial memory', *Journal of Experimental Child Psychology*, 64: 67–78.

Kalliala, M. (2006) *Play Culture in a Changing World*. Buckingham: Open University Press.

Karmiloff-Smith, A. (1992) *Beyond Modularity: A Developmental Perspective on Cognitive Science*. Cambridge, MA: MIT Press.

Karnes, M., Shwedel, A. and Williams, M. (1983) 'A comparison of five different approaches for educating young children from low-income homes', in M. Karnes, A. Shwedel and M. Williams, *As the Twig is bent ... Lasting Effects of Pre-school Programmes*. Hillsdale, NJ: Erlbaum. pp. 133–70.

Karrby, G. (1989) 'Children's conceptions of their own play', *International Journal of Early Childhood Education*, 21 (2): 49–54.

Keats, D.M. (1997) *Culture and the Child*, London: John Wiley & Sons.

Kellett, M. (2005) *How to Develop Children as Researchers: A Step by Step Guide to Teaching the Research Process*. London: Paul Chapman.

Kelly, C. (2007) *Children's World: Growing up in Russia 1890–1991*. New Haven: Yale University Press.

Kemp, A. (2003) *National Research Register Protocol: Analysis of Injury Data to Compare Injury Rates in Children Living on a Designated Local Authority Caravan Site with Rates in an Area of a Similar Size and Demographic Profile.* Publication ID: M0054081473. National Research register, Issue 1.

Kendall, L. and Harker, L. (eds) (2002) *From Welfare to Wellbeing: The Future of Social Care.* London: Institute of Public Policy Research.

King, R. (1979) *All Things Bright and Beautiful? A Sociological Study of Infant Classrooms.* Bath: Wiley.

Kohli, R. (2007) *Social Work with Unaccompanied Asylum Seeking Children.* London: Palgrave/Macmillan.

Konner, M. (1991) *Childhood: A Multicultural View.* London: Ebury Press.

Korbin, J. (ed.) (1981) *Child Abuse and Neglect: Cross-cultural Perspectives.* Los Angeles, CA: University of California Press.

Kottak, C.P. (1994) *Anthropology: The Exploration of Human Diversity* (6th edition). New York: McGraw-Hill.

Kuh, D., Hardy, R., Langenburg, C., Richards, M. and Wadsworth, M. (2002) 'Mortality in adults aged 26–54 years linked to socioeconomic conditions in childhood and adulthood: post war birth cohort study', *British Medical Journal,* 325: 1076–80.

Kuhn, T. (1970) *The Structure of Scientific Revolutions,* (2nd edition). Chicago, IL: University of Chicago Press.

Kumar, R.C. (1997) '"Anybody's child": severe disorders of mother-to-infant bonding', *British Journal of Psychiatry,* 171: 175–81.

Laevers, F. (1995) *An Exploration of the Concept of Involvement as an Indicator for Quality in Early Childhood Education.* Dundee: Scottish Consultative Council on the Curriculum.

Lamb, M. (1997) *The Role of the Father in Child Development.* New York: Wiley.

Laming, Lord (2003) *The Victoria Climbié Inquiry Report.* London: The Stationery Office.

Landreth, G. (2002) *Play Therapy: The Art of the Relationship.* London: Brunner-Routledge.

Langacker, R.W. (1987) *Foundations of Cognitive Grammar: Theoretical Prerequisites.* Stanford, CA: Stanford University Press.

Langacker, R.W. (1991) *Concept, Image, and Symbol: The Cognitive Basis of Grammar.* Berlin and New York: Mouton de Gruyter.

Langsted, O. (1994) 'Looking at quality from the child's perspective', in P. Moss and A. Pence (eds), *Valuing Quality in Early Childhood Services: New Approaches for Defining Quality.* London: Paul Chapman.

Lareau, A. (2000) 'Social class and the daily lives of children: a study from the United States', *Childhood,* 7 (2): 155–71.

Lareau, A. (2003) *Unequal Childhoods: Class, Race and Family Life.* Berkeley, CA: University of California Press.

Lawrence, W.G. and Robinson, P. (1975) An innovation and its implementation: Issues of evaluation. Tavistock Institute of Human Relations: document no. CASR 1069 (unpublished). Cited in E. Miller (1993) *From Dependency to Autonomy: Studies in Organization and Change.* London: Free Association Books.

Leathard, A. (1990) 'Backing a united front', *Health Services Journal*, 100: 1776, 29 November.

Leathard, A. (1994) *Going Inter-professional: Working Together for Health and Welfare*. London: Routledge.

Lee, N. (2001) *Childhood and Society: Growing Up in an Age of Uncertainty*. Buckingham: Open University Press.

Leontiev, A. (1981) *Problems of the Development of Mind*. Moscow: Moscow University Press.

Lerner, R.M. (1998) 'Theories of human development: contemporary perspectives', in W. Damon (Series ed.) and R.M. Lerner (Vol. ed.), *Handbook of Child Psychology (Vol. 1): Theoretical Models of Human Development* (5th edition). New York: Wiley.

Leslie, A.M. (1987) 'Pretense and representation: the origins of "theory of mind"', *Psychological Review*, 94: 412–26.

LeVine, R.A. and Miller, P.M. (1990) 'Commentary', *Human Development*, 33: 73–80.

LeVine, R.A. and New, R. (eds) (2008) *Anthropology and Child Development: A Cross-cultural Reader*. Oxford: Blackwell.

Lewendon, C.J. and Maconachie, M. (2002) 'Why are children not being immunised? Barriers to immunisation uptake in South Devon', *Health Education Journal*, 61 (3): 212–20.

Lewis, M.D. (2000) 'The promise of dynamic systems approaches for an integrated account of human development', *Child Development*, 71: 36–43.

Lewis, V., Kellett, M., Robinson, C., Fraser, S. and Ding, S. (eds) (2004) *The Reality of Research with Children and Young People*. London: Sage.

Lieberman, J.N. (1977) *Playfulness: Its Relationship to Imagination and Creativity*. London: Academic Press.

Lieven, E. (1994) 'Crosslinguistic and crosscultural aspects of language addressed to children', in C. Gallaway and B.J. Richards (eds), *Input and Interaction in Language Acquisition*. Cambridge: Cambridge University Press.

Lieven, E., Behrens, H., Spears, J. and Tomasello, M. (2003) 'Early syntactic creativity: a usage-based approach', *Journal of Child Language*, 30: 333–70.

Lieven, E., Pine, J.M. and Baldwin, G. (1997) 'Lexically based learning and early grammatical development', *Journal of Child Language*, 24: 187–219.

Lifton, B. (1988) *King of Children: A Biography of Janusz Korczak*. New York: Farrar, Straus and Giroux.

Lindon, J. (2001) *Understanding Children's Play*. Cheltenham: Nelson Thomas.

Linthwaite, P., Sampson, K., Longfield, A. and Tarling, R. (1983) *The Health of Traveller Mothers and Children in East Anglia*. London: Save the Children Fund.

Livingstone, S. (2002) *Young People and New Media*. London: Sage.

Lowe, N. (2002) *White, Carr and Lowe: The Children Act In Practice*. London: Butterworth Tolley.

Lubeck, S. (1986) *Sandbox Society*. London: Falmer Press.

Lust, B. (2006) *Child Language: Acquisition and Growth*. Cambridge: Cambridge University Press.

Lutz, W.J., Hock, E. and Kang, M.J. (2007) 'Children's communication about distressing events: the role of emotional openness and psychological attributes of family members', *American Journal of Orthopsychiatry*, 77 (1): 86–94.

Lyons-Ruth, K. and Zeanah, C. (1993) 'The family context of infant mental health I, Affective development in the primary caregiving relationship', in C.H. Zeanah Jr (ed.), *Handbook of Infant Mental Health*. New York: Guilford Press.

MacDonald, P.F. (2007) 'The MMR vaccine controversy – winners, losers, impact and challenges', *British Journal of Infection Control*, 8 (1): 18–22.

MacIntyre, C.R. and Leask, J. (2003) 'Immunization myths and realities: responding to arguments against immunizations', *Journal of Paediatric Child Health*, 39: 487–91.

Malaguzzi, L. (1993) 'History, ideas and basic philosophy', in C. Edwards, L. Gandini and G. Forman (eds), *The Hundred Languages of Children: The Reggio Emilia Approach to Early Childhood Education*. Norwood, NJ: Ablex Publishing.

Mallory, B. and New, R. (eds) (1994) *Diversity and Developmentally Appropriate Practices: Challenges for Early Childhood Education*. New York: Teachers College Press.

Mandalakas, A. (2001) 'The greatest impact of war and conflict', *Ambulatory Child Health*, 7: 85– 95.

Mandell, N. (1991a) 'The least-adult role in studying children', in F.C. Waksler (ed.), *Studying the Social Worlds of Children: Sociological Readings*. London: Falmer Press.

Mandell, N. (1991b) 'Children's negotiation of meaning', in F.C. Waksler (ed.), *Studying the Social Worlds of Children: Sociological Readings*. London: Falmer Press.

Mandler, J.M. (1992) 'How to build a baby: II. Conceptual primitives', *Psychological Review*, 99: 587–604.

Marshall, D., O'Donaghue, S. and Kline, S. (2007) 'Families, food and pester power: beyond the blame game?', *Journal of Consumer Behaviour*, 6: 164–81.

Masson, J. and Morris, M. (1992) *Children Act Manual*. London: Sweet & Maxwell.

Masten, A.S. and Coatsworth, J.D. (1998) 'The development of competence in favourable and unfavourable environments: lessons from research on successful children', *American Psychologist*, 53 (2): 205–20.

Matyka, K. and Malik, S. (2008) 'Management of the obese child – application of the NICE guidelines', *The British Journal of Diabetes and Vascular Disease*, 8: 178–82.

Mayall, B. (ed.) (1994) *Children's Childhoods: Observed and Experienced*. London: Falmer.

Mayall, B. (2000) 'Conversations with children: working with generational issues', in P. Christensen and A. James (eds), *Research with Children*. London: Routledge Falmer.

Mayall, B. (2002) *Towards a Sociology for Childhood: Thinking from Children's Lives*. Buckingham: Open University Press.

Mayall, B. and Petrie, P. (1977) *Minder, Mother and Child*. London: Institute of Education.

Maybin, J. and Woodhead, M. (eds) (2003) *Childhoods in Context*. Chichester: John Wiley.

Mayes, L.C. (1995) 'Substance abuse and parenting', in M.H. Bornstein (ed.), *Handbook of Parenting, Volume 4: Applied and Practical Parenting*. Mahwah, NJ: Lawrence Erlbaum Associates.

McCullough, M. (2007) 'Integrating children's services: the case for child protection', in I. Siraj-Blatchford, K. Clarke and M. Needham (eds), *The Team Around the Child*. Stoke-on-Trent: Trentham Books.

McGuire, J. (1991) 'Social interactions of young, withdrawn children in day nurseries', *Journal of Reproductive and Infant Psychology*, 9: 169–79.

McNeill, D. (1966) 'The creation of language by children', in J. Lyons and R.J. Wales (eds), *Psycholinguistic Papers: The Proceedings of the 1966 Edinburgh Conference*. Edinburgh: Edinburgh University Press.

McShane, J. (1991) *Cognitive Development: An Information Processing Approach*. Oxford: Blackwell.

Mda, Z. (2002) *The Heart of Redness*. London: Picador.

Meadows, S. (1993) *The Child as Thinker: The Development and Acquisition of Cognition in Childhood*. London: Routledge.

Menzies Lyth, I. (1995) 'The development of the self in children in institutions', in J. Trowell and M. Bower (eds), *The Emotional Needs of Young Children and their Families: Using Psychoanalytic Ideas in the Community*. London: Routledge.

Mikhailovich, K. and Morrison, P. (2007) 'Discussing childhood overweight and obesity with parents: a health communication dilemma', *Journal of Child Health Care*, 11: 311–22.

Mikulincer, M. and Shaver, P.R. (2007) *Attachment in Adulthood: Structure, Dynamics, and Change*. New York: Guilford Press.

Miller, E.J. and Rice, A.K. (1967) *Systems of Organization: Task and Sentient Systems and their Boundary Control*. London: Tavistock Publications.

Miller, L. (2008) 'Developing professionalism within a regulatory framework in England: challenges and possibilities', *European Early Childhood Education Research Journal*, 16 (2): 255–68.

Miller, P.H. (2002) *Theories of Developmental Psychology* (4th edition). New York: Worth Publishers.

Miller, R. and Bizzell, R. (1983) 'The Louisville experiment: a comparison of four programmes', in M. Karnes, A. Shwedel and M. Williams, *As the Twig is Bent...Lasting Effects of Pre-school Programmes*. Hillsdale, NJ: Erlbaum.

Minujin, A., Delamonica, E., Davidzuik, A. and Gonzalez, E.D. (2006) 'The definition of child poverty: a discussion of concepts and measurements', *Environment and Urbanization*, 18: 481–500.

Mooney, A. (2003) 'Mother, teacher, nurse? How childminders define their role', in J. Brannen and P. Moss (eds), *Rethinking Children's Care*. Buckingham: Open University Press.

Morrow, V. (1994) 'Responsible children? Aspects of children's work and employment outside school in contemporary UK', in B. Mayall (ed.), *Children's Childhoods: Observed and Experienced*. London: Falmer Press.

Morrow, V. (1998) *Understanding Families: Children's Perspectives*. London: National Children's Bureau.

Morrow, V. and Richards, M. (1996) 'The ethics of social research with children', *Children & Society*, 10 (2): 90–105.

Mortimer, H. (2001) *Special Needs and Early Years Provision*. London: Continuum.

Moses, L.J., Baldwin, D.A., Rosicky, J.G. and Tidball, G. (2001) 'Evidence for referential understanding in the emotions domain at twelve and eighteen months', *Child Development*, 72 (3): 718–35.

Moss, P. and Penn, H. (1996) *Transforming Nursery Education*. London: Paul Chapman.

Moss, P. and Petrie, P. (2002) *From Children's Services to Children's Spaces*. London: Routledge Falmer.

Moyles, J. K. (2005) *The Excellence of Play*. Maidenhead: Open University Press.

Moyles, J.K. (2006) *Effective Leadership and Management in the Early Years*. Maidenhead: Open University Press.

Mrazek, P.J. and Mrazek, D.A. (1987) 'Resilience in child maltreatment victims: a conceptual exploration', *Child Abuse & Neglect*, 11 (3): 357–66.

Muijs, D., Aubrey, C., Harris, A. and Briggs, M. (2004) 'How do they manage? Research in leadership in early childhood', *Journal of Early Childhood Research*, 2 (2): 157–69.

Murray, L. and Trevarthen, C. (1985) 'Emotional regulation of interactions between two-month-olds and their mothers', in T.M. Field and N.A. Fox (eds), *Social Perception in Infants*. Norwood, NJ: Ablex.

Muscroft, S. (ed.) (1999) *Children's Rights: Reality or Rhetoric? The UN Convention on the Rights of the Child – The First Ten Years*. London: Save the Children.

Najman, J., Behrens, B., Anderen, M., Bor, W., O'Callaghan, M. and Williams, G. (1997) 'Impact of family type and family quality on child behaviour problems: a longitudinal study', *Journal of the American Academy of Child and Adolescent Psychiatry*, 36 (10): 1357–65.

National Assembly for Wales (2000) *Working Together to Safeguard Children: A Guide to Inter-agency Working to Safeguard and Promote the Welfare of Children*, Cardiff: National Assembly for Wales.

National Assembly for Wales (2001) *Child and Adolescent Mental Health Services: Everybody's Business–Strategy Document*. Cardiff: National Assembly for Wales.

National Children's Bureau (2005) *Children and Young People's Views on Health and Health Services: A Review of the Evidence*. London: NCB.

National Institute for Clinical Excellence (NICE) (2006) *Obesity Guidance on the Prevention, Identification, Assessment and Treatment of Obesity in Adults and Children*. London: NICE.

National Research Council and Institute of Medicine (2000) *From Neurons to Neighbourhoods: The Science of Early Childhood Development*. Washington, DC: National Academy Press.

Nederveen Pieterse, J. (2004) *Globalization and Culture: Global Melange*. Oxford: Rowman and Littlefield.

New Zealand Ministry of Education (1996) *Te Whariki: Every Childhood Curriculum*. Wellington, NZ: Learning Media Ltd.

Newton, M. (2002) *Savage Girls and Wild Boys: A History of Feral Children*. London: Faber and Faber Ltd.

NHS Health Advisory Service (1995) *Together We Stand: The Commissioning Role and Management of Child and Adolescent Mental Health Services*. London: HMSO.

NICHD Early Child Care Research Network (2002) 'Child-care structure –> process –> outcome: direct and indirect effects of child-care quality on young children's development', *Psychological Science*, 13: 199–206.

NICHD Early Child Care Research Network (2006) 'Infant–mother attachment classification: risk and protection in relation to changing maternal caregiving quality', *Developmental Psychology*, 42 (1) 38–58.

Ninio, A. and Snow, C. (1999) 'The development of pragmatics: learning to use language appropriately', in T.K. Bhatia and W.C. Ritchie (eds), *Handbook of Language Acquisition*. New York: Academic Press.

Nivala, V. (2000) 'Leadership in general leadership theory', in V. Nivala and E. Hujala (eds), *Leadership in Early Childhood Education*. Oulu, Finland: Oulu University Press.

Nivala, V. and Hujala, E. (eds) (2000) *Leadership in Early Childhood Education*. Oulu, Finland: Oulu University Press.

Noriuchi, M., Kikuchi, Y. and Senoo, A. (2008) 'The functional neuroanatomy of maternal love: mother's response to infant's attachment behaviors', *Biological Psychiatry*, 63: 415–23.

Nutbrown, C. and Clough, P. (2006) *Inclusion in the Early Years: Critical Analyses and Enabling Narratives*. London: Sage Publications.

Obholzer, A. with Miller, S. (2004) 'Leadership and followership and facilitating the creative workplace', in C. Huffington, D. Armstrong, W. Halton, I. Hoyle and J. Pooley (eds), *Working Below the Surface: The Emotional Life of Contemporary Organisations*. London: Karnac.

O'Brien, M., Alldred, P. and Jones, D. (1996) 'Children's constructions of family and kinship', in J. Brannen and M. O'Brien (eds), *Children in Families: Research and Policy*. London: Falmer.

Ochs, E. (1985) 'Variation and error: a sociolinguistic approach to language acquisition in Samoa', in D.I. Slobin (ed.), *The Crosslinguistic Study of Language Acquisition*, Vol. I. Hillsdale, NJ: Erlbaum.

Ochs, E. and Schieffelin, B.B. (1995) 'The impact of language socialization on grammatical development', in P. Fletcher and B. MacWhinney (eds), *The Handbook of Child Language*. Oxford: Blackwell. pp. 73–94.

Odofsky, J.D. (ed.) (1987) *Handbook of Infant Development*. New York: Wiley.

Oerter, R. (1993) *The Psychology of Play: An Activity Oriented Approach*. Munich: Quintessenz.

Office of the Deputy Prime Minister (2006) *Definition of the Term 'Gypsies and Travellers' for the Purposes of the Housing Act 2004*. London: HMSO.

Ofsted (1993) *First Class: The Standards and Quality of Education in Reception Classes*. London: HMSO.

O'Hagan, K. (2006) *Identifying Emotional and Psychological Abuse: A Guide for Childcare Professionals*. Buckingham: Open University Press.

Okri, B. (1991) *The Famished Road*. London: Cape.

O'Neill, O. (1992) 'Children's rights and children's lives', in P. Alston, S. Parker and J. Seymour (ed.), *Children, Rights and the Law*. Oxford: Oxford University Press.

Organisation for Economic Co-operation and Development (OECD) (2001) *Starting Strong: Early Childhood Education and Care*. Paris: OECD.

Organisation for Economic Co-operation and Development (OECD) (2004) *Starting Strong: Curricula and Pedagogies in Early Childhood Education and Care: Five Curriculum Outlines*, Directorate for Education, OECD: www.oecd.org/dataoecd/23/36/31672150.pdf (accessed 6 March 2009).

Organisation for Economic Co-operation and Development (OECD) (2006) *Starting Strong II: Early Childhood Education and Care*. Paris: OECD.

Osborn, A., Butler, N.R. and Morris, A.C. (1984) *The Social Life of Britain's Five-year-olds*. London: Routledge and Kegan Paul.

Øvretveit, J. (1990) *Cooperation in Primary Health Care*. Uxbridge: Brunel Institute of Organisation and Social Studies.

Øvretveit, J., Mathias, P. and Thompson, T. (1997) *Interprofessional Working for Health and Social Care*. London: Macmillan.

Owen, S. (2006) 'Training and workforce issues in the Early Years', in G. Pugh and B. Duffy (eds), *Contemporary Issues in the Early Years: Working Collaboratively for Children* (4th edition). London: Sage.

Owen, S. (2003) 'The development of childminding networks in Britain: sharing the caring', in A. Mooney and J. Statham (eds), *Family Day Care: International Perpectives on Policy, Practice and Quality*. London: Jessica Kingsley.

Palincsar, A.S. and Herrenkohl, L.R. (1999) 'Designing collaborative contexts: lessons from three research programs', in A.M. O'Donnell and A. King (eds), *Cognitive Perspectives on Peer Learning. The Rutgers Invitational Symposium on Education Series*. Mahwah, NJ: Erlbaum.

Parent, S., Normandeau, S. and Larivee, S. (2000) 'A quest for the Holy Grail in the new millennium: in search of a unified theory of cognitive development', *Child Development*, 71: 860–1.

Parton, N. (2006) *Safeguarding Childhood: Early Intervention and Surveillance in a Late Modern Society.* London: Palgrave Macmillan.

Pascal, C. and Bertram, A. (1995) *Evaluating and Developing Quality in Early Childhood Settings: A Professional Development Programme.* Worcester: Amber Publishing Co. Ltd.

Pascal, C. and Bertram, A. (1997) 'A conceptual framework for evaluating effectiveness in early childhood settings', in M.K. Lohmander (ed.), *Researching Early Childhood, Vol. 3, Settings in Interaction.* Gothenburg: Göteborg University, Early Childhood Research and Development Centre. pp.125–50.

Payne, M. (2000) *Teamwork in Multiprofessional Care.* London: Macmillan.

Pedro-Carroll, J. (2001) 'The promotion of wellness in children and families: challenges and opportunities', *American Psychologist*, 56 (11): 993–1004.

Pellegrini, A. (1991) *Applied Child Study: A Developmental Approach* (2nd edition). Hillsdale, NJ: Lawrence Erlbaum Associates.

Penn, H. (2005) *Unequal Childhoods: Young Children's Lives in Poor Countries.* London: Routledge.

Penn, H. (2007) 'Childcare market management: how the United Kingdom Government has reshaped its role in developing early childhood education and care', *Contemporary Issues in Early Childhood*, 8 (3): 192–207.

Penn, H. (2008) 'Working on the impossible: early childhood policies in Namibia', *Childhood*, 15 (3): 379–395.

Penn, H. and Maynard, T. (forthcoming) *Siyabonana – We All See One Another.* Edinburgh: Children in Scotland.

Percy-Smith, B. (2002) 'Contested worlds: constraints and opportunities growing up in inner and outer city environments of an English Midlands town', in L. Chawla (ed.), *Growing up in an Urbanizing World.* London: Earthscan.

Perner, J. (1991) *Understanding the Representational Mind.* Cambridge, MA: MIT Press.

Peterson, C. and Siegal, M. (1995) 'Deafness, conversation, and theory of mind', *Journal of Child Psychology and Psychiatry*, 36: 459–74.

Petrie, P., Boddy, J., Cameron, C., Wigfall, V. and Simon, A. (2006) *Working with Children in Care: European Perspectives.* Buckingham: Open University Press/ McGraw Hill.

Pew Survey of Global Attitudes (2008) *Unfavorable Views of Jews and Muslims on the Increase in Europe.* Available at http://pewglobal.org/reports/display.php?ReportID=262 (accessed 6 March 2009).

Phillips, D. and Ochs, K. (eds) (2004) *Educational Policy Borrowing: Historical Perspectives.* Oxford: Symposium Books.

Piaget, J. (1951) *Play, Dreams and Imitation in Childhood.* London: Routledge & Kegan Paul.

Piaget, J. (1952) *The Origins of Intelligence in Children.* New York: Norton.

Piaget, J. (1965) *The Child's Conception of Number.* New York: Norton.

Piaget, J. (1969) *The Child's Conception of the World*. Totowa, NJ: Littlefield & Adams.

Piaget, J. and Inhelder, B. (1969) *The Psychology of the Child*. New York: Basic Books.

Pilcher, J. and Wagg, S. (eds) (1996) *Thatcher's Children? Politics, Childhood and Society in the 1980s and 1990s*. London: Falmer Press.

Pink, S. (2007) *Doing Visual Ethnography: Images, Media and Representations in Research*. London: Sage.

Pinker, S. (1984) *Language Learnability and Language Development*. Cambridge, MA: Harvard University Press.

Pinker, S. (1994) *The Language Instinct: How the Mind Creates Language*. London: Penguin Books.

Pollard, A. (ed.) (1987) *Children and their Primary Schools: A New Perspective*. Lewes: Falmer Press.

Popkewitz, T. (2004) 'Foreword', in G. Steiner-Khamsi (ed.), *The Global Politics of Educational Borrowing and Lending*. New York: Teachers College Press.

Pramling, I., Sheridan, S. and Williams, P. (2004) 'Chapter 2: Key issues in curriculum development for young children', in OECD, *Starting Strong Curricula and Pedagogies in Early Childhood Education and Care: Five Curriculum Outlines*, Directorate for Education, OECD: www.oecd.org/dataoecd/23/36/31672150.pdf (accessed 6 March 2009).

Premack, D. and Woodruff, G. (1978) 'Does the chimpanzee have a theory of mind?', *Behavioural and Brain Sciences*, 4: 515–26.

Prendiville, S. (2008) Bringing the Beach Indoors: A Study Investigating Sand and Water Play Opportunities in Infant Classrooms in the Republic of Ireland. Unpublished Masters thesis, University of Limerick.

Preston, G. (2008) 'Education and child poverty', in J. Strlitz and R. Lister (eds), *Why Money Matters: Family Income, Poverty and Children's Lives*. London: Save the Children.

Prout, A. (2005) *The Future of Childhood*. London: Routledge Falmer.

Prout, A. and James, A. (1990) 'A new paradigm for the sociology of childhood? Provenance, promise and problems', in A. James and A. Prout (eds), *Constructing and Reconstructing Childhood: Contemporary Issues in the Sociological Study of Childhood*. London: Falmer Press.

Pugh, G. and Duffy, B. (eds) (2006) *Contemporary Issues in the Early Years* (4th edition). London: Sage Publications Ltd.

Pugh, R. (1997) 'Change in British social work: the lure of post-modernism and its pessimistic consequences', in B. Lesnik (ed.), *Change in Social Work*. Aldershot, Arena. pp. 89–109.

Pugh, R. and Gould, N. (2000) 'Globalisation, social work and social welfare', *European Journal of Social Work*, 3 (2): 123–38.

Purdy, L. (1992) *In Their Best Interest? The Case Against Equal Rights for Children*. Ithaca, NY: Cornell.

Qualifications and Curriculum Authority (QCA) (2000) *Curriculum Guidance for the Foundation Stage*. London: QCA., Reference QCA 00/587.

Qvortrup, J. (2005) 'Varieties of childhood', in J. Qvortrup (ed.), *Studies in Modern Childhood: Society, Agency, Culture*. Basingstoke: Palgrave Macmillan.

Qvortrup, J., Bardy, M., Sgritta, G. and Wintersberger, H. (eds) (1994) *Childhood Matters: Social Theory, Practice and Politics*. Aldershot: Avebury.

Ramani, G..B. (2005) Co-operative play and problem solving in pre-school children. Unpublished Doctoral thesis, University of Pittsburgh.

Rawson, D. (1994) 'Models of inter-professional work: likely theories and possibilities', in A. Leathard (ed.), *Going Inter-professional: Working together for Health and Welfare*. London: Routledge.

Reason, P. and Bradbury, H. (2006) *Handbook of Action Research*. London: Sage.

Rice, A. (1958) *Productivity and Social Organisation*. New York and London: Garland Publishing.

Rich, D. (2002) 'Catching children's stories', *Early Education*, 36: 6.

Richardson, K. (1998) *Models of Cognitive Development*. Hove, East Sussex: Psychology Press.

Roaf, C. (2002) *Coordinating Services for Included Children: Joined up Action*. Buckingham: Open University Press.

Roberts, H. (2000) 'Listening to children and hearing them', in P. Christensen and A. James (eds), *Research with Children*. London: Routledge Falmer. pp. 225–40.

Roberts, R. (2002) *Developing Self-esteem in Young Children*. London: Paul Chapman/Sage.

Roberts-Holmes, G.P. (2004) 'I am a little bit brown and a little bit white: a dual heritage young boy's playful identity construction', *Race Equality Teaching*, 23 (1): 15–20.

Robertson, J. and Robertson, J. (1989) *Separation and the Very Young*. London: Free Association Press.

Robinson, C. and Kellett, M. (2004) 'Power', in S. Fraser, V. Lewis, S. Ding, M. Kellett and C. Robinson (eds), *Doing Research with Children and Young People*. London: Sage.

Robinson, K. and Diaz, C. (2006) *Diversity and Difference in Early Childhood Education: Issues for Theory and Practice*. Buckingham: Open University Press.

Robinson, V.M. (2006) 'Putting education back into educational leadership', *Leading and Managing*, 12 (1): 62–75.

Robson, S. (1993) 'Best of all I like choosing time. Talking with children about play and work'. *Early Child Development and Care*, 92: 37–51.

Rodd, J. (1996) 'Towards a typology of leadership in the early childhood professional of the 21 century', *Early Child Development and Care*, 120: 119–26.

Rodd, J. (1997) 'Learning to be leaders: perceptions of early childhood professionals about leadership roles and responsibilities', *Early Years*, 18 (1): 40–6.

Rodd, J. (1999) *Leadership in Early Childhood*. Buckingham: Open University Press.

Rodd, J. (2006) *Leadership in Early Childhood: The Pathway to Professionalism*. Buckingham: Open University Press.

Rodham, H. (1976) 'Children under the law', in A. Skolnick (ed.), *Rethinking Childhood: Perspectives on Development and Society*. Boston: Little, Brown.

Rogoff, B. (1989) 'The joint socialization of development by young children and adults', reprinted in P. Light, S. Sheldon and M. Woodhead (1991), *Learning to Think. Child Development in Social Context 2*. London: Routledge.

Rogoff, B. (1990) *Apprenticeship in Thinking: Cognitive Development in Social Context*. New York: Oxford University Press.

Rogoff, B. (2003) *The Cultural Nature of Human Development*. Oxford: Oxford University Press.

Rogoff, B., Chavajay, P. and Matusov, E. (1993) 'Questioning assumptions about culture and individuals. Commentary of Michael Tomasello, Ann Cale Kruger and Hilary Horn Ratner', *Behavioural and Brain Sciences*, 16: 533–4.

Rogoff, B. and Morelli, G. (1993) 'Perspectives on children's development from cultural psychology', in M. Gauvain and M. Cole (eds), *Readings on the Development of Children*. New York: Scientific American Books.

Roopnarine, J., Lasker, J., Sacks, M. and Stores, M. (1998) 'The cultural context of children's play', in O. Saracho and B. Spodek (eds), *Multiple Perspectives on Play in Early Childhood*. New York: New York Press.

Rosser, R. (1994) *Cognitive Development: Psychological and Biological Perspectives*. Needham Heights, MA: Allyn & Bacon.

Rost, J.C. (1991) *Leadership in the Twenty-First Century*. New York: Praeger.

Rost, J.C. (1993) 'Leadership development in the millennium', *The Journal of Leadership Studies,* 1 (1): 92–110.

Rubin, K.H., Fein, G.G. and Vandenberg, B. (1983) 'Play', in P.H. Mussen and E.M. Hetherington (eds), *Handbook of Child Psychology, Vol. 4*. Basel: S. Karger.

Ruffman, T., Perner, J., Naito, M., Parkin, L. and Clements, W. (1998) 'Older (but not younger) siblings facilitate false belief understanding', *Developmental Psychology*, 34: 161–74.

Ruffman, T., Slade, L., and Crow, E. (2002) 'The relation between children's and mothers' mental state language and theory-of-mind understanding', *Child Development*, 73: 734–51.

Rutter, M. (1985) 'Resilience in the face of adversity: protective factors and resistance to psychiatric disorder', *British Journal of Psychiatry*, 147: 598–611.

Rutter, M. (1995) 'Clinical implications of attachment concepts: retrospect and prospect', *Child Psychology and Psychiatry*, 36 (4): 549–71.

Sameroff, A.J., Seifer, R., Baldwin, A. and Baldwin, C. (1993) 'Stability of intelligence from preschool to adolescence: the influence of social risk factors', *Child Development*, 64: 80–97.

Sammons, P., Sylva, K., Melhuish, E., Siraj-Blatchford, I., Taggart, B. and Barreau, S. (2007) *Effective Pre-school and Primary Education 3–11 Project (EPPE 3–11): Influences* on *Children's Attainment and Progress in Key Stage 2: Social/Behavioural Outcomes in Year 5. Full Report*. London: Institute of Education, University of London.

Sampson, G. (2005) *Educating Eve. The 'Language Instinct' Debate*. New York: Continuum International.

Sanders, R. (1999) *The Management of Child Protection Services: Context and Change*. Aldershot: Arena.

Sanders, R., Colton, M. and Roberts, S. (1999) 'Child abuse fatalities and cases of extreme concern: lessons from reviews', *Child Abuse and Neglect*, 23(3): 257–68.

Sanders, R., Jackson, S. and Thomas, N. (1996) 'The Police role in the management of Child Protection Services', *Policing and Society*, 6: 87–100.

Sanders, R., Jackson, S. and Thomas, N. (1997) 'Degrees of involvement: the interaction of focus and commitment in area child protection committees', *British Journal of Social Work*, 27: 871–92.

Sanders, R. and Pope, P. (2008) 'Restructuring social welfare in Wales', in V. Fortunato, G. Friesenhahn and E. Kantowicz (eds), *Social Work in Restructured European Welfare Systems*. Rome: Carocci.

Saracho, O. (1991) 'Educational play in early childhood', *Early Child Development and Care*, 66: 45–64.

Saracho, O. and Spodek, B. (1998) *Multiple Perspectives on Play in Early Childhood*. New York: New York Press.

Save the Children (2006) *Righting the Wrongs: The Reality of Children's Rights in Wales*. Cardiff: Save the Children.

Sawyer, R. (2003) 'Emergence in creativity and development', in R. Sawyer, V. John-Steiner, S. Moran and D. Feldman (eds), *Creativity and Development*. Oxford: University Press.

Sayer, T. (2008) *Critical Practice in Working with Children*. London: Palgrave/Macmillan.

Schaffer, H.R. (2004) *Introducing Child Psychology*. Oxford: Blackwell.

Schieffelin, B. (1994) 'Language acquisition and socialization: three developmental stories and their implications', in B. Blount (ed.), *Language, Culture, and Society*. Illinois: Waveland Press Inc.

Schneider, W. and Pressley, M. (1997) *Memory Development between 2 and 20* (2nd edition). Mahwah, NJ: Erlbaum.

Scholl, B. and Leslie, A. (1999) 'Modularity, development and theory of mind', *Mind and Language*, 14: 131–53.

Schön, D. (1983) *The Reflective Practitioner: How Practitioners Think in Action*. New York: Basic Books.

Schön, D. (1987) *Educating the Reflective Practitioner*. San Francisco, LA: Jossey-Bass.

Schultz, E. and Lavenda, R. (1990) *Cultural Anthropology: A Perspective on the Human Condition* (2nd edition). St Paul, MN: West Publishing.

Schultz, J. (1995) *The Knowledge of Childhood in the German Middle Ages, 1100–1350.* Philadelphia, PA: University of Pennsylvania Press.

Schweinhart, L.J., Barnes, H.V. and Weikart, D.P. (1993) *Significant Benefits: The High/Scope Perry Preschool Study through Age 27.* (Monographs of the High/Scope Educational Research Foundation, 10).Ypsilanti, MI: High/Scope Press. PS 021 998.

Schweinhart, L.J., Montie, J., Xiang, Z., Barnett, W., Belfield, C. and Nores, M. (2005) *Lifetime Effects: The High/Scope Perry Preschool Study through Age 40.* Ypsilanti, MI: High/Scope Press.

Schweinhart, L.J. and Weikart, D.P. (1997). 'The High/Scope Preschool Curriculum Comparison Study through age 23', *Early Childhood Research Quarterly*, 12: 117–43.

Selleck, D. and Griffin, S. (1996) 'Quality for the under-threes', in G. Pugh (ed.), *Contemporary Issues in the Early Years* (2nd edition). London: Paul Chapman/Sage.

Selwyn, J. (2000) 'Fetal development', in M. Boushel, M. Fawcett and J. Selwyn (eds), *Focus on Early Childhood: Principles and Realities.* Oxford: Blackwell.

Serpell, R. (1993) *The Significance of Schooling: Life Journeys in an African Society.* Cambridge: Cambridge University Press.

Seung Lam, M. and Pollard, A. (2006) 'A conceptual framework for understanding children as agents in the transition from home to kindergarten', *Early Years: Journal of International Research and Development,* 26 (2): 123–41.

Seymour-Smith, C. (1986) *Macmillan Dictionary of Anthropology.* London: Macmillan.

Shahar, S. (1990) *Childhood in the Middle Ages.* London: Routledge and Kegan Paul.

Shakeshaft, C. (1989) *Women in Educational Administration.* Beverley Hills, CA: Sage Publications.

Shook Slack, K., Hall, J.L., McDaniel, M., Yoo, J. and Bolger, K. (2004) 'Understanding the risks of child neglect: an exploration of poverty and parenting characteristics', *Child Maltreatment*, 9: 395–408.

Siegel, D. (1999) *The Developing Mind.* New York: Guilford Press.

Siegler, R.S. (1976) 'Three aspects of cognitive development', *Cognitive Psychology*, 8: 481–520.

Siegler, R.S. (2000) 'The rebirth of children's learning', *Child Development*, 71: 26–35.

Siegler, R.S., DeLoache, J. and Eisenberg, N. (2003) *How Children Develop.* New York: Worth.

Siencyn, S.W. and Thomas, S. (2007) 'Wales', in M.M. Clark and T. Waller (eds), *Early Childhood Education and Care: Policy and Practice.* London: Sage.

Sigelman, C.K. and Rider, E.A. (2008) *Life-Span Human Development* (6th edition). London: Thomson Wadsworth.

Singer, P. (1995) *Animal Liberation* (revised edition). London: Pimlico.

Singer, P. (2001) *Unsanctifying Human Life: Essays on Ethics.* Oxford: Blackwell.

Siraj-Blatchford, I. (1999) 'Early childhood pedagogy, practice, principles and research', in P. Mortimore (ed.), *Understanding Pedagogy and its Impact on Learning.* London: Paul Chapman.

Siraj-Blatchford, I. (2001) 'Diversity and learning in the early years', in G. Pugh (ed.), *Contemporary Issues in the Early Years* (3rd edtion). London: Paul Chapman.

Siraj-Blatchford, I. (2007) 'Creativity, communication and collaboration: the identification of pedagogic progression in sustained shared thinking', *Asia-Pacific Journal of Research in Early Childhood Education*, 1 (2): 3–23.

Siraj-Blatchford, I. (2008) 'Understanding the relationship between curriculum, pedagogy and progression in learning in early childhood in Hong Kong', *Journal of Early Childhood Education*, 7 (2): 6–13.

Siraj-Blatchford, I. and Clarke, P. (2000) *Supporting Identity, Diversity and Language in the Early Years*. Milton Keynes: Open University Press.

Siraj-Blatchford, I., Clarke, K. and Needham, M. (2007) *Team Around the Child: Multi-agency Working in the Early Years*. Stoke on Trent: Trentham Books.

Siraj-Blatchford, I. and Manni, L. (2006) *Effective Leadership in the Early Years Sector (ELEYS) Study*. London: General Teaching Council for England.

Siraj-Blatchford, I. and Manni, L. (2008) '"Would you like to tidy up now?" An analysis of adult questioning in the English Foundation Stage', in *Early Years: An International Journal of Research and Development*, 28 (1): 5–22.

Siraj-Blatchford, I. and Sylva, K. (2004) 'Researching pedagogy in English preschools', *British Educational Research Journal*, 30 (5): 713–30.

Siraj-Blatchford, I., Sylva, K., Muttock. S., Gilden, R. and Bell, D. (2002) *Researching Effective Pedagogy in the Early Years DfES Research Report 365* Queen's Printer. London: HMSO.

Siraj-Blatchford, I., Sylva, K., Taggart, B., Sammons, P. and Melhuish, E. (2003) *Technical Paper 10: Case Studies of Practice in the Foundation Stage*. London: Institute of Education.

Siviy, S.M. (1998) 'Neurobiological substrates of play behaviour in the structure and function of mammalian playfulness', in M. Berkoff and J.A. Byers (eds), *Animal Play: Evolutionary, Ecological and Comparative Perspectives*. Cambridge: Cambridge University Press.

Skinner, B.F. (1957) *Verbal Behavior*. New York: Appleton-Century-Croft.

Slee, P.T. and Shute, R.H. (2003) *Child Development: Thinking about Theories.* London: Arnold Publishers.

Smart, C., Neale, B. and Wade, A. (2001) *The Changing Experience of Childhood: Families and Divorce*. Cambridge: Polity.

Smilanksy, S. (1968) *The Effects of Sociodramatic Play on Disadvantaged Preschool Children*. New York: Wiley.

Smith, P.K. and Vollstedt, R. (1985) 'On defining play; an empirical study of the relationship between play and various play criteria', *Child Development,* 56: 1042–50.

Snow, C.E. (1977) 'Mothers' speech research: from input to interaction', in C.E. Snow and C.A. Ferguson (eds), *Talking to Children: Language Input and Acquisition*. Cambridge: Cambridge University Press.

Social Services Inspectorate/Department of Health (1996) *Children in Need: Report of an SSI National Inspection of SSD Family Support Services 1993/1995*. Leeds: DoH.

Sokolov, J. and Snow, C. (1994) 'The changing role of negative evidence in theories of language development', in C. Gallaway and B.J. Richards (eds), *Input and Interaction in Language Acquisition*. Cambridge: Cambridge University Press.

Solomon, G.E.A. and Johnson, S.C. (2000) 'Conceptual change in the classroom: teaching young children to understand biological inheritance', *British Journal of Developmental Psychology*, 18: 81–96.

Soyinka, W. (2000) *Ake: The Years of Childhood*. London: Methuen.

Speier, M. (1976) 'The adult ideological viewpoint in studies of childhood', in A. Skolnick (ed.), *Rethinking Childhood: Perspectives on Development and Society*. Boston, MA: Little Brown.

Spelke, E.S. (1994) 'Initial knowledge: six suggestions', *Cognition*, 50: 431–55.

Spencer, H. (1859) *Education*. London: Williams and Norgate.

Spencer, H. (1873) *Principles of Psychology*. New York: Appleton.

Spillane, J., Halverson, R. and Diamond, J.B. (2001) 'Investigating school leadership practice: a distributed perspective', *Educational Researcher*, 30 (3): 23–8.

Springer, K. and Keil, F.C. (1991). 'Early differentiation of causal mechanisms appropriate to biological and non-biological kinds', *Child Development*, 62: 767–81.

Sprott, J.E. (1994) 'One person's "spoiling" is another's freedom to become: overcoming ethnocentric views about parental control', *Social Science and Medicine*, 38 (8): 1111–24.

Stainton-Rogers, W. and Roche, J. (1994) *Children's Welfare and Children's Rights: A Practical Guide to the Law*. London: Hodder & Stoughton.

Statham, J. (1986) *Daughters and Sons: Experiences of Non-sexist Childraising*. Oxford: Blackwell.

Steele, M., Steele, H. and Fonagy, P. (1995) 'Associations among attachment classifications of mothers, fathers and infants', *Child Development*, 67: 541–55.

Stein, M. (2006) 'Research review: young people leaving care', *Child and Family Social Work*, 11 (3): 273–80.

Stein, M. and Carey, K. (1986) *Leaving Care*. Oxford: Blackwell.

Steiner-Khamsi, G. (ed.) (2004) *The Global Politics of Educational Borrowing and Lending*. New York: Teachers College Press.

Steiner-Khamsi, G. and Stolpe, I. (2006) *Educational Import: Local Encounters with Global Forces in Mongolia*. New York: Palgrave MacMillan.

Stephens, W.B. (1998) *Education in Britain, 1750–1914*. Basingstoke: Macmillan.

Stern, D.N. (1985) *The Interpersonal World of the Infant*. New York: Basic Books.

Stipek, D.J. and Byler, P. (1997) 'Early childhood education teachers: do they practice what they preach?', *Early Childhood Research Quarterly*, 12: 305–25.

Stipek, D. and Ogano, T. (2000) *Early Childhood Education*. Los Angeles, CA: UCLA: Center for Healthier Children, Families and Community.

Strandell, H. (2000) 'What is the use of children's play: preparation or social participation?', in H. Penn (ed.), *Early Childhood Services. Theory, Policy and Practice*.
Buckingham: Open University Press.

Striano, T. and Rochat, P. (1999) 'Developmental link between dyadic and triadic
social competence in infancy', *British Journal of Developmental Psychology*, 17:
551–62.

Sturrock, G. (2003) 'Towards a psycholudic definition of playwork', in F. Brown (ed.),
Playwork: Theory and Practice. Buckingham: Open University Press.

Sulzby, E. (1989) 'Assessment of writing and of children's language while writing', in
L. Morrow and J. Smith (eds), *The Role of Assessment and Measurement in Early
Literacy Instruction*. Englewood Cliffs, NJ: Prentice- Hall.

Sulzby, E. and Teale, W. (1991). 'Emergent literacy', in R. Barr, M. Kamil, P. Mosenthal
and P.D. Pearson (eds), *Handbook of Reading Research* (Vol. 2). New York: Longman.

Sure Start (2002) *Birth to Three Matters: A Framework to Support Children in their Earliest
Years*. London: DfES.

Sutton-Smith, B. (1979) *Play and Learning*. New York: Gardnet Press.

Sutton-Smith, B. (1997) *The Ambiguity of Play*. Cambridge, MA: Harvard University
Press.

Sutton-Smith, B. and Kelly-Byrne, D. (1984) 'The idealisation of play', in P.K. Smith
(ed.), *Play in Animals and Humans*. Oxford: Basil Blackwell.

Sutton Trust (2007) *Recent Changes in Intergenerational Mobility in the UK: A Summary
of Findings*, www.suttontrust.com/reports/summary.pdf (accessed 26 September
2008).

Sylva, K., Blatchford, P. and Johnson, S. (1992) 'The impact of the National
Curriculum on pre-school practice', *International Journal of Early Education*, 21 (1):
41–51.

Sylva, K., Bruner, J.S. and Genova, P. (1976) 'The role of play in the problem solving
of young children 3–5 years old', in J.S. Bruner, A. Jolly and K. Sylva (eds), *Play:
Its Role in Development and Evolution*. Penguin: New York.

Sylva, K., Melhuish, E.C., Sammons, P., Siraj-Blatchford, I. and Taggart, B. (2004) *The
Effective Provision of Pre-School Education (EPPE) Project: Final Report*. London:
DfES/Institute of Education, University of London.

Sylva, K., Melhuish, E., Sammons, P., Siraj-Blatchford, I., Taggart, B. and Elliot, K.
(2003) *The Effective Provision of Pre-School Education (EPPE) Project: Findings from the
Pre-school Period Summary of Findings*. London: DfES.

Sylva, K., Siraj-Blatchford, I., and Taggart, B. (2006) *Early Childhood Environmental
Rating Scale – Extension (ECERS-E)* (2nd edition). Stoke on Trent: Trentham Books.

Takhvar, M. (1988) 'Play and theories of play: a review of the literature', *Early Child
Development and Care*, 39: 221–44.

Teale, W. and Sulzby, E. (eds) (1986) *Emergent Literacy: Writing and Reading*. Norwood,
NJ: Ablex.

Theakston, A., Lieven, E., Pine, J. and Rowland, C. (2001) 'The role of performance limitations in the acquisition of verb argument structure', *Journal of Child Language*, 28: 127–52.

Thelen, E. and Smith, L.B. (1994) *A Dynamic Systems Approach to the Development of Cognition and Action*. Cambridge, MA: Bradford/MIT Press.

Thomas, L., Howard, J. and Miles, G. (2006) 'The effectiveness of playful practice for learning in the early years', *The Psychology of Education Review*, 30 (1): 52–8.

Thomas, N. (2002) *Children, Family and the State: Decision-making and Child Participation*. Bristol: Policy Press.

Thomas, N. (2005) *Social Work with Young People in Care: Looking After Children in Theory and Practice*. London: Palgrave Macmillan.

Thomas, N. and O'Kane, C. (1998) *Children and Decision-making: A Summary Report*. Swansea: University of Wales Swansea, International Centre for Childhood Studies.

Thomas, S., Thomas, S., Nafees, B. and Bhugra, D. (2004) '"I was running away from death" – the pre-flight experiences of unaccompanied asylum seeking children in the UK', *Child: Care, Health and Development*, 30 (2):113–22.

Thompson, N. (2000) *Study Guide: Postqualifying Child Care Programme for Wales – Module 3: Working with Community and Professional Networks*. Swansea: University of Wales Swansea.

Thompson, N. (2002) *Building the Future: Social Work with Children, Young People and their Families*. London: Russell House Publishing.

Thomson, B. (2006) *Growing People. Learning and Developing from Day to Day Experience*. Oxford: Chandos Publishing.

Thomson, P. (ed.) (2008) *Doing Visual Research with Children and Young People*. London: Routledge Falmer.

Thorne, B. (1993) *Gender Play: Girls and Boys in School*. New Brunswick, NJ: Rutgers University Press.

Tomasello, M. (1992) *First verbs. A Case Study of Early Grammatical development*. New York: Cambridge University Press.

Tomasello, M. (2000) 'Do young children have adult syntactic competence?' *Cognition*, 74: 209–53.

Tomasello, M. (2003) *Constructing a Language: A Usage-based Theory of Language Acquisition*. Cambridge, MA: Harvard University Press.

Tomlinson, J. (1999) *Globalization and Culture*. Cambridge: Polity Press.

Trawick-Smith, J. (1997) *Early Childhood Development: A Multicultural Perspective*. Englewood Cliffs, NJ: Merrill/Prentice Hall.

Trevarthen, C. and Aitken, K.J. (2001) 'Infant intersubjectivity: research, theory, and clinical applications', *Journal of Child Psychology and Psychiatry and Allied Disciplines*, 42 (1): 3–48.

Trevarthen, C., Aitken, K., Papoudi, D. and Robarts, J. (1998) *Children with Autism: Diagnosis and Interventions to Meet their Needs*. London: Jessica Kingsley.

Turner, E.S. (1976) *Boys will be Boys: the Story of Sweeney Todd, Deadwood Dick, Sexton Blake, Billy Bunter, Dick Barton et al.* Harmondsworth: Penguin.

Tzuriel, D. (1999) 'Parent–child mediated learning interactions as determinants of cognitive modifiability: recent research and future directions', *Genetic, Social and General Psychology Monographs,* 125: 109–56.

UNESCO (2007) *Education for All (EFA) Monitoring Report 2007.* Paris: UNESCO.

UNICEF (2005) *The State of the World's Children.* New York: UNICEF.

UNICEF (2007) *Press Release: Child Deaths Fall Below 10 Million for the First Time,* www.unicef.org/media/media_40855.html (accessed 2 October 2008).

United Nations (UN) (1989) *Convention on the Rights of the Child, General Assembly resolution 44/25* www.unhchr.ch/html/menu3/b/k2crc.htm (accessed 6 March 2009).

United Nations Committee on the Rights of the Child (2006) *General Comment No. 7, Implementing Child Rights in Early Childhood,* CRC/C/GC/7.

Valsiner, J. (2000) *Culture and Human Development.* London: Sage.

Volling, B.L. and Belsky, J. (1992) 'Infant, father and marital antecedents of infant–father attachment security in dual-earner and single-earner families', *International Journal of Behavioural Development,* 15: 83–100.

Vygotsky, L. (1933) *Play and its role in the Mental Development of the Child,* Voprosy psikhologii, 1966, No. 6, trans. Mulholland, C., Psychology and Marxism Internet Archive 2002: www.marxists.org/archive/vygotsky/works/1933/play.htm (accessed 6 March 2009).

Vygotsky, L. (1978) *Mind in Society: The Development of Higher Mental Processes.* Cambridge, MA: Harvard University Press.

Vygotsky, L. (1981) 'The genesis of higher mental functions', in J.V. Wertsch (ed.), *The Concept of Activity in Soviet Psychology.* Armonk, NY: Sharpe.

Vygotsky, L. (1986) *Thought and Language.* Cambridge, MA: MIT Press.

Vygotsky, L. (2004) 'Imagination and creativity in childhood', *Journal of Russian and East European Psychology,* 42 (1): 4–84.

Wadsworth, M. and Butterworth, S. (2006) 'Early life', in M. Marmot and R.G. Wilkinson, *Social Determinants of Health.* Oxford: OUP.

Waksler, F.C. (1991a) 'Dancing when the music is over: a study of deviance in a kindergarten classroom', in F.C. Waksler (ed.), *Studying the Social Worlds of Children: Sociological Readings.* London: The Falmer Press.

Waksler, F.C. (ed.) (1991b) *Studying the Social Worlds of Children: Sociological Readings.* London: Falmer Press.

Waksler, F.C. (1996) *The Little Trials of Childhood and Children's Strategies for Dealing with Them.* London: Falmer Press.

Walkerdine (1990) *Schoolgirl Fictions.* London: Verso Books.

Walvin, J. (1982) *A Child's World: A Social History of English Childhood, 1800–1914.* Harmondsworth: Penguin Books.

Wang, C.C.D.C. and Mallinckrodt, B.S. (2006) 'Differences between Taiwanese and U.S. cultural beliefs about ideal adult attachment', *Journal of Counseling Psychology*, 53 (2): 192–204.

Waniganayake, M. (2000) *Leadership in the Early Years: New Directions in Research*. Keynote presentation to Professional Development conference. Melbourne, January 2000.

Warming, H. (2005) 'Participant observation: a way to learn about children's perspectives', in A. Clark, P. Moss and A. Kjorholt (eds), *Beyond Listening: Children's Perspectives on Early Childhood Services*. Bristol: Policy Press.

Watson, R.J. (1994) 'Affective tone in a toddler measured during transitions between multiple caregivers', *Early Child Development and Care*, 97: 135–44.

Weikart, D. (2000) *Early Childhood Education: Needs and Opportunity*. Paris: UNESCO: International Institute for Educational Planning.

Wellman, H. (2002) 'Understanding the psychological world: developing a theory of mind', in U. Goswami (ed.), *Handbook of Childhood Cognitive Development*. Oxford: Blackwell.

Wellman, H., Cross, D. and Watson, J. (2001) 'Meta-analysis of theory-of-mind development: the truth about false belief', *Child Development*, 72: 655–84.

Wellman, H. and Gelman, S.A. (1998) 'Knowledge acquisition in foundational domains', in D. Kuhn and R.S. Siegler (Vol. eds), Cognition, language, and perceptual development, Vol. 2 in W. Damon (Gen. ed.), *Handbook of Child Psychology*. New York: Wiley.

Wells, G. (1986) *The Meaning Makers: Children Learning Language and Using Language to Learn*. London: Hodder and Stoughton.

Welsh Assembly Government (2004) *Children and Young People: Rights to Action*. Cardiff: Welsh Assembly Government.

Welsh Assembly Government (2005) *National Service Framework for Children, Young People and Maternity Services*. Cardiff: WAG.

Welsh Assembly Government (2006) *Safeguarding Children: Working Together Under the Children Act 2004*. Cardiff: Welsh Assembly Government.

Welsh Assembly Government (2008) *The Foundation Phase*. Available at http://new. wales.gov.uk/topics/educationandskills/policy_strategy_and_planning/104009-wag/foundation_phase/?lang=en (accessed 12 March 2009).

Welshman, J. (2006) 'Searching for social capital: historical perspectives on health, poverty and culture', *The Journal of the Royal Society for the Promotion of Health*, 126: 268–74.

Werner, E.E. (1996) 'Vulnerable but invincible: high-risk children from birth to adulthood', *European Child and Adolescent Psychiatry*, 5 (suppl. 1): 47–51.

Westcott, M. and Howard, J. (2007) 'Creating a playful classroom environment', *Psychology of Education Review*, 31 (1), 27–34.

Whalley, M. and the Pen Green Team (2000) *Involving Parents in Their Children's Learning*. London: Paul Chapman.

White, L.A. (1959) *The Evolution of Culture: The Development of Civilization to the Fall of Rome*. New York: McGraw-Hill.

Whitebread, D. and Jameson, H. (2005) 'Play, storytelling and creative writing', in J. Moyles (ed.), *The Excellence of Play*. Buckingham: Open University Press.

Whitehurst, G., Falco, F., Lonigan, C.J., Fischal, J.E., DeBaryshe, B.D., Valdez-Manchaca, M.C. and Caufield, M. (1988) 'Accelerating language development through picture-book reading', *Developmental Psychology*, 24: 552–9.

Whitehurst, G. and Lonigan, C. (1998) 'Child development and emergent literacy', *Child Development*, 69 (3): 848–72.

Williams, C. (2007) *Social Policy for Social Welfare Practice in a Devolved Wales*. Birmingham: Venture Press.

Williams, J. (2008) *Child Law for Social Work*. London: Sage.

Wimmer, H. and Perner, J. (1983) 'Beliefs about beliefs: representations and constraining function of wrong beliefs in young children's understanding of deception', *Cognition*, 13: 103–28.

Wing, L. (1995) 'Play is not the work of the child: young children's perceptions of work and play', *Early Childhood Research Quarterly*, 16: 209–36.

Winnicott, D.W. (1971) *Playing and Reality*. London: Routledge Classics.

Wolman, J., Skelly, E., Kolotourou, M., Lawson, M. and Sacher, P. (2008) 'Tackling toddler obesity through a pilot community based family intervention', *Community Practitioner*, 81 (1): 28–31.

Wood, D. (1998) *How Children Think and Learn: The Social Contexts of Cognitive Development* (2nd edition) Malden, MA: Blackwell.

Wood, D., Bruner, J.S. and Ross, G. (1976) 'The role of tutoring in problem-solving', *Journal of Child Psychology and Psychiatry*, 17: 89–100.

Woodhead, M. (1999) 'Reconstructing developmental psychology: some first steps', *Children and Society*, 13 (1): 3–19.

Wooldridge, A. (1994) *Measuring the Mind: Education and Psychology in England, 1860–1990*. Cambridge: Cambridge University Press.

World Health Organisation (1948) *Constitution of the World Health Organisation*. Geneva: WHO.

World Health Organisation (1986) *The Ottawa Charter for Health Promotion*. Ottawa: WHO.

World Health Organisation (2004) *The Importance of Care-giver Child Interactions for the Survival and Health Development of Young Children: A Review*. Department of Child and Adolescent health and Development. Geneva: WHO.

World Health Organisation (2006) *Obesity and Overweight*. Available at: www.who.int/mediacentre/factsheets/fs311/en/index.html (accessed 6 March 2009).

Worsfold, V.L. (1974) 'A philosophical justification for children's rights', *Harvard Educational Review,* 44 (1): 142–59.

Written Answers (2007) Wednesday, 21 November 2007 *Children, Schools and Families. Children's Centres: Privatisation.* Available at www.theyworkforyou.com/wrans/ (accessed 6 March 2009).

Wyness, M. (2006) *Childhood and Society: An Introduction to the Sociology of Childhood.* Basingstoke: Palgrave Macmillan.

Yaqub, S. (2002) '"Poor children grow into poor adults": harmful mechanisms or over-deterministic theory?', *Journal of International Development,* 14: 1081–93.

Young, B. (2005) 'The obesity epidemic reviewed', *Young Consumers,* 6 (4): 50–5.

Zigler, E., Gilliam, W.S. and Jones, S.M. (2006) *A Vision for Universal Preschool Education.* New York: Cambridge University Press.

INDEX

This index is in word-by-word order. Authors are included where there is significant discussion in the text.

Research Methods Books from SAGE

Read sample chapters online now!

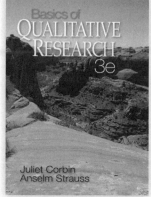

Basics of QUALITATIVE RESEARCH 3e

Juliet Corbin
Anselm Strauss

The Mixed Methods Reader

Vicki L. Plano Clark ▪ John W. Creswell

DOING QUALITATIVE RESEARCH USING YOUR COMPUTER

A PRACTICAL GUIDE

CHRIS HAHN

SECOND EDITION
INTERVIEWS
Learning the Craft of Qualitative Research Interviewing

Steinar Kvale
Svend Brinkmann

DISCOVERING STATISTICS USING SPSS THIRD EDITION

ANDY FIELD

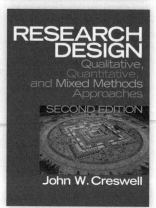

RESEARCH DESIGN
Qualitative, Quantitative, and Mixed Methods Approaches

SECOND EDITION

John W. Creswell

www.sagepub.co.uk

The Qualitative Research Kit

Edited by Uwe Flick

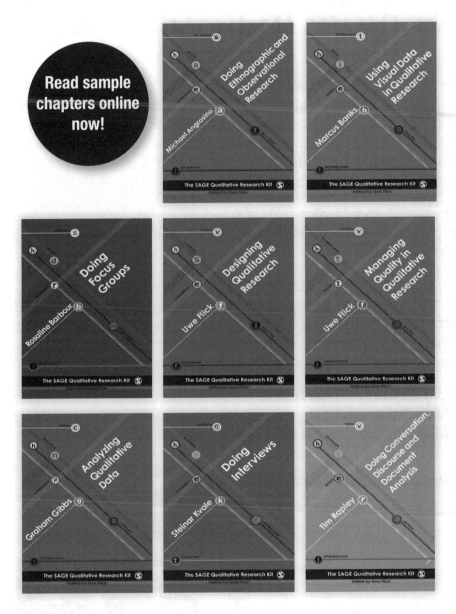

Read sample chapters online now!

Doing Ethnographic and Observational Research — Michael Angrosino — The SAGE Qualitative Research Kit — Edited by Uwe Flick

Using Visual Data in Qualitative Research — Marcus Banks — The SAGE Qualitative Research Kit — Edited by Uwe Flick

Doing Focus Groups — Rosaline Barbour — The SAGE Qualitative Research Kit — Edited by Uwe Flick

Designing Qualitative Research — Uwe Flick — The SAGE Qualitative Research Kit — Edited by Uwe Flick

Managing Quality in Qualitative Research — Uwe Flick — The SAGE Qualitative Research Kit — Edited by Uwe Flick

Analyzing Qualitative Data — Graham Gibbs — The SAGE Qualitative Research Kit — Edited by Uwe Flick

Doing Interviews — Steinar Kvale — The SAGE Qualitative Research Kit — Edited by Uwe Flick

Doing Conversation, Discourse and Document Analysis — Tim Rapley — The SAGE Qualitative Research Kit — Edited by Uwe Flick

www.sagepub.co.uk

THE LIBRARY
NEW COLLEGE
SWINDON
WITHDRAWN

Supporting researchers for more than forty years

Research methods have always been at the core of SAGE's publishing. Sara Miller McCune founded SAGE in 1965 and soon after she published SAGE's first methods book, *Public Policy Evaluation*. A few years later, she launched the Quantitative Applications in the Social Sciences series – affectionately known as the 'little green books'.

Always at the forefront of developing and supporting new approaches in methods, SAGE published early groundbreaking texts and journals in the fields of qualitative methods and evaluation.

Today, more than forty years and two million little green books later, SAGE continues to push the boundaries with a growing list of more than 1,200 research methods books, journals, and reference works across the social, behavioural, and health sciences.

From qualitative, quantitative and mixed methods to evaluation, SAGE is the essential resource for academics and practitioners looking for the latest in methods by leading scholars.

www.sagepublications.com